FAKING LIBERTIES

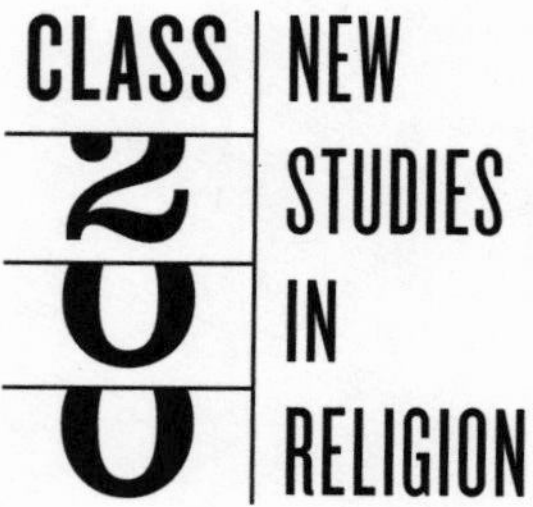

EDITED BY Kathryn Lofton AND
John Lardas Modern

FAKING LIBERTIES

Religious Freedom in American-Occupied Japan

JOLYON BARAKA THOMAS

The University of Chicago Press
Chicago and London

The University of Chicago Press, Chicago 60637
The University of Chicago Press, Ltd., London

Published 2019
Printed in the United States of America

28 27 26 25 24 23 22 21 20 19   1 2 3 4 5

ISBN-13: 978-0-226-61879-1 (cloth)
ISBN-13: 978-0-226-61882-1 (paper)
ISBN-13: 978-0-226-61896-8 (e-book)
DOI: https://doi.org/10.7208/chicago/9780226618968.001.0001

Library of Congress Cataloging-in-Publication Data
Names: Thomas, Jolyon Baraka, author.
Title: Faking liberties : religious freedom in American-occupied Japan / Jolyon Baraka Thomas.
Description: Chicago ; London : The University of Chicago Press, 2019. | Includes bibliographical references and index.
Identifiers: LCCN 2018037454 | ISBN 9780226618791 (cloth : alk. paper) | ISBN 9780226618821 (pbk. : alk. paper) | ISBN 9780226618968 (e-book)
Subjects: LCSH: Freedom of religion—Japan—History—20th century. | Japan—History—Allied occupation, 1945–1952.
Classification: LCC KNX2472 .T48 2019 | DDC 323.44/2095209044—dc23
LC record available at https://lccn.loc.gov/2018037454

♾ This paper meets the requirements of ANSI/NISO Z39.48–1992 (Permanence of Paper).

For Kimberley Anh

CONTENTS

PROLOGUE

The Drums of War

> On September the 11th, enemies of freedom committed an act of war against our country. Americans have known wars, but for the past 136 years they have been wars on foreign soil, except for one Sunday in 1941. Americans have known the casualties of war, but not at the center of a great city on a peaceful morning.
>
> Americans have known surprise attacks, but never before on thousands of civilians.
>
> All of this was brought upon us in a single day, and night fell on a different world, a world where freedom itself is under attack.
>
> GEORGE W. BUSH (2001)[1]

BY NOW IT IS A FAMILIAR story. A surprise attack on American territory perpetrated by fanatical pilots wrought unprecedented material destruction and an unimaginable loss of life. Even as the smoke rose from the ashes, the American president spoke to the nation to assuage its fears and to assure the people that justice would be served. Whereas only a few people had pounded the drum of war before the attack, suddenly the press resonated with its staccato rhythm. The person on the street demanded vengeance. She was out for blood. The American people were ready for war, and the enemy would have no place to hide.

The story in the preceding paragraph is familiar not only because it is an account of the fervor that swept through the United States in the wake of the 11 September 2001 attacks, but also because virtually the same response characterized the American response to the Japanese attack on Pearl Harbor. I do not claim that the events were historically identical. With almost exactly sixty years between them, they effectively took place in different worlds. Yet there is a striking parallel between 9/11 and the Japanese attack on Pearl Harbor of 7 December 1941. Both attacks resulted in devastating loss of life and property. Both galvanized Americans and created fertile ground for a militarist, racist jingoism that was striking in its suddenness and fervor. In both cases, influential observers identified religion as the prime motivator for the attack (Islam in the case of 9/11; Shintō in the case of Pearl Harbor). As America went to war in response, the promotion of religious freedom appeared as a way of turning such "bad religion" into "good religion." The religiously motivated enemy spurned freedom. It was the duty of the United States to militarily chastise this intractable foe, to bomb him into submission, and then in the course of military occupation to educate him about the true nature of liberty. In the process, the enemy's wife, his sister, and his child would be freed from the tyrannical grip of his illiberal ideology. In the process, the enemy himself would be transformed. Gentled. Made quiescent. Indeed, how could it be any other way? Such was the power of American Religious Freedom™.

Just as US president George W. Bush drew parallels between Pearl Harbor and 9/11 in his 20 September 2001 speech to Congress declaring the onset of the "War on Terror," some American neoconservative policy makers looked back at the Allied Occupation of Japan (1945–52) in search of a model for how the Muslim-majority nations of southwestern and central Asia might be democratized. Yet as historian of United States–Japan relations John Dower presciently argued in February 2003, the invasion and occupation of Iraq that followed would not and could not reproduce the Japanese success story in the way that many policy makers evidently hoped.[2] For all the parallels between the respective onsets of the Pacific War and the War on Terror, fundamental cultural and historical differences militated against reproduction of the unique circumstances that allowed the Japanese to "embrace defeat."[3]

I chose to study religious freedom during the Allied Occupation out of fascination with post-9/11 depictions of religious freedom as a panacea for the global ills of terrorism, Islamism, and sectarianism. My account in the following pages is not presentist, but it does have messages for readers today. Studying how the story of religious freedom in Japan has been told—

and paying close attention to who has done the telling—reveals that appeals to religious freedom have powerful political effects far beyond the tasks of making marginal religious organizations safe from persecution or freeing innocent people from the grip of oppressive ideology. Upon investigation, it becomes disturbingly clear that as much as religious freedom solves problems of inequity and oppression, it engenders new ones. This is true in international contexts, when occupying armies free religion at the point of a gun. It is also true in domestic contexts, when majoritarian claims often serve as tools for the suppression of religious minorities.

The Allied Occupation of Japan was technically a multinational endeavor, but it was essentially an American project that aimed to introduce religious freedom to Japan as a preliminary step in the democratization of the Asian country. While a number of scholars have written about the Occupation and its legacy, when I began my own preliminary research into this important period I found myself curious about the prehistory of the Occupation as much as the Occupation itself. If the American occupiers made the eradication of "State Shintō" and the promotion of religious freedom two of their primary objectives, what exactly existed before the Occupation? To what images of Shintō and statecraft were the occupiers responding? To what extent did these images correspond with reality? Finally, to what extent were scholars of religion complicit in the creation of those images prior to the Occupation, and how and why have scholars of religion perpetuated those images since?

The question of how religious freedom was conceived and protected in Japan prior to the Occupation therefore became an unavoidable topic. While the occupiers disparaged Japan's wartime regime as being both religiously intolerant and theocratic, Japan's 1889 constitution had included a clear guarantee of religious freedom. By the time the occupiers arrived on the archipelago, Japan had enjoyed more than fifty years of constitutional law in which freedom of religion existed both on the books and as a matter of vigorous public debate.

In this book, I juxtapose the presurrender religious freedom legal regime with that of the Allied Occupation to show that prewar and wartime Japanese practices of religious freedom were extraordinarily normal. I show that Occupation policies were at least as draconian as they were emancipatory. Indeed, throughout the book I regularly use oxymoronic language to highlight the paradoxes that I find endemic in the religious freedom endeavor. I show that religious freedom is not an ethereal *principle* that is applied to a situation or introduced to a nation. Rather, freeing religion is a mundane *project* subject to political machination and discursive manipulation.

To forestall misunderstanding at the outset, I personally celebrate religious freedom as an ideal. I think religious freedom is worth striving for. However, if religious freedom is a project rather than a principle, then like all projects it is only as effective as the people pulling it off. Like all projects, it is only as coherent as the operative terms that inform it. Like all projects, religious freedom necessitates compromise, collaboration, and contestation.

CONVENTIONS

JAPANESE TERMS ARE REPRESENTED IN A modified Hepburn system, italicized and with macrons representing all long vowels: *shūkyō*. Commonly known terms and place names (Tokyo) are unitalicized and rendered without diacritics. All instances of the word "Shintō" do appear with the macron, however, and all instances of the word "Hawaiʻi" appear with the *ʻokina* indicating a glottal stop between the last two vowels. (The adjective "Hawaiian" appears without the *ʻokina*.) Like *kami*, the words "god(s)" and "buddha(s)" remain uncapitalized throughout unless I am quoting a source that capitalizes them. When it is capitalized, the last refers exclusively to the historical founder of the Buddhist order ("the Buddha").

The problematic phrase "State Shintō" appears so frequently that it would be ludicrous to put scare quotes around every instance. I have added quotes at the first instance in each chapter and have otherwise restricted my usage to places where I refer to the phrase itself or where I juxtapose State Shintō with other concepts.

Biographical dates are given on first mention in each chapter and otherwise as appropriate, but only for people who are deceased. (The abbreviation "d.u." indicates that biographical dates are unknown to me.) I have not included military rank, aristocratic titles, or clerical status of individuals unless necessary. Otherwise unmarked references to "the war" indicate the conflict between Japan and the United States ("the Pacific War"). The "Fifteen Years' War" indicates Japan's conflicts in Asia and the Pacific from 1931 to 1945.

I have used the term "transsectarian" as a general descriptor of many of the groups under investigation here and as a translation of the Japanese term *chōshūha* (lit., "surpassing sects and factions"). More precisely, I use "transsectarian" to indicate groups that were designed to overcome sectarian doctrinal differences while maintaining denominational distinctiveness vis-à-vis other religions; "transdenominational" indicates cooperation and collaboration between different religions (e.g., between Buddhism and Christianity). "Latitudinarianism," a stance of showing no preference for specific forms of belief or ritual practice, glosses the phrase *jiyū hōnin shugi*, which might be awkwardly translated as "a policy of leaving people free to do as they please." "Sacerdotalism" is my translation for *kyōkenshugi*, a term used by some lay Buddhist intellectuals to criticize clerics' supercilious attitudes or claims to ultimate doctrinal authority.

Throughout, I refer to "religions policy" and "religions legislation." This may seem unnatural when the adjective "religious" could do. My usage matches the language of my primary documents, both English and Japanese. For example, the Occupation agency tasked with overseeing religious freedom policy was called the "Religions and Cultural Resources Division," or "Religions Division," not the "Religious Division." Similarly, while *shūkyō* can be translated as both the singular "religion" and the plural "religions," I have translated the Shūkyō Seido Chōsa Kai as the "Religions System Investigation Committee" because this executive branch focus group was tasked with developing one comprehensive legal system to encompass Japan's multifarious religious denominations, sects, and teaching assemblies.

INTRODUCTION

The Universal Particularity of Religious Freedom

> There is not absolute religious liberty in Japan to-day, as there is not in any modern state, but one can say that on the whole the citizens of modern Japan *enjoy religious liberty.*
>
> AUGUST KARL REISCHAUER (1927)[1]

> Until the day in 1946 when the divinity of the Emperor was formally denied in an Imperial Rescript, there was in principle no basis in Japan for freedom of belief.
>
> MARUYAMA MASAO (1946)[2]

THE MAPS WERE ONE OF THE things that struck me when I first moved to Japan in 2002. Japanese maps push the continents of the world to the periphery of the familiar Mercator projection, leaving the vast expanse of the Pacific Ocean to dominate the center. The visual effect is that the tiny Japanese archipelago captures one's attention first, especially because the familiar banana shape of the four main islands is often depicted in a striking red. There is a clear political message in these maps. Japan is at the center of the world.

Who ever said that the Americas had to be at the center of a world map? Who decided that the world's largest landmass should be split in two? The map on the wall of the apartment where I spent my first few months living in Tokyo grabbed my attention and forced me to rethink my orientation to the globe. While I quickly adjusted to my new geographic reality, it took me considerably more time and greater familiarity with the Japanese language to absorb how this striking visual depiction of Japan—the red archipelago situated both at the edge of the world and at its center—matched a common discursive practice.

There is a long tradition of orientalist and auto-exoticizing language in the study of Japan. We frequently read about how Japan is the quintessential Other, a land of paradox, a land simultaneously characterized by hidebound tradition and radical futurity. Japanese people eagerly contribute to portrayals of Japan's essential weirdness as a way of reinforcing national identity and pride. Paeans to inscrutability, rustic simplicity, cutting-edge electronics, superflat art, hyperreal fiction, and unconventional sexuality all represent a Japan that bursts at the seams, overburdened with its overwhelming Japaneseness. In the Japanese language, pervasive references to JAPAN shroud personal opinion under the comfortable mantle of national disposition, social consensus, or climate: Japanese people do not dance. Japanese people can "read the air" (*kūki o yomu*) and can communicate without words (*ishin denshin*). Preposterously, Japan is supposedly unique because it has four distinct seasons.

Beyond the archipelago, there is a whole industry devoted to disseminating images of "wacky Japan." Canadian pop stars mangle Japanese terminology while prancing through the iconic Tokyo neighborhoods of Shibuya and Harajuku accompanied by impassive background dancers (it turns out that Japanese people dance after all).[3] YouTube channels curate the latest Japanese television advertisements. Journalists report on cuddle clubs, old couples who do adorable things with their robotic pets, and Buddhist bars.[4] If the story captures some sort of apparent contradiction between timeless tradition and zany progressiveness, all the better.[5]

In the case of religion, too, scholars and journalists often treat Japan as exceptional. Japanese religiosity breaks all the rules. The number of religious adherents recorded in annual government statistics regularly exceeds the population of Japan by tens of millions of people, but personal professions of belief and affiliation reported in nongovernmental surveys hover at about 20 percent.[6] Religious edifices are ubiquitous, but most people who visit these sites do not call their ritual activities "religion."[7] Some scholars have even used the Japanese case to call for the utter dismantling of religion as an analytic category.[8]

Religious freedom is yet another place where Japanese practices frequently appear as an exception to the global rule. Historians have often highlighted the circumscribed language of Japan's 1889 constitutional guarantee of religious freedom as evidence that Japan got religious freedom wrong.[9] Historians and scholars of religion have described the prewar persecution of individuals for their religious beliefs in dramatic martyrs' narratives.[10] Police suppression of marginal religious movements and the passage of legislation designed to streamline the bureaucratic administration of religions in the 1930s feature as evidence that Japan abrogated its constitutional guarantee of religious freedom.[11] Many have argued that the 1889 constitutional guarantee was false, and that Japan did not experience genuine religious freedom until the American-led occupiers decreed it in autumn 1945.[12]

While the coercive nature of the prewar and wartime Japanese regime cannot be denied, it is striking that previous scholarship has treated Japanese practices of religious freedom as peculiar or has described imperial Japan's draconian police work as particularly egregious. In our received accounts, *Japan* is the problem. Meanwhile, the concept of religious freedom gets a free pass. Religious freedom appears as an anodyne principle that Japanese political leaders distorted and that Japanese religious leaders failed to protect.[13]

Yet upon investigation, it becomes clear that religious freedom anywhere is fundamentally characterized by a lack of feasibility and, to put it strongly, is inherently unjust. The very mechanisms that offer protection to some religious practices will make others unassailable matters of "custom" or "civic ritual," "conventional wisdom" or "common sense."[14] Informal understandings of religious authenticity creep into legislation, law enforcement, and jurisprudence.[15] Secular law—to the extent that something called "secular law" can even exist—renders religion comprehensible and controllable, but it also reifies dominant understandings of religion.[16] Constitutional religious freedom clauses inevitably run up against injunctions to preserve public order. There is simply no way to offer or enjoy unfettered religious freedom.[17]

Rather than treating Japan as the unfortunate exception to a global rule, in this book I show that prewar and wartime Japan actually exemplified the normal functioning of legal regimes characterized by religious freedom.[18] Japanese governance in the first half of the twentieth century was repressive because it was secularist, not because it was dominated by Shintō as a state religion. Legal interpretations of religious freedom privileged certain ways of being and belonging over others, just as all interpretations of religious freedom do. Clerics and lay religious leaders used activism, lobbying, and legislation to secure their legal positions, just as all religious groups situated in secularist governance structures will. Policy makers and legislators based their decisions about how to free religion on their informal, inadequate, and inexpert working definitions of the term. They also turned to scholarly experts for advice, and those experts frequently injected normative ideas about "good" and "bad" religion into their policy proposals.

With the onset of the Allied Occupation in September 1945, religion was not abruptly freed with the deus ex machina arrival of the occupiers on the archipelago. It was not suddenly free just because the occupiers' 4 October 1945 Civil Liberties Directive decreed it. When the Occupation began the range of stakeholders grew and the meanings of some of the operative terms changed, but administrative and apologetic practices of freeing religion remained strikingly similar to those of the prewar and wartime period. Religious leaders bent the ears of policy makers. Policy makers asked academics for criteria they could use in determining what constituted legitimate religious practice. Scholars of religion and legal experts wrote op-eds and illustrated pamphlets telling people how to be religious and teaching them how to be free. Meanwhile, the formal disestablishment of what the occupiers called "State Shintō" (15 December 1945) and the promulgation of the "Peace Constitution" (3 November 1946) left unresolved the fundamental questions of what religion was and how this nebulous entity might be governed.

This book juxtaposes the presurrender religious freedom legal regime with that of the Allied Occupation to show that prewar and wartime Japanese practices of religious freedom were extraordinarily normal. It places Japan at the center of our global map. It shows that our shared history, like our geography, is rendered arbitrarily. Religious freedom did not travel from America to Japan during the Allied Occupation. It did not touch down when American boots hit the ground. Religious freedom was already there. It had been made in Japan along with the construction of the modern category *shūkyō* ("religion") in the late nineteenth century.[19] During the Occupation, Americans and their Japanese collaborators repackaged religious freedom as a universal human right.

THE COERCIVE NATURE OF FREEDOM

This book is about the inherently coercive nature of religious freedom. It is about how freeing religion constrains religious expression. It is about how freeing religion mobilizes the violent technologies of law enforcement and the punitive circumstances of military occupation. It is about how the ideal of religious freedom as it appears in law, policy making, and legislative lobbying always designates some remainder (rituals, commitments to empirically unverifiable realities, relationships with nonobvious entities) as not-religion. It is about how the practice of freeing religion invites the production of scholarship that designates certain institutions and practices as religion and, ineluctably, describes some other groups and activities with other terms. It is about how that same scholarship, while ostensibly neutral and re-descriptive, frequently makes activist value judgments.

My argument is not about the "impossibility of religious freedom," but rather about the politics and ethics of who gets to define the operative terms.[20] I am an equal opportunity critic. I take scholars, clerics, bureaucrats, and individuals across the political spectrum equally to task for using a lofty yet ambiguous phrase to pursue their parochial agendas. While the project is unabashedly politically motivated and admittedly may have political effects, I am resolute in being historically descriptive. For reasons that will become clear in the telling, mine is deliberately not an activist project. It is nevertheless prescriptive regarding scholarly method. I argue that scholars need to pause before evaluating specific religions or particular secularist formations according to unexamined criteria. While I do not pretend to be impartial, I do advocate a type of reflection that rejects some long-standing and widespread presuppositions about what religion is and about how religious people should behave. Specifically, I do not presume that religion is intrinsically altruistic, apolitical, or ascetic. I do not take it for granted that religion makes good people do bad things, nor do I assume that bad people sublimate their violent tendencies with religious language. I reject the notion, long favored in American policy-making circles, that religion is a guise masking reactionary politics.

I am a scholar of Japan, but my story is also about America. While I readily acknowledge that American military power makes the United States uniquely influential in the post-WWII world, I do not assume that American religious freedom is special. I emphatically reject the notion that the

American brand of religious freedom is universal. Instead, I suggest that the putatively unique qualities of the American approach to religious freedom are accidents of history that were partially shaped by American interactions with others, both in wartime and in peace. My linguistic skill set and familiarity with Japanese religious history led me to focus on Japan, but others could tell a similar story regarding American religious freedom as it has been constructed in relationship to Catholicism, Islam, or communism, both in America and elsewhere.[21]

Most directly, this book is about Japan. However, I reject commonly held assumptions about Japan's relationship with religious freedom that continue to appear in journalism, scholarship, and undergraduate textbooks. Specifically, I dispute the intertwined notions that Japanese policy makers somehow got religious freedom wrong in Article 28 of the 1889 Meiji Constitution, that Japanese religious leaders never properly understood religious freedom until the implementation of the American-drafted "Peace Constitution" in 1947, or that for the seventy-odd years since Japan's defeat the Japanese right wing has been avidly poking holes in the fragile screen separating religion from the Japanese state.[22]

For example, I show that the category of State Shintō had to be constructed to fit American military strategy and foreign policy during and immediately after the Pacific War (1941–45) at least as much as Shintō doctrine had to be molded to match expansionist ideology during Japan's Fifteen Years' War (1931–45). Without apologizing for Japan's imperialist misadventures and wartime atrocities, I demonstrate that narratives treating the Meiji constitutional legal regime as a perversion of the "principle" of religious freedom make an analytical mistake in treating religious freedom as perennial, universal, and uniform. Without going to the extreme of assuming that the Occupation policy makers were ill-intentioned, I show that they established a number of double standards when it came to freeing different types of religiosity.

Religious freedom lay at the heart of fundamental Occupation reforms in the fields of Japanese governance, education, and social life. But the centrality of the phrase in Occupation policy was belied by the ambiguity with which it was interpreted and received. Not everybody agreed on what religious freedom was or how it should be protected, but despite significant differences of opinion the occupiers were unanimous in claiming that Japan had lacked "real" religious freedom prior to their arrival. One side effect of this victors' narrative was that Japan's previous relationship with religious freedom was largely effaced.

In the first half of this book, I uncover the local history of religious freedom in prewar and wartime Japan. But as my chapter on the experiences of Japanese Americans in the interwar United States suggests, my story is also a global one. It is about the geopolitics of religious freedom, about how easily the seemingly benign idea of freeing religion abroad can be linked to imperialist projects and may have deleterious consequences.[23] Law freeing religion constrains what religion can look like and whose religion counts.[24] In domestic situations and in transnational contexts alike, the operative definitions of religion and freedom favored by policy makers, priests, and police structure the privileges granted to specific groups.[25]

Because operative definitions of religion matter, this book is also about the politics of religious studies. It is about how those of us who professionally study religion in a nonconfessional mode allow our work to be used in policy making. Some of us even seek out the attention of policy makers as a way of proving the relevance of our inquiry. I do not call for a hasty retreat into the ivory tower by making our research politically anodyne or administratively impractical, but I do argue that we must be cognizant and explicit about the politics we champion when we discuss religion-state relations in any time or place.

Indeed, I wrote this book with a keen awareness of how scholarly narratives render historical change in the dramatic language of decline and efflorescence, antagonism and reconciliation.[26] The structure of the story is mine, but I recount my tale by translating, summarizing, and juxtaposing the words of historical figures who weighed in on the idea of religious freedom during the time that Japan's first constitutional guarantee of religious freedom was in place (in the Meiji Constitution, promulgated in 1889 and in effect from 1890 until it was suspended at the onset of the Occupation in 1945). These historical characters were not necessarily liberal heroes who championed religious freedom based on their unimpeachable commitments to lofty democratic principles, but neither were they necessarily chauvinists who sublimated their persecution of others through the language of religious freedom. My story is not about how principled men fought the law and won, nor is it about how principled men fought the law and lost. Rather, it is about how interested parties bent the word of the law to their political wills and made it accommodate their doctrinal and political agendas. It is, however, unfortunately almost entirely about *men*: I searched the archive in vain for the voices of women who weighed in on the issues I discuss. That is not to say that women did not care about religious freedom or had nothing to say about it, but in my primary sources they mostly appear as supporting characters (translators and other clerical staff working in the Occupation Religion and Cultural Resources Division, for example) if they appear at all.

By situating what I call the Meiji constitutional regime as a form of secularism with a legitimate and robust set of protections for religious freedom, I reject the essentialism that reduces complex social phenomena to simplistic catchphrases ("State Shintō") or ethnocentric models ("the Japan-style relationship between religion and the state").[27] This reframing has the salutary effect of making Japan important neither because it is the exception to the Western rule and therefore illegitimate (the State Shintō model) nor because it is a woefully misunderstood victim of the quasi-colonial imposition of the foreign category of religion (the "unique Japanese secularity" model).[28] I show instead that Japanese people have played significant roles in structuring global conceptions of religious freedom and ideal religion-state relations even as they have applied global norms and concepts to local circumstances.

Finally, by juxtaposing modern Japan and the United States, I show that while cultural differences and historical contingency elicit variant approaches to freeing religion, religious freedom regimes share structural similarities because they demand that stakeholders define religion in order to free it. I show that early attempts to render religious freedom as a human right were a natural outcome of the inherently transnational Allied Occupation, but I also show that human rights talk came into use unevenly. I focus particularly on how scholars of religion played a crucial role in constructing a universal religious anthropology that could support the new human rights claims by positing religiosity as the irreducible core of humanity. I also show how academic rhetoric that was born in the administrative circumstances of the Occupation came to structure a postwar politics of religious freedom that has had global and lasting effects.

OVERVIEW OF THE BOOK

At the risk of obfuscating the significant continuities in the governance of religions that exist across the prewar, wartime, and Occupation eras, I have divided this book into two parts. The book is organized chronologically, but readers who are most interested in American foreign policy and the role of religious freedom in the Occupation will probably prefer to begin in part 2 (starting with chapter 5) and then return to the prewar and wartime period documented in part 1. While this reading strategy breaks the book's chronology, it does not substantially alter the narrative. In fact, the book could easily be organized the other way around.

The two-part organization also facilitates another reading strategy, which is to pair chapters 1 and 5, 2 and 6, and so forth. As the matching titles suggest, each of these chapter pairs deals with a specific issue, specifically: 1) the nature of secularism and concomitant implications for religious freedom, with particular emphasis on Shintō (chapters 1 and 5); 2) differences in how competing interest groups interpreted religious freedom, with a focus on collaborative and contested relationships between transsectarian groups and state actors (chapters 2 and 6); 3) the tension between the universalist aspirations of religious freedom language and particularist applications thereof (chapters 3 and 7); and 4) the role of religious studies scholarship in demarcating "good" and "bad" versions of religion (chapters 4 and 8).

My argument will stand whether one chooses to read the book chronologically, thematically, or by beginning with the Occupation in part 2 and then returning to its prehistory in part 1. Readers who are interested in law will notice that each chapter focuses on particular legal problem, but I must note at the outset that most of my data comes from debates about legislation, law enforcement, and policy rather than jurisprudence (I do not, for example, spend much time on the Tokyo War Crimes Tribunal).[29] This is a side effect of how I encountered my sources in the archive rather than a programmatic research decision. I leave it to others to conduct a more robust historical analysis of case law under what I call the Meiji constitutional regime.[30]

Part 1 shows that while the oppressive nature of the war years was real, the claim that Japan lacked religious freedom prior to the onset of the Occupation is simply incorrect. The chapters of this section show that competing Japanese interest groups engaged in a robust, disputatious conversation about religious freedom during the entirety of what I call the Meiji constitutional period (1890–1945). Chapter 1 describes the Meiji constitutional regime as a secularist system, showing how governance of religions reflected ongoing, essentially anxious attempts to establish and maintain a workable religion/not-religion paradigm.[31]

Following the broad historical and theoretical overview offered in chapter 1, the remaining chapters of part 1 offer a roughly chronological account. In chapter 2, I show that Buddhists began to develop theories of religious freedom and ideal religion-state relations in the late 1890s in response to the perceived threat of "mixed residence," a policy under which foreign

Christians would be granted the unprecedented right to live side by side with Japanese nationals. I also show that while Buddhists were nearly unanimous in their opposition to an 1899 governmental attempt to strictly administer religions through proposed legislation, different Buddhist interest groups advanced competing visions of religious freedom in their attempts to scuttle the controversial bill.

Chapter 3 shifts across the Pacific to the American territory of Hawaiʻi. I show that Japanese American Buddhists developed homegrown theories of religious freedom in the broader context of internal debates about the desirability of "Americanization" (*beika*) and contemporaneous American concerns about whether Japanese language schools run in conjunction with Buddhist missions interfered with Japanese Americans' cultural assimilation. Chapter 4 compares three radically different interpretations of religious freedom held by politically active Buddhists in the first two decades of the Shōwa era (1926–89), showing that received narratives of Buddhist resistance, complicity, and martyrdom are excessively simplistic.

As the preceding paragraph suggests, Buddhist primary sources dominate the first half of the book, and most of the Buddhists who appear in the text hail from the Jōdo Shinshū (True Pure Land sect). This focus on Buddhist sources is partially because Buddhism dominated the Japanese religious landscape and therefore dictated understandings of mainstream religiosity. The focus on Shinshū thinkers is mostly accidental, but it also reflects a long-standing sectarian tradition of theorizing about the proper relationship between sovereign and Buddhist law.[32]

At any rate, these Buddhist sources offer stunning insight into the actual position of Shintō in Japanese social and political life during the Meiji constitutional period. Rather than suggesting that Buddhists saw themselves as subordinate to an ascendant State Shintō, my sources show that Shintō was never fully established as a state religion in the way that the occupiers would later claim.[33] To the extent that they acknowledged the idea of Shintō as a national religion, Buddhists rejected it as preposterous. This was true even as some of them accepted that shrine rites unproblematically constituted a kind of patriotic civic ritual. This attitude was not a violation of Buddhist doctrine, nor was it a misunderstanding of religious freedom. Collectively, the chapters of part 1 show that it was a systematic application of both.

Part 2 focuses on Occupation policies regarding religion. In chapter 5, I briefly introduce the basic policy orientations of presurrender planning before showing that the category State Shintō was artificially constructed in the first few months of the Occupation to serve as a foil for the religious freedom the occupiers were instructed to establish. In chapter 6, I argue that Occupation governance of religion exhibited significant continuities with the wartime regime despite the occupiers' insistence that they were teaching the Japanese people to desire religious freedom; I also demonstrate that the occupiers seriously disagreed on the question of how to define religious freedom. In chapter 7, I show that the postwar reconfiguration of religious freedom as a human right took place because Occupation policy makers, Japanese legal experts, and scholars of religion were situated in a peculiar legal situation that demanded universalizing language. Chapter 8 makes a reflexive turn by looking at how the Occupation directly affected postwar religious studies, both in Japan and globally. I show that postwar scholarship generated in Japan helped define the political contours of the new conception of religious-freedom-as-human-right by creating globally influential visions of "good" and "bad" religion.[34]

The book concludes with some reflections on the academic field of religious studies and its complicated relationship with religious freedom in the post-9/11 world. While I would rather live in a world in which policy makers listen to scholars of religion than one in which they did not, I regard the mobilization of religious studies expertise in police work and foreign policy with suspicion. I am not so naive as to assume that scholars of religion can generate scholarship that is entirely divorced from our own political commitments, but I am concerned that religious studies scholars' contributions to policy making can unwittingly serve as vectors for missionary work and apologetic projects in ways that we do not intend. Perceptions of crisis and concern with proving our relevance may compel us to advance prescriptive claims in the guise of neutral advice. The conclusion therefore offers some thoughts about how scholars of religion might responsibly approach religious freedom with a firm sense of where the protean and porous line lies between politically prescriptive claims and re-descriptive aims. The epilogue uses musical metaphor and a lyrical tone to trace the autobiographical factors that brought me to this project.

MAKING RELIGION TO FREE IT

Of necessity there are points in this book where I make functionalist arguments about the role of the religion/not-religion distinction in Japanese and American imperial governance. But I am concerned less with social and political *function* than with the constructed, contingent, and contested nature of what Tisa Wenger calls "religious freedom talk."[35] Focusing on the importance of the category "religion" in shifting conceptions of religious freedom, throughout this book I follow a precedent set by Markus Dressler, Arvind-Pal S. Mandair, and Elizabeth Shakman Hurd by investigating three rhetorical stances vis-à-vis religion: the supposedly dispassionate, re-descriptive gaze of the scholar or the journalist (expert religion/religion-making from outside); the bureaucrat's anxiety that religion may be a potentially oppressive or subversive force (governed religion/religion-making from above); and the apologetic concern on the part of clerics or adherents that the state make decisions conducive to religious flourishing (lived religion/religion-making from below).[36] Each chapter of this book traces how scholars, journalists, bureaucrats, clerics, and lay religious leaders "made" religion and, in so doing, demarcated the scope of religious freedom and identified its potential beneficiaries.

Religion-making traffics not only in the twin concepts of "religion" and "the secular," but also in associated concepts such as "superstition," "magic," "spirituality," and "science."[37] Although any of these terms might perform a religion-making function, none is guaranteed to appear in any given primary source. This creates an interpretive challenge in that some acts of religion-making have to be apprehended when the word "religion" itself is not used. By extension, some demarcations of the limits of religious freedom will happen through processes of religion-making that do not make explicit mention of the words "religion" or "freedom." There are places in this book where I have necessarily made my arguments about religious freedom through reference to policies, scholarship, lobbying, and legislation that did not always explicitly discuss religious freedom as such. For example, academic and bureaucratic attempts to suppress or control "superstitions" and the debates over the ideal "religions system" for modern Japan served as proxies for discussions of religious freedom in that they drew the boundaries of religion and liberties alike. Accordingly, throughout the text I do not refer to the mutually constitutive categories of "religion" and "the secular," but rather to "religion" and "not-religion."

A final point to make before I turn to the content chapters is that religious freedom has a material quality and a tactile feel. To the extent that "it" is a single thing (I do not think that it is), then it is about access to land. It is about who gets to cut down that tree over there. It is the precise size of the debris left over after police have demolished a building (less than one foot, in the case of the Special Higher Police suppression of Ōmotokyō in 1935).[38]

Religious freedom is the racialization of human bodies; it is a tool for rendering potentially unruly populations docile. Religious freedom is sensual. It is the familiar scent of incense wafting from a temple reminding Japanese Americans in Hawaiʻi of their ancestral home; it is the alien look of a Christian burial ground situated on Japanese soil. Religious freedom is corporeal and affective. It is the feeling of bowing to the imperial portrait at a Japanese school or the physical practice of mastering the Japanese language in an American classroom. It is the twinge of guilt or the sense of righteousness one feels when burning someone else's cherished family altar, the perplexity that greets the scratchy sound of a divine emperor declaring that he is all too human in a widely publicized radio address. My evidence below is primarily textual and discursive, but the real-world impacts of the essays, lectures, and op-eds I cite were very tangible, if not always sensible.

A PREOCCUPATION WITH RELIGIOUS FREEDOM

01

THE MEIJI CONSTITUTIONAL REGIME AS A SECULARIST SYSTEM

> If the "Shintō" of the proponents [of making Shintō the national religion] indicates the Great Divine Way [*kannagara no daidō*], then it is neither a national religion [*kokkyō*] nor a popular religion [*minkyō*]. As long as one is a Japanese citizen, it [the Great Divine Way] is one's conviction, the object of one's respect, and the inexhaustible article of faith. However, what we must understand is that the Great Divine Way is not a religion. If it was a religion, because belief is free [under the constitution], then that article of faith and that respect [characteristic of the Great Divine Way] would be circumscribed. The general meaning of the Great Divine Way is different; it is the supreme directive to Japanese people. More than a supreme directive, it is the same as [being] "Japanese." From the moment we are born, it suffuses the bodies and spirits of us Japanese. In contrast to this, Sect Shintō, Buddhism, and Christianity are religions. Because they are religions, according to the point established by the constitution, "Japanese subjects shall, within limits not prejudicial to peace and order, and not antagonistic to their duties as subjects, enjoy freedom of religious belief." Therefore the arguments for national and popular religions enter into the problem of constitutional revision, and should not be taken lightly.
>
> ANDŌ MASAZUMI (1942)[1]

IN AN 1872 OPEN LETTER PENNED in English and submitted to Japanese prime minister Sanjō Saneyoshi (1837–91), famed statesman Mori Arinori (1847–89) wrote the following:

> Among many important human concerns, the one respecting our religious faith appears to be the most vital. In all the enlightened nations of the earth, the liberty of conscience, especially in matters of religious faith, is sacredly regarded as not only an inherent right of man, but also as a most fundamental element to advance all human interests.
>
> It is a strange and grievous fact that we fail to find in the whole history of the long and glorious continuance of our intelligent race, a trace of the recognition in any form of this sacred right. It is even more remarkable, amid the wonderful progress we now behold, that our people are not as yet quite earnest and thorough in their consideration of this important subject.[2]

Mori went on to propose that the Japanese government establish proper laws "by which all the proper rights of man shall be recognized and protected from violence," and that it establish an educational system "by which the whole condition of our people shall be so elevated that their moral strength will sufficiently protect their rights, even without the additional dry and unsatisfactory shield of the written law of the state."[3]

The problem that Mori aimed to address was epistemological as much as it was legal. To think of religious freedom as a right that needed to be protected, one needed the modern concept of religion: exclusivist, private, belief-centric, a universal genus of which there were many competing species.[4] To think of religious freedom as an "inherent right of man," one needed to think of rights as inalienable (even as one also thought of them as endangered).[5] As Japan's first ambassador to the United States, Mori was keenly aware of these issues. He knew that solving some of Japan's most pressing diplomatic concerns, such as revising unequal treaties, hinged on them (hence the simultaneous publication of his missive in both English and Japanese).

By the time Japanese oligarchs promulgated the Meiji Constitution in the name of the emperor in February 1889, Mori and his colleague Itō Hirobumi (1841–1909) had successfully made the case that incorporating a provision for religious freedom in the national charter would definitively mark Japan as one of the few "civilized" nations of the world.[6] But Mori was stabbed on the very day that the new constitution was promulgated, and he died the following day. The assassination of one of Japan's foremost champions of religious freedom at the hands of an ultranationalist who was purportedly enraged by Mori's alleged disrespectful comportment at the

Ise Shrines could easily seem to presage the demise of religious freedom in Japan.

Indeed, although the Meiji Constitution incorporated a clause guaranteeing freedom of religious belief that was similar in wording and scope to the constitutions of many contemporaneous European constitutional monarchies, scholars writing in the postwar period have frequently suggested that the Japanese clause was inherently flawed.[7] Some have argued that the architects of the Meiji state failed to understand "real" religious freedom and therefore unnecessarily circumscribed this crucial civil liberty through the language of civic duties. They also claim that the constitutional clause proved to be ineffective at protecting the rights of marginal groups such as Christians or members of the many religious confraternities, sects, and movements that flourished in the late nineteenth and early twentieth centuries.[8] Many have also argued that the small degree of religious freedom the constitution guaranteed was attenuated, and then wholly abandoned, in the years following its promulgation.

For example, the "clash of education and religion" debates that followed the Christian educator Uchimura Kanzō's (1861–1930) principled refusal to bow before the imperial portrait in 1891 revealed significant disagreements about how to balance the "duties of subjects" with the provision for religious liberty.[9] Subsequent police crackdowns on marginal movements such as Renmonkyō (late 1890s) and Ōmotokyō (1921 and 1935) seemed to confirm that "real" religious liberty in Japan breathed its last breath along with its former champion Mori in 1889.[10] When Japan lost the Pacific War and the Allied Occupation began, the occupiers in charge of religions policy repeatedly claimed that Japan had no genuine tradition of religious freedom. Japanese modernizers made similar claims in support of their own reformist projects.[11] In these postwar accounts, Japanese religious freedom was born with Mori's 1872 missive and died with him the day after the Meiji Constitution was promulgated. Religious freedom, the story goes, only returned to life when the benevolent American occupiers swooped in to Japan at the close of the war, liberating Japan's citizens from their oppressive and theocratic government.

There are very good reasons to question this pat narrative, particularly because it clearly served the political purpose of justifying Occupation reforms related to religion. If we only look at historical sources generated during the Occupation and in the first several decades after it, then Japan during what I will call the Meiji constitutional period appears wholly bereft of religious freedom.[12] If, however, we examine sources from the Meiji constitutional period itself, we find instead a surfeit of discussion about religious freedom and ideal religion-state relations. Japanese people were not ignorant of religious freedom. In fact, they were deeply concerned about it and were constantly trying to figure out how to make it work. Because they had adopted the category of "religion" in their diplomatic relations and because they had formally separated religion from politics in constitutional law, Japanese people *had* to distinguish religion from not-religion. The problem was that not everyone agreed on where to draw the line. The religion/not-religion distinction established in Japanese constitutional law prompted ongoing anxiety about how to separate religion from other aspects of social and political life. This uncertainty prompted a range of stakeholders to weigh in on the vexing question of whether compulsory participation in shrine rites constituted infringement on the right to religious liberty.[13]

This background chapter tracks the ebbs and flows of this contentious discourse in broad strokes by focusing on how debates about religious freedom revealed the shifting and diverse religion/not-religion distinctions that undergirded the Meiji constitutional regime.[14] Subsequent chapters of part 1 focus on particular legal debates in which specific interest groups defined and defended religious freedom as they understood it. I show that religious freedom is not simply a matter of constitutional law or national policy, but is rather determined at subnational scales in response to disputes over property, privileges, and precedent.[15] I also show that Japan's relationship with religious freedom was not aberrant in comparison to global norms. Japanese interest groups tactically imported and adapted interpretations of religious freedom based on their interpretations of what worked for "civilized" North American and European nations. In chapter 3, I show through examples of Japanese immigrant experiences in the United States that American perspectives on religious freedom were just as incoherent as Japanese practices were. Collectively, the chapters of part 1 thoroughly undermine the occupiers' claim that they understood religious freedom and that their Japanese counterparts did not.

To make this claim stick, I first have to prove that prewar and wartime Japan was repressive not because it was dominated by a state religion, as has commonly been assumed, but rather because the religion/not-religion arrangement adopted in the Meiji Constitution allowed politicians, policy makers, priests, and police to designate certain practices as deserving of protection and others as inimical to peace and order. It was the act of discriminating between religion and not-religion that allowed for draconian crackdowns on particular movements and apparent infringements on religious liberty, not the dominance of what scholars before me have called "State Shintō." Put differently, what we know today as State Shintō was a *symptom* of a deeper conceptual arrangement, not the *cause* of illiberal practices of governance.[16] As Yijiang Zhong has stated, the modern Japanese state "should not be understood as a peculiar case in which an irrational and religious form of divine authority was mobilized to justify an authoritarian modern state." Instead, "the formation of the ambivalent political authority in Meiji Japan was a process galvanized by the imperative to devise and institute the mutually constituting categories of the religious and the secular, in order to construct the formally secular, public, political authority of the modern nation-state."[17]

Japanese secularity was not weird. It was normal. It is the normalcy of the Japanese religion/not-religion distinction that should disturb us, not the peculiar qualities of theocratic State Shintō. There is no doubt whatsoever that the prewar and wartime Japanese state was unjust. Police surveilled and suppressed religious groups. Religious leaders died in prison. But our diagnosis of why this state of affairs was even possible has been deeply flawed.

DEMARCATING THE MEIJI CONSTITUTIONAL PERIOD

The common claim that the Occupation introduced religious freedom where there previously was none is ideologically driven more than it is factually correct. It overlooks a mountain of historical evidence that indisputably demonstrates that Japanese people argued vociferously throughout the time the Meiji Constitution was in effect about what religious freedom meant and how it could best be secured. In addition to debating the meaning of the words "religion" and "freedom" and what it meant to juxtapose them, stakeholders attempted to define a constellation of related terms such as superstition, morality, tradition, and civic ritual. While Article 28 of the Meiji Constitution clearly circumscribed the guarantee of religious freedom offered to Japanese imperial subjects through its references to "duties" and "peace and order," it did not deny them that freedom outright, nor was its language particularly strict in comparison with other constitutions of the time.[18]

To my knowledge few have systematically examined this period when

Japan's first constitutional guarantee of religious freedom was in effect as a discrete historical era, but there are compelling reasons to do so.[19] The period from 1890 to 1945 was bookended by interactions with the United States (especially) and European nations in which the concept of religious freedom played a major role. It opened with the Japanese government's overt attempt to appeal to the international community by providing a constitutional guarantee of religious freedom as one mark of Japan's entry into the ranks of "civilized" nations.[20] It closed when the occupiers suspended the Meiji Constitution at the formal onset of the Occupation.

The subsequent promulgation of the American-drafted "Peace Constitution" in November 1946 was designed to replace the previous Japanese system of religion-state relations with a new democratic system characterized by what the occupiers understood as "real religious freedom." Understandably, this watershed legal-historical moment has attracted considerable academic attention and remains a hotly contested point in contemporary Japanese politics. I take up the ramifications of the American reforms in the second half of this book, but my unconventional periodization in the first half focuses attention on the broad characteristics of the legal regime that preceded this stunning Occupation intervention into Japanese political life.

My periodization also serves as a corrective for the fact that many studies of modern Japanese religions have focused on the Meiji era (1868–1912) at the expense of sustained engagement with broader time spans.[21] Conversely, some scholars specializing in the history of Shintō and its relationship with the state have treated the entirety of the period from 1868 to 1945 as a single historical period, often making the inaccurate assertion that Shintō served as Japan's national religion throughout that time.[22] The former approach artificially divides up history according to imperial reign dates and therefore obscures legal and political continuities across different eras of imperial rule. The latter approach articulates history according to two drastic political transitions (the "restoration" of direct rule to the emperor in 1868; the "democratization" of Japan in 1945), but it obscures significant conceptual, legal, and political shifts that took place both during and across the Meiji (1868–1912), Taishō (1912–26), and early Shōwa (1926–89) eras. Many of these shifts were associated with major changes in the position of religion in Japanese society, law, and politics.[23] Here I will trace a few of the main dynamics that contributed to the prevailing understandings of religion and law in the period under question, providing a brief overview of the prehistory of the Meiji Constitution before I discuss the impact of the formal establishment of religious freedom in constitutional law.

The Prehistory of the Meiji Constitutional Religious Freedom Clause

The 1889 provision of a constitutional religious freedom clause represented a major change from the Japanese government's earlier attempts to establish a single "national teaching."[24] Historically, the tradition we now call Shintō had only recently come into its own as a discrete religion distinct from Buddhism, with a series of purifying moves beginning in the fourteenth century culminating in the forceful separation of Shintō and Buddhism following the political revolution of 1868.[25] After the political transition "restoring" the emperor to direct rule in 1868, a brief period of anti-Buddhist violence known as *haibutsu kishaku* ("destroy the buddhas; expel Śākyamuni") ensued. During this time, proponents of making Shintō the national religion advocated the utter rejection of Buddhism as a foreign creed unsuitable to the Japanese national character.[26]

By the time the anti-Buddhist fervor died down in the early 1870s, the architects of the modern Japanese state began experimenting with religion and education as methods for fostering a new sense of national identity. This effort characterized the Great Promulgation Campaign (*Taikyō senpu undō*) that took place between 1872 and 1884, when the state enrolled Shintō priests, Buddhist clerics, and popular entertainers in the project of disseminating a vague "national teaching" to the populace through standardized lectures on the three basic doctrines of "revering the gods and loving the country," "following the principle of heaven and the way of humanity," and "dedicating oneself to the emperor and honoring and protecting the court."

The project was fraught from the outset. In the wake of the anti-Buddhist persecution of the late 1860s, Buddhist commitment to the new "national teaching" campaign was understandably muted. The Japanese state had also intervened in Buddhist affairs by bypassing clerical authority in matters of marriage and diet. The *nikujiki saitai* edict of 1872 gave priests permission to eat meat and to marry, effectively annulling a long-standing legal arrangement in which Buddhist clerics were regarded as separate from ordinary citizens due to their ascetic commitments.[27] Buddhists resented state intrusion into what they saw as their traditional jurisdictions and the perquisites that accompanied clerical status. Controversial land reforms in the 1870s and 1880s exacerbated these tensions when the state expropriated public lands that had previously been leased to Buddhist organizations in a long-term arrangement with the Tokugawa government.[28] Governmental interference in shrines' and temples' customary rights to land and property would recur during the Meiji constitutional period (see chapter 4) and under the Occupation (see chapter 6). A new governmental policy of tolerating Christianity after centuries of prohibition further complicated the tense relationship between Buddhist and Shintō priests, spurring battles over customary rights and over the proper definition of "religion."[29]

The anti-Buddhist campaigns of the early Meiji years and Buddhists' negative reactions to state initiatives fostered a dramatic increase in efforts at transsectarian organization. Stunned by the vociferous attacks on their tradition and freshly motivated to secure their rights and privileges from the state, Buddhist intellectuals began a series of initiatives designed to prove the value of their tradition to Japanese society. Precept revival movements emphasized Buddhist probity as a way of counteracting claims of widespread degeneracy.[30] Transsectarian newspapers like *Meikyō shinshi* appealed to a broad Buddhist audience, reflecting the political reality that Buddhists needed to band together in the face of widespread calumny. Against the backdrop of these transsectarian collaborations, Buddhists of the Jōdo Shinshū (True Pure Land Sect) were particularly influential in pushing for more clarity in the relationship between religion and politics, religion and education, and religion and national morality.[31] Later chapters will show that Shinshū thinkers continued to play an outsized role in public debates about how to draw the line between religion and not-religion.

Even as Buddhists circled the wagons to protect their customary rights and defend their collective reputation, the newly created Shintō religion was starting to come apart.[32] Disputes between rival lineages over the rankings of deities in the Shintō pantheon in 1879–80 resulted in the bifurcation of Shintō into an "official" *nonreligious* cult of the Japanese state (centered on the imperial ancestor Amaterasu and the Ise Shrines) and an "unofficial" *religious* congeries of sects and confraternities devoted to specific shrines and their deities.[33] By 1882, Shintō priests were no longer allowed to serve as doctrinal instructors in the Great Promulgation Campaign, and the division between the "official" and "unofficial" aspects of Shintō became partially formalized. Thereafter, "shrine rites" would be the official cult of the imperial Japanese state, while "Sect Shintō" would designate the various confraternities and teaching assemblies dedicated to native *kami*. In 1884 the government finalized the disambiguation of the religious world by designating national rites (*kokka no sōshi*) as Japan's suprareligious political orthodoxy while treating Sect Shintō, Buddhism, and Christianity equally as "religions." The 1889 Constitution of the Great Empire of Japan formalized this new arrangement with the provision of religious liberty in Article 28.[34]

Notably, while foreign observers occasionally expressed concern about Christian missionaries' abilities to do their work, they generally seem to have thought of Japan's constitutional guarantee of religious freedom as legitimate.[35] Equally notable is the fact that the aforementioned policy shifts took place in response to public remonstrations with the government advanced by prominent Buddhist intellectuals such as Shimaji Mokurai (1838–1911) and Ōuchi Seiran (1845–1918). The shifts not only reflected disputed understandings of "public" and "private" and how religion fit within them; they also reflected competition between various governmental factions who favored policies of freeing religious belief or tolerating religious difference.[36] This pattern of public dissent and internal dispute remained unchanged after the Meiji Constitution went into effect in 1890.

THE SECULARIST MEIJI CONSTITUTIONAL REGIME

Using terminology that matches my name for the period, I designate as the "Meiji constitutional regime" the legal and political system that was established with the implementation of the Constitution of the Empire of Japan in 1890 and disestablished at the onset of the Allied Occupation in September 1945.[37] This legal regime featured Japan's first formal constitutional guarantee of religious freedom, and I argue that it must be understood as inherently secularist insofar as it was premised on the presupposition that "religion" could and should be separated from "not-religion." I distinguish here between "religion" and "not-religion" rather than between "religion" and "the secular" because conceptions of "religion" appeared in juxtaposition with a host of other terms such as "superstition," "morality," "customs," "rituals," "festivals," and "rites," any of which might been coded as "religion" or as "not-religion," depending on who was doing the interpreting. I should also mention that by this time the Japanese term *shūkyō* had been thoroughly established as the accepted translation for the English word "religion," but the term *sezoku*, nowadays translated as "the secular," had not yet come into consistent usage.[38]

My argument that the Meiji constitutional regime was secularist is consistent with scholarship that has focused on secularism as a political ideology and set of associated legal and administrative practices.[39] In this view, a supposedly neutral social field ("the secular") lies under the jurisdiction of the state, and religions feature as private entities that may influence, but are nevertheless purportedly separate from, this neutral field.[40] The state assumes control over the realm of indisputable fact and unquestionable political authority, while groups designated as religions vie for jurisdiction over nonempirical fields.

But I am less concerned with "the secular" as the artificial field that policy makers envision as prior to and independent of "religion" than I am with the ongoing and perennially uncertain activity of discriminating between "religion" and "nonreligion."[41] States draw distinctions between religion and not-religion in the name of adopting a policy of noninterference in religions' affairs, but in doing so they inevitably make doctrinal claims and adjudicate empirically unverifiable matters.[42] Agents of states recognize certain groups, practices, and ideas as legitimate "religions" while dismissing others as illegitimate "superstitions" or "cults." State representatives also premise legislation, law enforcement, and jurisprudence on majoritarian definitions of religion, which may be tacit or intuitive rather than explicit.[43] In turn, religious groups may "speak up" to state authority in order to have their legitimacy recognized. They may also form transsectarian or transdenominational organizations that can influence policy makers' understandings of what constitutes mainstream religiosity. Policy makers and religious leaders alike may then turn to scholars to adjudicate these religion-making practices, in this case from an ostensibly neutral position "outside" of garden-variety theological and political claims.[44]

If *secularism* designates the ideology that undergirds this legal-political-academic arrangement, then *secularity* in my account refers to the paradoxical situation in which the act of sequestering religion from not-religion constantly begs the question of how the operative terms should be defined.[45] Secularity is therefore not the mere absence of religion, nor is it the progressive diminution of religion in public life ("secularization"), nor is it simply a state of affairs characterized by the assumption that mundane concerns supersede transcendent ones. Secularity is, rather, the state of being uncertain about what counts as religion and what does not. Secularity is anxious.

The Meiji constitutional regime was *normatively* secularist because the constitution explicitly drew a distinction between the realm of religion and the ostensibly neutral field of society (although the figure of the emperor as head of state and Shintō high priest constituted a gray zone, as it does in the postwar constitution).[46] It was *functionally* secularist because the religion/not-religion distinction dictated social, legal, and political life, with real effects on human bodies, populations, and the demarcation of property: some things appeared as special, sacrosanct, tax exempt; others did not.[47]

But most importantly for my argument, various stakeholders collectively *constructed* the Meiji constitutional regime as secularist by drawing the lines between religion and not-religion in pursuit of their specific administrative and apologetic projects.

I find the language of secularism useful because, to paraphrase Hussein Ali Agrama, I am interested in how Japanese people asked and answered the question of where to draw the line between religion and politics, how they assumed that such a line could be drawn in the first place, and how they used such demarcations to establish a range of rights and duties, including religious freedom. Indeed, the Japanese case perfectly exemplifies Agrama's point that "what best characterizes secularism is not a separation between religion and politics, and not simply state regulation of religion, but an ongoing, deepening entanglement in the *question* of religion and politics, for the purpose of identifying and securing fundamental liberal rights and freedoms."[48]

The Meiji constitutional regime was secularist in precisely this sense, and the ways that different interest groups mobilized the concept of religious freedom show that the question of how to separate religion from politics remained perennially vexing and forever unanswered. As Benjamin Schonthal has argued in the case of Buddhist-majority Sri Lanka, this ongoing tension does not mark the failure of constitutionalism. Rather, "the endurance and depth of conflicts over religion are, counterintuitively, the partial consequence of creating and relying on constitutional law in the first place."[49] Finbarr Curtis has similarly suggested about religious freedom specifically that "without conflict among political actors, there would be no need to define a discreet [*sic*] area of social life called religion and then insist that it should be protected. Conflict is not what happens when already formed religions bump into each other in public life; conflict makes religions."[50]

Under the Meiji constitutional regime, it was quite common for the language of religious freedom to be used at cross-purposes by competing groups, but it was decidedly not the case that nobody talked about religious freedom, nor was it the case that clerics were ignorant of the concept. Diplomats, priests, and scholars of religion had equally compelling but essentially conflicting reasons for interpreting religious freedom as an international norm, as a customary right, or as a flimsy legal fiction. Policy makers, legislators, and police discriminated between "religion" and "not-religion" as they established law and as they enforced it.

The potentially counterintuitive point here is that secularist governance is intrinsically oppressive at least as much as it is potentially emancipatory.

The Meiji constitutional regime was indisputably repressive, but it was repressive because the always-unresolved question of how to define religion left open the possibility that groups and practices that *appeared to be religion* were not in fact religion at all. This was equally true for marginal movements (which police could suppress as "lascivious heresies," *inshi jakyō*) and shrine rites (which moralists could describe as nonreligious civic duties).[51]

What about State Religion?

As I will show in more detail near the end of this chapter, the question of whether citizens' compulsory participation in shrine rites constituted a national religion or a type of nonreligious civic ritual was one particularly contentious topic over which various Japanese stakeholders spilled lots of ink. Indeed, the obvious preponderance of Shintō-derived rituals and ideas in Japanese public life during the Meiji constitutional period is one of the main reasons scholars before me have depicted the Meiji constitutional regime as theocratic and illiberal. Their reasonable assumption has been that the utter dominance of one religion in public life could only have happened at the expense of religious liberty. But while the Japanese secular was clearly constructed in conjunction with conceptions of sovereignty, territory, and divine kingship derived from classical Shintō mythology and early modern exegeses thereof (what Jason Josephson has called the "Shintō secular"), modern Buddhist apologetic claims calling for a more thoroughgoing separation of the spheres of religion and politics also contributed to the protean forms Japanese secularism ultimately took.[52] Internal and external pressures from Christians also meant that Japanese secularity developed in relation to a set of international legal norms and practices associated with Christianity-centric concepts of "civilization" and "religious freedom" favored by the Western imperial powers.[53] By the time of the creation of the 1889 constitution and the promulgation of the Imperial Rescript on Education in 1890, the Japanese government had instituted a system in which certain empirically unverifiable propositions (imperial divine descent) and ritual practices (paying reverence to the emperor) appeared as nonnegotiable aspects of citizenship and public life. Meanwhile, administrators relegated "religion" (*shūkyō*, a term that now indicated Buddhism, "Sect Shintō," and Christianity) to the private sphere, regarding it as a matter of elective affiliation and personal belief.[54]

When viewed in conjunction with the preconstitutional push to make Shintō Japan's "national teaching," at first glance this compromise seems to have established a sort of emperor-centric state religion in that it based political reality on empirically unverifiable claims. The constitution rendered the emperor "sacred and inviolable," and educators and moralists exhorted citizens to pay reverence to his divine ancestors who appeared in the Japanese mythic histories *Kojiki* and *Nihon shoki*. Schoolchildren participated in compulsory shrine visits and the government administered shrines as public institutions. It was for these reasons that British observer Basil Hall Chamberlain published a short tract with the Rationalist Press in 1912 that described the "invention of a new religion" in which bureaucrats professed belief even though they knew it was "not true."[55] This invented tradition came to be known in English as "Mikadoism" (see chapter 3) and, during the Occupation, as State Shintō (see chapter 5).

What appeared to the freethinker Chamberlain as a new religion, however, was in actuality a developing secularist system.[56] Japanese policy makers set up a putatively neutral public sphere of civic ritual and designated certain types of beliefs and commitments as "religious" (and therefore equal before and protected by the law) while treating others as either required "patriotic duties" or forbidden "superstitions." This ideological project facilitated the management of claims to transcendent authority by placing some of those claims within the exclusive jurisdiction of the state and permitting others to survive in the form of tolerated "religions."[57] Japan's constitutional arrangement therefore matched the language of other monarchies that had recently adopted constitutional law: royal authority derived from transcendent principles usually associated with "religion" while representative democracy governed the temporal realm.[58]

This arrangement became further entrenched over the first four decades of the twentieth century through a series of administrative shifts that further disaggregated shrine rites from "religious" Shintō. First, the government separated the administration of shrines from that of religions with the establishment of the Shrine Bureau and Religions Bureau in the Home Ministry (1900). Next, a government-led program of shrine mergers beginning in 1906 affected how local shrines appeared in a national hierarchy of state ritual institutions, negatively impacting local shrine finances and often forcing priests (who were now underpaid employees of the state) to seek additional income by providing "religious" ritual services on the sly. The separation of shrine rites from "religion" was further accomplished with the move of the Religions Bureau (Shūkyō Kyoku) to the Ministry of Education while leaving the Shrine Bureau (Jinja Kyoku) within the Home Ministry (1913).

Meanwhile, imperial pageantry and public monuments reinforced the perception that imperial mythology was historical fact.[59] Ideologues reconfigured the Ise Shrine complex as an imperial mausoleum (late 1800s), actively promoted the idea that Yasukuni Shrine in Tokyo served as the final resting place for Japan's deified war dead, and established Meiji Shrine as a new imperial mausoleum in the late 1910s (figure 1; the shrine was commissioned in 1912 and completed in 1920).[60] These ideological efforts intensified as Japan entered a period of fifteen years of uninterrupted war. For example, the Ministry of Education's 1937 pamphlet *Kokutai no hongi* (*The Cardinal Principles of the Body Politic*) rendered imperial mythology as indisputable historical fact, and shrine visits became increasingly compulsory by the late 1930s.

These administrative initiatives of the executive branch troubled the religion/not-religion distinction even as they established and reinforced it. This problem of how to define religion also appeared in contemporaneous legislative endeavors. In the decades following the promulgation of the constitution, there were repeated, frequently abortive, attempts to pass legislation that would clarify the relationship between religions and the state and streamline the otherwise piecemeal laws and regulations related to the administration of religions (policy makers made formal attempts to pass such legislation in 1899, 1927, 1929, 1935, and 1939; see chapters 2 and 4).[61] Such legislation would secure a superior position for the state above particularist religious claims, exclude "superstitious" practices from the purview of "proper religion," and at the same time mobilize religious ideas and institutions for the purposes of nation-building. This project, described in contemporaneous sources as an attempt to establish a comprehensive "religions system" (*shūkyō seido*) became particularly exigent in the context of Japan's Fifteen Years' War (1931–45), when policy makers looked to religious organizations as potential sources of spiritual mobilization or viewed them as possible hotbeds of sedition. The exceptional circumstances of the war years also provided rationales for expanding or contracting operative legal definitions of public order, sovereignty, and individual rights and liberties.

What about Civil Religion?

The Meiji constitutional period was characterized by rupture, discontinuity, and a considerable amount of experimentation, but one consistent feature of the legal regime was a reluctance on the part of Japanese political leaders to formally establish a state religion. Indeed, they never actually did. What, then, are we to do with the obvious preponderance of Shintō-derived ideas and ideals in public school education and other aspects of civic life? At first glance, Robert Bellah's concept of "civil religion" seems to be an elegant answer to this question because it explains how religious ideas can dominate public life even in the absence of a formally established national creed.[62] However, the concept of civil religion presupposes that "religion" is a unique category of human experience, emotionally suasive and foundational to personal identity, and therefore always-already antecedent to group belonging and politics.[63]

Could it actually be so? Whereas Bellah imagined religion as a unique, transhistorical entity that could foster social cohesion, I would argue that "religion" only comes into existence through the discursive activity of naming, demarcating, and classifying. Indeed, scholars working on the emergence of "religion" in Japanese history have irrefutably shown that this naming and classifying was fundamental in the formation of the modern Japanese polity, and that interest groups' mobilization of things deemed "religious" (or *not* religious) for the sake of fostering social cohesion is best understood as a by-product of this political process.[64] To suggest that the Meiji constitutional regime was dominated by a civil religion would be to problematically assume that the spheres of religion and politics were stable. But legal experts, clerics, policy makers, and academics all disagreed vehemently with one another about this very thing.

In this sense, it seems important to me that Bellah seems to have invented the American civil religion even as he described it for the first time in his classic 1967 article, and it is crucial that he seems to have developed the concept in conjunction with his years-long study of Japan.[65] Adopting the position of the academic capable of standing outside religion and politics and objectively analyzing both, Bellah selected a series of prophets (Lincoln), patriarchs (Jefferson), national sacrifices (the Kennedy assassination), and jeremiads (opposition to the developing conflict in Vietnam). His vision was expansive and his politics relatively progressive for his day, but the supposedly capacious "civil religion" that he described was also exclusivist and framed by the horizons of his historical perception. Bellah lamented the plight of the Negro, but apparently did not think to include his own contemporaries Dr. Martin Luther King or Malcolm X in his list of American prophets. He regarded the phrases "under God" and "in God we trust" as timeless national commitments, conveniently overlooking the fact that these words had only been formally adopted in the Pledge of Allegiance and as the national motto in the mid-1950s as part of America's anticommunist ideology. He highlighted the construction of war memorials as national shrines and treated classical American political oratory as part of a national canon, but the shrines he included and the lectures he selected all reflected his preexisting notion of the constituent elements of religion. He wrote:

> What we have, then, from the earliest years of the republic is a collection of beliefs, symbols, and rituals with respect to sacred things and institutionalized in a collectivity. This religion—there seems no other word for it—while not antithetical to and indeed sharing much in common with Christianity, was neither sectarian nor in any specific sense Christian.[66]

There seems no other word for it. For Bellah, it was inconceivable that social cohesion could take place without religion, and it was obvious to him that politicians' habitual references to "God" were fundamentally religious even if nonsectarian. But I would argue that Bellah's functionalist argument was undermined by the essentialist presuppositions about religion and politics on which it relied. I would furthermore submit that the same problem attends what might be understood as the inverse of Bellah's "civil religion," namely, the concept of State Shintō.[67] Simply put, both "civil religion" and "State Shintō" assume that religion and politics are discrete entities that mix. But is it not the case that these analytical terms represent anxious secularist attempts to fix boundaries, establish limits, to settle what is "really religion" once and for all?

What's Wrong with State Shintō?

Scholars before me have advanced a number of different interpretations trying to explain the centrality of imperial mythology and shrine rites to Japanese political life during what I call the Meiji constitutional period. These approaches differ from one another in how they imagine historical causality and global political norms: Did religious commitments structure authoritarian political forms and thereby lead Japan to war, or did cynical operatives abuse religious ideas for political ends? Is religious freedom a universal principle that looks the same everywhere, or is it a localized practice that reflects dominant conceptions of religion in a particular time and place?

Scholars have also differed on whether to attribute responsibility for totalitarian politics to elites alone or to the masses who supported elite projects. In some cases, they have focused on the national scale at the expense of investigating the narrow-bore objectives of competing interest groups; in others, cultural and national differences have disappeared in light of imagined universals. The result is an incoherent and largely inconclusive discourse characterized by contested definitions, tedious debates about periodization, competing understandings of scale, and serious differences of opinion about how narrowly or capaciously to parse operative terms.[68]

Building on the Occupation diagnosis that Japan was dominated by a state religion at the expense of religious freedom, advocates of what I will term the State Shintō approach have depicted the separation of religion from politics as a timeless, universal principle. In such accounts, Japanese people either never properly understood this universal principle or the principle temporarily appeared in Japanese constitutional law only to be immediately overtaken by a particularistic ideology associated with a uniquely Japanese religion. Proponents of this view have called this aberrant arrangement "State Shintō," using the term to imply the cynical abuse of religious ideas for political ends.[69] For them, Japanese policy makers distorted the benign ideas of a quaint indigenous religion to suit their imperialist agendas and militarist goals.

While there is no doubt that policy makers mobilized ideas associated with traditional *kami* veneration in the service of nation-building, the State Shintō approach problematically assumes that Shintō-derived ideas were uniformly influential, spreading from the top down to the masses through the mediating agents of school and shrine. Some historians have rightly questioned this top-down approach by showing how the Japanese population supported state-building initiatives from the bottom up and how members of Japan's educated middle class wedded their parochial aims to those of the state.[70] Such bottom-up approaches have the benefit of showing that political responsibility during the Meiji constitutional period was distributed more evenly than the classic State Shintō model would suggest.[71] Rather than depicting rank-and-file Japanese citizens as passive victims of a manipulative state, alternative accounts of ideology and governmentality in the Meiji constitutional period have shown that Japanese citizens actively contributed to the manufacture of state propaganda.[72] Other accounts have shown that even though imperial propaganda was pervasive and apparently persuasive, small acts of resistance like graffiti show that not all Japanese people bought into the official orthodoxy of the time.[73]

Another alternative to the State Shintō narrative has featured in a series of publications by scholars affiliated with training institutions for Shintō priests such as Kokugakuin University (Tokyo) and Kōgakkan University (Ise).[74] Using evidentiary historiography to trace the actual political strength wielded by Shintō institutions, this strain of scholarship has highlighted the asymmetrical power dynamics of the Occupation as a major contributing factor in the development of the received concept of State Shintō.[75] In this view, the occupiers failed to recognize the existence of a unique "Japan-style relationship between religion and politics" (*Nihongata seikyō kankei*) in the process of formulating Occupation religions policy.[76] Specifically, proponents argue that the Shintō Directive of 15 December 1945 mistook a workable political system for an oppressive regime because the occupiers who drafted it were convinced of their own cultural superiority. The Occupation therefore marked a tragic point when a distinctly Japanese mode of governance was lost.

While often excessively defensive of the clearly repressive wartime regime, this scholarly corrective anticipated by several decades the flurry of anglophone scholarship in the 2000s and early 2010s on "secularisms" and "varieties of secularism."[77] Specialists in the modern history of Shintō used the Japanese case to show that the United States did not have a monopoly on "real" secularism, that Occupation policy established double standards whereby Japanese practices were held to stricter account than contemporaneous American ones, and that the uneven nature of postwar geopolitics has made it difficult for Japanese people to practice a culturally specific but nevertheless legitimate secularism.[78] The most theoretically sophisticated contributions to this strain of scholarship have built upon Talal Asad's critique of secularism as a project whereby "nonmodern peoples are invited to assess their adequacy," suggesting that Japanese people today are the victims of quasi-colonial American conceptual violence.[79]

Some scholars have also used painstaking historical documentation to show that State Shintō did not solidify as a system of governance—if it ever solidified at all—until just before the onset of the Pacific War.[80] Their research has effectually refuted the claim that State Shintō was the defining feature of Japanese governance from 1868, when imperial loyalists "restored" the Meiji emperor as the leader of Japan, until 1945, when the Shintō Directive supposedly abolished all links between Japanese religion and statecraft. In its most carefully substantiated versions, the critique is an irrefutable rebuke to the received narrative about the alleged dominance of Shintō in prewar and wartime Japanese political life.[81]

Those who prefer the State Shintō model have responded to these critiques by showing how Shintō ideas permeated the populace through compulsory public school education and by arguing that the postwar survival of the imperial institution allowed State Shintō to continue into the present.[82]

Some scholars have also described the postwar political activities of lobbies like the Shintō Seiji Renmei (Shintō Association for Spiritual Leadership) as a revival of the "public religion" of the wartime past.[83] A few scholars have also engaged with cutting-edge theories of secularism, acknowledging the secular nature of the Japanese state while using "State Shintō" more narrowly to describe how political authorities used Shintō to disseminate state ideology.[84]

The Problem of Scale and the Promise of a Constructivist Approach

Many very smart people fundamentally disagree on the State Shintō issue. This impasse results, I argue, from partially overlapping but inherently contradictory claims based on irreconcilable functionalist and essentialist understandings of religion. It also results from a problematic focus on the national scale at the expense of examining the competing claims of individual stakeholders and interest groups operating at other scales. Ironically, the terms of the debate highlight the point that I made above about the unanswerable question that lies at the heart of secularism. In their attempts to definitively draw the line between religion and politics by establishing what counted as "real religion" and what counted as political ideology, scholars exemplify the anxiety that characterizes all secularist religion-making projects.[85]

Wherever they stand on the State Shintō issue, scholars often make *functionalist* claims about the relationship between religion and governance, and they frequently make *essentialist* claims about Shintō, Japan, or both: A quaint ethnic religion *was expropriated* for political ends, or an essentially Japanese method of governance *was misunderstood* as a distortion of a universal principle. But as the passive constructions italicized in the previous sentence suggest, it is difficult to attribute agency with any accuracy when specific historical actors go unnamed. The existence of the religion/not-religion distinction in constitutional law prompted a series of conflicts wherein specific stakeholders defined these operative terms more or less capaciously and juxtaposed them with third terms such as "superstition," "heresy," and "morality" that helped grant both "religion" and "not-religion" greater conceptual clarity.[86] It is not enough to simply describe secularism as a state project, nor is it enough to reduce the complicated politics of secularist governance to the workings of a totalitarian state religion. We have to identify the stakeholders and clarify their agendas to figure out how they variously drew the boundaries between the mutually dependent categories of religion and not-religion.

Whether or not observers take State Shintō to be a real thing and independent of whether they treat religious freedom as a universal principle or a culturally specific ideal, most existing scholarship on the religion-politics distinction in the Meiji constitutional period has focused on the national scale, giving undue weight to the idea that all Japanese people interpreted religious freedom and religion-state relations in the same way. However, even a cursory survey of the historical archive makes it clear that competing interest groups understood ideal relationships between religions and the state in myriad ways. These stakeholders discriminated between "religion" and "not-religion" because they lived in a political and legal system that demanded it. Rather than treating this system as a perversion of secularist politics ("State Shintō") or as a parochial "Japan-style relationship between religion and politics," I regard the Meiji constitutional regime as a paradigmatic example of how the parsing of religion and not-religion works. Aside from the geographic setting and the specific terminology that was used, little was "Japanese" about it.[87]

My point is that a functionalist focus on the relationship between religion and politics at the national scale gets in the way of a more compelling set of questions. Rather than asking what work religion did politically or how cynical politicians used religion as a tool to mobilize the masses, we can ask instead who made claims about how religion should be separated from Shintō, why specific interest groups favored one vision of the ideal relationship between religion and politics over another, and what sort of euphemisms and metaphors helped stakeholders imagine and define the religion/not-religion distinction. In the remainder of this chapter, I will pursue these questions through several specific examples of people trying to clarify the relationship between religion, politics, and Shintō in light of the constitutional religious freedom guarantee. I am not interested in the *essence* of religious freedom as a legal norm, nor am I interested in the emancipatory or repressive *function* of state policies that instantiated or violated that norm. Rather, I want to know who *made* the religion/not-religion distinction that lies at the heart of religious freedom talk, how they did so, and for what reasons.[88] I intend to show that religious freedom was invented in Japan, over and over and over again.

OF RITES AND RIGHTS

Because the criteria used to designate some practices as "religious" and others as patriotic duty were both ambiguous and protean throughout the Meiji constitutional period, the legal distinction between religion and not-religion invited repeated attempts at clarification. The vexing question of whether Shintō was properly understood as a religion, whether shrine rites constituted "Shintō," and whether shrine rites were a nonreligious civic ritual system would remain unresolved all the way through the Pacific War, with attempts to draw the lines between religion and secular, religion and Shintō, and Shintō and secular resulting in some torturous, often unconvincing, logic on all sides. Crucially, virtually every argument about these issues that I encountered in the Japanese-language archive made obligatory reference to the constitutional religious freedom clause. Japanese agents active during the Meiji constitutional period habitually situated their arguments within the legally normative presupposition that policy initiatives and legislative changes should take place *within* the scope of the constitutional religious freedom guarantee. They just disagreed on what counted as religion, and therefore disagreed about which practices and people deserved protection.[89]

As a way of showing the stunning diversity of takes on the question of how to parse religion and not-religion, I offer here several examples of religious freedom talk from around the time of the Fifteen Years' War (1931–45). One of the main problems engendered by the religion/not-religion divide was the vexing question of whether participation in shrine rites was compulsory, whether making shrine visits compulsory constituted an infringement on the constitutional religious freedom clause, and whether there was any real difference between "civil" rites and "religious" rituals.[90] These debates had both domestic impacts and diplomatic ramifications. The state made shrine visits obligatory for schoolchildren (and therefore for schoolteachers) from around 1900, prompting a series of questions about whether paying obeisance at shrines constituted religious practice and therefore violated students' and teachers' religious freedom.[91] Forced obeisance at shrines was also part of Japanese assimilation practices in colonies like Korea and Taiwan.[92] While shrine rites therefore had a compulsory aspect, imperial propaganda depicted veneration at shrines as model behavior (figure 1), as part of daily routine (figure 2), and as a pleasurable leisure activity (figure 3).

Because they drew negative attention from missionaries and other expatriates, obligatory participation in shrine rites complicated Japan's diplomatic relationships and created tensions with powerful international organizations like the Roman Catholic Church. They also begged the ultimately unanswerable legal question of whether outward physical comportment impacted private belief. Most observers agreed that it would have been untoward and unconstitutional for the Japanese government to force *belief* on citizens in the face of Article 28, but they differed on whether the physical act of bowing at shrines constituted religious practice.[93]

Minobe Tatsukichi (1930): The Ambiguous Legal Status of the Shrine System

Minobe Tatsukichi (1873–1948) was a constitutional law professor who is perhaps most famous for his 1935 purge from Tokyo Imperial University as a result of his controversial "emperor as an organ of the state" theory.[94] Five years before he was forced to resign his prestigious post, Minobe published a short piece in the religious newspaper *Chūgai nippō* about how Japan might reconcile the "shrine system" (*jinja seido*) with constitutional law. Minobe's piece was published on 20 May 1930, a little more than a year after the government had failed to pass comprehensive religions legislation (see chapter 4). After that controversial religions bill died in committee, the government convened a group of experts to determine once and for all whether shrine rites were religion. The committee met numerous times between 1929 and 1932, but members were ultimately unable to come to a definitive answer to this vexing question.[95]

Minobe's roughly contemporaneous piece was similarly inconclusive. He seems to have wanted to argue both sides of the question of whether Shintō constituted religion and whether the government's preferential treatment of Shintō shrines infringed on religious freedom. He lamented the fact that the position of shrine and imperial rites had not been clearly stated in the constitution when it was written, but he suggested that as long as the position of shrines was not formally established in constitutional law, the only course of action was to supplement the terse language of the religious freedom clause with reference to custom and historical precedent.

But precedent was also problematic. Although shrines were administered separately from religion at the time he was writing, Minobe reminded his readers that this was a relatively recent development that had only taken place within their living memories. Even in the early Meiji era, shrines had been administered *as religions* alongside Buddhist temples under the jurisdiction of the Shrine and Temple Bureau (Shaji Kyoku) of the Home Ministry. By highlighting how the ambiguous legal status of shrines was a problem engendered by very recent administrative changes, Minobe implied that the treatment of shrines as nonreligious institutions was a flimsy legal fiction at best.

This did not mean, however, that Minobe thought that shrine rites infringed on religious freedom. If one were to treat Shrine Shintō as a religion, he averred, then it would properly be considered a national religion and should regarded as the official religion of the empire. However, if Shrine Shintō were to be formally treated as Japan's national religion in this way, then it would necessarily come into conflict with Article 28 of the constitution, which guaranteed one of the most important rights enjoyed by Japanese citizens. Yet it could not be interpreted that the state had adopted a stance wholly distant from religion. Indeed, while religious freedom encompassed freedom of belief, freedom of religious expression, freedom of religious association, and the principle of separation of religion from the state, Minobe argued, few constitutional democracies actually practiced religious freedom in such an absolute sense.

Japan was no exception. Shrine rites served as national observances and shrines received special protection and oversight from the government. It therefore could *not* be said that religion and the state were totally separate. Under existing national law, Minobe argued, the Japanese government had not yet thoroughly separated religion from the state, but instead maintained a special relationship with specific religions (i.e., Shintō shrines). By giving preference to shrine rites, the state effectively created a national religion, but it did not infringe upon Article 28. Shrine rites were national religion only insofar as the state took it upon itself to administer and fund shrines, not in the sense that the state could force Shintō *belief* upon the people.

For Minobe, preferential treatment for shrines could occur because it was virtually impossible to have absolute separation of religion from the state. Like many of his contemporaries, Minobe drew a distinction between what the government could demand of people's bodies (bowing at shrines) and what it could force into their minds (belief in Shintō deities or imperial divine descent). He acknowledged that religious freedom in an ideal, theoretical sense would involve total separation of religion from the state, but he also pragmatically argued that few constitutional democracies actually practiced such thoroughgoing separation. The preferential treatment that shrines enjoyed was therefore neither unusual in comparison to other constitutional democracies, nor was it unconstitutional. Indeed, Minobe seemed quite sanguine about the state's ability to maintain a de facto national religion without compromising the constitutional guarantee of religious freedom.

The Catholic Church (1936): The Patriotic Duties of Catholics

Minobe Tatsukichi's argument worked in part because he avoided specific hot-button issues and wrote in the abstract terms of legal theory. But in the political background of his short piece was an ongoing debate about whether participation in shrine rites constituted a violation of religious liberty. At the time he wrote, visits to shrines were mandatory for schoolchildren and colonial subjects, but technically were optional for adults in the metropole. This created a complicated situation for private religious schools like Sophia University, a Jesuit school that became embroiled in a serious conflict with the government over the issue of students and their teachers paying obeisance at shrines. As Kate Wildman Nakai has argued in a compelling pair of articles on the issue, the Japanese Ministry of Education could not force students to venerate shrines, but it *could* withhold military liaison teachers from the school as punishment, thereby denying students access to a major source of postgraduation networking and advancement.[96] The issue of paying obeisance at shrines filtered up to the upper echelons of the Catholic Church, prompting the Vatican to issue concrete instructions to Catholics in Japan.

A papal instructional document issued on 25 May 1936 called on Catholic missionaries to "acknowledge and respect the devotion and love of the Japanese for their country and also to teach these sentiments to the faithful lest in patriotism they be inferior to the other citizens."[97] The document then stressed the Japanese government's commitment to "the principle of religious freedom" and approvingly reiterated the government's claim that there was a real distinction between expressions of loyalty to "National Shintō" and "the religious cult of Shintoism." It furthermore stressed that the Ministry of Education had already affirmed in 1932 that compulsory shrine visits had "no other purpose than to manifest visibly [students'] sentiment of fidelity to and love of country."[98] After discussing several other legal precedents and expressing concern over the negative impact on the faith in Japan should Catholics be seen as unpatriotic or untrustworthy, the document directed clerics in Japan to instruct the faithful that it was lawful for Catholics to join in ceremonies held at national shrines.[99]

This papal communiqué may seem craven in that it forced Catholics to conform with national law, but as Hans-Martin Krämer has pointed out, in the late 1930s and early 1940s many Christian organizations (Protestant and Catholic alike) remained relatively sanguine about the Japanese government's preferred religion/not-religion distinction.[100] As Japan and the United States entered a bellicose relationship, however, the voices of those who decried "national" or "state" Shintō as a threat to Christians' religious liberty came to have greater influence on international perceptions of the issue. Protestant missionaries were at the forefront of this critical discourse.[101]

Kōno Seizō (1938): Clarifying the "Unity of Rites and Rule"

Christians had obvious reasons to be worried about whether participation in shrine rites was a dereliction of faith. But proponents of Shintō also had reason to worry about where the state drew the line between "national rites" and "religious rituals" and what that meant for the sanctity of shrines. As a number of observers pointed out in the 1930s, shrine priests were also in a difficult situation because as "nonreligious" caretakers of national monuments they technically were not supposed to perform the "religious" rituals that their local parishioners wanted.

About a year after the publication of the 1937 Ministry of Education book *Kokutai no hongi* (*Cardinal Principles of the Body Politic*), scholar of Shintō Kōno Seizō (1882–1963) wrote a pamphlet entitled *Our Body Politic and Shintō*. The pamphlet put forward a rationale for why shrines should be considered "public" and why shrine rites did not infringe upon freedom of religious belief. Kōno scrupulously defined his terms. By disambiguating the semantically related words "rites," "ritual," "governance," "festival," and "religion," he attempted to bring greater clarity to commonly repeated phrases such as "the unity of rites and rule" (*saisei itchi*) that seemed to collapse the religion-politics distinction on which the constitution depended.

> The "rites," that is "festivals" in [the phrase] "the unity of rites and rule" is not so-called religion, but rather the rituals of our nation, our national rituals [*kokurei*]. From the beginning, ritual [*rei*] has been an area that was particularly developed in the Orient, and moral consciousness has emerged from the fusion of such ritual with popular customs [*kokumin no fūshū*] to become national customs; if one adds religious sentiment to this, rites [*saishi*] develop. The reason that rites [*saishi*] comprise much

> of ritual [*rei*] lies herein. However when one also adds political relationships to this, then national rituals [*kokurei*] are developed. Shrine rites belong to this category. Among the national rituals [*kokurei*] of our nation the most important are the enthronement and Daijōsai festivals, in other words the great august [i.e., imperial] rituals. Among the national rituals those that have extremely limited religious elements are the national observances [*kokugi*]. There are times when the "national rituals" and the "national observances" are used synonymously, but in either case these should be distinguished from religion.[102]

Kōno's focus was semantic more than it was legal. He advanced a narrow argument that could support his claim that the unity of rites and rule did not constitute an infringement on the right to religious freedom. Unlike his contemporary Minobe Tatsukichi (the law professor), his presentation did not focus on abstract principles such as rights and liberties, but rather on the concrete situations and terminological distinctions that caused consternation and confusion about the scope of constitutional law. If Minobe had spoken in somewhat abstruse terms about how shrine rites could be legally interpreted as indisputably religious, public, and nevertheless unproblematic from the standpoint of religious freedom, Kōno suggested that the rites themselves were *not* religious and therefore not legally problematic.

Andō Masazumi: Shrines Are Not Religion; the "Great Divine Way" Is Secular

A final approach in my nonexhaustive list of viewpoints on the issue also viewed shrine rites as civic ritual, but did so by disaggregating religious "Shintō" from the secular "Great Divine Way" (*kannagara no daidō*). On 20 December 1941, in his dual capacity as a member of the House of Representatives and chairperson of the Greater Japan Buddhist Youth Association Federation, Andō Masazumi (1876–1955) published a book on the necessity of Buddhist reform that included a five-page appendix entitled "Shrines Are Not Religion."[103] Published less than two weeks after Japan declared war on the United States, *Readiness for the Final Battle and Japanese Buddhism: A Proclamation of Unified Buddhism* (*Kessen taisei to Nihon Bukkyō: Zen'itsu Bukkyō no teishō*) envisioned ideal religion-state relations as Japan set about establishing a new world order.

Andō was a laicized Buddhist priest who had served as a journalist before becoming an elected official. His blueprint for Buddhist reform in

Readiness for the Final Battle was premised on the idea that Buddhism could serve the nation best if outmoded practices were abandoned and Buddhists worked together to provide spiritual and ideological support for the war effort. He criticized recent calls to make Shintō the national religion and questioned religious studies scholars' assertions that shrine rites were indisputably religious.[104] Andō preferred to think of shrine rites as a form of timeless civic ritual, while the lay-centric, this-worldly Buddhism that had existed in Japan since the sixth century was perfectly suited to supporting the body politic *as religion*. Buddhism was also uniquely prepared to support the Japanese imperial project because it formed the common religious heritage of diverse peoples of Asia that Japan aimed to lead.

Andō's appendix, "Shrines Are Not Religion," was composed as a public response to a statement that Fujisawa Chikao (1893–1962) had made at a recent meeting of the Central Cooperation Committee (Chūō Kyōryoku Kaigi). Fujisawa had allegedly argued that Shintō should be treated as Japan's national religion while Buddhism, Christianity, and Islam should be regarded as "popular religions" or "religions of the people" (*minkyō*). According to Fujisawa, making such a distinction would ensure that the people were not estranged from shrine rites. Andō strongly agreed with Fujisawa that maintaining strong connections between the people and shrines was of the utmost importance in exigent times, but he questioned whether it was wise to treat "shrines" (he put the word *jinja* in quotation marks) as "religion," and a national religion at that. To do so would undermine the theoretical basis that allowed shrine rites to be universally observed by all Japanese. Moreover, Andō argued, treating Shintō as Japan's national religion would also render meaningless Article 28 of the Constitution of the Empire of Japan. In guaranteeing freedom of religious belief, Andō pointed out, the constitution had effectively denied the possibility of establishing a national religion. For Andō, participation in shrine rites was a sine qua non of Japanese citizenship, but shrine rites did not conflict with religious commitments because they constituted a universal practice rather than the elective, private beliefs characteristic of religion. Shrine rites were expressions of patriotism, not religion.

Andō repeated this line of argumentation in multiple publications over the next several years. For example, in a 1 January 1944 issue of the popular Buddhist magazine *Daihōrin* (*Great Dharma Wheel*), Andō argued against national purists who wanted to eliminate Buddhism as a foreign religion while elevating Shintō to the status of Japan's national religion. Arguing that Buddhism was essential to Japanese culture while pointing out that Shintō had only recently been purified of Buddhist elements, Andō drew a distinction between what he called *kannagara no daidō* (the "Great Divine Way") and Shintō. As a euphemism for imperial rule, the former served as a nonnegotiable component of Japanese citizenship; the latter was merely one religion among several. While the intellectual content of this "Great Divine Way" remained vague, in Andō's usage it represented the incontrovertible, secular truth implicitly acknowledged by all Japanese citizens. By contrast, religions were important vehicles for social edification, but they represented private commitments that were protected by Article 28 (see this chapter's epigraph).

Andō's public debates with others in popular newspapers and religious journals suggest that while some people in the early 1940s may have thought that Japan *needed* a national religion, few seem to have thought that Japan already *had* one. If he was arguing against people who were advocating *making* Shintō Japan's national religion in 1941, 1942, and 1944 (three instances in which I found Andō disagreeing with the proponents of the Shintō-as-national-religion stance), then this suggests that Shintō was never established as a national religion in wartime Japan. This is not merely a semantic point. Andō's debates with proponents of making Shintō Japan's national religion reveal not only that Shintō was not *legally* designated Japan's national religion, but also that it did not *functionally* serve as Japan's de facto national religion. If it had, Andō's interlocutors would presumably have had nothing to complain about.

Staring at the Sun

Readers will have noted that even though discussions of shrine rites as civic rituals regularly connected the observances to the imperial house, the connections were oblique rather than direct. Indeed, many of the people who weighed in on the shrine rites issue appealed to the idea of imperial divinity without really making the imperial house the object of *religious* veneration, and euphemistic language (e.g., Andō's "Great Divine Way" and Kōno's "national rituals") allowed for the vague association of the emperor with transcendental, timeless principles without categorizing imperial rites as religion. Just as imperial pageantry established a set of protocols in which imperial subjects were to view the emperor but not do so directly, disquisitions about religious freedom during the Meiji constitutional period tended to sacralize the imperial house without connecting it to the potentially destabilizing category of religion.[105] After all, Article 28 of the imperially decreed Meiji Constitution suggested that religious belief and affiliation was elective, so to render veneration of the emperor as religious ran the risk of making it optional (indeed, this was Andō's concern). As Isomae Jun'ichi has argued, this anxiety created a sort of blind spot in Japanese thinking about the religion/not-religion divide: The refulgent descendants of the sun goddess Amaterasu shone brightly but were ironically quite difficult to see.[106]

THE VIOLENCE OF SECULARISM

Collectively, the various attitudes regarding the shrine rites issue described above show that there was no single approach to how the lines should have been drawn between religion and not-religion during the Meiji constitutional period. It was the very fact that the criteria were fuzzy and the legal categories blurry that made the Meiji constitutional regime secularist in the sense I outlined above. Utter anxiety about the relationship between religion and not-religion dominated the period. This anxiety came to the fore in aspects of public life such as public school education and national ceremonies that affected almost all Japanese citizens and colonial subjects.

To be clear, treating the Meiji constitutional regime as secularist does not deny its coercive character. If anything, secularisms are doubly coercive in that they demand both belief and unbelief. Constitutionalization, legislation, jurisprudence, and policy making regularly designate some claims as universally accepted facts and treat other claims as optional choices that are tolerated in public contexts.[107] The rationales undergirding such distinctions are not necessarily logical, consistent, or just.

Secularisms also delimit a range of nonnegotiable acceptable and unacceptable practices and demand conformity through law enforcement (legally legitimated acts of violence or the threat of exercising such violence).[108] In secularist systems, citizens are required to acknowledge the premise that public space is doctrinally neutral, and that private faith-based commitments should have minimal impact on public discourse. Clearly such idealized scenarios rarely work out this way in actual practice (religious interest groups exert political pressure on politicians, for example). Nevertheless, the point here is that secularist political systems determine ideologically and physically coercive distinctions between religion and not-religion. Many of the parties cited above wanted to strictly separate private conscience from public comportment, although as a number of scholars have argued, comportment itself may also foster moral and ethical dispositions.[109] Indeed, critics of State Shintō have feared not that people bowed at shrines because they believed, but that they came to believe because they bowed at shrines.[110]

Although secular states supposedly limit governmental power to a neutral public realm, religion influences the state not only in the political pressure that religious lobbies bring to bear on state policy, but also in the legitimizing tactics that states use to shore up political authority. For example, in the contemporary United States civic rituals such as presidential inaugurations and material artifacts such as currency refer to an abstract "God" that is unambiguously Protestant Christian in origin.[111] In prewar and wartime Japan, the Shintō-derived ideas of imperial divine descent and of Japan as a divine nation were presented in public school education as historical fact.[112] Such political practices derive in part from governmental attempts to affix legal authority, extralegal norms, and moral codes to transcendent ideals.[113] Many of these sources of transcendence are related to, or derive from, empirically unverifiable claims that would otherwise be called religion.[114] These legitimizing tactics often reflect majoritarian religious viewpoints, sometimes at the expense of minority positions.[115]

Freeing religion can therefore be brutal. While religious freedom language theoretically guarantees freedom to all, in practice policy makers and police prioritize the rights and privileges of some groups over others. They may even use the language of religious freedom to rationalize repressive policies. For example, the police crackdowns on marginal religious movements that occurred periodically during the Meiji constitutional period should be understood not as violations of religious freedom as a universal principle, but rather as one outcome of the combination of the state's capacity to discriminate between "religion" and "not-religion" and its monopoly on maintaining public order.[116] The crackdowns could be justified by designating marginal movements such as Ōmotokyō and Hitonomichi as not really religious, and therefore not actually protected under constitutional law. Similarly, the ignominious imprisonment of Sōka Kyōiku Gakkai leader Makiguchi Tsunesaburō (1871–1944) in July 1943 happened not because Makiguchi was a principled martyr who indefatigably championed religious freedom, but because Gakkai exclusivist approaches to religious practice (such as burning others' cherished religious paraphernalia) proved that zealous Gakkai members disturbed the peace (see chapter 4).

The language of religious freedom also has homogenizing effects, fostering isomorphism among those religions that *are* officially tolerated by the state. To receive governmental acknowledgment and ensure equal treatment, religious organizations have to make themselves legible by adopting specific forms of organization, establishing representatives who serve as official mediators between clerical and political authority, and recognizing the supremacy of temporal law over religious doctrine (see chapter 6). Religious leaders are always free to refuse, and some groups may choose to reject the category of "religion" altogether. But whether groups adopt the category or not, under a secularist regime the agents of the state will always reserve the right to designate some groups as "real religions" (and therefore deserving protection as contributors to the public good), others as "false religions" (and therefore deserving suppression or surveillance as potential threats to public order), still others as not really religion at all (and therefore beyond the purview of any religious freedom guarantee).

COMPETING SECULARIST VISIONS AND THE ALLIED OCCUPATION

In the context of cross-cultural interactions like the Allied Occupation of Japan, some forms of secularist logic will seem strange to those who are embedded in others. Secularisms can be mutually unintelligible. It is certainly true that during the Meiji constitutional period Japanese religious leaders, legislators, and bureaucrats understood religious freedom and religion-state relations in ways that would have been counterintuitive to the Americans who were setting postconflict policy as the Pacific War drew to a close. For example, the long-standing Buddhist vision of a mutually reinforcing relationship between sovereign law and Buddhist dharma was almost certainly anathema to Americans ensconced in a strong political tradition of rejecting royal authority and an equally strong Protestant skepticism of clerical authority. Indeed, as I show in chapter 3, white Americans looked askance at Japanese Buddhist immigrants because they associated Buddhism with "Mikadoism," which they saw as a sort of Japanese popery.

However, Japanese visions of religion-state relations were neither inauthentic nor illegitimate because they differed from the American variety. Japanese policy makers and religious leaders distributed the capacities of religion and the state somewhat differently from their American counterparts. Like the Americans of the time, they sometimes took empirically unverifiable claims as political truths and historical facts. But they nevertheless drew substantive distinctions between religion and governance. They embraced religious freedom as an ideal, challenged its interpretation, and appealed to the constitutional religious freedom clause in support of their respective initiatives. This happened with such regularity throughout the Meiji constitutional period that the received claim that Japan lacked religious freedom simply falls apart.

WHO NEEDS RELIGIOUS FREEDOM?

> Ah, why would our country alone welcome foreign religions and regard traditional religions, which rightly preserve the spiritual unity of the citizenry, so coolly? In the next issue we will observe actual examples from the various countries, take up the traditional prerogatives accorded to Buddhism, and explain the truth of this. Here we proclaim that religious freedom does not at all clash with prejudice in the treatment of foreign and domestic religions, and we thereby dispel the misconceptions of the world.
>
> Unsigned editorial (probably written by Chikazumi Jōkan; 1899)[1]

ON THE MORNING OF 14 DECEMBER 1899, debate raged on the floor of Japan's House of Peers. Under discussion was a controversial religions bill (Shūkyō hōan) that had been advanced on 9 December by the cabinet of Prime Minister Yamagata Aritomo (1838–1922). The prime minister opened the debate by explaining the cabinet's position. Arguing that the government had already recognized religious freedom in Article 28 of the 1889 constitution, and furthermore indicating that the government was committed to upholding that clause, Yamagata claimed that the bill was designed to clarify the special provisions necessary when considering the freedom of religious groups as opposed to the other types of juridical persons outlined in the Civil Code of 1898. While Yamagata did not clarify what specifically constituted the "different nature" of religions in comparison to other groups, he argued that the various contemporaneous debates about the role of religion vis-à-vis the state could be resolved through legislation that monitored the "external" functions of religion such as incorporation and the staging of public events. The bill would thereby ensure peace and order, fulfilling one of the government's prime responsibilities.[2]

Responses to the bill in the House of Peers were mixed, and the initial debate that followed Yamagata's opening speech took over two hours. House members expressed perplexity about the necessity of the bill; many also expressed trepidation about the confusion that would inevitably arise over particular stipulations. Irritation mounted as debate dragged well beyond the usual lunch break at noon, and the discussion was finally tabled with the establishment of an investigative committee of fifteen members who would review the legislation.[3]

When the bill was brought up again in the late morning of 27 February 1900, a vigorous conversation ensued that would take up nearly the entire day.[4] Members returned from an hour-long lunch break with renewed vigor and the bill was debated from quarter past one until nearly five in the afternoon. The parliamentary stenographer dutifully recorded shouted interjections and moments when the chamber erupted in response to some comment or another. When finally put to a vote late in the afternoon, the measure failed: 121 votes against to 100 in favor.[5]

The fractious drama that unfolded on the legislative stage at the turn of the century was a microcosm of a larger debate playing out in contemporaneous Japanese society about how the concept of religious freedom should be interpreted and applied. The debates over the bill reflected the recent historical emergence of a sophisticated set of Buddhist theories about ideal religion-state relations that took for granted the secularist discrimination between religion and not-religion outlined in the 1889 Meiji Constitution. Buddhist responses to the Yamagata bill also show how the trans-sectarian Buddhist groups that had developed in defensive response to the anti-Buddhist campaigns of earlier decades began to split into factions and lobbies representing competing Buddhist political interests in the last years of the nineteenth century.[6] These new factions were divided on the issue of whether the best legal position for Buddhists was close to, or distant from, the Japanese state.

Geopolitics played a role in these debates. The anticipated influx of Christian missionaries that attended Japan's revised treaties with European and North American powers brought with it a new set of ideas and ideals about religion-state relationships. Buddhists responded to these domestic issues and diplomatic pressures by theorizing about religion-state relations in newly sophisticated ways. They agreed that they needed cutting-edge theories of religious freedom to press their case with the state, but they disagreed vehemently with one another about which interpretations worked best.

THE DOMESTIC GEOPOLITICS OF RELIGIOUS FREEDOM

This chapter has two objectives. First, I examine Buddhist responses to three legal issues that cropped up in the last few years of the nineteenth century in order to show that Japanese Buddhists were clearly aware of global practices of religious freedom and regularly cited international precedents in support of their legal claims. They often invented traditions in making their points, but just as Japanese policy makers like Mori Arinori (1847–89) appealed to global civilizational standards to make religious freedom into an administrative priority (see chapter 1), Buddhists similarly referred to the practices and policies of other countries such as Germany, France, and the United States while trying to secure customary and civil rights.

My second aim is to show that while Buddhists were keenly interested in the problem of religious freedom, their multifarious responses to legal issues show that they were not united in their interpretation of the constitutional religious freedom clause. Together, these arguments substantiate a claim that I made in chapter 1, which is that Shintō did not function as a national religion during the Meiji constitutional period. Buddhist discourse on religious freedom at the turn of the century shows that secularism remained hotly contested, and Shintō-derived practices and ideals were not yet central to public life. Buddhists of the time did not see Shintō as Japan's national creed; in fact, they generally treated Shintō as beneath their notice.

The first legal issue at stake was the Sugamo Prison chaplain affair, in which Christian warden Arima Shirōsuke (1864–1934) summarily dismissed four Buddhist chaplains at the Sugamo Prison in northern Tokyo and replaced them with a single Christian minister, citing the constitutional religious freedom clause and budgetary constraints as rationales. The second issue was the onset of "mixed residence" (*naichi zakkyo*) with foreigners that was a result of bilateral treaty revisions that began taking effect in 1898. In securing long-sought revisions to unequal treaties, the Japanese government adopted relatively lax religious freedom provisions for non-Japanese residents. The new provisions established double standards in which foreign Christians enjoyed liberties denied to local Buddhists. The third issue, described briefly above, was a controversial religions bill advanced by the Yamagata Aritomo cabinet in December 1899 that would have subjected Japan's religions to draconian oversight had the bill actually become law.

Debates over prison chaplaincy, mixed residence, and the Yamagata religions bill offered Buddhist leaders new opportunities to formally theorize about religious freedom and religion-state relations. They frequently cited cutting-edge principles drawn from the "civilized" nations of Europe and North America to make their cases, advocating for the best kind of religious freedom they could envision within the horizons of their own historical and cultural perceptions. They made majoritarian claims when it was convenient, but they also adopted the role of the persecuted minority when necessary. They often did both simultaneously.

These diverse Buddhist responses to legal controversies at the turn of the century also show that competing interest groups injected their parochial objectives into the term "religious freedom," shifting their operative definitions of religion, rights, and liberties to suit their needs. To speak of interest groups in this way is not necessarily to speak in terms of religions, denominations, or sects. It is not simply the case that Buddhist, Christian, and Shintō constituencies differed in their responses to the Yamagata proposal, nor is it only the case that sectarian differences led to different Buddhist approaches to the Yamagata proposal, although that is partially true.[7] While the groups described below all spoke about Buddhism, their perceptions of what counted as genuine Buddhism, who was authorized to speak for Buddhists, and how Buddhism would benefit state, society, and individuals varied considerably. Furthermore, pragmatic collaboration on the political project of defeating unpalatable legislation obscured fundamental points of disagreement about the scope of legal concepts such as rights, liberties, and privileges. Some groups preferred to articulate their positions about religious freedom in terms of threats to traditional religious authority. Others decried state interference in religions' affairs. Each was prepared to use religious freedom as a shield when protecting its own interests; each wielded religious freedom as a weapon to smash perceived opponents.

Below, I distinguish between three types of religious freedom that appeared in Buddhist discourse of the day. *Statist* approaches gave preference to the governmental prerogative to grant or rescind religious freedom based on the state's perception of the public good. *Corporatist* approaches prioritized customary privileges for Buddhism as Japan's majority religion. Finally, *latitudinarian* approaches treated religious freedom as a civil liberty devolving upon individuals rather than groups. By showing that religious freedom was many things to many people, these categories correct for the tendency to treat religious freedom as an ahistorical, universal principle that Buddhists misunderstood and that the Japanese state incorrectly applied.

THE SUGAMO PRISON CHAPLAIN INCIDENT

"I was appointed to the Sugamo Prison as a chaplain in October 1895, but as of early September of this year I count as one of the four chaplains who was dismissed from that prison."[8]

So began Buddhist priest Tōgō Ryōchō (d.u.) in an impassioned lecture recorded on 15 November 1898. Tōgō's indignant speech outlined the shady circumstances behind the Sugamo warden's peremptory dismissal of four Buddhist chaplains and subsequent replacement of them with a single Christian minister. Delivered over three days in the last half of November 1898, Tōgō's series of lectures served as an opportunity for his Buddhist audience to reflect on whether the new constitutional guarantee of religious freedom was working for them. Given that the dismissal of the Buddhist chaplains had been justified by the warden's citation of the constitutional religious freedom clause, the dispute over the prison chaplaincy served as a proxy battle for a larger dispute over the scope of the constitutional guarantee. Of particular concern for Buddhists was whether the right to practice Christianity, a minority foreign religion, would be allowed to trump the freedom to practice Buddhism (the dominant Japanese religion at the time).[9]

According to Tōgō's account, warden Arima Shirōsuke, a recently baptized Christian, had announced his intent on 5 September 1898 to establish a new chaplaincy system in which there would be two modes of ministering to the spiritual needs of Sugamo's inmates. The first would be to install chaplains in charge of general moral instruction, while the second would be to employ chaplains specializing in specific religious doctrines. In making this distinction between general morality and specific religiosity, Arima called attention to the problematic particularism of religious commitment while also implying that "general moral instruction" would supersede denominational difference. The warden had also appealed to the constitutional principle of religious freedom to justify his hiring of Tameoka Kōsuke (1864–1934), the minister of Reinanzaka Church in Tokyo's Minato Ward who had baptized Arima himself just four months prior.[10] At the same time, Arima cited budget constraints as a rationale for discharging the four Buddhist chaplains who had been employed at the prison for years.

Tōgō's indignant speech served to vent his evident frustration with having been unceremoniously fired. But the disgruntled priest was also building a case around the concept of religious freedom. Strikingly, however, he did not argue that his religious freedom had been infringed upon, as one might expect. Rather, he argued that Arima's appeal to the constitutional religious freedom clause made a categorical mistake in treating a foreign, minority religion as a beneficiary of the religious freedom guarantee. The problem for Tōgō was that Christianity had never been formally recognized in Japanese law as a Japanese religion. He could therefore claim that Christianity was not actually protected by the constitution.[11]

Tōgō assumed that official governmental recognition was a prerequisite for religious groups or individuals to enjoy the religious freedom enshrined in the constitution. In his eyes, a particular religion had to be officially acknowledged as valid before the religious freedom clause would go into effect. In the absence of this sort of governmental recognition, people would of course be free to believe whatever they wanted, but their abilities to make religious freedom claims in public matters (such as the oversight of the prison chaplaincy) would be nonexistent. Tōgō also assumed that religious freedom disputes should be resolved through attention to the relative numerical strength of the religion or religions in question, meaning that minority religions like Christianity were less deserving of religious freedom than those in the majority (namely, Buddhism). Tōgō could therefore confidently state that Arima profoundly misunderstood the constitutional religious freedom clause because he assumed that religious freedom guarantees should be based on historical precedent and majority status.

Tōgō's argument reflected a growing consensus among some Japanese Buddhists about the proper relationship between religion and the state, but his attitude should not be mistaken for a reactionary Buddhist response to the recent arrival of religious freedom as a global legal norm. In fact, the pamphlet in which Tōgō's speeches appeared concluded with an appendix surveying the religious freedom laws of various European nations, highlighting the fact that nearly all of these "civilized" countries discriminated in some way between minority and majority religions by designating some as "officially recognized religions" (*kōninkyō*). Japanese Buddhists like Tōgō skillfully used examples from the civilized nations of western Europe to argue that *real* religious freedom was based on precedent, numerical strength, and customary privileges.

The Buddhist obsession with legal recognition at the close of Japan's nineteenth century made explicit one of the tacit presuppositions of religious freedom law. For religious freedom to work, specific groups and practices must be made legally legible. They must be acknowledged in the eyes of the state to exist, and they must be recognized as deserving of legal protection. The furor over the Sugamo Prison chaplains' summary dismissal concentrated Buddhist attention on this recognition issue. Buddhist activists pushed the state to clarify just which groups were deserving of religious freedom and which were not, expecting to prove once and for all that Christianity would be slotted into the latter category. As they called for this legal clarification, Buddhists did not hesitate to remind policy makers, in a thinly veiled political threat, that the majority of Japanese citizens were Buddhists and therefore potentially disgruntled voters.

Under sustained Buddhist opposition, the Sugamo decision was eventually reversed through a 4 March 1899 vote on the floor of the House of Commons. Buddhists successfully made the claim that the majority of the Sugamo inmates were Buddhist and therefore required the services of Buddhist clerics.[12] This legislative victory marked a turning point in the domestic politics of religious freedom in Japan. The Sugamo Prison chaplain incident galvanized clerics and Buddhist lay intellectuals, fostering among them concern that Christian minorities might successfully use the language of religious freedom to undermine the customary privileges of Japan's Buddhist majority. With the Sugamo Prison chaplain incident of 1898, the Buddhist battle over the meaning of religious freedom began in earnest.[13]

THE THREAT OF MIXED RESIDENCE

Buddhists were keenly aware that government officials' desire to revise the famously unequal treaties signed with the foreign nations when Japan opened up to trade in the mid-nineteenth century might have negative repercussions for them. While securing equal treaties at the expense of enhanced religious freedom protections for foreign residents in Japan probably seemed like a small price to pay for members of the executive branch, for Buddhist clerics it presented the unpalatable prospect that incidents like the Sugamo Prison chaplain affair were just the tip of the iceberg. If *Japanese* Christians like Arima could cause so much trouble, how much more so could foreign missionaries with unfettered access to the Japanese interior? As they responded to the prospect of mixed residence with foreigners, Japanese Buddhists tactically adopted religious freedom language and adapted it to their exclusionary project of diminishing Christian clout, if not keeping Christians out.

Buddhist concerns about religious freedom in this context prompted disquisitions on constitutional law and national character, on the relationship between law and morality, and on the relative importance of precedent and progress. While Japanese Buddhists could not stop treaty revisions from taking effect in 1899 and therefore could not stop the influx of foreign Christians, they *could* move the goalposts in terms of how religious freedom was understood. They did so with alacrity and ingenuity. They also established precedents for debates over religious freedom in ensuing decades, offering typologies and terminology that would periodically resurface in later disputes over comprehensive religions legislation.

Buddhist disquisitions on mixed residence did not necessarily use the language of religious freedom explicitly. For example, prominent lay Buddhists such as Ōuchi Seiran (1845–1918), Inoue Enryō (1858–1919), and Katō Totsudō (1870–1949) gave lectures in 1897 that rendered the mixed residence issue in moral terms rather than legal ones.[14] These speakers tended to treat mixed residence as an opportunity to prove the moral superiority of Buddhism over Christianity; they also encouraged their audiences to think about how mixed residence with foreign Christians could prepare Buddhists for the propagation of Buddhism abroad. At the same time, they tended to downplay legal interpretations of religious freedom. Ōuchi argued, for example, that to focus too much on legal language would be to cede ground to foreign Christians on their own conceptual turf, while Inoue and Katō both suggested that Western legal arrangements were based on Christian principles that did not apply to Japan's inherently Buddhist mentality.

One Buddhist who did contribute explicitly legal analysis to the discussion was Jōdo Shinshū Honganji-ha priest Fujishima Ryō'on (also Tangaku, 1852–1918), who published a roughly one-hundred-page pamphlet in April 1899 on the subject of how the religious freedom recently guaranteed in Article 28 of the Meiji Constitution should work in the context of the revised treaties that allowed for mixed residence. *New Treatise on State and Religion* offered an extended analysis of religion-state relations and an impassioned assessment of the potential negative effects of mixed residence on Buddhism and Buddhists.[15] Fujishima had studied in France in the early 1880s, and he peppered his text with references to cutting-edge French scholarship on the issue.

Offering a typology that would become quite popular among Buddhists in the coming years, Fujishima divided religion-state relations into four types: theocracy (rule by religion), systems of state religion (as in the case of the Anglican Church), systems of "complementarity" in which religion and state support one another, and latitudinarian systems such as the one found in the United States. Fujishima rejected theocratic and state religion systems outright, but he also rejected latitudinarian systems as fundamentally flawed. Such permissive systems did not provide sufficient strictures on religions, Fujishima opined, and the case of the United States showed that it was not uncommon for unwholesome new religions and lax moral practices to arise as a result.[16] Naturally, the best course was to adopt a system of complementarity between state and religion: Buddhism would be officially recognized as a religion and offered particular perquisites, while "new religions" like Christianity were given a lower status if they were acknowledged at all. Fujishima spoke approvingly, for example, of how French Jews were technically granted religious freedom, but Judaism was not given officially recognized religion (*kōninkyō*) status under the new French constitution.[17]

Fujishima's pamphlet addressed the threat of mixed residence explicitly at the close of a chapter calling for the establishment of an "officially recognized religion" (*kōninkyō*) system. Pointing out that Japanese state policies regarding religion remained inconsistent despite the 1889 promulgation of the Meiji Constitution, Fujishima claimed that miscellaneous laws related to religion continued to subject Buddhism and Shintō to undue restriction even as Christianity enjoyed tacit license from the state. At a time when Japan was renegotiating its treaties with foreign powers, it was of the utmost importance to unify a religions policy that was otherwise lacking a guiding principle. For Fujishima, to adopt a latitudinarian system would be unquestionably detrimental to Japan because of the subversive nature of the new religions that would inevitably arise under such a legal arrangement. Japan therefore needed to adopt a system of officially recognized religions before the revised treaties went into effect. Moreover, in the absence of a system of officially recognized religions, pernicious double standards in the treatment of local and foreign religions could remain in place. Citing the 1898 Franco-Japanese Commerce Treaty as one example, Fujishima pointed out that Christians would be likely to use the second clause granting foreign citizens freedom of conscience and freedom to erect places of worship as a mode of infiltrating the country. He cited the treaty as follows:

> Article Two. Citizens of each of the two signatory countries shall enjoy complete freedom of conscience in the territory of the other country, and in accordance with the laws and regulations may construct and maintain [religious] edifices [*dōu*] and may also perform worship in public and private. According to these terms, citizens of these countries have the

> right to be buried in cemeteries befitting their religious customs. If there should not be appropriate cemeteries in existence, they shall be established and respectfully maintained.

With this clause, the treaty effectively granted French Christians the right to construct places of worship without seeking advance permission, whereas Buddhists and Shintō priests were still required to seek permission from the Home Ministry to construct edifices of any kind. While other treaties may have been less specific in their clauses related to religion, Fujishima claimed, other countries would certainly follow France's lead in making unreasonable demands on the Japanese government that could only elicit consternation from the Japanese people. Rather than allowing this to happen, Buddhists should force the state to adopt a system of officially recognized religion and thereby ensure the primacy of Buddhism in national law.

The Significance of Mixed Residence for Buddhist Conceptions of Religious Freedom

Fujishima's proposals, which existed as part of a broader contemporaneous Buddhist discourse about the mixed residence issue, were clearly intended to place Buddhism in a superior position to Christianity through legal maneuvering (the adoption of a *kōninkyō*, or officially recognized religion, system prior to the onset of mixed residence).[18] While Buddhists like Fujishima clearly recognized that they could not stop the treaty revisions from taking effect, their theorization about religious freedom in preparing for the onset of mixed residence directly contributed to their subsequent push to scuttle the comprehensive religions bill advanced by the Yamagata Aritomo (1838–1922) cabinet in 1899. When the bill came under scrutiny in December of that year, Buddhists already had well-organized lobbies in place that could challenge legislation that seemed to run counter to Buddhist interests. Buddhists were able to use the same political networks and special interest publications they had developed in response to treaty revision and the Sugamo Prison chaplain incident to spread information about what such a bill might mean for Buddhists and how they could turn the outcome of a such a bill in their favor. Transsectarian Buddhist organizations lobbied legislators, organized petitions, and showed up en masse at the House of Peers to express disapproval. Yet it quickly became apparent that Buddhists were divided about what sort of religious freedom was best for their tradition.

COMPETING REACTIONS TO THE 1899 YAMAGATA RELIGIONS BILL

Although Buddhist political organizations that lobbied against the Yamagata bill invariably presumed to speak for all Buddhists (or all "real" Buddhists), in actuality their transsectarian rhetoric masked profound differences in how they conceived Buddhism's social and political role. It consequently affected how they understood religious freedom. For example, the Greater Japan Buddhist Youth Association (Dai Nippon Bukkyō Seinen Kai, founded 1894), one of the more vocal critics of the bill, represented a flourishing Buddhist youth culture largely active in the capital of Tokyo (rather than in the Kyoto area where the headquarters of most Buddhist sects were located).[19] Many of these young priests had been born after the Meiji Restoration of 1868 and therefore had no direct memory of the violent paroxysms that had dealt a near-fatal blow to Japanese Buddhism in the wake of that regime change.[20] Furthermore, in contrast to their older clerical counterparts, these younger Tokyo-based clerics tended to benefit from a type of modern education that balanced sacerdotal training in ritual and doctrine with fluency in Western political and philosophical concepts.[21] They also came of age at a time when Christians were exerting much greater social influence in Japan, and some of these young Buddhists eagerly adopted Christian ideals of social work and abstemiousness even as they rejected the appropriateness of Christianity's fit with the Japanese national character.[22]

Additionally, the growing trend of "lay centrality" placed additional pressure on traditional sources of Buddhist authority.[23] Journalists, politicians, disaffected and laicized priests, doctors, educators, and other educated individuals used the burgeoning print media and flourishing culture of Buddhist oratory (*enzetsu*) to absorb and disseminate ideas about Buddhism. With the rise of evidentiary historiography and philology, clerics were no longer understood as absolute authorities on matters of Buddhist doctrine and history.[24] Nonordained intellectuals began writing authoritatively about Buddhism, presaging the rapid increase in scholarship by lay Buddhists who derived their authority from academic credentials rather than clerical status.[25] Against this backdrop, it was unlikely that all Buddhists would have shared the same political views regarding controversial legislation like the Yamagata bill. While the Buddhist publications cited below can only provide a narrow window into the actual diversity of contemporaneous Buddhist opinion, they make it quite clear that Buddhist approaches to religious legislation and the associated topic of religious freedom were far from uniform.

Statist, Corporatist, and Latitudinarian Approaches to Religious Freedom

Comparison of Buddhist transsectarian publications generated in response to the Yamagata bill suggests that significant ideological differences manifested in what appear to have been at least three distinct interpretations of "religious freedom" championed by Buddhists at the time. Statist visions of religious freedom treated it as circumstantial state-granted right and acknowledged the state's prerogative to determine when expressions of religious faith infringed upon the government's duty of maintaining peace and order.[26] In contrast, corporatist interpretations treated religious freedom as a customary privilege based on precedent, regarding egalitarian policies as threats to the esteemed positions of traditional religions boasting majority status. Finally, latitudinarian approaches regarded religious freedom as a civil liberty that granted freedom of conscience to individuals and freedom from state intervention to religious groups.

This tripartite typology of attitudes regarding religious freedom is admittedly schematic and somewhat reductive. To be clear, all three types bore some degree of overlap in any given publication or elocution. Each was subject to change according to context and circumstance. The constitutional provision of religious freedom may have been somewhat statist because it reserved the right for the state to maintain "peace and order" and enjoined Japanese citizens to not let religious commitments interfere with their "duties as subjects," but it was also open to interpretation as competing interest groups and powerful political lobbies encouraged the state to clarify operative conceptions of "religion," "rights," and the relationship between imperial subjecthood and democratic citizenship.[27]

Religious Freedom as a Circumstantial Right: Defenders of the Yamagata Religions Bill

Article 28 of the Meiji Constitution legally instantiated a particular interpretation of religious freedom that gave a greater degree of latitude to the prerogatives of the state than it did to individuals or to groups. The promulgation of the Imperial Rescript on Education in 1890 and the furor that followed the 1891 Uchimura Kanzō lèse-majesté incident (known as the "clash of education and religion," *kyōiku to shūkyō no shōtotsu*) attest to the fact that some scholars, religious leaders, and legislators preferred to concentrate transcendent power in the person of the emperor and the authority of the state as opposed to dividing transcendence with the newly "private" realm of religion.[28] This statist interpretation of religious freedom reserved the right of the state to place the "duties of subjects" and "peace and order" above their government-granted ability to profess a particular faith and behave accordingly in public. In this view, religious freedom was an indulgence provisionally granted to subject-citizens by the state but also subject to circumstantial revocation. To give an example, the well-documented journalistic persecution of marginal religions such as Tenrikyō and Renmonkyō that occurred in the last decade of the nineteenth century tended to presume the guilt and illegitimacy of these religions; contemporary calls for their eradication appealed to the state's duty to maintain peace and order.[29] Similarly, Inoue Tetsujirō's famous indictment of Christianity as being incompatible with public school education—a highly publicized response to the aforementioned Uchimura Kanzō lèse-majesté incident—drew new lines between public duty and private faith while redistricting "morality" as falling under the jurisdiction of the state.[30] But even though the wording of Article 28 of the Meiji Constitution clearly gave priority to the state in adjudicating the proper balance between rights and duties, the Yamagata Aritomo cabinet attempted to clarify the issue by advancing new legislation on the subject. The attitudes exemplified in the text of the bill and the stances adopted by its defenders illustrate what I am calling "statist" religious freedom here.

In the draft religions bill (Shūkyō hōan) dated 9 December 1899, the cabinet offered a legislative vision that restricted the scope of the constitutional religious freedom clause. The bill was couched in bureaucratic language that explicitly limited religions' freedom of assembly and left the determination of what counted as a religion up to the narrow definition provided by the state. It reflected Yamagata's preference for authoritarian approaches that concentrated as much power as possible in the state, and in the person of the emperor specifically.[31]

The bill was largely written in negative language that constrained rights and liberties rather than outlining specific duties, a fact reflected in the majority of the fifteen clauses comprising the first chapter, "Overview [*sōsoku*]." For example, the first clause read, "those corporations and associations that publicly promulgate religion and perform religious ceremonies but do not conform with this law may not become juridical persons."[32] After defining which groups would count as "churches" and "temples" (Clauses 2 and 3), the bill stipulated that any corporation or association that attempted to incorporate other associations already recognized as churches or temples could not in turn be recognized as such (Clause 4, effectively cutting off religions' ability to amalgamate). Those that already belonged to an existing group could not split off to become groups of their own (Clause 5, forestalling schism).[33] Religious groups that wished to organize a public assembly for religious purposes were required to receive permission from the appropriate government office at least twenty-four hours in advance. While periodic or regular observances did not require such permission, the government reserved the right to change the terms without notice (Clause 8). Any activity deemed a threat to peace and order, destructive of morals and customs, or in opposition to the duties of subjects was subject to revocation or revision by the government (Clause 9).[34] While religious buildings and lands were exempt from taxation (Clause 12), the government reserved the right to define which were eligible (Clause 13). All religions were required to comply with bureaucratic directives (Clause 14). In a particularly powerful clause, if religions were found to be in breach of the law or if it was deemed to be in the public interest, their legal recognition as religions and all associated permissions could be revoked by the responsible government office.[35] In short, the definition of "public interest" could be expanded and contracted to suit any number of cases.[36]

The remaining five chapters of the bill laid out specifics regarding churches and temples (chapter 2), sects and denominations (chapter 3), clerics (*kyōshi*, chapter 4), and penalties and regulations (*bassoku*, chapter 5). An appendix indicated the government's intention that the law should replace prior government directives regarding Buddhism, Shintō, and religion (Clause 47), and that all religious organizations should have conformed to the law within a year of its enactment (that is, by no later than July 1901).[37]

Curiously, this appendix did not make any explicit reference to the constitutional religious freedom clause when it referred to "prior government directives regarding Buddhism, Shintō, and religion." This striking absence suggests two possible intentions on the government's part. On the one hand, the executive branch may have intended to clarify the ambiguously worded religious freedom clause, which left a great deal of latitude in interpretation. If this was the case, then the draft bill was hardly a step in the right direction. One of the main criticisms of the bill on the floor of the House of Peers was that it was vague and easily prone to misinterpretation.[38] On the other hand, the Yamagata cabinet may have intended to replace the constitutional religious freedom clause with a new law that amounted to a de facto constitutional revision.[39] Whatever the case, for the Yamagata cabinet, religious freedom was simply a privilege that was provisionally granted to citizens and groups, meaning that it could be revoked at the government's whim.

While this attitude was primarily evident among policy makers in the executive branch, some Buddhists apparently accepted it as natural. For example, in a short letter to the editor of the Buddhist journal *Meikyō shinshi*, the lay Buddhist legal expert Katō Totsudō (1870–1949) argued for the statist vision of religious freedom advocated by the Yamagata cabinet, suggesting that the bill needed tweaking but was a step in the right direction.[40] Other Buddhist clerics were apparently inclined to support the bill in return for promises of preferential governmental treatment.[41]

Corporatism and Customary Privileges: The "Officially Recognized Religion" Camp

Buddhist authorities who were eager to curry favor with the government embraced the Yamagata cabinet's statist interpretation of religious freedom, but other interest groups interpreted religious freedom as a customary right. In this case, religious freedom was not a principle of egalitarian or neutral treatment, but precisely the opposite: it would preserve the perquisites traditionally granted to occupational groups such as clergy (tax exemption, for example) or to specific religions such as Buddhism.[42] Buddhists of the day were probably particularly inclined to think of rights in customary terms because of the economic issue of land reform (see Clauses 12 and 13 above). Recent changes regarding the taxation and ownership of temple lands and graveyards had brought to Buddhists' collective attention that the political changes of the Meiji era had significant economic impacts on their incomes. Land that temples had managed for generations abruptly changed legal status, and customary rights changed into formal property rights based on documented and verifiable claims to ownership.[43] Buddhist conceptions of religious freedom were at least partially influenced by this economic issue.

Whatever the reasons, the concept of officially recognized religion (*kōninkyō*) came to be promoted with much greater force after the Sugamo Prison chaplain incident galvanized clerics and lay Buddhists alike to assert the unique relationship between Buddhism and the state. Contemporaneous Buddhist publications featured detailed explications of how a *kōninkyō* system would work.

Superficially, *kōninkyō* advocacy seems to represent a peculiar approach to religion-state relations unique to Japan.[44] However, just as the

Japanese constitution's provision of religious freedom actually matched the language of contemporary European constitutions, the Japanese advocates of the *kōninkyō* concept drew much of their inspiration from observation of the countries of western Europe.[45] Proponents argued that a *kōninkyō* system acknowledged the importance of precedent while also distinguishing trustworthy religions such as Buddhism from untrustworthy foreign religions like Christianity.[46]

For example, in a 16 December 1899 *Meikyō shinshi* editorial by Jōdo Shinshū priest and chief editor Andō Tetsuchō (better known as Masazumi, 1876–1955) entitled "Our 'Officially Recognized Religion,'" the journal argued that the constitutions of all lawful nations of the world included some clause or statement regarding religions systems.[47] However, although Japan had entered the ranks of such nations thirty years prior with the Meiji Restoration, it had not yet established a transparent religions system. As debates raged about whether such a system would be for the sake of religion or for the sake of the state, many confused state religion (*kokkyō*) with officially recognized religion (*kōninkyō*), and some confused a latitudinarian policy with a *kōninkyō* policy, thinking that such a policy would treat all religions in the country equally. Lamenting this state of affairs, Andō felt compelled to clarify the outlines of a religious system and to advocate the adoption of a *kōninkyō* arrangement. Although he did not cite Fujishima directly, Andō offered a similar typology of religion-state relations that rejected systems of state religion as oppressive and latitudinarian systems as excessively permissive. The only country that had tried to the latter approach was the United States, where new religions like the Church of Jesus Christ of Latter-day Saints (informally, the Mormons) violated the law and flouted conventional ethics through the practice of plural marriage. Andō sarcastically scoffed that such a "system" was clearly dangerous to the nation.

However, he argued, it was possible to avoid both extremes of adopting a national religion, on the one hand, or adopting libertarian latitudinarianism on the other. A *kōninkyō* system would strike the sweet spot between these extremes by adjusting regulations to match the relative strength and influence of each of the religions in the country. The success of the *kōninkyō* arrangement could be seen in the German example of designating religions as "Alpha" and "Beta" types, with the Alpha variety granted status as public juridical persons and oversight over their own affairs, and those of the Beta variety given status as private juridical persons. Those that lacked formal organization or were of minimal influence were treated as Gamma religions and were managed through regular ordinances regarding public gatherings and meetings. Andō argued that such a system was based on the principle of religious freedom and embodied the aim of separation of religion and the state, but did not separate state from religion absolutely, but to just the right degree, thereby solving the problems shared by state and religion in an orderly way.

Andō's editorial then generated a set of criteria for determining which religion(s) might qualify for *kōninkyō* status in Japan. Not surprisingly given the venue and his Buddhist audience, Andō concluded that it was only Buddhism that had the numerical influence, historical longevity, and moral probity to pass muster as Japan's officially recognized religion. He concluded by claiming that a *kōninkyō* system operated under the crucial premise of granting religious freedom while also fixing the currently faulty apparatus for administering religion. By setting up the systems of state religion and latitudinarianism as minority positions taken by a tiny number of countries, Andō also implied that the *kōninkyō* arrangement was the global norm. It was also no accident that Andō's criteria for *kōninkyō* status left room for Buddhism alone to fill the role of *kōninkyō*, nor was it an accident that his list effectively foreclosed the possibility that Christianity or the Shintō sects might achieve formal recognition.

Strikingly, Andō made no explicit mention of Shintō. This was no doubt partly a function of the fact that he was writing for a transsectarian Buddhist newspaper. But it was also due to what seems to have been a general point of agreement among Buddhists at the time: The recently reinvented Shintō tradition was not even worthy of mention in the context of discussions of state religion or officially recognized religion. This historical fact undermines the postwar narrative that Shintō had already achieved the status of national religion by this time. Had Shintō been the national religion, then presumably proponents of making Buddhism Japan's sole *kōninkyō* would have articulated their arguments by first delegitimizing Shintō or by acknowledging that systems of national religion and officially recognized religions could coexist. While Buddhists were divided about whether establishing Buddhism as Japan's only officially recognized religion was proper or desirable, in general they do not seem to have seriously considered the idea that Shintō could serve as Japan's national religion. They clearly did not regard Shintō as already occupying that role. This is a crucial historical point that has until recently gone largely overlooked.[48]

At any rate, Andō Masazumi and his journal, *Meikyō shinshi*, were by no means the only voices that called for the establishment of Buddhism as Japan's officially recognized religion. Jōdo Shinshū cleric Chikazumi Jōkan

(1870–1941) was another.[49] Originally from a small Buddhist temple serving a farming community in what is now Shiga Prefecture, Chikazumi demonstrated his intellect from an early age and attracted the attention of the Shinshū leadership. On Kiyozawa Manshi's (1863–1903) recommendation, he traveled to Tokyo as a representative student of the Otani-ha branch of the sect.[50] There, he studied at the First Higher School and joined in founding the Greater Japan Buddhist Youth Association (Dai Nippon Bukkyō Seinen Kai) in 1894, where he served as secretary. Chikazumi studied under Inoue Tetsujirō (1855–1944) at Tokyo Imperial University, graduating with a bachelor's degree in Western philosophy in July 1898.[51] In September 1898 he began protesting the Sugamo Prison chaplain incident.[52]

This experience apparently prompted Chikazumi's founding of the lay-centric Buddhist Citizens' Alliance Association (Bukkyō Kokumin Dōmei Kai) on 29 October 1898.[53] Chikazumi renamed the group the Greater Japan Buddhist Alliance Association (Dai Nippon Bukkyōto Dōmei Kai) in May 1899. The group disseminated ideas about ideal religion-state relations in a bimonthly periodical, *Seikyō jihō* (*State and Religion Times*), that ran from 1 January 1899 until 8 December 1903. Each issue included a prominent display of the group's founding principles and an anonymous editorial regarding some aspect of religion-state relations. Other sections included essays, a society column, and other miscellanea.[54] After the initial debate regarding the Yamagata religions bill in the House of Peers in December 1899, the association devoted its resources to distributing fifty-five thousand copies of a handbill advocating its defeat.[55]

Just as Andō Masazumi's *Meikyō shinshi* editorial had tactically made use of foreign examples, a *Seikyō jihō* editorial titled "Misinterpretations of Religious Freedom" skillfully wielded citations from documents such as the Japan-France Treaty and the laws regarding religion in France, Prussia, Austria, and Bavaria (at that time a sovereign kingdom within the German Empire) to argue against the Yamagata proposal.[56] Opening the editorial with the claim that Yamagata was taking advantage of Japanese citizens' ignorance of religious freedom to push forward legislation that would ultimately serve the narrow interests of the cabinet, the author lamented the fact that the prime minister merely served as an intermediary who introduced interpretations of religious freedom that clearly originated from foreign powers.

Instead of a state-centric system, the author continued, freedom of conscience (freedom of belief) should be strictly separated from the administration of religions. For example, France's religions law guaranteed freedom of assembly, exemption from military conscription, corporate status for religious edifices, and financial support for clerics, but only for recognized groups: Catholics, Protestants, Lutherans, Reformers, and—in Algeria (Arujinia in the original)—Muslims.[57] As long as they did not interfere with the national interest, other groups could perform religious rites in private or seek special permission to perform such rites in public. The government reserved the right to dissolve marginal groups, and they had no right to assemble without government permission. In particular, smaller groups like Jews were forbidden from collaborating with foreign religions, and they could not achieve juridical person status. Whereas in France's reasonable system Japanese traditions would be subject to similar oversight due to their status as foreign religions, under the proposed Japanese law French Catholics could receive the same treatment as local Buddhists in Japan. The author dismissed this possibility as risible.

Around the time this editorial appeared, publication of *Seikyō jihō* became rather erratic as Chikazumi worked tirelessly to lobby the government. Articles in the small number of issues published during this time reiterated the themes of the 29 December 1899 editorial cited above. In January Chikazumi published, under his own name, a tract called *Shūkyō hō ronsan* (*A Critical Treatise on the Religions Bill*). This was closely followed by a sixty-one-page anonymous pamphlet entitled *Our Opinion [Regarding] Opposition to the Religions Bill.*[58] Although the logic of this remarkable document was not always coherent, it encapsulated a major distinction between the statist approach to religious freedom put forward in the Yamagata religions bill and the corporatist approach to religious freedom favored by some Buddhists. The author (almost certainly Chikazumi) suggested that a religions bill that treated all religions equally would ignore the important issue of historical precedent. Rights should be based on tradition rather than on universal principles that obfuscated historical circumstances and cultural particulars. Hence his disparaging references to egalitarianism and his dismissal of giving foreign religions equal treatment in the name of religious freedom.

Both Andō and Chikazumi advanced a "Goldilocks" version of religious freedom that saw a *kōninkyō* system as a perfect middle ground between statism and latitudinarianism. These attitudes did not constitute ignorance of the importance of religious freedom. Rather, they represented a tactical interpretation of religious freedom designed to secure an advantageous position for Buddhists through the legal framework of customary rights. *Kōninkyō* proponents pursued this domestic agenda by making tactical references to the practices of "civilized" European nations like France and Germany, undercutting the government's ability to appeal to foreign precedent or diplomatic considerations to advance draconian religious legislation.

Religious Freedom as a Civil Liberty: The Fellowship of Puritan Buddhists

At roughly the same time that Chikazumi was vigorously lobbying the government and printing handbills opposing the proposed religions bill, another Buddhist movement was emerging in Tokyo in response to the proposed legislation. However, whereas Chikazumi's Greater Japan Buddhist Alliance Association tended to adopt a conservative stance that sought to preserve Buddhist prestige by aligning Buddhism with the state through a *kōninkyō* arrangement, the Bukkyō Seito Dōshikai (Fellowship of Puritan Buddhists) sought to preserve Buddhist liberty by guaranteeing Buddhist freedom from governmental oversight.[59] They articulated their civil libertarian vision in the pages of the magazines *Bukkyō* (*Buddhism*, which published fellowship tracts for about a year between February 1899 and March 1900) and *Shin Bukkyō* (*New Buddhism*, established by fellowship members in July 1900 and published monthly until August 1915). Fellowship members were suspicious of state intervention into religious affairs and more likely than many of their contemporaries to advocate egalitarian treatment of religions. At the same time, however, their critiques of "superstitions" (*meishin*) allowed them to designate certain groups as "not-religion" and therefore not deserving of freedom.

The Fellowship of Puritan Buddhists was a group of disaffected young priests and lay intellectuals that coalesced in Tokyo in the midst of the furor over the Yamagata religions bill. In a retrospective published in 1910, Sakaino Kōyō (1871–1933) recalled that the original impetus for the movement derived from an 1894 meeting of Furukawa Rōsen (1871–99), Sugimura Jūō (1872–1945, also Sojinkan), and others who formed the Tokyo-based Keiikai (Warp and Woof Society), although some of the founding members' acquaintance with one another traced back to an even earlier progressive Buddhist group based in Kyoto known as the Hanseikai (Temperance Society, founded 1886).[60] The Keiikai journal, *Bukkyō* (*Buddhism*, published 1889–1902), had taken a notoriously caustic stance vis-à-vis the clerical establishment by pushing for institutional reform.

In 1899, Keiikai members split into two factions regarding the *kōninkyō* issue: Chikazumi Jōkan and Kashiwahara Buntarō (1869–1936) advocated the elevation of Buddhism—and only Buddhism—to *kōninkyō* status, while others advocated either elevating both Buddhism and Christianity to such status or abandoning the idea of "officially recognized religion" altogether.[61] With these significant differences of opinion as impetus, the Keiikai unanimously agreed to disband at a meeting held on 5 February 1899.[62] One week later, on 12 February, those who had represented the anti-*kōninkyō* camp—Andō Hiromu (1876–?), Sakaino Kōyō, Takashima Beihō (1875–1949), and Tanaka Jiroku (1869–?)—gathered in a small, dark room in Takashima's humble Tokyo lodgings and created the Bukkyō Seito Dōshikai (Fellowship of Puritan Buddhists), composing a five-article list of principles:

1. We believe in the original principles of Buddhism.
2. We anticipate the fundamental reform of society through the arousal of faith.
3. We insist on free inquiry into Buddhism.
4. We abolish all superstitious beliefs.
5. We do not acknowledge the necessity of preserving prior religious systems.[63]

In response to the contemporaneous push to make Buddhism an officially recognized religion, the members of the fellowship added a sixth point about rejecting state interference in religious affairs. This additional principle, "We abolish all governmental protection and oversight of religions" was temporarily added to the platform by March 1899 when the existence of the group was first publicized in an anonymous *Bukkyō* editorial.[64] It later became a permanent fixture.[65]

Although the members had hoped to turn the journal *Bukkyō* into the official organ for the fellowship, negotiations with editor Kaji Hōjun (1864–1920) broke down and the members were forced to establish their own journal.[66] In the time between the initial formation of the group in early 1899 and the publication of the first issue of *Shin Bukkyō* (*New Buddhism*) in July 1900, the furor over the Yamagata religions bill galvanized the group and provided a ready-made raison d'être for these self-described "progressive Buddhists" (*shinshin Bukkyōto*) who had espoused stances that were consistently critical of both the Buddhist clerical establishment and the state.[67] The group was able to capitalize on the indignation that greeted the Yamagata bill by appealing to young intellectuals who favored more latitudinarian stances than those evidenced by the older clerical establishment or the *kōninkyō* faction.

Takashima Beihō later recalled that prospective members were banging down the door in their eagerness to join the group following a promulgation of its formation in *Bukkyō* on 15 March 1899, but the founding members made a policy to apply stringent standards to membership, rejecting first-time applicants as a matter of course.[68] Fellowship members' reformist attitudes, their antisacerdotalism, and their support of latitudinarian state policies vis-à-vis religion were hardly commonplace. Members initially treated the group as a secret society to protect themselves from potential fallout associated with these unpopular positions.[69] While this caution derived at least as much from youthful exuberance as from any serious threat to members' physical well-being or social standing, their reformist stance had serious repercussions for those who came from clerical backgrounds. Hence the members' adoption of code names (e.g., "Mr. 68") and secret passwords.[70]

Immediately following the 15 March 1899 *Bukkyō* editorial announcing the establishment of the fellowship was a second editorial entitled "A Different Perspective on Officially Recognized Religion." The article began by saying that, in the face of the threat of mixed residence with foreign Christians, a number of people had begun to advocate the treatment of Buddhism as Japan's officially recognized religion (*kōninkyō*). However, the editors felt that Buddhism should not be officially recognized, but should instead be the subject of a latitudinarian policy. After all, the author continued, what does "officially recognized" mean anyway? Citing the fact that legal scholars exhibited great differences of opinion about the respective purviews of civil and private law, the author dismissed a *Seikyō jihō* definition of officially recognized religion as being legally untenable and conceptually vague. Moreover, to seek state acknowledgment of religions was to invite statutory oversight, thereby placing religion in a subordinate position to the state.

Moving on to criticize recent editorials in *Meikyō shinshi* that had been calling for the acknowledgment of Buddhism as Japan's officially recognized religion, the author indicated that such editorials had emphasized that such status would not benefit Buddhism but would be of great benefit to the state. With evident incredulity, the author wondered what might motivate any Buddhist to act in such a manner. While such an initiative coming from the state would be understandable, would it not be strange to have Buddhists themselves calling for such oversight? Moreover, given that Buddhism effectively enjoyed state recognition while Christianity did not, was it not odd that Buddhists claimed to be languishing while Christianity was flourishing?

Ultimately, the editorial opined, neither Buddhism nor Christianity should be treated as an officially recognized religion. If both were treated as *kōninkyō*, then Christianity would be given undue preferential treatment because of the government's evident desire to appease foreign powers. As such, there could be no way to treat the two religions equally other than to adopt a stance of liberal latitudinarianism. Although some might complain that this would put Buddhism at a disadvantage as mixed residence policies went into effect, the writer scoffed that a Buddhism incapable of competing with Christianity on a level playing field was no Buddhism at all.[71]

The caustic tone of this editorial and its willingness to call out contemporaneous publications and groups such as *Seikyō jihō* and *Meikyō shinshi* was characteristic of *Bukkyō*. As the editorial announcing the formation of the fellowship had suggested, "old Buddhism" was superstitious, hypocritical, mendacious, and reactionary.[72] Combating this religion of fogies and fakes, the new fellowship claimed to not be one of those quasi-political movements seeking personal benefit, but rather a purely religious movement based on faith.[73]

This last claim is rather suspect, for the fellowship almost immediately formed its own political lobby, the Liberal Buddhist Alliance Association (Jiyū Shugi Bukkyōto Dōmei Kai). The lobby aimed to reject the Yamagata religions bill while simultaneously countering the claims of the *kōninkyō* faction. This political project was exemplified in a 24 January 1900 *Bukkyō* opinion piece attributed to the association called "An Opinion in Response to the Religions Bill." It began:

> We lament the fact that inveterate Old Buddhists and pigheaded priests do their utmost to preserve their temples through political power and try to conserve the outward forms of their sects and factions out of fears that other religions might infringe on their own territory. We have completely opposed the officially recognized religion philosophy and have rejected governmental protection and interference for quite some time. Now, as the Religions Bill has been submitted, we liberal and progressive Buddhists announce a few of the points we see in the outlines of that Bill, and we intend to call for transparent, public criticism of it.[74]

In its first point following this somewhat bombastic introduction, the article reproduced the language of the sixth point in the fellowship platform: "We reject all sorts of political protection and interference regarding religion." The anonymous author suggested that as long as religions did not infringe upon morals or public order, the government should adopt a passive, rather than active, approach to managing religions. The article then went on to say that the association approved of the fact that the Yamagata bill ostensibly treated Buddhism and Christianity equally, but hastily added that the bill failed to actually treat the two equally because of significant terminological differences regarding definitions of priests, churches, temples, and the like. Going on to outline specific clauses that should be cut or modified, the document made clear that it was less opposed to the spirit of the law than it was to the advocacy of a *kōninkyō* system that greeted its submission in the House of Peers. That is, the Liberal Buddhist Alliance Association was not opposed to the statist thrust of the Yamagata bill nearly as much as it was opposed to the conservative attitudes behind calls for official state recognition of Buddhism.

In sum, these "progressive" Buddhist activists were not concerned about being placed in a subordinate position vis-à-vis Japan's national religion of Shintō. They were concerned that the *wrong Buddhists* would speak on behalf of their tradition, inadvertently inviting excessive governmental oversight. By admitting to the superiority of temporal law over private religious affiliation, they acknowledged the power of the state to determine the boundaries of religion. Their concern was that the state listen to *them* about what sort of religion deserved to be free.

Members of the fellowship would later recall the turn-of-the-century attempts to pass a religions bill in the Diet as crucial to the formation of the organization, but again it was not the possibility of passage of the bill itself that was the issue, but rather the *kōninkyō* debate.[75] Sakaino Kōyō and other founding members would extol the efforts of the fellowship in resisting clerical obduracy in their periodic retrospectives in *Shin Bukkyō* and other religious magazines, but the extent to which the Liberal Buddhist Alliance Association was actually successful in countering the *kōninkyō* faction is unclear.[76] After the fellowship changed its name in 1903 to the Shin Bukkyōto Dōshikai (Fellowship of New Buddhists), members would repeatedly claim that they had been on the right side of history. In the numerous historical retrospectives featured in the pages of *Shin Bukkyō*, it became obligatory to make some reference to the *kōninkyō* faction as representative of the "old Buddhism" against which these "New Buddhists" had been struggling.[77]

The fellowship's rhetoric has made the group attractive to postwar scholars seeking evidence of a prewar liberal tradition that challenged state power, but members were less politically progressive than a superficial reading of their rhetoric would suggest.[78] They denied the legitimacy of groups and practices that they deemed "superstitious," and their resistance to state intervention in religious affairs was not based on an unambiguous commitment to universalist principles.[79] Furthermore, there was a marked move to more conservative stances among these bearers of Buddhist youth culture as they entered middle age. By the Taishō era (1912–26), these self-avowed progressives partnered with policy makers in the Home and Education Ministries to advance a conservative political philosophy that envisioned Buddhism at the center of Japanese public life. Ultimately, they moved much closer to the *kōninkyō* camp than their rhetoric at the turn of the century would have suggested.[80]

VARIETIES OF RELIGIOUS FREEDOM IN JAPAN AT THE TURN OF THE CENTURY

All of the parties involved in the debates described above exhibited an intense preoccupation with the problem of religious freedom, and their discussions about the meaning and scope of religious freedom took place through the inherently democratic processes of free speech, protest, and parliamentary procedure. The important question at stake in this chapter is therefore not *whether* Japan exhibited religious freedom at the turn of the century (it clearly did) or *if* Buddhists actually understood the concept (they did, albeit in multifarious ways). Rather, my concern is with how various interest groups tactically defined "religion" and "freedom." Focusing on competing interpretations of religious freedom in Buddhist responses to the Yamagata religions bill and the legal disputes that preceded it leads to an inescapable conclusion that is not limited to the historical case discussed here: Religious freedom is never just one thing. "It" is not simply granted in constitutional law; nor is "it" expanded or contracted through legislation. "It" is neither protected nor infringed upon by law enforcement. Rather, *religious freedoms* are always-already plural. Controversies over legislation and policy like the ones described above inevitably reflect divergent interpretations concerning what needs to be freed and who needs to be protected.

Such controversies were not limited to Japan. Just as Japanese Buddhists looked askance at the influx of reprobates from overseas who might sully Japanese morals or enjoy privileges that even Japanese citizens did not enjoy, white landowners in the American territory of Hawaiʻi looked at the swelling Japanese immigrant population as a threat to American identity. Chapter 3 examines American rhetoric around religious freedom by focusing on controversies over land, language, and labor on the Hawaiian island of Oʻahu in the 1910s and 1920s.

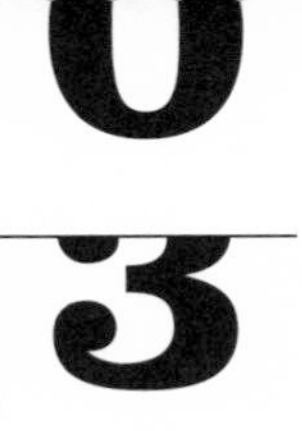

3

DOMESTIC PROBLEMS, DIPLOMATIC SOLUTIONS

The task of Americanization is a difficult one, even under the most favorable conditions. It is made doubly difficult by the influence of the Japanese teachers, many of whom do not speak the English language, nor have they the viewpoint of the American in the ideals that are dearest and holiest to him—his religion and his patriotism.

It seems to me that if we Americans have learned our lesson from the past few years [presumably referring to World War I], we should know that it is absolutely wrong that any great number of people should remain un-Americanized within our midst. We must help them to assimilate and to develop a true love and respect for our American ideals and ideas. This will not be done through the Japanese language school. What compatibility is there between Mikado worship, ancestor worship, and the teaching of democracy?

ANONYMOUS TEACHER (1920)[1]

IN A 6 NOVEMBER 1921 ARTICLE in the *Los Angeles Times*, former governor of the territory of Hawaiʻi Charles J. McCarthy (1861–1929) described Japanese immigrants on the Pacific archipelago as maintaining national characteristics and allegiance "most stubbornly."[2] Japanese did not associate with "whites of any nationality, do not intermarry with the other races, and do not accept the Christian religion except to a limited extent," McCarthy wrote. They "maintain their own language, schools, newspapers and religious organizations. These exercise a most powerful influence upon the Japanese, and they have always taught, written and preached loyalty to Japan and reverence for its institutions and culture."[3] McCarthy lamented control of the mother country over even second-generation children, whose allegiance to Japan was "doubly strong in that it is interwoven with and fostered by the national religion of which the Mikado in his heaven-born descent is the head."[4]

It may come as a surprise that McCarthy was referring not to the tradition we now know as "State Shintō," but rather to Buddhism. He was not alone in his disparaging assessment. College of Hawai'i professor Vaughan MacCaughey (1887–?) had already made a similar argument in the education journal *School and Society* in January 1919. Pointing out that Japanese students comprised about 40 percent of the student population in Hawai'i and that almost all of these students attended Japanese language schools run by "reactionary Buddhist priests," MacCaughey wrote that "the variety of Buddhism dominant in Hawai'i is medieval, ultra-superstitious and intensely Japanese. Mikado-worship and veneration of antique superstitions are prominent features of the system. Its inimical effects on the efforts of the public schools toward genuine Americanization are obvious, even upon cursory examination."[5]

MacCaughey seems to have had no particular expertise in public school education, but shortly after he published his piece in *School and Society*, Governor McCarthy appointed MacCaughey as Hawai'i's superintendent of public instruction. Counteracting the alleged anti-Americanism of the Japanese language schools became MacCaughey's pet project during the four years of his tenure, and because the position of superintendent was appointed rather than elected, MacCaughey could make major policy changes with considerable impunity.[6] At his formal request, the US Department of the Interior dispatched a commission of education specialists to survey Hawai'i's educational system in October 1919. Behind the request lay a tacit understanding that the commissioners would find indisputable evidence proving that the Buddhist-run Japanese language schools were inimical to Americanization.[7] True to this implicit mandate, the commission's July 1920 report suggested that the schools should be closed:

> Although the commission recognizes the inherent right of every person in the United States to adopt any form of religious worship which he desires, nevertheless it holds that the principle of religious freedom to which our country is unswervingly committed does not demand that practices and activities must be tolerated in the name of religion which

> make the task of training for the duties and responsibilities of American citizenship a well-nigh hopeless one. The commission, therefore, feels no hesitancy in recommending as a first and important step in clearing away the obstacles from the path of the Territorial public-school system that all foreign-language schools be abolished.[8]

Although outright abolition of the Japanese language schools ultimately proved to be politically unfeasible, the commissioners' report provided a rationale for a major policy change. Four months after the report's publication, Governor McCarthy signed Act 30 during a special session of the territorial legislature. The act placed the Japanese language schools under the direct supervision of MacCaughey's Department of Public Instruction. It imposed severe financial limitations on the schools, restricted eligibility for instruction to teachers with near-native fluency in English who could pass an ideological purity test, and ensured that students' Japanese language training would not exceed one hour per day.[9] Subsequent revisions in 1923 and 1925 placed further restrictions on the schools, gradually raising the age at which students could even begin attending.[10]

These onerous and clearly discriminatory laws remained in place until 21 February 1927, when the US Supreme Court decided in *Farrington v. Tokushige* that voluntary associations of Japanese Americans had a constitutional right to maintain private language schools if they so desired. Although the word "religion" did not appear in the Court's decision, the educational dispute was at heart a dispute over religious freedom. The Japanese American litigants' legal strategy before the Supreme Court rested on the Fourteenth Amendment right to equal treatment rather than the religious freedom guaranteed by the First Amendment, but behind their approach lay sophisticated theorization about religious freedom generated by the Honolulu-based Buddhist leader Imamura Yemyō (1867–1932).[11] Imamura tried to use the American ideal of religious freedom to help Japanese people bypass racial discrimination. Despite his strenuous efforts, the Supreme Court decision implicitly confirmed that Japanese Americans, like some other racial minorities, could not take full advantage of America's religious freedom guarantee.[12]

This chapter has three aims. First, I use the experiences of Japanese American immigrants in the American territory of Hawai'i to demonstrate that American practices of religious freedom in the interwar years were just as incoherent as Japanese governance of religion during roughly the same time period. By focusing on practices of religious freedom under American empire, my discussion sets up later chapters that describe the American occupiers' conceit that they had real religious freedom while the Japanese did not. Looking at how white Americans treated Japanese religious minorities in Hawai'i during the 1910s and 1920s also shows how the later Occupation was an extension of long-standing American imperial ambitions and racist thinking.

Second, although Japan had ostensibly "proved" its civilized status by including religious freedom guarantees in its modern constitution and in several bilateral treaties, Japanese diplomats repeatedly had to demonstrate that Japan truly respected the religious freedom of Christian missionaries living in Japanese territories. This diplomatic problem came to a head in the wake of World War I, when Japanese attempts to include a racial equality clause in the League of Nations charter led to spurious accusations that their ulterior motive was to eradicate global religious freedom protections. Simply put, racist double standards impeded the ability of Japanese representatives to effectively deploy the language of religious freedom in Japan's international relations, presaging how the occupiers would later dismiss existing Japanese practices of religious freedom as false.

Finally, whereas chapter 2 showed that debates over religious freedom within Japan pitted Buddhist majoritarian claims against the rights of an upstart Christian minority, the language school issue shows that even though Japanese American Buddhists sometimes used religious freedom as an apologetic tactic to gently challenge the majoritarian claims of American Christians, they were ultimately unable to use religious freedom talk as a legal strategy in court.

RELIGIOUS FREEDOM IN AMERICAN LIFE

Who deserves religious freedom? Despite the prominent position of the religious freedom concept in America's founding myth, this question has not had an easy answer for most of American history.[13] At specific historical moments, members of particular denominations have enjoyed religious freedom, have been denied it, or have enjoyed such a degree of mainstream privilege that they have had the luxury of not even thinking about it. Centered on the Puritan quest for free religious exercise, the national myth suggests that religious freedom made America and that the American version of religious freedom made the United States without peer.[14] Indeed, many people over the course of America's short history have claimed that Americans perfected religious freedom, if not that we created it.[15]

But we can tell a different story.

Focusing on the transatlantic passage of the Puritans from religious oppression, the national myth of American religious freedom centers attention on the North Atlantic world, reinforcing the notion that our present secular age was born in Europe.[16] Yet there is a transpacific story of American religious freedom that also deserves to be told.[17] While European intellectual and legal precedents clearly informed American ideals and practices of religious liberty, American conceptions of religious freedom were just as much a product of imperial encounters in the American West and the Pacific.[18] The American-led Allied Occupation of Japan was in many respects a natural, though hardly inevitable, outcome of a decades-long push to use religious freedom talk to justify American control of new territory.[19]

For example, religious freedom featured prominently in early treaties between the sovereign Kingdom of Hawai'i and the United States, and missionaries' civilizationalist rhetoric presumed the superiority of Christianity to local customs and traditions.[20] American weaponization of religious freedom as a diplomatic tool also directly influenced Japan's rapid legal and political changes of the mid-nineteenth century.[21] After all, it was American warships that demanded that the Japanese shogunate open Japan's ports for trade after centuries of relative seclusion, and it was American negotiators who included demands for religious freedom and extraterritoriality clauses related to religious practice in Japan's first modern treaties.[22] As briefly discussed in chapter 2, when the Japanese government aimed to renegotiate treaties with the United States and European powers in the last decade of the nineteenth century, the powers extracted concessions from the Japanese regarding religious freedom that gave rights to foreigners that even Japanese people did not possess.

As the United States wielded religious freedom as a tool of empire in sovereign Pacific states such as the Kingdom of Hawai'i and the former Spanish colony of the Philippines, the urgency of learning how to manipulate this powerful implement of international law was not lost on Japanese diplomats.[23] It is therefore hardly surprising that Japanese religious and political thinkers regularly situated their practices against an American model in the late nineteenth and early twentieth centuries. This is not to say that Japanese thinkers regarded American religious freedom as an unambiguous good. As I showed in chapter 2, the United States often appeared in Japanese Buddhists' accounts not as a staid bastion of "real" religious freedom, but rather as a laughably lax country where latitudinarian policy invited the efflorescence of "lascivious heresies" like Mormonism.

But American power was real, and the influence of American legal and political ideals was especially palpable in the wake of World War I. As nations settled into a new postwar geopolitical arrangement dominated by Wilsonian visions of global concord, Japanese representatives eagerly demonstrated their respect for religious liberty on the international stage even as they sought global guarantees of racial equality that would ultimately be denied to them.[24] One of the problems they faced was a vitriolic contemporaneous discourse about the putative threat of "Mikadoism," an artificially concocted national religion of emperor worship that many European and American observers associated with Buddhism. Policy makers in Japanese territories had to repeatedly prove that American missionaries were not substantially burdened by governmental policies, while American diplomats disingenuously regarded Japan's quest for racial equality in international relations as a ploy to eliminate religious freedom. The crucial role imperial Japan played in the interwar period as a non-European military power with growing colonial holdings deserves attention because the Pacific War and the subsequent Occupation reflected the American conceit that Americans enjoyed religious freedom while Japanese people did not. In the 1910s and 1920s Japanese representatives and their non-Japanese sympathizers showed time and again that Japan actually *had* religious freedom, but their ability to be heard on this point was directly related to the racial hierarchies that dominated geopolitics.

Against the backdrop of the diplomatic problem wherein Japanese representatives strained to prove that Japan was truly "civilized" and beholden to the principle of religious freedom, anti-Japanese sentiment in America reached a fever pitch. Fears about Japanese religiosity as antithetical to "Americanism" formed a crucial part of this anti-immigrant animus. Forced into a defensive position, Japanese Americans experimented with religious freedom claims as a way of proving their right to live in America unmolested. Writing in both English and Japanese, Buddhist clerics used religious freedom talk to prove just how American Japanese people could be. Unfortunately for them, the widespread association of Buddhism with "Mikadoism" and "Mikadoism" with anti-Americanism interfered with their ability to use religious freedom claims effectively. Whereas other minorities like Jews were able to use religious freedom talk to avail themselves of the privileges of whiteness, Japanese Buddhists' religion proved too strange and too threatening for them to circumvent American racial hierarchies. To return to the language school issue that sits at the heart of this chapter, Japanese Americans may have won at the Supreme Court in 1927, but they did so without the help of religious freedom.

HAWAI'I'S JAPANESE IMMIGRANT POPULATION AND THE PROBLEM OF ASSIMILATION

The late nineteenth and early twentieth centuries witnessed several waves of Japanese emigration to the Americas. In Hawai'i, the main influx of Japanese immigrants took place between 1885 and 1907, when the governments of Japan and the United States established their 1907 "Gentlemen's Agreement" that curtailed Japanese contract labor migration.[25] Although the Japanese government agreed to not issue passports for new émigrés, the quasi-legal arrangement precipitated the practice of recruiting "picture brides" for male agricultural laborers, contributing to a swelling second-generation population.[26] By law, these Nisei were American citizens who had voting rights. They could also own property. Anxieties quickly arose among the white landowning class in Hawai'i concerning whether the primary allegiance of this second-generation population was to the country of their birth (the United States) or to that of their parents (Japan). Many members of this white landowning class were descendants of Christian missionaries who had successfully used religious freedom talk to snap up native Hawaiian land and incorporate it into an export-driven economy of plantation labor and strict racial stratification.[27] Religious freedom had worked well for them, but now they feared that giving too much freedom to Japanese laborers might threaten their precious property.

Initially, the Japanese population in Hawai'i tended not to intermarry with members of other ethnicities.[28] Yet working with other foreign-born laborers and communicating with white landowners necessitated a certain degree of cultural and linguistic homogenization.[29] Despite these homogenizing imperatives, the Japanese community brought their distinctive cultural traditions with them. Recognizing that Japanese abroad required clerical care, by the 1890s some of the Japanese Buddhist sects began dispatching clerics to minister to overseas populations.[30] In many cases, the clerics were not only responsible for ritual care, but also took on prominent roles regarding education, including teaching the Japanese language to the second-generation children of first-generation immigrants.[31] Buddhist temples came to serve as community centers.[32] They also provided shelter to laborers who were in periodic disputes with plantation bosses.[33]

The association of Buddhism with labor strikes, on the one hand, and an unassimilable foreign language, on the other, generated a series of economic, racial, and legal conflicts on the archipelago in the 1910s and early 1920s.[34] Even relatively sympathetic "Japan hands" like Sidney L. Gulick (1860–1945), who had years of experience living in Japan and considerable facility with the Japanese language, viewed Buddhist temples with suspicion. Gulick regarded Buddhist priests as political reactionaries who propounded superstitious emperor worship and ancestor veneration.[35] In Gulick's voluminous and influential writings on immigration and assimilation, Buddhism appeared as nationalistic and intensely "Japanese."

For members of the white landowning class, Buddhism came to represent a type of undiluted and unassimilable aspect of Japanese culture that was inimical to Americanization. Because of widespread perceptions that the Buddhist-run Japanese language schools fostered anti-American sentiment by teaching a nationalistic religion that made American-born Japanese children beholden to the Japanese emperor rather than the land of their birth, in the late 1910s white plantation owners and some Japanese pro-assimilation collaborators began a concerted effort to eradicate language schools once and for all. Rooted in economic anxieties that the swelling Japanese population could soon control both land and labor, opposition to the language schools also stemmed from a growing discourse in the 1910s about the threat of "Mikadoism."

THE BIRTH OF "MIKADOISM"

An explosion of articles in English-language newspapers and magazines around 1912 described the creation of a "new national religion" in Japan. The most prominent of these was a Rationalist Press Association pamphlet by Basil Hall Chamberlain (1850–1935) called *The Invention of a New Religion*.[36] Chamberlain described the Japanese people as fundamentally irreligious and generally perplexed by the "strangely superstitious" attitudes of Europeans. However, "this same agnostic Japan is teaching us at this very hour how religions are sometimes manufactured for a special end—to subserve practical worldly purposes," Chamberlain wrote. He dubbed this new religion "Mikado-worship and Japan-worship."[37]

Chamberlain's pamphlet was polemical and its claims somewhat exaggerated for rhetorical, even comedic, effect. "The new Japanese religion consists, in its present early stage, of worship of the sacrosanct Imperial Person and of His Divine Ancestors, of implicit obedience to Him as head of the army . . . [and] of a corresponding belief that Japan is as far superior to the common ruck of nations as the Mikado is divinely superior to the common ruck of kings and emperors," Chamberlain wrote.[38] While rank-and-file peasants still remained devoted to the Buddhism of their ancestors, Chamberlain argued, the governing class had revivified selected components of the otherwise moribund Shintō tradition to emphasize loyalty to the throne and insinuate the state in both private and public life.[39] Shintō priests now buried the dead and married the living; schoolchildren now paid obligatory obeisance to the illustrious deified emperors at shrines. Disturbingly for Chamberlain, the "go-ahead" people destined for positions of future leadership in Japan and its colonies appeared to be most beholden to this new ideology.[40]

While it is difficult at great historical distance to trace Chamberlain's direct influence on other writers of the day, it seems that the basics of his narrative proved appealing even to those who harbored less antipathy to religion than he evidently did. For example, the July 1912 issue of *Current Literature* suggested that the new national religion described by Chamberlain was inimical to the religious freedom established in the 1889 Meiji Constitution.[41] Musing on a previous abortive attempt to install Christianity as the national religion, the article suggested that Japanese people were now in desperate need of moral direction. It was supposedly this lamentable state of affairs that had prompted the government to try to unite the people in Mikado worship. The article disapprovingly referred to the government-sponsored "Three Religions Conference" of 25 February 1912, which had brought representatives of Buddhism, Christianity, and Sect Shintō together with prominent scholars of religion such as Anesaki Masaharu (1873–1949) and representatives from the Home and Education Ministries to discuss how religions could set aside theological differences in service of uplifting national morality.[42] Citing a writer at the *Japan Weekly Chronicle*, the author of the *Current Literature* piece suggested that the conference had effectively demanded that Buddhists and Christians subordinate their religious commitments to the new national religion of "Mikadoism."[43] It was these sorts of critiques that would prove to be of such concern to the educators in Hawai'i who saw Japanese language schools as fronts for the dissemination of anti-American ideology.

The *Current Literature* article appeared just before the 30 July 1912 death of Emperor Meiji. The ensuing pomp and circumstance apotheosizing the deceased monarch confirmed for foreign observers that they were witnessing the birth of a new national religion. Under the title "Japan's New Epoch," the *Christian Science Monitor* wrote on 29 August 1912:

> Europeans and Americans, who have been wont to say that modern Japan is irreligious, must revise their estimate in view of events arising from the recent change of rulers. Scenes of religious reverence and supplication that have "no parallel in history," according to one observer, have been witnessed by Occidental onlookers. An Emperor that, for the people, took rank as a demi-god while he lived, is now elevated to the position of a deity, and as such will now "do more than ever for fair Japan."[44]

This mildly disparaging assessment would seem to foreshadow a critique of Japanese irrationality á la Chamberlain, but the *Monitor* went on to suggest that while destructive "secularizing factors" remained harmful to theism in Japan, "out from the people's recent enforced dwelling on the ultimate issues of a great sovereign's career, and on his relation to the creator of all, good must come."[45] This rather sanguine reaction to the theater of state suggests that while ardent critics like Chamberlain saw Japan's new political ideology as both inherently irrational and as a cynical distortion of essentially religious ideas for political ends, others saw in the Japanese pageantry of imperial death a laudable stepping-stone to Christian faith.

If for the *Christian Science Monitor* Mikado worship merely presaged the inevitable conversion of the Japanese people to Christianity, for sympathetic professional observers like William Elliot Griffis (1843–1928) this "Mikadoism" was a profound and workable ethical system in its own right: "Mikadoism is the symbol of all that is dear to the Japanese; yet, like all social forces, whether religion, or the magic of a great name, or the national flag, the dogma is often abused by its so-called friends, is made an unnecessary engine of cruelty, or is debased to selfish or mercenary purposes," Griffis wrote.[46] Griffis was convinced, where Chamberlain was not, of the profound efficacy of what he termed "Mikadoism" as a national ethic that fused religion and politics. While he used the term positively in his 1915 book, "Mikadoism" became useful shorthand in the battle against Japanese Americans, both in Hawai'i and on the mainland.[47]

The "Mikadoism" trope created a diplomatic problem for Japan in two ways. First, Japanese leaders had to prove that Christians living in Japanese territories were not forced to subsume their commitments to the new "national religion" that foreign correspondents described. Second, Japanese diplomats and prominent representatives of the Japanese American community such as Buddhist priests had to forestall American concerns that Japanese Americans' affection for the emperor would lead to seditious activity. I will take these two problems up in turn.

RELIGIOUS FREEDOM AS A DIPLOMATIC PROBLEM

As American nationalism increased during World War I, Japanese leaders found themselves on the defensive, forced to defend Japan's commitment to global norms and forced to prove time and again that they deserved a seat at the table with the other Great Powers.[48] Policy makers in Tokyo saw the racist treatment to which Japanese émigrés and their children were subjected in America. They witnessed with serious concern the passage of exclusionary laws about land rights and property in places like California in the 1910s.[49] Cultural intermediaries like Dōshisha University professor Sidney L. Gulick spoke frequently to American audiences about how the "Yellow Peril" that Americans perceived at home was matched by an even greater "White Peril" experienced by Japanese, Chinese, and other Asians who had seen their nations invaded, colonized, carved up, or subjected to humiliating unequal treaties over the previous several decades. In an address delivered sometime in early 1914, Gulick argued that "the treatment of the Japanese in some parts of Christendom is galling to their pride and national dignity" and that California's 1913 antialien legislation had "deeply wounded the entire Japanese people."[50]

Gulick had a large platform for his message. He delivered his remarks as part of a multicity speaking tour sponsored by the Federal Council of Churches after spending three months in California observing conditions there in summer 1913. He also delivered expert testimony to the US Senate Committee on Immigration and Naturalization on 31 January 1914. While he proposed to the committee a formal amendment to limit immigration to no more than 5 percent of those already naturalized, Gulick also highlighted for members the fact that anti-Japanese vitriol in California worked directly against American interests in Japan and created the impression of American hypocrisy concerning both rights and Christian values. He argued that his fellow missionaries in Japan complained about American racist sentiment as a hindrance to their work, and he mentioned that in the current legal situation Japanese laws regarding foreign labor and foreign land ownership were far more egalitarian than those in California.[51] While he was circumspect in his criticisms, Gulick made it clear that American domestic policy lagged far behind the ideals that the United States was projecting to the world.

To highlight the potential embarrassment America faced on the global stage, Gulick cited a May 1913 article by a Professor Nagai in Tokyo as follows:

> If the white races truly love peace and wish to preserve the name of Christian nations they will practice what they preach and will soon restore to us the rights so long withheld. They will rise to the generosity of welcoming our citizens among them as heartily as we do theirs among us. We appeal to the white races to put aside their race prejudice and meet us on equal terms in brotherly co-operation.[52]

As Nagai's comments suggest, the concepts of racial equality and religious freedom were crucial diplomatic tools that the Japanese used to put pressure on Americans, albeit with mixed success. Embarrassingly, rather than successfully eliciting attitudinal change by highlighting religious freedom and racial equality as global norms, these spokespeople frequently found themselves in the uncomfortable position of having to prove to supercilious Americans that *Japan* was truly civilized. Assemblages of race and religion worked to preserve white American superiority within American territory while maintaining American hegemony in the Pacific.[53]

To give an example of how Japanese spokespeople were forced to "speak up" to American power and constantly assure Americans that Christian missionary efforts in Japan would not be hampered, in a 29 August 1918 address to the American Bar Association, Miyaoka Tsunejirō stressed that the Japanese national charter protected rights like religious liberty:

> There is no law in Japan that relates to the limitation of faith or that gives preference to any form of religion. As there are so many temples and shrines of Buddhist and Shintō religion in the country, there is naturally a large body of statutes and regulations relating to the secular administration of sects or the enjoyment of property rights by ecclesiastical corporations. The wording of Article 28 of the Constitution of Japan is [otherwise] so simple and direct that it requires no supplementary legislation to give effect to its provision. Freedom of belief is only limited by the condition that the belief shall not be prejudicial to peace and order,

> nor incompatible with the duties which an individual as a Japanese subject owes to the sovereignty of the Empire.[54]

This was apparently a newsworthy statement. Under the headline "Constitution of Japan Reviewed: Mr. Miyaioka [*sic*] of Tokyo Declares before American Bar Association Religious Freedom Is Fundamental in His Country," the *Christian Science Monitor* quoted Miyaoka's speech approvingly, albeit redacting the part of his claim about the "statutes and regulations relating to the secular administration of sects."[55] Miyaoka concluded his speech by assuring his audience that the "Japanese people are not the kind of people to quietly submit to the invasion of their rights and the curtailment of personal liberty."[56]

As Miyaoka's supplicatory tone suggests, the experiments with global governance and national self-determination that characterized the years immediately following the Great War (1914–18) allowed Japan to be both included in, and excluded from, international deliberations concerning the intertwined concepts of racial equality and religious freedom.[57] While Japan had proven itself an equal to the Great Powers by defeating Russia (1905) and annexing Korea (1910), the country's geopolitical status remained ambiguous due to prevailing contemporaneous hierarchies of race and religion.[58] The diplomatic kerfuffle that attended the Japanese request to include a racial equality clause in the League of Nations charter exemplifies this contradictory position. The Japanese delegation, smarting in response to the discriminatory treatment Japanese émigrés were then receiving both in Hawai'i and on the American West Coast, sought explicit language that would guarantee people of Japanese heritage equal treatment before the law. The American delegation resisted the Japanese proposal, alleging that the Japanese were using racial equality claims to delimit global protections for religious liberty.[59]

This perplexing reaction to the Japanese request provoked an indignant response from Matsuoka Yōsuke, senior secretary to the Japanese delegation to the Paris Peace Conference, on 8 April 1919. He wrote:

> The Japanese Commission, under no conditions, intends to block the inclution [*sic*] of a universal Religious Liberty Clause in the constitution of the League of Nations. Such a thought never entered the minds of the Commissioners. On the contrary, we are in hearty sympathy with the inclusion of such a clause.
>
> Religious intolerance has been a prolific source of wars and interna-

> tional strife in the past, and this is the opportunity to write Religious Liberty indelibly into the constitution of the world.[60]

With the benefit of historical hindsight, this is a striking statement. At the conclusion of the Pacific War, the American occupiers would claim that the Japanese had no real commitment to religious liberty and could not even understand the concept. But at the highest levels of diplomacy, Japanese spokespeople like Matsuoka spoke with evident sincerity about the importance of promoting religious freedom worldwide. In discussions with American audiences about Japanese law, lawyers like Miyaoka also stressed that Japan was a safe place for religions of all stripes.

Administrators in Japan's colonies were similarly keen to present their policies as conducive to religious freedom. For example, the *Christian Science Monitor* reported on 16 June 1920 that recent Japanese reforms in the administration of its Korean colony had introduced a degree of religious freedom, allowing for religious instruction and providing mechanisms for the corporate holding of mission and religious property.[61] Certainly this piece of evidence should not suggest that Japan's colonies were devoid of problems related to religious liberty. For example, Japanese assimilation techniques in Seoul included compulsory visits to Shintō shrines that many Koreans clearly resented.[62] But disputes about whether obligatory obeisance at shrines in Japan's colonies constituted violations of religious freedom matched similar debates over terminology and law that were taking place in the metropole at around the same time (see chapter 1). The point here is that Christian missionaries were clearly able to successfully pressure the Japanese Government-General in Korea to grant them rights that Korean imperial subjects had trouble claiming.

To summarize the foregoing, non-Japanese observers viewed the creation of Japan's "new religion" of "Mikadoism" with a combination of bemusement, perplexity, and consternation. But for the most part, "Mikadoism" was a problem for people in far-off foreign lands and for the American missionaries who worked there. The American territory of Hawaiʻi was different. By the early interwar period, the Japanese population numerically outstripped all others on the islands, including the native Hawaiians. Nisei were American citizens who technically had voting rights, and when the language school issue began heating up in 1918, some of these second-generation children had already reached the age of majority. Many more would do so by the early 1920s. According to Nisei children themselves, within their own families, national loyalties were divided. Some of their siblings and parents retained exclusive allegiance to Japan. Others fully embraced the United States as their home.[63] Judging by the tenor of Japanese-language newspapers like *Nippu jiji* (the *Japanese-Hawaiian Times*), both first- and second-generation Japanese held a cosmopolitan outlook that looked simultaneously to Japan in the west and the American mainland in the east as bastions of "civilization." It was this combination of demographic change and ambivalent allegiance that so exercised former governor McCarthy in his 1921 screed in the *Los Angeles Times* cited at the opening of this chapter.

BUDDHIST DEMOCRACY AND CHRISTIAN ASSIMILATION

It was also in the context of major demographic change that educators like Vaughan MacCaughey began pushing for the abolition of the Japanese language schools once and for all. A professor at the College of Hawai'i who published papers on such varied topics as tropical flora, island geography, the physical characteristics of the ancient Hawaiians, and "race mixture" in Hawai'i, MacCaughey seems to have had varied interests that coalesced around the eugenicist biological science prevalent in his day. In his writings on education, MacCaughey advocated a brand of American public school education that envisioned Christianity as the lifeblood of American ideals and political life: "True Americanization can not bloom in a Buddhist Oriental household," he wrote, and "Hawai'i can not be American until she truly Christianizes her population, and makes dominant *the Christian home*."[64]

Honolulu-based Jōdo Shinshū bishop Imamura Yemyō found this sort of attitude puzzling. In his May 1918 English-language pamphlet *Democracy According to the Buddhist Viewpoint*, he wrote:

> Those who are not very well acquainted with the teachings and history of Buddhism are apt to regard it as advocating autocracy or absolutism. This is far from the truth. For the ethical, philosophical, and religious ideals of Buddhism, as manifesting themselves in the history of those nations where it has been most prospering, directly contradict the criticism, and are in perfect harmony with the principles of democracy. In fact, what-

> ever democracy there is in the East, it derives its power and support from Buddhism.[65]

Imamura went on to argue that the community established by the Buddha was inherently democratic, and that over the course of history not a single drop of blood had been spilled in the name of Buddhism.[66] Both of these claims were patently false, but Imamura's immediate purpose was to forestall critique of Buddhism as antidemocratic and un-American. He was a quick study of American traditions and a creative interpreter of Buddhist doctrine. Over the next few years, he worked tirelessly to reconcile Buddhist teachings with America's egalitarian ideals.

It is unclear whether MacCaughey and Imamura were in direct conversation over the language school issue, but shortly after Imamura's 1918 English-language article appeared, MacCaughey published a piece in the educational journal *School and Society* that countered Imamura's claim by describing Buddhism as undemocratic and portraying the Buddhist-run Japanese language schools as "narrow, superstitious shrines for Mikado worship."[67] In MacCaughey's view Buddhism was a direct obstacle to Americanization whereas Christianity was conducive to it.

While MacCaughey's explicit association of Christianity with American civil life is hardly surprising for the time in which he wrote, it *is* surprising that he and other critics of the Japanese language schools singled out the relatively progressive Jōdo Shinshū denomination as uniquely guilty of propounding a doctrine of fealty to the Japanese throne. After all, it was Shinshū adherents who had pushed for greater clarity in the separation of religion from the state in the early years of the Meiji political experiment.[68] As I will show in chapter 4, Shinshū thinkers in Japan continued to be active theorists of religious freedom all the way through the Pacific War. However, the official 1920 report on the educational situation in Hawai'i commissioned by MacCaughey and Governor McCarthy singled out Jōdo Shinshū as particularly inimical to democracy. The report even mentioned Imamura by name, depicting him as a puppet master who could control the vast majority of the archipelago's Japanese population at will:

> The Nishi Hongwanji is by far the strongest Buddhist sect in the islands, as it is in Japan, embracing about 75,000 members of the island population. This sect in Japan is controlled by a cabinet formed of high priests at whose head stands the "Hoss," or chief priest. The Hoss is held in very high esteem by members of the sect, who honor him as they would a

> living Buddha. The Hoss is represented in the islands by a "Kantoku" (Bishop Imamura), who has absolute authority over the priests and teachers of the sect as well as over its members, controlling the whole body, according to a Japanese authority, "as easily as one moves his fingers."[69]

Given that the relatively conservative, even nationalistic, traditions of Shingon and Nichiren Buddhism received brief attention, but little criticism, in articles like MacCaughey's and the reports on the territorial educational situation that he commissioned, it seems plausible that the critics' antagonism to Jōdo Shinshū stemmed primarily from their reliance on the accounts of Japanese Christian Okumura Takie (1865–1951) and his son, Umetarō (d.u.), in developing their reports.[70] In a long-standing battle over the allegiances of Honolulu's Japanese population, Okumura Takie represented a sort of respectability politics that saw Christianization as the only path to full assimilation, while the Buddhist Imamura tactically used American political ideals as tools to dismantle prejudicial treatment.[71] While there is no "smoking gun" to prove it, evidence strongly suggests that the Okumuras' personal differences with Imamura Yemyō (including, perhaps, jealousy concerning the latter's popularity and influence) informed governmental policy: Umetarō served as a translator for the politically powerful Hawai'i Sugar Planters' Association and was an informant for intelligence services on the islands.[72]

The hostility to Buddhist language schools was sparked by American nationalism and then fanned into flame by the Okumuras and other prominent Japanese who favored full-blown assimilation.[73] An additional factor that fed fuel to the fire was not language, but labor. Imamura publicly sided with striking sugarcane plantation workers in a dispute that shut down O'ahu's sugar plantations for about six months in 1920, while Okumura argued that the workers should acquiesce to the demands of capital.[74] The strongest push to shutter the Japanese language schools coincided with this labor dispute.[75] Abortive attempts to pass legislation that would render the Japanese language schools illegal had already begun in 1919, but the strike of early 1920 prompted concerted collaborations between nationalist, assimilationist, and capitalist interests that led to the passage of draconian legislation and, ultimately, to a battle at the Supreme Court.[76]

Of Labor and Language: The 1920 O‘ahu Sugar Strike and Its Repercussions

Although the swelling Japanese population contributed directly to the economic productivity of the Hawaiian Islands, a combination of political and economic factors conspired to render Japanese immigrants as threats. The 1920 O‘ahu Sugar Strike (January–July), in which tens of thousands of protesting Japanese and Filipino laborers were forcibly evicted from their plantation homes, brought these issues to a head. Whereas in previous years striking laborers of one ethnicity had been replaced by strikebreakers of another, in this case Japanese joined hands with striking Filipinos rather than breaking the strike.[77] The newfound solidarity seemed to reinforce the fears of members of the Hawai‘i Sugar Planters Association (HSPA) that Japanese laborers could use their superior numbers to upset the carefully constructed racial hierarchy that then dominated the islands. In an implicit nod to the racialized notions of plantation work that dominated the American popular imagination, the Japanese language press used the language of a "slavery system" (*dorei seido*) to discuss the plight of underpaid Japanese laborers.[78]

The HSPA staunchly refused to hear Japanese workers' 4 December 1919 appeal, in which they wrote that although they considered "it a great privilege and pride to live under the Stars and Stripes, which stands for freedom and justice, as a factor of this great industry and as a part of the labor of Hawaii," nevertheless they were suffering under a paltry wage of seventy-seven cents a day.[79] Rebuffed by the HSPA in their polite request for higher wages, the newly formed Japanese laborers' union continued to press for their demands, but the landowners were unrelenting. On 19 January 1919, Filipino workers struck, and Japanese laborers joined the strike four days later. Because Japanese workers struck one day after Imamura Yemyō and other priests had submitted a letter to the HSPA asking the planters to accommodate the workers' demands, HSPA representatives concluded that Buddhist agitators were the masterminds behind Japanese workers' grievances.[80]

The plantation owners responded to the strike on 14 February by evicting laborers from their homes on the plantations, prompting a massive influx of suddenly homeless people into Honolulu, where voluntary associations provided shelter and aid even as a deadly strain of influenza swept the islands.[81] (Imamura Yemyō's Jōdo Shinshū mission provided shelter to the striking workers; Okumura Takie's Christian church did not.)[82] After months of stalled negotiations that were no doubt exacerbated by the flu, the Japanese Federation of Labor acquiesced and returned to work, having extracted only paltry concessions from the HSPA.

Just as this high-stakes debate over labor was intensifying, the education commissioners who had been called from the mainland submitted their report on the state of education in the territory of Hawai'i. The report singled out the Buddhist-run Japanese language schools as serious obstacles to assimilation and called for their abolition. While a minority of white schoolteachers argued that the schools were forces for good in their communities, overall their sentiments toward the language schools were antagonistic. As the list of anonymous quotes gathered by the researchers suggests, many teachers saw the language schools as Buddhist, the Buddhists as nationalists, and the nationalism of the Buddhist schools as a contributing factor in strife between Japanese labor and the capitalist class: "The Japanese schools, under cover of religious instruction, teach the children loyalty to their Emperor and country. The Japanese language schools must go, if we are to teach the young Japanese to become Americans," one teacher argued.[83] Another said that some Japanese teachers may appear to "lean the right way," but that "the older ones, whose schools are a part of the Buddhist mission, are in the majority. They . . . teach a kind of divided allegiance theory, which fits a child to be an American for the time being—a Japanese should the occasion arise."[84] These critiques must be understood in light of the labor disputes of the day and the aforementioned fears on the part of white landowners that enfranchised Nisei might pool their resources and snap up valuable plantation land.

The HSPA Attempts to Solve the Labor Problem by Changing National Immigration Policy

Even after the labor situation was temporarily resolved and the language schools hobbled by Act 30 of the Territorial Legislature (24 November 1920), the anxiety on the part of the white landowning class that Japanese people might take over the lucrative sugar industry remained. In June and July 1921, the House of Representatives Committee on Immigration and Naturalization held a series of hearings on labor problems in Hawai'i. The chair of the committee was state of Washington representative Albert Johnson (1869–1957), the congressperson later responsible for drafting the infamous Immigration Act of 1924 that abolished immigration from Asia and subjected Asian Americans to discriminatory treatment.

Johnson's committee heard first from Walter F. Dillingham (1875–1963), chairman of the Hawaiʻi Emergency Labor Commission. Dillingham argued that the agricultural industries of Hawaiʻi faced a labor shortage due in part to ex-migration from the islands to California and in part to a recent effort on the part of the Japanese to seize the means of production by purchasing land outright (the law allowed America-born Japanese children of immigrants the right to purchase land, and sometimes first-generation parents bought land in the names of their children).[85] Because past attempts to hire Negroes had been unsuccessful and white laborers were unsuited to work in Hawaiʻi's tropical climate, Dillingham cited an appeal written by recently retired Governor Charles McCarthy suggesting that the federal government allow for some creative solution to the labor shortage such as allowing for an ad hoc admission of relatively docile Chinese laborers or possibly importing labor from Europe. In the background of his testimony, of course, was the committee's awareness that the Japanese-Filipino labor strike of 1920 had threatened the productivity of Hawaiʻi's sugar industry. While the Filipinos had struck first, the committee and the representatives of Hawaiʻi's white landowning class seemed to agree that it was the Japanese who were the real problem.

The day after Dillingham's testimony, recently appointed Governor Wallace R. Farrington (1871–1933) argued before the committee that the recent dispute between the HSPA and the Japanese Federation of Labor had been acute and "of a different nature than ordinary strikes on the mainland" because it became a "nationalistic movement" fomented by an "alien element."[86] His testimony was corroborated by HSPA lobbyist Royal D. Mead (d.u.), who claimed that the Japanese Federation of Labor had not a single laborer on its directorate and was composed primarily of newspapermen and agitators who were not American citizens.[87] As his testimony continued the following day, Mead argued that Japanese people were unassimilable, presenting a significant labor problem that could best be resolved by importing a large number of white laborers.[88] He also claimed that the labor strike of the previous year had been fomented by Buddhist priests in charge of the Japanese language schools.[89]

To summarize, Japanese Americans were trapped between the inflated image of "Mikadoism" as a sort of virulent emperor worship, landowners' fears about retaining control over property and labor in the lucrative Hawaiian sugar industry, and racist thinking that depicted the Japanese as conniving and loyal only to their own kind. Buddhism was caught in the crossfire because of the oft-repeated assumption that Japanese people in Hawaiʻi simply did the bidding of Buddhist leaders, because Buddhists appeared to be behind the labor strike, and because Buddhist-run language schools appeared to be ideological training camps for little Japanese insurgents. In such circumstances, it is no surprise that Jōdo Shinshū Bishop Imamura Yemyō would deploy religious freedom talk apologetically. By encouraging his Japanese counterparts to appeal to one of the principles that Americans held most dear, Imamura tried to make it easier for them to avoid racist treatment.

RELIGIOUS FREEDOM AS A DIPLOMATIC SOLUTION

Written at the height of the O'ahu Sugar Strike and published in the same year that the House of Representatives Committee on Immigration and Naturalization conducted its hearings, Imamura's 1921 Japanese-language pamphlet titled *On the American Spirit* began as follows:

> In America religious freedom [*shūkyō no jiyū*] is guaranteed in the constitution, and it is not a topic for one such as me to problematize [*aete mondai to subeki mondai de wa nai*]. However, among the many people of the world it is not the case that there are none who, in the name of [America as] a Christian nation, reject Buddhism out of compromise and conservatism. And such people do not spend even a word on religious freedom in Japan or [the topic of] Buddhism versus Christianity [there]. As residents in American territory, I think that we must firmly uphold the national law and preserve public order. At the same time, we should not refrain from declaring the rights we hold in our international relations, and we should not hesitate in proclaiming and disseminating the articles of our absolute faith. Now, in response to emotional slander and groundless persecution, we should furthermore not hesitate in enlightening such ignorance.[90]

Imamura's apologetic tract was published not only in the wake of the sugar strike of 1920, but also in the context of intensifying, vehement debates within Hawai'i's Japanese immigrant community about whether it was better to "Americanize" (*beika*) or whether it was better to retain discrete Japanese cultural traditions.[91] Pitted against Christian evangelist Okumura Takie in a bitter dispute over assimilation, Imamura favored Americanization as he understood it, but he resisted Okumura's interpretation of Americanization as Christianization.[92] Imamura acknowledged the racial hierarchies that dominated American life and lamented the chauvinistic nationalism that had attended the recent Great War (1914–18), but he suggested that Japanese residents in Hawai'i could prove their value to their adopted land if they embodied American political values while simultaneously maintaining their Buddhist heritage. Upholding and celebrating religious freedom would allow Japanese living in Hawai'i to counter racist stereotypes by appealing to the principle Americans held most dear.

As Imamura put it, independence of conscience and religious freedom were the essential articles of faith undergirding the American spirit.[93] Describing what he termed "Americanism" in three basic points, he said 1) that the persecution or slander of others' denominations or sects was an abuse of American ideology; 2) that the American project was by its very nature imperfect and therefore ongoing; and 3) that it was not assimilationist in the sense of eliminating difference, but was rather accommodationist in the sense of viewing all rivers as flowing into the great sea or seeing the myriad stars sprinkled across the magnificent sky.[94] Looking at the sheer number and diversity of the churches and synagogues dotting Fifth Avenue in New York, he said, one could sense the essential commitment to religious liberty that inspired America.[95]

Imamura used this paean to the American spirit to apologetic ends. While some white Americans might view Buddhism as antithetical to America because it was not monotheistic and because it was foreign, if one surveyed the world one would see that very few countries (Japan included) continued to maintain their original "ethnic" religions. Instead, "world religions" such as Buddhism and Christianity had come to dominate religious life. In such circumstances, both in Japan and in the United States it had become national policy to adopt a stance of freedom of conscience and religious liberty. Indeed, Imamura argued, discriminating against someone because of his religion was widely considered in America to be even worse than racial discrimination.[96] His implication was that those who would discriminate against Japanese Americans on racial or religious grounds were actually engaging in fundamentally anti-American behavior. The lesson for his Japanese counterparts was that countering anti-Japanese discrimination with claims about the importance of respecting religious difference could attenuate racial discrimination.

Turning to the language school issue, Imamura suggested that America was a nation of immigrants and that recent calls to close foreign language schools were mere by-products of the nationalistic fervor that had attended the recent Great War.[97] He highlighted the fact that America was founded on both liberalism and cosmopolitanism, and that the ability to speak multiple languages contributed to the expansiveness of one's worldview without interfering with one's allegiance to country. He then cited none other than P. P. Claxton saying, at a meeting of the Americanization Committee, that while "those who are in America must study English," that did not mean "that they may not study the languages of other countries."[98] By citing the words of the education commissioner who had just recommended the total closure of the Japanese language schools in this way, Imamura highlighted the utter hypocrisy of the Americanization movement.

Imamura exhorted his readers to pay no mind to the claims that America was a Christian nation, to not refrain from talking about their faith, to be pragmatic about Buddhism's real social benefits, to be progressive in outlook, and to not become discouraged when encountering American discrimination.[99] When one applied these ideas to the current Japanese language school problem, Imamura argued, the point was similar: Just because America was an English-speaking nation, that did not mean that people must forgo their right to speak other languages.[100]

Imamura then returned to the topic of religious freedom in earnest:

> We must know that at the same time that America is a country of religious freedom, it is also a country of freedom of expression and a country of free critique. Therefore we must always be prepared to hear free criticism of the faith we uphold and of the education we are currently establishing. In America, whether it be the words of the President or the decisions of the Supreme Court, whatever the case may be, one may freely criticize [them] without reservation and can frankly censure [them]. In the same way, we must be prepared to expect that various sorts of criticisms will appear as a matter of course from a certain type of gentleman in response to foreign religions or the activities of foreigners. If there are those who fear this sort of unrestrained critical attack, we must say that they are not suited to life in American territory. To say more: In cases where this free expression becomes popular opinion [*yoron to nari*], when it becomes the majority decision, those who live in a democratic country must always acknowledge that they have a duty to abide by it;

> such mental preparation [*kokoroe*] is of the utmost necessity. . . . But even as we follow the laws adopted by the majority, we must hold our faith and without reservation continue to spread it.[101]

Imamura's tract was written in Japanese for a Japanese audience, but the message was clear. No less than other immigrants, Japanese American Buddhists deserved the same rights and protections as other transplants to American soil. Throughout his text, Imamura cited founding fathers like Benjamin Franklin (1706–90) and Thomas Jefferson (1743–1826), demonstrated deep familiarity with American history, and boasted of having toured major American cities across the continent in autumn 1919. Writing as both a Japanese Tocqueville observing American democracy from without and as a Buddhist apologist experiencing American hypocrisy from within, Imamura argued that Japanese people living in American territories had every right to enjoy the American promises of freedom of speech, conscience, and belief. Imamura did his utmost to prove that Japanese Americans wanted religious freedom, deserved it, and had their own well-developed theories about it.[102] He also exhorted his Japanese readers to exercise their freedom of religion even as they accommodated themselves to the promises, premises, and perils of living in the land of the free. Implicitly, he also encouraged Japanese political leaders at home to take up his arguments about religious freedom when advocating on behalf of their Japanese brethren living abroad. That the foreword to his book was penned by the politically connected Tokyo Imperial University Buddhologist Takakusu Junjirō (1866–1945) helped to reinforce this appeal for political support from the folks back home.

About half a year after Imamura penned the preface to his book, the first of several territorial statutes was passed limiting the ability of Japanese people in Hawaiʻi to maintain Japanese language schools on the islands (Act 30). Subsequent laws further restricting the activities of the language schools and establishing linguistic competency and ideological purity tests for teachers put Imamura's suggestion to abide by the whims of the majority to the test. No doubt Imamura chafed when the United States passed the Immigration Act in 1924.

But true to his word, Imamura and his allies used the tools of American democracy to press their case. While Imamura was initially slow to join a litigation effort challenging Act 30 spearheaded by newspaperman Fred Makino Kinzaburō (1877–1953), he drastically improved the plaintiffs' ability to afford their legal fees when he eventually lent Honolulu Hongwanji support to the cause.[103] Imamura and his fellow plaintiffs successfully won a Supreme Court case about the Japanese language school issue in 1927 because they used the American promises of freedom and equality to highlight the obviously discriminatory intent of the anti–language school acts of the early 1920s.[104] Ultimately, however, their victory came not because they successfully made claims about religious freedom, but because they made use of the equal protection clause of the Fourteenth Amendment (extended to the territory of Hawai'i through the Fifth Amendment).

MacCaughey and McCarthy's campaign against the Japanese language schools was clearly premised on the idea that the (mostly Buddhist) schools promoted seditious religious ideology, but the Supreme Court decision made no explicit mention of religion. Instead, the justices referred to American minorities' legitimate rights to maintain private educational institutions funded by voluntary associations. While further research on the particulars of the case is necessary, the plaintiffs' legal strategy seems to have reflected Imamura's pragmatic recognition that the association of Buddhism with the language schools could very well work against their cause.[105] In other words, even though Imamura knew that the language of religious freedom *could* work to undermine American racial hierarchies, he (or the legal team) seem to have understood that making a religious freedom claim might backfire because Buddhism was widely perceived to be too weird and too threatening to mainstream American life.

Imamura's 1921 book therefore proved prescient. He knew that people in American territory had every legal right to engage in proselytism and teaching of foreign languages under the law, but the nature of the decision also reinforced the racial hierarchies of the day: Some American minorities were able to avail themselves of the language of religious freedom; others were not.[106] Indeed, Imamura had included a diagram in his essay "On the American Spirit" that outlined the racial hierarchies of his adopted home. Anglo-Saxons sat at the top of a pyramid, while Japanese languished near the bottom, superior only to (and partially overlapping with) blacks.[107] The *Farrington v. Tokushige* decision reflected the difficulties racial and ethnic minorities had in using the language of religious freedom to bypass the constraining categories of race.

CONCLUSION

Scholars of American religions have irrefutably demonstrated that Americans have historically used the concept of religious freedom to exclude at least as much as we have used it to accommodate: What Tisa Wenger calls "religious freedom talk" has always been linked to differential access to resources that reflects shifting American hierarchies of ethnicity and race.[108] Over the country's short history, some American minorities such as Jews and Catholics successfully used religious freedom talk to supersede ethnic difference and therefore avail themselves of the privileges of whiteness. Others, such as African Americans and Native Americans, have experienced the benefits of religious freedom talk rarely and unevenly, if at all.[109] These discrepancies and disparities are as intrinsic to American religious freedom as religious freedom is integral to the national narrative of America as the "land of the free."[110]

The experiences of Japanese people living in American territory have rarely featured in critical accounts of the uneven distribution of America's religious freedom guarantee, but like other racial minorities, Japanese Americans' phenotypic traits and radical religious differences from the Christian majority interfered with their ability to use religious freedom talk effectively.[111] Both in domestic contexts related to the language school issue and in diplomatic contexts related to global visions of the new postwar order, Japanese people tactically made claims that showed that they could beat the Americans at their own religious freedom game. Imamura Yemyō could use the language of religious liberty to show that Japanese Americans were both law-abiding and eager to partake of America's bounty. Matsuoka Yōsuke's claim that the Japanese push for a racial equality clause in the League of Nations charter was not inimical to, but rather supportive of, religious liberty tried to appeal to Americans' higher virtues. Within the assemblages of race and religion that characterized American empire and the geopolitics of "civilization," however, the claims of both men fell on deaf ears. This point is important because Japanese claims about religious freedom would similarly fail to find audience with American policy makers at the close of World War II. As the chapters of part 2 will show, Americans simply assumed that Japanese people *could not* understand religious freedom.

The irony here is striking. The double standards to which Japanese Americans were subjected regarding the language school issue were obvious, and the fact that religion did not feature in the *Farrington v. Tokushige* decision even though the initial complaints about the language schools were based almost exclusively on anti-Buddhist animus showed that only some Americans were allowed to make religious freedom claims. The experiences of Japanese Americans showed definitively that the imperial United States was hardly the bastion of religious liberty that the occupiers would later claim.

The suspicion that Buddhism was intimately linked to "Mikadoism" lingered, and then intensified, once Japan and the United States went to war. After the Japanese surprise attack on Pearl Harbor, the first Japanese people targeted for arrest were Buddhist priests.[112] In the wake of the bombing, ordinary Japanese Americans were hard-pressed to prove that they were not foreign agents. Their homes changed as they discarded religious accoutrements that suggested that they were beholden to the empire.[113] Their faith changed as they abandoned their long-held religious commitments in desperate efforts to prove themselves truly American. While Japanese people living in Hawai'i escaped mass incarceration, their counterparts on the mainland landed in internment camps after President Franklin Delano Roosevelt's (1882–1945) infamous Executive Order 9066.

These policies represented both racial and religious discrimination, giving lie to the American conceit that Americans "had" religious freedom while Japan lacked it. While the American government "prioritized and attempted to enforce freedom of religion" in the internment camps, it did so within a restrictive regime that forced adherents to collapse sectarian distinctions into just three religions: Buddhism, Protestantism, and Catholicism. Selectively drawing on the claims of the Japanese government, the War Relocation Authority designated Shintō as nonreligious, and therefore not eligible for freedom.[114]

Meanwhile, American military officers treated Japanese Americans who wanted to support the war effort as potential double agents.[115] Intelligence officers pumped volunteers for information but gave them little chance to serve. Ethnicity was cause for suspicion; religion was reason for discrimination: Volunteers for military duty received a point in favor of their applications if they claimed to be Christian, but lost a point if they were Buddhists and lost *three* points if they claimed Shintō as their religion.[116]

Of course, the Americans did have good reason to be suspicious of Japanese claims that religious freedom was protected. By the time of the Pacific War, Christian missionaries based in Japan were alleging that state policies interfered with religious freedom, and police crackdowns on marginal religious movements in the 1920s and 1930s had certainly given the impression that only some religions in Japan were actually free. In the immediate wake of the war, the occupiers would also point to the 1939 Religious Organizations Law as the final nail in the coffin of whatever religious freedom actually existed in Japan, suggesting that this law subjected religions to draconian oversight.

But the story is much more complicated than a declensionist narrative of creeping fascism would suggest, particularly because academic experts and foreign service officers based in Japan repeatedly assured anglophone audiences that Japanese ways of governing religion were not particularly problematic. For example, in a 1 December 1927 article in *The Chinese Recorder* newspaper, prominent scholar of Japan August Karl Reischauer (1879–1971) confidently asserted that Japanese people enjoyed religious liberty.[117] No modern state could offer wholly unfettered religious freedom, Reischauer said, but to the extent that any state could offer maximal freedom while still maintaining peace and order, Japan was doing just fine.

Reischauer's comments in late 1927 took place against the backdrop of a spate of articles in missionary publications and anglophone newspapers addressing rumors that the Japanese Ministry of Education was considering new legislation concerning the management of religions. On the whole, these articles shared Reischauer's confidence. If the law were going to interfere in religions' affairs, for the most part the negative effects would not redound onto Christian churches, but would instead affect Buddhist organizations and their finances.[118] Taking the public statements of Ministry of Education officials at face value, most anglophone newspapers reported that the proposed legislation would perform some legislative housekeeping that should make administration of religious affairs easier for bureaucrats and religious leaders alike.[119]

Certainly there were some who sounded tocsins of alarm. A few Christian outlets feared that the law gave the state too much power to interfere in religions' affairs with impunity.[120] Missionaries aimed to preserve their rights to proselytize without hindrance. But Reischauer's sanguine article was published immediately after the defeat of one Ministry of Education proposal in 1927 and just before a follow-up initiative began in 1928. Religious freedom was safe in Japan, he averred, just as religions in Japan were safe from state harm. When a version of the legislation was finally passed about a decade later, confident Americans based in Japan cabled the US Department of State that the law was nothing to worry about, did not infringe upon American missionaries' religious freedom, and merely served to streamline existing laws while preventing the ability of "fly-by-night religious promoters" to abuse the category of religion to fleece unwitting victims.[121] All of this is to say that while Americans at home may have been critical of "Mikadoism" and suspicious of Japanese people's ability to really practice religious freedom at all, experts situated on the ground assured those who would listen that Japanese practices of religious freedom were not all that different from those of any other "civilized" country.

My cases in the next chapter all come from this period between 1925 and 1945, when Japanese policy makers repeatedly attempted to pass comprehensive religions legislation akin to the Yamagata bill that had died in the House of Peers in February 1900 (see chapter 2). In 1925 the Ministry of Education created a "Religions System Investigation Committee" in order to pursue the prospect of passing comprehensive religions legislation. The committee's deliberations resulted in several abortive attempts to create such a bill (in 1927, 1929, and 1935), but it was not until 1939 that the legislation finally passed. In most postwar histories, these executive branch initiatives have appeared as pieces of evidence proving that the Japanese state aimed to restrict religious liberties or even to abrogate the constitutional religious freedom clause altogether. But in their time, these initiatives were subject to competing interpretations that reflected wildly divergent understandings of religion, freedom, and the proper relationship between religions and the state. In the next chapter, I gather these diverse perspectives together by listening to activist oratory in public halls, eavesdropping on bureaucrats' policy making in the Ministry of Education, reporting on lawmakers' grandstanding in the diet, and questioning cops' attempts to fix the meaning of religious freedom once and for all in the interrogation chamber.

4

IN THE ABSENCE OF RELIGIOUS FREEDOM

> One can only wonder what the effect would have been on Japanese society, including the government, if even a few hundred Buddhist priests had spoken out or, more important, taken action against the war on religious grounds. As [James] Ketelaar has observed: "[Buddhism] was indeed one, if not the only, organization capable of offering effective resistance to state policy." Large-scale resistance, of course, never occurred, but those few Buddhists who did oppose Japan's war policies demonstrated that resistance was possible if one were prepared to pay the price. Each and every Japanese Buddhist did have a choice to make.
>
> BRIAN VICTORIA, citing James Ketelaar (1997)[1]

BRIAN VICTORIA'S COUNTERFACTUAL speculation in his 1997 book *Zen at War* exemplifies a widespread tendency in scholarship on religion-state relations in the first two decades of the Shōwa era (1926–45). Some scholars have pointed out that policy makers frequently tried to mobilize the ideological power of religion for the purposes of social cohesion and control, and have shown that representatives of mainstream religious organizations responded to these top-down initiatives by aligning themselves with social edification projects.[2] Other scholars have shown that marginal religions, such as Ōmotokyō, experienced devastating police persecution.[3] Many have decried the 1939 Religious Organizations Law as the death knell of religious freedom in wartime Japan.

But we would make a mistake if we assumed that all state initiatives were unambiguously intrusive, that all religious leaders were unquestioningly compliant, or that the various pieces of religions legislation advanced during this period simply aimed to control religions without also safeguarding their constitutional rights. The historical record shows that many government policy makers were conscientious about safeguarding religions' interests and were aware that comprehensive religions legislation would be subject to the constitutional provision of religious freedom.[4] Parliamentary records, committee deliberations, and briefings for party members show that for the most part, legislators and government officials tried to solve vexing administrative problems through legal means that remained within the confines of constitutional law.[5] Extant pamphlets and handbills also show that a variety of Buddhist organizations protested proposed legislation just as they had at the time of the Yamagata bill at the turn of the century.[6] Virtually all of these publications made reference to the importance of religious freedom.

Nevertheless, postwar scholarship on this period has frequently presented the situation as one characterized by the dismal failure or total absence of religious freedom protections. In such narratives, Japanese policy makers misunderstood the very idea of religious freedom.[7] In these accounts, Japanese religious leaders ignored the principle of religious freedom, willingly capitulating to state authority out of political expediency.[8] These stories invariably portray state authority as evil and structure our expectation that religious leaders had a sacred duty to combat that evil by mounting public resistance based on progressive principles.[9] This freedom fighter trope has so deeply influenced the search for evidence of political resistance that vociferous, very public challenges to controversial legislation have gone almost entirely unnoticed.[10] Similarly, the resistance/complicity binary encourages us to interpret the actions of people who worked within the corridors of power as quietist or even overtly hostile to religious freedom, when in fact they seem to have understood their own actions quite differently.

As exemplified in Victoria's quote above, scholars have tended to assume that resistance is the only way religions should have engaged with the state and that such resistance should have occurred in a progressive or libertarian mode, securing maximal freedom for individuals while diminishing authoritarian power. This presupposition is frequently presented in some variation on a counterfactual question: Why did Buddhists fail to resist the oppressive religions legislation that bound them so firmly to the state?[11]

The question undoubtedly serves a valuable function in emic discussions of Buddhist doctrine and idealized visions of "engaged Buddhism."

However, the presentist nature of the question makes it unanswerable through standard historiographic methods. The conclusion that Buddhists failed to resist is a foregone one, so the historical investigation becomes moot. The counterfactual question of why Buddhists failed to resist also contravenes the principle of doctrinal neutrality that presumably distinguishes nonconfessional religious studies from theology. In other words, the question problematically assumes that all Buddhist political actions should have been premised on progressive principles.[12]

Below I challenge the intertwined assumptions that Buddhist resistance to controversial religions legislation was necessarily politically progressive, that Buddhist complicity with state initiatives required capitulation to illiberal principles, that state suppression of religious movements completely ignored the transcendent principle of religious freedom, or that victims of police persecution were all martyrs who championed religious liberty.[13] Through examinations of very different perspectives on religious freedom embodied by three lay, laicized, or lay-leaning Buddhist leaders, I make the potentially counterintuitive claim that the draconian legislation and law enforcement of the early Shōwa era was largely *democratic* insofar as it was characterized by free speech, parliamentary procedure, surveys of popular opinion, and respect for the rule of law. The problem is that what constitutes the "rule of law" varies, and laws and law enforcement are only as good as the definitions that inform them.

RESISTERS, COLLABORATORS, MARTYRS

I first use the figure of Chikazumi Jōkan (1870–1941) to argue that the complicated question of how Buddhists went about protecting their religious freedom is best understood if we abandon the normative presupposition that Buddhists should have resisted religions legislation out of commitment to either liberal principles or to specific Buddhist doctrines.[14] Chikazumi's resistance to proposed religions legislation in the late 1920s was framed in reactionary terms. Unlike his erstwhile friend Andō Masazumi (1876–1955), Chikazumi argued that egalitarian treatment of religions was a problem, not a solution.[15] In this chapter he features as an example of *free speech* even though his interpretations of religious freedom seem illiberal today.

For his part, Andō spent the period between 1926 and 1945 skillfully navigating between protecting Buddhist interests and facilitating greater governmental oversight of religions. As a legislator in Japan's House of Commons, a junior bureaucrat in the Ministry of Education, and as leader of numerous transsectarian Buddhist organizations in wartime, Andō imagined a near-future utopia in which Buddhism would play a crucial role in Japanese social and political life, both for citizens in the metropole and for imperial subjects in Japan's colonies. Whereas Chikazumi denounced the egalitarian stance associated with liberal politics, Andō considered himself a liberal through and through. It may therefore come as a surprise to know that he proudly facilitated the passage of the Religious Organizations Law of 1939.[16] Postwar scholars have generally regarded the Religious Organizations Law as a formal abrogation of Japan's constitutional guarantee of religious freedom.[17] In his time, however, Andō saw the Religious Organizations Law as a model piece of legislation that protected and expanded the rights of religions and even protected marginal movements from persecution by the state while staying within the bounds of the constitutional religious freedom guarantee. Andō therefore features here as an example of *legislative process* and high-minded *policy making*.

I read Andō somewhat sympathetically, even if some of his claims about religious freedom seem disingenuous. I do not deny, as he might have, the existence of draconian policing in the early Shōwa era. Police targeted religious groups, infiltrated them, and subjected them to surveillance. They were so effective at this that some marginal groups disappeared; others barely survived the war. Andō would probably have regarded this as a natural state of affairs in which "real" religion triumphed over deleterious superstitions. However, in turning from Andō's pet topic of religions policy to the concrete particulars of law enforcement, I show that at least one famous instance of police suppression of a marginal religious group offers another potentially counterintuitive lesson on religious freedom. In the 1943 suppression of the Sōka Kyōiku Gakkai (Value Creation Education Study Association), the police were able to rationalize their intervention by appealing to the idea of maintaining peace and order. Behind this rationale lay the fact that Gakkai members had been infringing on others' freedom to worship as they chose by discarding and burning cherished religious paraphernalia.

When he was arrested for exhorting people to commit such crimes, Gakkai leader Makiguchi Tsunesaburō (1871–1944) apparently did not attempt to exonerate himself by appealing to the constitutional religious freedom clause.[18] Makiguchi's arrest and interrogation therefore serve as an example of the tenuous balance between *law enforcement* and *civil liberties*. We can critique the wartime surveillance state and can cast aspersions on the punishments meted out to individuals who did not acquiesce to Japan's suprareligious orthodoxy, but we must acknowledge the uncomfortable truth that cops are always caught between their duty to preserve public order and their duty to protect civil rights. For better or worse, they frequently generate operative definitions of rights and duties that deem some groups suspect while giving others a free pass.

My purpose is neither to condone nor to condemn the attitudes of the historical figures I discuss here. Instead, I mean to show that while religious freedom existed as both a conceptual ideal and as a legal principle throughout the war years, it was interpreted quite differently depending on the positions and commitments of the individuals and groups in question. The renewed attempt to pass comprehensive religions legislation that began in 1927 and continued up until the passage of the Religious Organizations Law in 1939 provides good insight into the diverse interpretations of religious freedom propounded by various stakeholders at the time.

THE RENASCENT RELIGIONS BILL (JANUARY 1929)

At a meeting of the Religions System Investigation Committee held on 10 January 1929, chairperson Hiranuma Kiichirō (1867–1952) opened the meeting by situating the committee's task in a long line of governmental efforts to clarify the relationship between the Japanese state and religious organizations.[19] Whereas recent efforts at establishing comprehensive religions legislation had failed due to public opposition and procedural failures, Hiranuma argued, the time had come to finally establish a law that would harness the ideological power of religion and ensure that it served the needs of the state.

Hiranuma then turned the floor over to Minister of Education Shōda Kazue (1869–1948) to explain the purpose of the legislation in more detail. Shōda's comments added some necessary nuance to Hiranuma's authoritarian opening remarks. It was impossible to *control* religion insofar as that would constitute an infringement on the constitutional guarantee of freedom of conscience, Shōda clarified, but it was possible to *regulate* religions in their external manifestations as public bodies. Thus, one change introduced in the new bill was titular. Unlike the failed "Religions Law" advanced by former minister of education Okada Ryōhei (1864–1934) in 1927, the legislation would now be called the "Religious *Organizations* Law"

(Shūkyō *Dantai* Hō). The new bill also corrected for a major shortcoming of the Okada bill, which had been unnecessarily intrusive in religions' private affairs. Moreover, splitting off a section of the previous bill regarding shrines' and temples' customary rights to governmental land removed a compelling economic incentive for religions to support the bill, meaning that some of the more strident criticisms of the recently failed Okada bill could be countered.[20]

Shōda was technically responsible for the legislation in his capacity as Minister of Education, but he let his junior consultant, Andō Masazumi, outline the particulars for the committee. Andō was the perfect person to explain the new bill because he came from a clerical background (he had been ordained as a Jōdo Shinshū priest) and could therefore speak with authority about the concerns of priests. He also had a keen sense of how to gauge public opinion due to decades of professional work as a journalist, and he had been widely considered an eloquent speaker even as a young man.[21] He also understood the intricacies of the legislative process due to years of work as a legislator in the House of Commons. He could therefore speak both *about* religion from an administrative standpoint and *for* it from a confessional one.

Andō's interpretation of the proposed legislation was quite sanguine, and as he walked the committee through the particulars of the bill, he argued that it removed restrictions on religious organizations rather than saddling them with new ones. He drew attention to the bewildering hodgepodge of mutually contradictory laws that confronted clerics when they wanted to do simple things like construct new buildings, and he reminded his audience that religions performed a valuable social function by fostering morality and by providing legitimate alternatives to "lascivious heresies" (*inshi jakyō*) like Ōmotokyō and Tenri Kenkyūsho. Passing comprehensive legislation would therefore help religions contribute to the public good.

With the benefit of historical hindsight, it may seem odd that a laicized Buddhist priest like Andō would speak so positively on behalf of the government's position. Although the 1929 bill would die in committee just as its 1927 precursor had, in postwar historiography the Shōda bill has appeared as an important precursor to the dastardly 1939 Religious Organizations Law that allegedly stripped Japanese individuals of their constitutional right to religious freedom in the context of Japan's "Total War."[22] In most received accounts, craven Buddhist priests failed to mount significant resistance to these legislative initiatives, while manipulative militarists successfully positioned Shintō as Japan's suprareligious political orthodoxy.[23] Reading

Andō's remarks to the committee in light of this narrative, our options are either to assume a sort of false consciousness in which Andō did not fully understand the threat the proposed legislation posed to his own religious tradition, or to acknowledge that our received accounts may be flawed.

I take the latter approach, but I do not take Andō at his word. Andō brashly implied that he spoke *for* the religious world, but his erstwhile friend Chikazumi Jōkan made a veritable career of vehemently denying this claim. Chikazumi remonstrated with Andō both publicly in print and in private correspondence, suggesting that Andō had abandoned his religious principles in the service of promoting an unfeasibly egalitarian model of religious freedom. The two friends ultimately had a bitter falling out over the issue. Although they were both Jōdo Shinshū priests who shared a commitment to lay outreach and political activism, their radically divergent interpretations of religious freedom proved to be incommensurable.

CHIKAZUMI JŌKAN'S BUDDHIST RESISTANCE

Chikazumi Jōkan appeared in chapter 2 as one of the chief proponents of the *kōninkyō*, or "officially recognized religion," stance during the debates on the Yamagata religions bill.[24] At that time, he headed a lay organization developed to operate in tandem with clerical efforts to defeat the Yamagata legislation. Immediately after the parliamentary failure of that bill in early 1900, the Jōdo Shinshū leadership sent Chikazumi to Europe and the United States in hopes that he might survey systems there and provide the sect with ammunition for future debates.

Chikazumi was gone for two formative years.[25] When he returned in March 1902, he launched a new phase of his career that focused more on religious outreach than on political activism. In June 1902, he initiated a donation campaign for the construction of his Kyūdō Kaikan (Seeking the Path Hall) and began offering weekly Sunday sermons.[26] While his journal *Seikyō jihō* (*State and Religion Times*) had continued publication in his absence, the journal discontinued publication in December 1903; Chikazumi replaced it with the more confessional journal *Kyūdō* (*Seeking the Path*) in February 1904. Both *Seikyō jihō* (published 1899–1903) and *Kyūdō* (1904–22) reflected Chikazumi's stance that Buddhism should serve as the basis for all aspects of Japanese cultural life in the same way that Christianity did in the countries of Europe and North America.[27] Whereas *Seikyō jihō* had reflected this position in its rigorous critique of contemporary religion-state relations, *Kyūdō* focused primarily on personal development and social edification.[28]

Chikazumi's political activism of earlier years was virtually nonexistent during the publication of *Kyūdō* (1904–22), with one important exception being his attempt to resist the "Three Religions Conference" organized by Vice Minister of the Interior Tokonami Takejirō (1867–1935) in 1912.[29] Chikazumi, Andō, and several members of the Fellowship of New Buddhists collaborated to resist this event, which they saw as a misguided attempt to facilitate greater government control of religion.[30] In this chapter I focus on a later phase of Chikazumi's life, when he tried to prevent the passage of the religious organizations bill advanced by Minister of Education Shōda Kazue (1869–1948) in 1929.

Resistance to the Shōda Religious Organizations Bill of 1929

There is little documentation of Chikazumi's resistance to the failed Okada religions bill of 1927. By his own account, he protested the legislation but could not mount an effective opposition movement before the bill died during a cabinet shake-up in April of that year.[31] However, when a slightly revised version of the Okada legislation appeared in 1929, Chikazumi poured his energy into its defeat.[32] From January to March of 1929, Chikazumi organized lecture meetings, released public statements denouncing the legislation, and published several scathing pamphlets.[33] He argued that because religious faith was absolute, any attempt to enforce egalitarian treatment of the three religions of Shintō, Buddhism, and Christianity in the name of religious freedom would actually infringe on the freedoms of the very people the law aimed to protect. For Chikazumi, equal treatment *was* discrimination.[34]

Before the proposed legislation had even been formally presented to the House of Peers for deliberation, Chikazumi published two pamphlets expressing his opposition. The first, dated 8 January 1929, was an autobiographical retrospective entitled *Shūkyō hōan hantai raireki* (*My History of Opposing Religious Legislation*).[35] Chikazumi opened his account by reflecting on the Yamagata bill of 1899. Acknowledging that the Yamagata bill included no small number of perquisites for Buddhists like tax exemption, Chikazumi said that Buddhists of the time were nevertheless willing to sacrifice such financial benefits out of principled opposition to the idea that Buddhism might be treated equally with Christianity. Confronting the looming reality of mixed residence, proponents of that bill had attempted to appease such foreign powers by adopting a foolhardy egalitarian policy. Yet the Buddhists of Japan united and fought the legislation tooth and nail, leading to its defeat in the House of Peers.

Reflecting positively on the defeat of the Yamagata bill at the hands of Japan's united Buddhists, Chikazumi lamented the fact that the recently failed Okada bill of 1927 had initially been advanced because of Buddhist entreaties to the government. Some members of the House of Commons had campaigned on platforms that linked the passage of comprehensive religions legislation to the prospect of the government selling confiscated property back to Buddhist groups at greatly reduced prices.[36] Eager to regain access to lands they considered rightfully theirs, Buddhist clerics joined ranks with these politicians and supported the religions legislation. Chikazumi claimed that the Religions System Investigation Committee was a gathering of such Buddhists and their ilk, and that committee had problematically operated on the premise of egalitarian treatment of religions from the outset. Like the earlier Yamagata bill, however, the Okada legislation was ultimately a flawed bill that paired strict supervision of religions with egalitarian treatment of the three religions (Buddhism, Shintō, and Christianity).

According to Chikazumi, the legislation currently being prepared by the committee in 1929 was nothing other than the revivified corpse of the very same Okada bill, although it was now called the "Religious Organizations Law" (rather than the "religions bill").[37] Chikazumi argued that promoting the legislation under any name ultimately amounted to an attempt to create a Buddhist political party and could only result in sullying Buddhist rectitude. Rumors that some members of the House of Commons who hailed from Shinshū Ōtani-ha backgrounds were drowning in this whirlpool of folly were particularly dismaying. Chikazumi was undoubtedly leveling criticism at his erstwhile friend Andō, who would later proudly claim responsibility for the change in the legislation's nomenclature.[38]

ANDŌ MASAZUMI'S BUDDHIST COMPLICITY

Andō Masazumi was born to a Jōdo Shinshū temple family in Tokyo in 1876; he took the tonsure ten years later in 1886.[39] He benefited from an advanced education, earning degrees at both Tetsugakukan (now Tōyō University) in

1895 and Tōkyō Senmon Gakkō (now Waseda University) in 1899. Andō became a writer for the influential religious journal *Meikyō shinshi* in 1894 and wrote for the journal until 1896, when he briefly participated in Kiyozawa Manshi's (1863–1903) attempt to reform Jōdo Shinshū.[40] Andō served as chief editor of *Meikyō shinshi* from 1899 to 1900; he also was the first editor of the Kanazawa-based newspaper *Seikyō shinbun* (*State and Religion News*).

Andō's journalistic career also extended beyond the religious press. He worked as a reporter for the *Yamato shinbun* for most of 1901 and then joined the *Nippon shinbun* in December of that year. Andō reported from the front lines during the Russo-Japanese War before joining the *Ōsaka asahi shinbun* in 1906. He returned to Tokyo in 1908 to serve as director and editor in chief of the *Tōkyō asahi shinbun*. He continued to maintain some affiliation with that paper until the early 1920s, although his political career soon eclipsed his journalistic one.

Andō's commitment to Buddhism was indisputable. For example, he established a Buddhist kindergarten on the grounds of Asakusa Honganji in 1902, and in 1910 he created the Tōkyō Bukkyō Gokoku Dan (Tokyo Buddhist Nation-Protecting Corps) and served as editor of that group's journal, *Seikyō shinron*.[41] However, Andō withdrew from the clergy on 24 June 1914 and embarked on a career in politics shortly thereafter.[42] After spending a couple of years as a local politician in Tokyo's Asakusa Ward, Andō became a member of the House of Commons (Shūgiin) in 1919. He was reelected ten more times in the course of his career. While continuing to participate in parliamentary politics, Andō served in various administrative capacities under Rikken Seiyūkai Party prime ministers Tanaka Giichi (1864–1929) and Inukai Tsuyoshi (1855–1932). From 1936 to 1940, Andō served as secretary-general of his party. Through the war years, he held several prominent positions as a leader of transsectarian Buddhist organizations and enjoyed considerable clout as a go-between for the religious and political worlds.[43]

Andō on Religious Legislation and the Topic of Religious Freedom

During the height of the furor over the Yamagata religions bill at the turn of the century, Andō had sharply criticized the proposed legislation. At that time, in his capacity as chief editor of the influential Buddhist journal *Meikyō shinshi*, Andō had advocated treating Buddhism as Japan's sole "officially recognized religion" (*kōninkyō*). A quarter of a century later, Andō began to modify his position.[44] In a lecture that was included in a 1926 Seiyūkai publication entitled *Lectures on Politics* (*Seiji kōza*), Andō demonstrated his facility with abstract argument in a methodical disquisition on the ideal relationship between religion and the state. Andō advocated the principle of separation of the two as the ideal policy for his party to adopt, but he also argued that there were limits to state toleration of religious difference. Citing the example of Mormon polygamy in America, he argued that if religion harmed customs, morals, or peace and order, it needed to be suppressed or banned. "Although the freedom of religious groups [*shūkyō no jiyū*] is respected," Andō argued, "the state cannot just let them be completely on their own."[45]

While Andō's 1926 speech indicated that he was not opposed to placing limits on religious freedom for the sake of peace and order, he was also opposed to the idea that religions legislation should merely make religious administration easier for bureaucrats while overlooking the needs and perspectives of religious organizations. His progressivist theory of religion-state relations no longer treated a pure *kōninkyō* system as the ideal one for Japan, but rather embraced a latitudinarian and egalitarian interpretation of religious freedom that included some pragmatic limits to keep potentially harmful religious practices in check. Andō's staunch resistance to excessive bureaucratic oversight of religions makes it easy to see how he and Chikazumi had previously collaborated in efforts to resist state interference in religions' affairs. Yet when Minister of Education Shōda Kazue resuscitated the failed Okada bill in 1928, Andō (now a cabinet official) abruptly embraced the legislation. He lost his friend Chikazumi in the process.[46]

THE RESISTANCE STRIKES BACK

In a 22 January 1929 pamphlet titled *Our Reason for Opposing the Religious Organizations Law*, Chikazumi argued that the Buddhist Alliance against the Religious Organizations Law (Shūkyō Dantai Hō Hantai Bukkyōto Dōmei) opposed the proposed legislation because of the fact that it treated Buddhism, Shintō, and Christianity equally.[47] The understanding of religious freedom that was being used as a rationale for the legislation was inherently flawed, he claimed, because equal treatment actually infringed on individuals' closely held beliefs. Moreover, because Buddhists constituted the majority of the population, they should not be treated according to the same criteria as Christian sects, most of which had their headquarters overseas.[48]

Chikazumi was not alone in having reservations about the proposed legislation. When the bill was brought up for debate in the House of Peers on 15 February 1929, Minister of Education Shōda Kazue faced a series of tough questions from legislators about the government's intent, how the proposed legislation fit with the constitutional religious freedom clause, and how the law might be used to discriminate between proper "religions" and "lascivious heresies." For example, Sakatani Yoshirō (1863–1941) commented that while he did not have any particular reservations about supporting the bill, he wanted to note that he had received many letters from respected religious leaders urging him to resist it. He also noted with some concern that letters from religious leaders urging him to support the legislation tended to have temples' economic interests primarily at heart.[49] As I will soon show, this economic issue was central to the critiques that some of Chikazumi's comrades were then leveling against the bill.

Sakatani's queries about how to distinguish between proper religions and "lascivious heresies" also raised the problem of how religion was to be defined in Japanese law. Shōda claimed that the authors of the bill had referred to Itō Hirobumi's (1841–1909) commentaries on the constitution as they considered the legislation, and had noticed, following Itō, that other countries' constitutions used different clauses for religious freedom (*shinkyō no jiyū*, freedom of conscience or belief) and corporate freedom (*dantai kessha no jiyū*, freedom of association or freedom of assembly). Thus, the law did not infringe on *belief*, but could regulate *incorporation*. Shōda also stressed that the spirit of religious freedom undergirded the bill and that the constitutional right to profess the religion of one's choice would not be infringed upon.[50]

Neither the sharp questions from Sakatani and his colleague Shirakawa Sukenaga (1871–1961; Shirakawa was a Shintō priest) nor Shōda's anemic responses were likely to assuage Chikazumi's concerns about the legislation.[51] Contemporary debates between legal scholars in the pages of the newspapers were also unlikely to satisfy him, for Chikazumi was clearly not interested in the recondite details of legal theory nor in what paternalistic government bureaucrats thought was best for religions.[52] Chikazumi wanted to ensure that Buddhism alone would be officially recognized as the one true religion for the Japanese people. Such an objective may have been unrealistic, but he thought that elective interpretations of religious freedom were based on a false principle of equality that ironically undermined *true* freedom of religious belief.

After the initial debates about the proposed legislation in the House of Peers, Chikazumi's lobbying group held a lecture meeting on 22 February 1929 featuring Chikazumi, Tokyo Imperial University law professor Ono Seiichirō (1891–1986), and manager of Heigo Press Takashima Beihō (1875–1949) as the headlining speakers. A handbill bearing the same date was either drawn up to encapsulate resolutions established at the meeting or printed up ahead of time and passed out to attendees. The handbill denounced the proposed Religious Organizations Law by saying that it violated the spirit of religious freedom. The full text of the handbill read:

> Resolution:
>
> Because the Religious Organizations Law aims to manage the various religions equally and interferes politically [in their affairs], it damages the essence of religion and abrogates the spirit of religious freedom. Therefore we oppose it and anticipate its repeal.
>
> Supplementary Resolution:
>
> Recently the leaders of the various Buddhist sects call themselves [our] representatives; the announcements they make in collaboration with Shintō and Christian leaders are not the general opinion of true and upright Buddhists. Here we denounce their presumptuous and deceitful acts and expect such to be abolished.
>
> 22 February 1929, at the Akasaka Tameike Sankaidō
>
> Buddhist Alliance against the Religious Organizations Bill[53]

As the supplementary resolution indicates, the indignation evident in this handbill derived from a complicated politics internal to the Buddhist tradition at least as much as it reflected concerns about religion-state relations in a more abstract sense. These internal disputes were not merely matters of philosophical disagreement. As Chikazumi's colleague Sakami Chūsei (d.u.) argued in a pamphlet published on 24 February 1929, sectarian leaders and some rank-and-file Buddhists seemed quick to align themselves with governmental initiatives for all the wrong reasons.[54] Many of these Buddhists had mistaken ideas about what they would gain from the government under the proposed law. Sakami argued that some Buddhists bought into the narrative of Buddhist degeneracy and supported the law out of a misguided sort of respectability politics, trying to prove Buddhist probity by supporting flawed legislation. Others naively believed the government officials who claimed that the bill offered them more freedom, while in fact the "freedom" offered by the bill put Buddhists on equal footing with the foreign religion of Christianity and would force Buddhists to accept governmental intrusion in their internal affairs. Meanwhile, accepting the law's designation of "juridical persons" (*hōjin*) might seem to be an elevation of Buddhist status, but in actuality it subjected Buddhists to civil laws from which they had previously been exempt. The government would also be allowed to monitor temple finances, meaning that even small mistakes in the ledger could lead to fines or imprisonment.

But the biggest issue was the "shrine and temple land restitution problem."[55] Many Buddhists were under the impression that the proposed legislation would return to them land that they had long held prior to the controversial land reforms of the 1870s and 1880s.[56] Sakami scoffed at such naïveté. While priests thought that the land would be returned free of charge, in actuality the government was offering to *sell* the land back to temples at reduced prices. The only plots that would actually be free were those tiny parcels of land that the government acknowledged as being used primarily for religious propagation and ritual activities. This meant that any land that temples customarily leased out to tenants for revenue (a major source of temple income) would have to be purchased. Such an arrangement might be fine for the tiny minority of very large rural temples that enjoyed steady incomes from ritual services, but the majority of small urban temples would suffer. The proponents of the legislation masked this fact, Sakami argued, by cooking up fake public opinion polls that prioritized the views of large temples that could afford to buy land back from the state.

Sakami wrote from the stance of a jaded legal scholar trying to enlighten his fellow Buddhists about the dangers of accepting the government's position at face value. For his part, Chikazumi was clearly incensed that the administration could so hastily dismiss religious interest groups that were not represented by the elite leaders of the various Buddhist sects who could actually afford the land-use arrangement proposed by the government. Chikazumi saw the government's language of elective religious freedom as a calculated ploy to distract the public from this fundamental economic issue. But he also disliked the governmental perspective on religious freedom as choice because it did not correspond with his perception of freedom of conscience, nor did it accord with what he thought of as international norms. This stance can be seen in another pamphlet that Chikazumi published on 2 March 1929:

> As the Religions Bureau of the Ministry of Education actually proclaimed in a pamphlet, it aims to conduct a religions policy of "tolerance of other religions," "egalitarian treatment," and so forth. Therefore it interprets religious freedom as the freedom of choice, and then lines up Buddhism, Shintō, and Christianity in front of the people and tells them to voluntarily choose one. In sum, it misconstrues so-called religious freedom as freedom of choice, and with this as a rationale, it ultimately aims to conduct a policy in which uniform treatment of the three religions forms the fundamental principle of the law. We must say that this oversteps the bounds of religious freedom. If anything, we must say that it forces a lack of freedom on each individual. This is proved by the fact that in none of the various countries of the world does such a law exist that treats the various sects and factions with one common "religions law" or "religious organizations law."[57]

Chikazumi probably have breathed a sigh of relief when the Shōda bill failed to pass in 1929, but he was immediately embroiled in another controversy when he began advocating reform of the Shinshū Ōtani faction in response to the 1928 defrocking of former head of the sect (*kanchō*) Kubutsu Shōnin (a.k.a. Ōtani Kōen, 1875–1943).[58] Chikazumi was stripped of his clerical rank on 23 July 1929 as a result of this activism, prompting him to launch a new, characteristically inveterate publication called *Shinkai kengen* on 15 January 1930.[59] Like Chikazumi's earlier periodicals, *Shinkai kengen* critiqued the mutual sullying of religion and politics and steadfastly admonished the sectarian leadership for dubious behavior.

The unfailingly apoplectic Chikazumi suffered a cerebral hemorrhage on 30 October 1931 and spent the last decade of his life as an invalid. Yet he continued to write as much as he was able, and when rumors began to spread that the Ministry of Education was considering advancing the Religious Organizations Law yet again in 1935, Chikazumi devoted a whole issue of *Shinkai kengen* to the topic (20 December 1935). Subsequent issues returned to the topic of sectarian reform, and *Shinkai kengen* continued in this manner until 20 November 1938, when the paper abruptly ceased publication shortly after the battlefield death of Chikazumi's eldest son. Shattered by the loss, Chikazumi himself died three years later on 3 December 1941. Because his publication activities ceased at around the same time that the Religious Organizations Law was being drafted, it is difficult to know how Chikazumi perceived the bill.[60] I surmise that his fierce opposition would have continued unabated.[61]

A REASONABLE RATIONALE

At roughly the same time that Chikazumi was protesting Minister of Education Matsuda Genji's (1876–1936) renewed initiative to pass comprehensive religions legislation in the pages of *Shinkai kengen* in late 1935, his former pal Andō Masazumi published a retrospective offering his own reasons for *supporting* the religions bill. Andō's reflections appeared in a November 1935 special issue of the religious journal *Uchū* (*Kosmos*) on the pros and cons of a Religious Organizations Law.[62] In the article, Andō reflected on his impressions of the various religions bills that had been advanced in Japan since the promulgation of the 1889 constitution.[63] For several decades after the Yamagata bill's defeat in 1900, Andō opined, the issue of religions legislation was largely overlooked. However, in 1926 and 1927, the Wakatsuki cabinet prepared to submit new religions legislation to the House of Peers. Minister of Education Okada Ryōhei was an ardent public proponent of establishing a formal religions system, and he was supported behind the scenes by Education Ministry Bureau of Religions chief Shimomura Juichi (1884–1965).[64]

Andō said he was chosen at that time to participate on the new Religions System Investigation Committee as a representative of the Seiyūkai political party. The bill that emerged from the committee's deliberations was privately shown to scholars, members of both legislative houses, bureaucrats, and representatives from each religious sect; it was only submitted to the House of Peers in 1927 after having worked through preliminary negotiations with each these groups. While the legislation may not have been perfect and although it had ultimately failed, it had been thoroughly vetted by experts and stakeholders.[65] By describing the thoroughgoing nature of the vetting process, Andō implied that Chikazumi's concerns were groundless.

While he thought that the general thrust of the 1927 Okada bill was quite different from that of the Yamagata bill of 1899, Andō admitted that it had harbored significant problems concerning the designation of religious status, how the administration of religions would be accomplished, the nature of the authority the Ministry of Education held over religions, the credentialing of clerics, the adjudication of doctrinal disputes, and the controversial issue of the restitution of temple property. In Andō's estimation it was clearly a bureaucrat's bill that did not take the interests of religions into account. Although the House of Peers Special Investigative Committee met three times to discuss the legislation and although the government offered to make significant revisions, the bill died before it was born.

Andō criticized the 1927 Okada bill as a bureaucrat's dream, but he then recalled that when new education minister Shōda Kazue asked for Andō's opinion about the bill in 1928, he announced himself an ardent proponent of the legislation. Reading between the lines of his retrospective, it seems that Andō probably recognized that the best way to ensure that the new bill took religions' needs seriously was to write the revisions himself. He spent the entire summer of 1928 collaborating with Vice Minister Awaya Ken (1883–1938) and aforementioned Religions Bureau chief Shimomura on the project. When the revised bill was put before the Religions System Investigation Committee on 10 January 1929, Andō was given the task of explaining the details of the proposed legislation.[66] He was the government official who best understood how to couch the legislation in terms that would appeal to all parties involved: bureaucrats, clerics, lawmakers, and police all needed to get behind the bill for it to work.

Andō recalled that the 1929 bill, like the 1927 version, was subject to a laborious process of vetting and debate that culminated in inconclusive clause-by-clause deliberations and sharp critiques. Eventually, his pet legislation died on 24 March 1929 in a state of "incomplete examination." While he acknowledged that there was some opposition to the bill outside of the Diet (elsewhere he acknowledged Chikazumi Jōkan's insistent letters and protestations), Andō claimed that it was not nearly as vociferous as the opposition to the earlier attempts, probably because this bill was rather liberal and acknowledged the sacrosanct essence of religion.[67] Andō claimed that he felt a great sense of personal responsibility for the defeat of the legislation, and while he had collaborated with Minister of Education Hatoyama Ichirō (1883–1959) on revising and resubmitting the legislation while serving as parliamentary vice minister of education in the Inukai cabinet (1931–32), the parliament was dissolved before the initiative could work.

Andō concluded his 1935 account by claiming that religions legislation was necessary to quell the rise of "superstition" and quasi-religious organizations, to streamline piecemeal laws and therefore make things easier on religious bodies, and to foster religious sentiment that could help Japan's citizens in a time of heightened anxiety concerning foreign affairs. But above all else, Andō argued that a religious organizations law must be liberal in spirit and must ultimately support the autonomy of religious organizations themselves.[68]

If Andō is to be believed, then he was personally responsible for some of the most significant changes in the wording and presentation of religions legislation that took place between 1927 and 1929. He therefore played a crucial role in formulating the secularist discrimination between religion and not-religion that was eventually enshrined in the 1939 Religious Organizations Law. If he is to be believed, then that law was not a dastardly attempt to rescind the constitutional guarantee of religious freedom, but actually an attempt to clarify the protections it offered. Some of Andō's contemporaries—Chikazumi among them—evidently thought of him as silver-tongued and two-faced, but by his own account he acted in order to protect religions, not punish them.

THE RELIGIOUS ORGANIZATIONS LAW

The extent to which Andō substantively contributed to the legislation in its final form remains a matter of some speculation, but his influence can be seen in two aspects of the Religious Organizations Law that finally passed in 1939. First, and crucially, the change in nomenclature from a "religions bill" to "religious organizations law" remained. Andō believed that this change preserved and protected religions' interests by making the limited scope of the legislation explicit. His understanding that religions legislation should focus on the external aspects of religion reflected his presupposition that religious freedom was inherently a matter of conscience, so that issues of official recognition and legal incorporation were disaggregated from the constitutional religious freedom guarantee.

Second, the distinction that Andō made in his retrospective between "religions," "newly arisen religions," and "superstitions" also appeared as a widely shared rubric and as a natural administrative distinction in the parliamentary deliberations about the 1939 law.[69] But if anything, the 1939 legislation was less severe than it might have been in that it allowed marginal movements to decide if they wanted to register themselves with the government as "religions" rather than leaving it up to the police to determine which groups were "religions" and which were "superstitions." Of course, registering with the state could subject marginal movements to additional scrutiny as easily as it could protect them from police intervention, but the law nevertheless left it up to voluntary associations themselves to seek recognition as religions so that they could benefit from the perquisites and prestige that attended such status. While skepticism regarding "superstitions" (*meishin*), "pseudo-religions" (*ruiji shūkyō*), and "recently arisen religions" (*shinkō shūkyō*) ran high during the entirety of the Meiji constitutional period and especially during the war years, policy makers' hopes that these organizations might be conscripted for ideological purposes appeared in Minister of Education Araki Sadao's (1877–1966) 24 January 1939 speech outlining the rationales behind the bill.[70] Notably, Araki also stressed that the drafters had taken pains to not infringe on the fundamental constitutional right to religious freedom in the slightest as they worked on the legislation. It was Andō himself who introduced the bill on the floor of the House of Commons two months later on 24 March 1939, urging its passage to wild applause.[71] Presenting his speech on the ten-year anniversary of the failure of the Shōda bill was no doubt personally satisfying.

One more point deserves attention regarding the oft-vilified 1939 legislation. Although the occupiers would later fault the Religious Organizations Law for restricting religious freedom, at the time it was passed foreign observers in Japan reported that most religious organizations, including foreign Christian missionaries, were quite sanguine about it.[72] The English-language *Japan Times Weekly* tersely noted that the numerous committee meetings that had preceded the bill's passage reflected the complexity of the issues the new law addressed, but that the attempts to control religions seen in previous iterations of the bill had been fully stripped from the new version.[73] Similarly, writing for mainline Protestant newspaper the *Christian Century* on 24 May 1939, American journalist Stuart Lillico (1909–?) wrote that the terms of the new law were "in no way severe" and that while the law harbored a potential threat in that it gave latitude to prefectural governors and the education minister in determining which groups would be eligible to register, otherwise it appeared "extremely impartial."[74]

US Department of State correspondence from the spring of 1939 also suggests that American diplomats readily accepted the Japanese explanation that the law was merely intended to clarify and rationalize matters of administrative procedure. The American legation understood the explicit aim of suppressing "pseudo-religions and fly-by-night religious promoters" to be a normal and natural objective.[75] Of course, this insouciance changed when Japan attacked the United States in December 1941, and during the Pacific War policing of religions became much more draconian. American missionaries eventually left Japan. But Japanese religious groups that did not conform with the wartime status quo lacked that option. They suffered as a result.

MARTYRDOM FOR RELIGIOUS FREEDOM? THE WARTIME SUPPRESSION OF SŌKA KYŌIKU GAKKAI

In the foregoing sections, Chikazumi Jōkan served as an example of Buddhist resistance to controversial religions legislation who rejected egalitarianism in legal articulations of religious freedom. I then showed that one of the architects of the 1939 Religious Organizations Law, Andō Masazumi, promoted the law because he thought of it as a liberal piece of legislation that would *protect* religious freedom. Turning now from Andō's abstract discussions of ideal religion-state relations to the concrete particulars of law enforcement, I show through the case of the Sōka Kyōiku Gakkai (Value Creation Education Association) that excessive focus on the resistance/complicity binary may detract from our ability to see who actually was promoting or protecting religious freedom in the instances when religious organizations were suppressed.[76]

Buddhists like Andō and Chikazumi did not "resist" the state in the sense of martyring themselves for their respective causes, but some groups and individuals did combat the official orthodoxy and risk persecution.[77] Yet I think it is crucial that some of these groups did not avail themselves of the legal language of religious freedom nearly as much as they appealed to the superior moral authority of religion. While it would be an overstatement to say that the language of religious freedom was unavailable to them, religious freedom was not yet understood to transcend or precede citizenship as a "human right" (see chapter 7). Appeals to religious freedom could therefore only occur within the confines of the national legal system as embodied by the constitution, while appeals to transcendent religious authority could challenge the system itself.

Sōka Kyōiku Gakkai

The Sōka Kyōiku Gakkai was established around 1928, although the name of the organization was first formalized on 18 November 1930 with the publication of the first volume of founder Makiguchi Tsunesaburō's (1871–1944) magnum opus *Sōka kyōiku taikei* (*Outline of Value-Creation Education*).[78] In the late 1920s, Makiguchi had been introduced to Nichiren Shōshū (the Correct Nichiren Sect), and he quickly recognized that the *Lotus sūtra* and the teachings of the thirteenth-century Buddhist saint Nichiren (1222–82) aligned with his pedagogical method of "value creation" (*sōka*). Makiguchi wanted to use education to create a Japan-centric global utopia based on the principles of the *Lotus sūtra*.

When Makiguchi and several other high-ranking leaders of Sōka Kyōiku Gakkai were arrested in July 1943, the initial report in the Special Higher Police monthly magazine *Tokkō geppō* suggested that Makiguchi had said several unpatriotic things concerning the emperor, the Imperial Rescript on Education, and the Ise Shrines. These crimes were punishable under the Peace Preservation Law (an originally anticommunist piece of legislation that was revised in 1941 to include thought crimes and lèse-majesté). Moreover, Makiguchi's followers had been attacking worship of anything other than the calligraphic mandala venerated by the Nichiren sect, burning and discarding others' talismans, amulets, and household altars in flagrant displays of exclusivist and single-minded devotion to their religious truth. In extreme cases, housewives would conduct such "eliminating the slander of the dharma" in their own homes while their husbands were out, leading to a concerning rise in divorce.[79]

The Special Higher Police arrested and convicted Makiguchi under the Peace Preservation Law in part because he had incited his followers to destroy others' religious paraphernalia. Safeguarding "peace and order" in this particular case meant attacking one religious group in order to protect the rights of other citizens to worship as they chose. While the Special Higher Police were probably not operating out of any high-minded principle of protecting religious freedom (they did not specifically mention safeguarding religious freedom as a rationale for the arrest), the effect of their actions was to draw a distinction between "acceptable" and "unacceptable" religious practice. Following the logic of Article 28 of the Meiji Constitution, preserving "peace and order" served to demarcate the purview of "religious freedom."

Makiguchi Tsunesaburō under Interrogation

Because Makiguchi died in prison in 1944, he would seem to represent an ideal example of principled resistance to state authority during the war years. Indeed, Sōka Gakkai literature has traditionally depicted him as a champion of religious freedom.[80] Yet when he was interrogated by the Special Higher Police in July and August of 1943, Makiguchi was more likely to appeal to the transcendent authority of the *Lotus sūtra* than he was to refer to the legal concept of religious freedom.[81] Under interrogation, he spoke without remorse about having directed upward of five hundred people to destroy amulets, talismans, and domestic altars, an admission that ensured that he would languish in prison for the short remainder of his life.[82]

Indeed, unlike his Buddhist contemporary Seno'o Girō (1889–1961), Makiguchi's principled resistance was not based on civil libertarian ideals or socialist ideas of equality.[83] In part this was because Makiguchi regarded the Constitution of the Empire of Japan as a mere "trace" of the original law of the Buddhist dharma.[84] The constitutional provision of religious freedom was therefore subordinate to the Nichiren Buddhist injunction to castigate those who failed to pay obeisance to the calligraphic mandala used as the central object of worship (*gohonzon*) in the Nichiren Shōshū sect to which Makiguchi belonged. For Makiguchi, the primary objective of his organization in the age of the declining dharma, or *mappō*, was to ensure that as many people as possible embraced the teachings of the *Lotus* as their sole faith. During his interrogation by the Special Higher Police, Makiguchi stated repeatedly that both the emperor above and the people below must accept the truth presented by the *gohonzon* of Nichiren Shōshū.[85]

The open-ended questions that begin the interrogation record suggest that the questioners aimed to get Makiguchi to speak candidly about his teachings in the hope that he would inadvertently divulge incriminating information. They need not have tried such subterfuge, for Makiguchi seemed wholly unconcerned with threats to his well-being.[86] He spoke at length about Nichiren Shōshū doctrine. Without any prompting, he acknowledged that he had referred to the emperor as an "ordinary man" (*bonbu*) and had directly encouraged followers to burn any religious accoutrements that might impugn the sanctity of the Nichiren Shōshū *gohonzon*.

Although he might have been expected to appeal to religious freedom as a way of minimizing his sentence or being acquitted, the interrogation records suggest that it was not the imprisoned Makiguchi who exhibited the greatest concern with religious freedom, but rather the anonymous investigator(s) who conducted the interrogation. Clearly the Special Higher Police were not worried about whether Makiguchi's arrest infringed on *his* religious freedom, but the rationale for his arrest indirectly highlighted the way that the concept of "religious freedom" operated in conjunction with its twin concept of "peace and order" in law enforcement during the Pacific War. Makiguchi's orders to his followers put the police in the uncomfortable position of having to determine the boundary between liberty and security, or between the conflicting religious freedoms of multiple parties.

My argument here is about effect rather than intention. The interrogation record offers no direct evidence that the Special Higher Police aimed to protect the religious freedom of the aggrieved victims who had been subject to the violent Gakkai intrusions into their homes. Yet the law enforcement aspect of religious freedom is premised on the state's legitimated use of violence to protect people's right to worship as they choose and—when necessary—to actually use that violence to intervene when one religious group threatens the religious freedom of another. In the case of Makiguchi's arrest, preserving "peace and order" was fundamentally a concern that some people's rights to worship as they wished were being trampled upon by the zealous Nichirenist lay Buddhists, with deleterious side effects like divorce.

A secondary point concerns the emperor and the question of how the ambiguous concept of lèse-majesté overlapped with the equally ambiguous concept of religious freedom. In the context of questioning Makiguchi about his ideal of converting the entire world to Nichiren Buddhism, the seemingly incompatible dictates of religious freedom and absolute imperial authority curiously aligned when the interrogator asked with evident surprise whether his majesty the emperor had any real choice in whether to venerate the Nichiren Shōshū *gohonzon*. Makiguchi's response was an unequivocal "no." While he was careful to indicate his respect for the emperor and clearly saw the emperor as playing a crucial part in the eventual conversion of Japan, there was no room for the emperor to adopt a different religious view. The anonymous interrogator's abrupt shift to a different line of questioning after this exchange makes it difficult to determine whether he found this response discomfiting (because it so explicitly challenged imperial authority) or satisfying (because it established Makiguchi's guilt beyond doubt).

While the Special Higher Police probably intended to stamp out heresies that denigrated the majesty of the sanctified *kokutai* and the imperial person (they referred to the destruction of Ise talismans as "sacrilege," after all), they found it equally important to *protect* religious freedoms insofar as they needed to preserve the rights of ordinary citizens to worship as they pleased. Protecting "peace and order" was, in this sense, protecting religious freedom.[87] The flamboyant actions of Makiguchi and his followers, such as burning and discarding valuable and emotionally laden domestic altars, were too blatant for the police to ignore. Those actions *did* disturb peace and order, and the right of Sōka Kyōiku Gakkai members to uphold their exclusivist commitment to what they saw as the true teaching had to be balanced against the right of others to worship as they saw fit. This tension between security and liberty is a perennial problem in the enforcement of legal guarantees of religious freedom, as is adherents' flagrant disregard for temporal law for the sake of their sincerely held beliefs. Seen in this light, Makiguchi appears in the interrogation record not as a martyr for religious freedom, but as a champion of a Buddhist exclusivism that had no need for such legal niceties.

MOVING BEYOND THE RESISTANCE/COMPLICITY BINARY

Brian Victoria was indisputably correct in one respect when he said that "each and every Japanese Buddhist did have a choice to make" about his or her relationship with the Japanese state during a period characterized by imperial expansion, draconian policing, and military adventurism. Buddhists in the early Shōwa era had choices. They could interpret religious freedom as a freedom of conscience that demanded preferential treatment for majority religions while excluding minority religions (Chikazumi). They could see religious freedom as something best protected by a paternal state that disaggregated the external aspects of religion from matters of conscience and belief (Andō). Or they could effectively dismiss religious freedom as a mundane concern that distracted from loftier soteriological aims (Makiguchi). This list is certainly not exhaustive, and no doubt other types of religious people envisioned religious freedom differently. But in their respective ways, each of the three cases examined above raises potentially counterintuitive ideas about religious freedom in early Shōwa era Japan.

The case of Chikazumi Jōkan showed that the question of why Buddhists failed to resist oppressive legislation is the wrong question. Chikazumi and his allies fiercely opposed unpalatable legislation by holding lecture meetings, writing letters to politicians, and publishing strident pamphlets. These lobbying efforts have probably been overlooked to date because Chikazumi's illiberal rhetoric does not easily match up with postwar expectations for what "resistance" might have looked like. His vision was based on an unwavering commitment to the separation of religion from politics, but if we expect proponents of religious freedom to espouse egalitarian stances as a matter of course, then we miss Chikazumi's vigorous activism on behalf of an illiberal and antiegalitarian freedom. Chikazumi ultimately lost in the debates over how to construct Japan's ideal religions system, but his case offers an example of Buddhist resistance to state policies that was not politically progressive.[88] He focused on the narrow aim of preserving customary rights for Buddhists while denying equal rights to adherents of foreign religions.

Like Chikazumi, Andō presents a potentially counterintuitive image to the postwar observer. His complicity with the top-down administrative projects of the Japanese state is indisputable. While in the postwar years he passed himself off as a pawn with little clout in the Japanese wartime hierarchy, it is clear that he was a prominent Buddhist layperson who eagerly participated in yoking Buddhism to the war effort and apparently had few qualms about using his status as a former Buddhist priest to encourage Buddhists to join in his political projects (or to convince policy makers and legislators that he had his finger on the pulse of the Buddhist world).[89] Yet in his contributions to the Religious Organizations Law, Andō also aimed to protect religious freedom as he understood it. If Chikazumi complicates the idea of liberal "resistance," Andō complicates the idea of quietist Buddhist compliance with statist agendas.

Finally, Makiguchi Tsunesaburō's story is superficially that of an unjustly persecuted martyr who died in prison protesting his religious freedom. But Makiguchi had little use for religious freedom when mounting his defense. His interrogators even provided him with a chance to invoke the Japanese constitution, presumably a prime opportunity to seek exoneration for his crimes through appeal to Article 28. But whatever the constitution might have said, for Makiguchi it was a mere trace of the true teaching represented by the *Lotus sūtra*. His staunch exclusivism did not allow for a worldview in which religious affiliation was a matter of choice.[90]

There is no doubt that the war years were oppressive, that the Japanese military and Special Higher Police engaged in atrocious acts, and that parties representing a wide range of demographics readily mobilized religious ideas to sanctify violence.[91] Religious groups were quashed. People died in prison. Clerics sacrificed significant material resources in support of

Japan's quixotic war.[92] The purpose of this chapter has not been to deny these historical facts, but rather to add nuance to accounts that have too readily described Buddhists in caricature: as myopic sycophants who sucked up to the state in pursuit of preferential treatment, as principled progressives who fought state power, or as martyrs who died for the sake of religious freedom.

Part 2 of this book will show how the idea that Japanese religious leaders were ignorant of religious freedom emerged as a way of justifying the Occupation policy of promoting religious freedom in Japan. It was only by arguing that religious freedom was absent that Occupation policy makers could set about the process of establishing it. However, while the occupiers were ostensibly teaching the Japanese people about the importance of religious freedom, in actuality both parties were learning to think of religious freedom in a whole new way.

FIGURE 1. Dai Nippon Teikoku Kōgun Imonkai (Society for the Consolation of the Imperial Army of the Great Japanese Empire), "Praying for the Imperial Army's Certain Victory (Inset: The Main Hall of Meiji Shrine)," n.d. The image from the period of the Fifteen Years' War (1931–45) depicts an older child leading younger children in bowing to the Meiji Shrine. Image courtesy of Special Collections and College Archives, Skillman Library, Lafayette College, and the East Asia Image Collection (http://digital.lafayette.edu/collections/eastasia/).

FIGURE 2. Kushida Naokan (d.u.), "Dawn Prayers at the Village Shrine," n.d. This postcard image from the period of the Fifteen Years' War (1931–45) depicts veneration at small local shrines as a part of daily routine. Image courtesy of Special Collections and College Archives, Skillman Library, Lafayette College, and the East Asia Image Collection (http://digital.lafayette.edu/collections/eastasia/).

FIGURE 3. Fukiya Kōji (1898–1979), "A Visit to Yasukuni Shrine," n.d. This postcard, included in a New Year's issue of the girls' magazine *Shōjo Club*, depicts shrine visits as a leisure activity for young women. The text reads: "Today Yukiko once again invited a friend to visit Yasukuni Shrine in Kudan [central Tokyo]. Walking home after expressing heartfelt thanks to the nation-protecting glorious spirits and wishing for the great victory of the imperial army, the early spring sunshine brightly illuminates their surroundings." Image courtesy of Special Collections and College Archives, Skillman Library, Lafayette College, and the East Asia Image Collection (http://digital.lafayette.edu/collections/eastasia/).

FIGURE 4. Norman Rockwell (1894–1978), "Save Freedom of Worship: Buy War Bonds," poster, Washington, DC, 1943. This popular propaganda poster, based on a "Four Freedoms" series originally published in the *Saturday Evening Post* in February 1943, treated the war as a battle for religious freedom. Image from University of North Texas Libraries, Digital Library, digital.library.unt.edu; crediting UNT Libraries Government Documents Department (digital .library.unt.edu/ark:/67531/metadc262/). Printed by permission of the Norman Rockwell Family Agency. © 1943 The Norman Rockwell Family Entities.

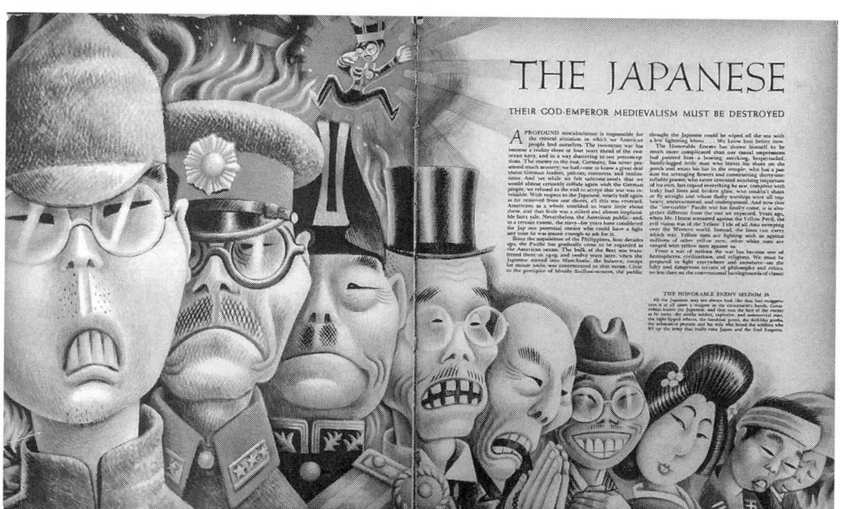

THE JAPANESE

THEIR GOD-EMPEROR MEDIEVALISM MUST BE DESTROYED

A PROFOUND miscalculation is responsible for the critical situation in which we American people find ourselves. The two-ocean war has become a reality three or four years ahead of the two-ocean navy, and in a way shattering to our preconceptions. The enemy to the east, Germany, has never presented much mystery; we had come to know a great deal about German leaders, politics, resources, and institutions. And yet while we felt subconsciously that we would almost certainly collide again with the German people, we refused to the end to accept that war was inevitable. With respect to the Japanese, nearly half again as far removed from our shores, all this was reversed. Americans as a whole troubled to learn little about them, and that little was a stilted and almost implausible fairy tale. Nevertheless, the American public—and, to a certain extent, the navy—for years have considered the Jap one potential enemy who could have a fight any time he was insane enough to ask for it.

Since the acquisition of the Philippines, four decades ago, the Pacific has gradually come to be regarded as *the* American ocean. The bulk of the fleet was transferred there in 1919, and twelve years later, when the Japanese moved into Manchuria, the balance, except for minor units, was concentrated in that ocean. Clear to the precipice of bloody disillusionment, the public thought the Japanese could be wiped off the sea with a few lightning blows . . . We know him better now.

The Honorable Enemy has shown himself to be much more complicated than our casual impressions had painted him—a bowing, smirking, bespectacled, bandy-legged little man who leaves his shoes on the porch and wears his hat in the temple; who has a passion for arranging flowers and constructing thirty-one-syllable poems; who never invented anything important of his own, but copied everything he saw, complete with leaky fuel lines and broken glass; who couldn't shoot or fly straight and whose flashy warships were all top-heavy, underarmored, and undergunned. And now that the "inevitable" Pacific war has finally come, it is altogether different from the one we expected. Years ago, when Mr. Hearst screamed against the Yellow Peril, the evil vision was of the Yellow Tide of all Asia sweeping over the Western world. Instead, the lines run every which way. Yellow men are fighting with us against millions of other yellow men; other white men are ranged with yellow men against us.

From a war of nations the war has become one of hemispheres, civilizations, and religions. We must be prepared to fight everywhere and anywhere—on the lofty and dangerous terrain of philosophy and ethics no less than on the conventional battlegrounds of classic

THE HONORABLE ENEMY SELDOM IS

All the Japanese may not always look like this, but exaggeration is at all times a weapon in the caricaturist's hands. Covarrubias knows the Japanese, and thus sees the face of the enemy as he turns—the toothy soldier, capitalist, and commercial man, the tight-lipped officers, the fanatical priest, the doll-like geisha, the submissive peasant and his wife who breed the soldiers who fill up the army that really runs Japan and the God Emperor.

FIGURE 5. *Fortune* magazine, "The Japanese: Their God-Emperor Medievalism Must Be Destroyed," February 1942. This two-page opening spread in *Fortune* featured Japanese stereotypes at the beginning of a long article on Japanese cultural traits and political history. The caption in the bottom right reads: "All the Japanese may not always look like this, but exaggeration is at all times a weapon in the caricaturist's hands. [Miguel] Covarrubias [the famous Mexican caricaturist, 1904–57] knows the Japanese, and thus sees the face of the enemy as he turns—the toothy soldier, capitalist, and commercial man, the tight-lipped officers, the fanatical priest, the doll-like geisha, the submissive peasant and his wife who breed the soldiers who fill up the army that really runs Japan and the God Emperor." When this image first appeared in *Fortune* in February 1942, the "fanatical priest" (*center right*) represented Buddhism, not Shintō.

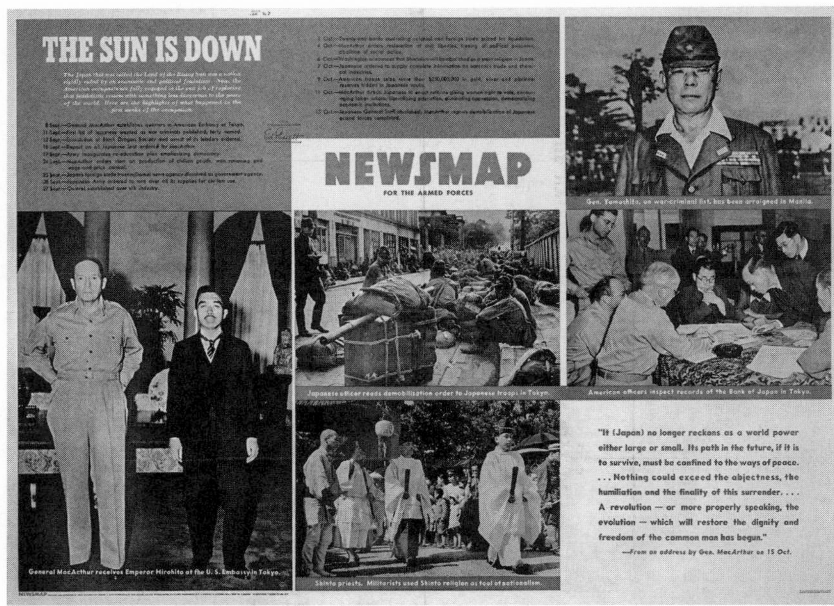

FIGURE 6. US Army Information Branch, "Newsmap for the Armed Forces: The Sun Is Down," New York, 22 October 1945. This infographic for military personnel breathlessly announces the rapid reforms conducted during the first six weeks of the Occupation. It makes note of the surprise US State Department announcement on 6 October 1945 that Shintō would be disestablished; an accompanying photo caption at the bottom center describes Shintō as a tool used by warmongering militarists. University of North Texas Libraries, Digital Library, digital.library.unt.edu; crediting UNT Libraries Government Documents Department. (Stable URL: http://digital.library.unt.edu/ark:/67531/metadc849/.)

FIGURE 7. US Army Information Branch, "Newsmap for the Armed Forces: End of a Myth," New York, 14 January 1946. This infographic for military personnel announces several of the "negative reforms" of the Occupation: formal disestablishment of Shintō, abolition of the "feudal land system," discontinuation of courses in geography, morals, and history in public schools, and the emperor's famed renunciation of his divinity. University of North Texas Libraries, Digital Library, digital.library.unt.edu; crediting UNT Libraries Government Documents Department. (Stable URL: http://digital.library.unt.edu/ark:/67531/metadc836/.)

FIGURE 8. Kitaura Keitarō (1887–1954), "Religious Freedom Is Protected (Constitution Article 20)," 1947. This image from an illustrated primer on the new constitution depicts the new legal guarantee of religious freedom by depicting three members of a family engaged in three different types of religious practice: The father (*right*) chants the title of the *Lotus sūtra*, the daughter (*top left*) sings a Christian hymn, and the son (*bottom left*) chants a Shintō *norito*. From Kitaura Keitarō, *Zukai kenpō* (Nara: Nara Nichinichi Shinbunsha, 1947).

THE OCCUPATION OF RELIGIOUS STUDIES

5

STATE SHINTŌ AS A HERETICAL SECULARISM

> In entering the war we, peoples who based our hopes for civilization upon the triumph of universalism and human freedom, were sending our armed forces against a mighty war machine. But of even greater importance, from a long range point of view, is the fact that we were opposing our ideals of the equality of man, of self-government, of freedom, and of peace, to powerful and contradictory ideas which must be charged with much of the responsibility for Japan's aggressive militarism—the Shintō conceptions that the islands of Japan, the people, and their ruler are divine, that their mission is to conquer the world, and that all peoples owe homage to the divine emperor whose authority is absolute.
>
> ROBERT OLESON BALLOU (1945)[1]

ON 6 JANUARY 1941, ALMOST EXACTLY eleven months before the Japanese bombing of Pearl Harbor, US President Franklin D. Roosevelt (1882–1945) delivered one of the most noteworthy foreign policy speeches of his career. Roosevelt justified America's material contributions to the war then raging on the European continent by suggesting that Americans were united with their European brethren in defense of what he termed the "Four Freedoms": freedom of speech, freedom of everyone to "worship God in his own way," freedom from fear, and freedom from want. Eager to convince isolationist Americans to redouble their efforts in supporting a war taking place on other shores, he closed his speech with the following rousing statement:

> This nation has placed its destiny in the hands and heads and hearts of its millions of free men and women; and its faith in freedom under the guidance of God. Freedom means the supremacy of human rights everywhere. Our support goes to those who struggle to gain those rights or keep them. Our strength is in our unity of purpose.
>
> To that high concept there can be no end save victory.[2]

The articulation of universal freedoms in Roosevelt's January 1941 State of the Union address marked the importance of religious freedom in American visions of why the conflict now known as the Second World War needed to be fought. It also happened to be the first time the phrase "human rights" was used in any major American policy statement. However, "human rights" functioned in the speech as a rhetorical flourish, not as a programmatic outline of foreign policy. Indeed, at the time many policy makers were unclear as to what the phrase meant.[3]

In the wake of the Japanese bombing of Pearl Harbor on 7 December 1941, the language of the "Four Freedoms" and the productively ambiguous concept of human rights came to serve a different purpose by rationalizing why Americans were fighting and dying for the sake of others abroad. Hostilities with the Japanese were structured from the outset by a dualistic understanding of a free America and a totalitarian Japan, and religious freedom in particular featured prominently in the racist propaganda blitz that accompanied the Pacific War (figure 4). American Christianity appeared opposite "ultranationalism," emperor worship, and a mystical and vaguely threatening *bushidō* (the way of the warrior). The image of the inscrutable, fanatical Japanese soldier who eschewed personal freedom in favor of his unthinking loyalty to an emperor with false presumptions to divinity served as a foil for the image of the enfranchised American citizen who was free to "worship God in his own way." Like all good propaganda, this approach thoroughly othered the enemy. It also created an American national identity that was freedom-loving and Christian (or, in a contemporaneously emerging phrase, "Judeo-Christian").[4]

Japan had expanded well into Asia and the Pacific by 1942 and seemed poised to take over all of Asia. The Cairo Declaration of November 1943 announced the cooperation of the United States, China, and Great Britain in forestalling this threat by guaranteeing Japan's swift and utter defeat. Surrender ultimately came in the wake of an indiscriminate firebombing campaign in spring 1945 and the Americans' unprecedented use of atomic weapons that August. These military strategies made no distinction between non-combatants and combatants. They operated from the presupposition that Japanese men, women, and children required terrifying punishment. Propaganda posters likened Japanese people to vermin and called for their extermination. Popular magazines painted the war as a clash of civilization and medieval barbarity (figure 5). In their defense of human rights, the Allies thoroughly dehumanized the Japanese enemy.[5]

Even as the American military systematically rendered Japan's metropolitan areas to ashes and killed hundreds of thousands of noncombatant citizens with devastating technology in the spring of 1945, policy makers began hashing out plans for a postwar occupation. Article 10 of the Potsdam Declaration of 26 July 1945 stressed that establishing religious freedom would be a fundamental aim in the rehabilitation of Japan after the island nation's inevitable surrender.[6] Upon Japan's unconditional surrender following Emperor Hirohito's (1901–89) 15 August 1945 declaration that the war was lost, the vision laid out in the Potsdam Declaration suddenly needed to become reality. Freedom of speech, religion, and thought needed to be guaranteed. Respect for human rights needed to be established.

But how? These lofty terms had to be clarified for the occupying army to do its recuperative work, but it would quickly become clear that the occupiers understood rights and freedoms in wildly divergent ways. Figuring out how to change Japanese hearts and minds was also no easy task, and determining whether any changes had actually stuck was almost impossible. The Allied Occupation of Japan began as a difficult project not because the Japanese were recalcitrant, but rather because the operative terms guiding Occupation policy were vague and because the occupiers themselves disagreed about priorities and guiding principles.

While the Occupation therefore exhibited contradictory impulses due to the conflicting initiatives of competing interest groups, some general policy orientations affected how the project of establishing religious freedom was linked to the broader project of democratization. In the civilizationalist framework preferred by Supreme Commander MacArthur and influential figures in the executive branch of the US government, democracy was a product of Christian culture that needed to be implanted in Japan.[7] Characterized first and foremost by a "religious freedom" that was really the freedom to worship the Christian god, this Christ-centric democracy would serve double duty as a replacement for Japan's prewar and wartime state cult and as a bulwark against the "godless communism" that was then flourishing on the Asian continent.

Although it exhibited global aspirations, this particularist understanding of religious freedom was intrinsically ill-suited for transnational application. Religious freedom was a crucial ingredient of the democratic brew that the occupiers prescribed for Japan's ills, but the recipe needed tweaking to be effective. It had to lose its American flavor and Christian odor.

The legal purview of religious freedom also needed to expand. The unique circumstances of the Occupation created a peculiar situation in which religious freedom could no longer be a right simply granted to citizens by their states. One national government dictated policy; another enacted it. Religious freedom therefore had to become something more than a mere civil liberty. It had to transcend the rights, privileges, and duties that attended national citizenship. It had to be made timeless. It had to become innate, universal, and unquestionable. In short, religious freedom had to become a human right.

Abstract theorization about religious freedom as a human right had taken place in rarefied contexts prior to the Occupation, but while Roosevelt had implied that "freedom to worship God in [one's] own way" was one of the human rights America aimed to protect, religious-freedom-as-human-right did not yet exist because nobody had figured out how to enforce it. It was only over the course of the Occupation that religious freedom actually became a human right in any concrete sense. My discussion of the Occupation in the next several chapters shows how religious freedom became a human right through collaborations between bureaucrats and academics, journalists and legal experts, Americans and their Japanese interlocutors. Simply put, the occupiers did not introduce the human right of religious freedom to a place where it was absent. Rather, the peculiar circumstances of the Occupation demanded that they cooperate with Japanese people in inventing it. This chapter outlines a first step in this process. My argument is that the occupiers invented the concept of "State Shintō" so that they could eradicate a state religion and replace it with religious freedom as a universal ideal.

THE CREATION AND DESTRUCTION OF STATE SHINTŌ

On 7 October 1945, the chief of the Far East Division of the US Department of State, John Carter Vincent (1900–1972), made a striking comment on NBC's "University of the Air" radio program. Unbeknownst to the policy makers in Tokyo who had just promulgated a civil liberties directive guaranteeing freedom of religion in Japan a mere three days before, Vincent casually outlined a drastic shift in State Department policy.[8] Whereas the people responsible for both presurrender and immediate postsurrender policy had generally avoided making any explicit, specific mention of Shintō in favor of advancing generic platitudes about the ideal of promoting religious freedom in Japan, Vincent made it clear that Shintō was to be the target of radical American intervention. "Shintoism insofar as it is a religion of individual Japanese is not to be interfered with," he proclaimed. "Shintoism, however, insofar as it is directed by the Japanese Government and is a measure enforced from above by the Government, is to be done away with. . . . Shintoism as a state religion, National Shintō, that is, will go."[9]

If the *New York Times* editorial page is any indication of national sentiment, then American audiences embraced Vincent's statement as an epochal first step in establishing "real religious freedom" in Japan.[10] However, it caught Occupation officials and their Japanese counterparts by surprise (see figure 6). A flurry of correspondence ensued as officials stationed in Japan sought to clarify a policy that had not been previously established as an official Occupation directive. Communication between Occupation diplomatic advisor Dean Acheson (1893–1971) and US secretary of state James F. Byrnes (1882–1972) finally confirmed, in line with Vincent's precipitous and very public statements, that the new policy was to eradicate "National Shintō" while not interfering with Shintō "insofar as it [was] a religion of individual Japanese."[11]

This administrative scramble for clarification of policy was followed by a momentous bureaucratic undertaking. Responding to the communiqué from the State Department, Occupation Civil Information and Education Section chief Ken R. Dyke (d.u.) instructed Lieutenant William K. Bunce (1907–2008) to draft a directive outlining the new policy. Unfortunately, Bunce was given little guidance as to how to proceed. Bunce was not only not an expert in religion of any sort, but he was also in the difficult position of having to navigate between the Scylla of promoting religious freedom and the Charybdis of eliminating the apparently privileged status granted to a specific religion.[12] Moreover, he was under pressure to complete the directive quickly.

By most accounts, Bunce performed his job as admirably as anyone might under such unenviable circumstances.[13] He undertook a crash course on Japanese religions, reading voraciously and consulting with University of Tokyo assistant professor of religious studies Kishimoto Hideo (1903–64).

Two months and many drafts later, he produced the "Staff Memorandum on State Shintō." This document served as the basis for the 15 December 1945 Shintō Directive that formally divorced Shintō from governance and public school education.[14]

The impact of the Shintō Directive was considerable. The effects on Japanese religious institutions and education were both immediate and profound, but the document also had an international impact in that it represented an opportunity for Americans to juxtapose "their" particular variety of religion-state relations with a Japanese variety. This act of juxtaposition was a watershed historical moment that initiated a global process of articulating how the ideal of religious freedom should operate in international relations and transnational contexts.

The 3 December 1945 Staff Memorandum on State Shintō was also a site for the confluence of academic, bureaucratic, and apologetic attempts to define "real religion" as apolitical and intrinsically personal. In portraying Shintō as an oppressive and particularist national religion, the memorandum provided a negative example against which the positive ideal of universal religious liberty could be set. The concept of State Shintō therefore played a crucial role in creating postwar understandings of religious freedom as a human right.

THE STAFF MEMORANDUM ON STATE SHINTŌ AND THE SHINTŌ DIRECTIVE

The Staff Memorandum on State Shintō encapsulated Bunce's reading of a range of anglophone scholarship by British, American, and Japanese scholars. It also reflected the significant influence of his regular conversations with University of Tokyo professor of religious studies Kishimoto Hideo, who acted as an unofficial advisor to the occupiers on matters of religion and Japanese culture throughout the Occupation.[15] Kishimoto remembered Bunce as an assiduous student who earnestly took notes during their one-on-one tutorials on the basics of Japanese religion.[16] However, the professor also recalled that Bunce was determined to find evidence that supported the official US government view that Shintō was merely a tool used in the service of fostering ultranationalism.[17]

This inflexibility may have been partially a facet of Bunce's personality. In his later role as head of the Religions Division, Bunce politely but steadfastly resisted various interest groups' attempts to inject their preferences into Occupation religions policy.[18] However, Bunce's intractability on the specific issue of Shintō also derived from his incontrovertible orders from the State-War-Navy Coordinating Committee to eliminate "National Shintō," which influential parties in the US State Department understood to be a uniquely deleterious system of militarism, nationalism, and religious ritual that characterized Japanese governance.[19]

Bunce's orders reflected fundamental inconsistencies and even basic factual errors in policy makers' understandings of Shintō.[20] As his colleague William Woodard would later point out, policy makers were initially inclined to collapse several different strains of thought and practice into the catchall category of "National Shintō."[21] In Bunce's drafts, residual racist tendencies also appeared in the designation of Shintō as "primitive" and the dismissive claim that Japanese people were unanimously and fanatically dedicated to this state religion.[22] Bunce labeled this with the pejorative phrase "State Shintō."

Although the phrase "State Shintō" swiftly came to enjoy widespread currency, conceptually it remained vague. In the memorandum, Bunce circularly defined State Shintō as both a manifestation of ultranationalism and as its source (how "ultranationalism" could be distinguished from garden-variety nationalism was unclear). In his presentation, this State Shintō served as a tool that political and military elites had cynically used to foster citizens' loyalty to the emperor and the state as Japan had modernized (figure 6).[23] As a side effect of this process, Bunce argued, the state had not truly granted religious freedom to Japanese subjects, but had only begrudgingly pretended to do so under tremendous international pressure. The Japanese state had also violated its own constitutional provision of religious freedom by demanding that citizens manifest their loyalty by paying reverence at shrines, which Bunce understood to be an unambiguously religious practice.

In the first paragraph of the memorandum, "The Problem Presented," Bunce outlined what was to become the official Occupation position as follows:

> *State Shintō* has been used by militarists and ultranationalists in Japan to engender and foster a military spirit among the people and to justify a war of expansion. While the defeat, surrender, and subsequent occupation of

> Japan have undoubtedly done much to destroy the potency of Shintoism as a political force, until Shintō is separated from the state and instruction in Shintō is eliminated from the education system, there will always be the danger that Shintō will be used as an agency for disseminating militaristic and ultra-nationalistic ideology. In order to obviate this danger, the Supreme Commander for the Allied Powers has been directed to accomplish the separation of Shintō from the state and the elimination of Shintō from the education system.[24]

The last sentence of this opening paragraph indicates that although Bunce's memorandum officially served as an unbiased *descriptive* analysis of Japanese religion-state relations that could inform policy, it was actually a *prescriptive* account tailored to support a foreordained policy objective. This may have been bad scholarship in that it was deterministic, but it served its true purpose by providing authoritative academic support for the Occupation edict that officially disaggregated Shintō from all aspects of political and public life (figure 7).[25] A *Time* magazine editorial published on 24 December 1945 observed that the 15 December 1945 Shintō Directive "was more than formal separation of Church and State. It was the first official U.S. attempt to draw the fine line between genuinely religious doctrine and social propaganda."[26] Publication of this editorial on Christmas Eve 1945 was no doubt symbolically resonant with many Christian Americans at the time, and the cover of the magazine featured a Christian nativity scene with the title "The Christmas Event: Peace on Earth among Men of Good Will." Similar juxtapositions of Christian majoritarianism with Americans' celebration of the eradication of Shintō nationalism would occur time and again throughout the Occupation period.

In hindsight the *Time* assessment might seem a hyperbolic vestige of wartime jingoism, but Bunce's memorandum and the Shintō Directive that followed it actually crystallized a process of definition in which the boundaries of religion and the secular were demarcated in an unprecedented fashion for parties on either side of the Pacific. While it was certainly not the first formal attempt to highlight how religion would be addressed in Occupation policy, the memorandum was more theoretically sophisticated than earlier presurrender plans. It was also more detailed than the initial postsurrender policy documents that had vaguely gestured to the importance of promoting religious freedom as one of a raft of civil liberties. The memorandum was the first attempt to indicate precisely why religious freedom needed to be promoted in Japan, why the Japanese government's claims about religion-state relations deserved suspicion, and why existing constitutional law and parliamentary legislation—which included an explicit guarantee of religious freedom and formal separation of religion from the state—needed to be revised.

THE RELIGIOUS FREEDOM/STATE SHINTŌ BINARY

Bunce's portrayal derived from a tension between academic and bureaucratic visions of religion-state relations. His position as a mid-level bureaucratic functionary assigned to generate a study with a foreordained conclusion meant that scholarly inquiry took a backseat to political expediency. Despite Japanese claims that religion was actually separated from the state and that religious freedom had been protected under existing Japanese law, Bunce averred that the Japanese political status quo was not authentically a system of separation at all, but rather a state religion. Through the pejorative phrase "State Shintō," Bunce described prewar and wartime Japanese religion-state relations as illegitimate.

At the same time that he offered this diagnosis, Bunce used the term "religious freedom" to designate an ideal relationship between religions, citizens, and the state. The interpretation of ideal religion-state relations that resulted was pluralist in the sense that it posited religious freedom as a matter of elective choice and idealized the peaceful coexistence of different religious groups under the irenic banner of the secularist state. It was immanentist in that it treated religious freedom as an innate right shared by all humans, regardless of citizenship or creed. It was also unprecedented in that it began the process of affixing guarantees of religious freedom beyond the jurisdiction of one particular state, although it left open the vexing question of how exactly religious freedom should be protected in the inchoate framework of universal freedoms that was gathering under the rubric of human rights around that time.[27]

Yet in writing the Staff Memorandum on State Shintō, Bunce faced a serious problem because Japan explicitly did *not* have a constitutionally designated state religion.[28] Technically, Japan already had legal separation of religion and state, no explicit mention in the constitution of a national religion, and a constitutional guarantee of religious freedom. In actual practice, the relationship between religious ideas and Japanese politics was somewhat ambiguous, with Shintō-derived ideas of imperial divine descent and shrine-based rituals forming a major part of Japanese civic life (see chapter 1). As Vincent's radio broadcast and subsequent policy directives made clear, influential American policy makers had seized upon this ambiguity to blame Shintō for Japanese militarism during the course of the war; they therefore anticipated disestablishment in their planning for Japan's surrender.[29] Prominent figures like Supreme Commander Douglas MacArthur had also diagnosed the problem of Japanese militarism as "basically theological."[30] Bunce therefore had to selectively interpret recent Japanese history to find a national religion that could be targeted for eradication. State Shintō had to be created to be destroyed.

Bunce's Dilemma

Bunce was a conscientious man. He was tasked with disestablishing a national religion, but targeting one religion for negative treatment in the name of promoting religious freedom would have been hypocritical. At the same time, because of his orders he could not accept at face value the idea that religious freedom was actually guaranteed and that religion was separate from the state under existing Japanese constitutional law. Treating the Japanese constitutional model as valid would also have invited the unpalatable conclusion that multiple, equally acceptable modes of religion-state relations coexisted. While the extent to which Bunce formally thought through this dilemma is unclear, it seems that Bunce settled on treating Shintō as Japan's totalitarian, ultranationalistic national religion as a way to thoroughly deny the legitimacy of the Japanese distribution of the capacities of religion and state. This move not only delegitimized whatever versions of religious freedom may have existed in prewar and wartime Japan, but also positioned the occupiers' version of religious freedom as universal and unimpeachable.

Bunce needed help to make this argument, so he turned to anglophone academic scholarship on religion produced by American, British, and Japanese scholars. This research was useful because it was authoritative and therefore lent legitimacy to the Occupation project. It was also useful because religious studies scholarship consistently described shrine rites and imperial ritual alike as "religion," undermining claims that such rites served as expressions of patriotism or civic duty. If Bunce represented a sort of bureaucratic secularist project in that he was trying to reduce the impact of a state religion on Japanese public life, the authoritative tone of the scholarship he was reading derived from a different kind of secularist vision in which the scholar stands "outside" and dispassionately identifies certain social and cultural phenomena as "religious" through re-descriptive language.[31] Bunce relied on this academic secularist stance in identifying the political-bureaucratic secular of prewar Japan (what he came to call "State Shintō") as improper. The same authoritative stance allowed him to identify the American political-bureaucratic secular (what he called "religious freedom") as the only valid option for postwar Japan. His dependence on scholars of religion for his historical evidence combined with his nonnegotiable directives from the US Department of State, leading him to identify the Japanese political system as a perversion of a universal norm.

Specifically, the bureaucratic mandate to limit the impact of religion on Japanese public life led Bunce to try to figure out just what Japanese religion was. He relied on research by scholars of religion, who tended to understand all ritual practices and all empirically unverifiable claims as inherently and unambiguously "religious." Christian missionary tendencies also exerted considerable influence on the anglophone scholarship that Bunce consulted, particularly the works of his main academic source D. C. Holtom (1884–1962).[32] The staff memorandum reflected Holtom's missionary apologetics by contrasting Shintō's alleged particularism with a set of abstract liberal principles associated with evolutionarily advanced "universal religions" like Protestant Christianity.

These various bureaucratic, academic, and apologetic impulses operated synergistically in Bunce's account, but not without internal tension. His superiors saw religion as a polluting influence on governance and vice versa, but they also saw religious freedom and separation of religion from the state as uniquely Western, even Christian, contributions to world civilization. Policy makers easily slid between these two idioms when discussing religious freedom and ideal religion-state relations for postwar Japan, often with confusing results.[33] Did Japan need to Christianize in order to institute democracy and experience "proper" religious freedom? If so, what kind of religious freedom worth the name demanded conversion to a particular religion?

As a way of threading a line between these mutually contradictory objectives, Bunce's memorandum adopted the strategy of treating Japan's ostensibly secularist existing system of religion-state relations as a national religion.[34] This allowed him to fulfill his professional duties (he had to eliminate a national religion) and provided a suitable rationale for predetermined Occupation reforms (promoting religious freedom). Bunce's strategy also had lasting consequences in that it used the category "State Shintō"—a category that until that point had not enjoyed consistent academic or bureaucratic usage within or outside of Japan—to designate one variety of religion-state relations as aberrant while using "religious freedom" to designate a different variety of religion-state relations as normative and universal.[35]

Exclusive Similarity and State Shintō as Heresy

Bunce settled on the language of State Shintō because the phrase allowed him to describe prewar and wartime Japanese claims about separation of religion and the state and protection of religious freedom as inherently flawed. This was an act of what Jason Ānanda Josephson has termed "exclusive similarity."[36] Briefly, as part of a larger argument about how the category of religion operates as a tool of statecraft, Josephson distinguished between "hierarchical inclusion," in which foreign or competing ideas are subsumed within a preexisting hierarchy as being simply different names for familiar concepts (he used the example of Japanese Buddhists understanding the Christian word *Deus* as just another name for the cosmic buddha Dainichi Nyorai), on the one hand, and "exclusive similarity," on the other. Whereas hierarchical inclusion accepts alternative viewpoints as essentially the same if outwardly different, exclusive similarity operates by treating alternative viewpoints as superficially similar but essentially different. Josephson applied this distinction to early encounters between Japanese and Europeans in which the abstract term "religion" was not yet established as a universal category that superseded cultural differences. In that historical context, both the Japanese and their Jesuit missionary counterparts had two options: they could treat the other as doing something essentially the same (Buddhism as a pale imitation of Christianity, for example), or they could treat the other as essentially different (Buddhism as heresy, from the Christian perspective).

Acts of exclusive similarity create categories such as "heresy" and "superstition" that in turn contribute to the construction of religious orthodoxy. Importantly, the creation of such orthodoxy is not limited to mere doctrinal distinctions, but also extends to the problem of whether religious or political authorities regard a certain set of beliefs and practices as acceptable "religion," spurious "superstition," or authoritative "science." Collectively, religion, the secular, and superstition form what Josephson has called a "trinary" of mutually constitutive forces.[37]

While Josephson's analysis focused on the category of religion in cross-cultural encounters, hierarchical inclusion and exclusive similarity can also take place in situations like the Occupation when competing secularist systems are juxtaposed and evaluated vis-à-vis one another. Bunce's study and the Shintō Directive that followed it used the phrase "State Shintō" to designate a particular variety of religion-state relations—the legal system enshrined in the Meiji Constitution and modulated through later legislation like the 1939 Religious Organizations Law—as similar to an implied norm but nevertheless illegitimate. Bunce acknowledged that the Japanese government had formally separated religion from the state but denied that the separation had been successful. This distinction was rhetorically effective because the very nomenclature of State Shintō implied that the target of critique was an oppressive, particularist religion that wedded religion to the state rather than separating religion from it. The one true model of religion-state relations and religious freedom existed among the Allied powers, and the self-appointed task of the American occupiers was to establish that model in Japan by eradicating the heretical abomination that currently existed.

THE SCHOLARSHIP THAT INFORMED THE STAFF MEMORANDUM ON STATE SHINTŌ

Tracing Bunce's citations of religious studies scholarship, in the remainder of this chapter I show how specific ideas were taken from their original contexts and used in the service of establishing the concept of "State Shintō" and then positioning that concept as the antithesis to "religious freedom." My aim is not only to show the provenance of the conceptual tools Bunce used to conduct his bureaucratic task of proving that Japan lacked religious freedom and therefore needed it, but also to show how religious studies expertise was marshaled in the service of formulating major international policy. This is important because the influence of religious studies scholarship on policy outlasted the Occupation and, as I will show in chapter 8, some intellectual orientations that developed during the Occupation continue to structure some of the rhetoric and discourse about global religious freedom today.

Bunce's Account

Bunce argued that the Japanese state gave Shintō undue political preference so that Shintō enjoyed preeminent status not only as a de facto national religion, but also as the ideological glue that undergirded Japanese militarism. He argued that religious freedom was paid mere lip service in the 1889 constitution, while in practice it was either ignored or violated. Together, these claims bolstered the Occupation initiative of designating certain ritual practices (venerating the emperor) and ideas (Japan as a divine nation) as essentially "religious" and therefore inappropriate in governance or public school education; they also provided theoretical rationales for positive Occupation reforms such as efforts to instill a "desire for religious freedom" in the Japanese people.

Bunce's memorandum cited a set of writings by British and American missionary-scholars such as W. G. Aston (1841–1911), Basil Hall Chamberlain (1850–1935), and D. C. Holtom (1884–1962), as well as books in English by Japanese scholars of religion such as Anesaki Masaharu (1873–1949) and Katō Genchi (1873–1965). Against the claim that shrine rites were civic rites rather than religious ritual, these scholars all deemed such rites as incontrovertibly part of Shintō and furthermore treated Shintō as "religion." While all of them also shared an evolutionary concept of religion that placed universalistic religions above "primitive" ones (usually, but not always, considered "national" or "ethnic"), they differed on how to position Shintō vis-à-vis other religions.

Shintō Is Primitive and Artificial: W. G. Aston and Basil Hall Chamberlain

Early twentieth century texts emphasized the primitive nature of Shintō because the emerging concept of world religions taxonomically organized religions by region and ranked them on a scale that invariably placed Protestant Christianity at the apex of religious evolution.[38] While specific criteria regarding how to position certain religions varied among scholars, by the turn of the century the basic rubric used by many scholars of religion placed "universal religions" above "ethnic" ones, with the presupposition that the particularism of ethnic religions such as Daoism and Shintō would lead to their eventual extinction, while the alleged universalism of missionary religions like Christianity (of course) and Buddhism (provided that it looked like Protestant Christianity) would ensure their survival. Bunce reproduced this view in the memorandum: "[State Shintō] does not, like a universal religion such as Christianity or Buddhism, center on the individual and thus transcend national boundaries. Of necessity, it is racialistic and nationalistic."[39]

Bunce reinforced this portrayal of Shintō's alleged particularity by reproducing D. C. Holtom's claim that Shintō was an outmoded religion that evolutionarily lagged behind occidental religions by some two to four thousand years.[40] He also cited British scholar W. G. Aston, who wrote in 1905 that Shintō was on the wane and that Christianity might eventually replace Japanese religions.[41] Aston, Holtom, and other British and American observers of Japan regularly referred to the "rudimentary" or "primitive" nature of Shintō in contrast to the advanced nature of Christianity. This conceptualization reappeared in Bunce's treatment of Shintō as "a primitive religion put to modern uses."[42]

Even as the memorandum portrayed Shintō as a crude instrument that could perform devastating ideological work, it also emphasized the artificial nature of modern Shintō in its indebtedness to Basil Hall Chamberlain's 1912 Rationalist Press Association pamphlet *The Invention of a New Religion*.[43] At a time when his compatriots were admiring Japan's rapid industrialization and wondering whether Japan might eventually eclipse Great Britain as the world's next great empire, Chamberlain wrote with awe and trepidation about the alacrity with which the Japanese populace had embraced the obviously fabricated ritual calendar and imperial mythology.[44] Chamberlain argued that the Japanese ruling class had shrewdly concocted an irrational state cult for the purposes of nation-building, a cult in which the state officials "believe even though [they] know it is not true."[45] Bunce cited Chamberlain's pamphlet in the memorandum to highlight the artificial and illegitimate nature of modern Shintō.[46]

Shintō Is Japan's Indigenous Religion: Anesaki Masaharu

British observers had some of the earliest words in the English-language scholarship on Shintō, but they certainly did not have the last. The Japanese academy had eagerly embraced the new field of the scientific study of religion in the middle of the Meiji era (1868–1912), and several young Japanese intellectuals traveled to Europe to study philology and comparative religion in the late nineteenth and early twentieth centuries.[47] Building upon the popularity of Inoue Tetsujirō's (1855–1944) lectures in the closing years of the nineteenth century, Tokyo Imperial University established a regular lecture (*kōza*) in religious studies (*shūkyōgaku*) in 1905 and a separate department for the subject in 1918.[48] Scholars in the university's Religious Studies Department became tremendously influential on Western understandings of Japanese religions over the first half of the twentieth century.[49] This was particularly true in the case of Anesaki Masaharu, who served as longtime chair of the department and who spent a year lecturing on Japanese religions and culture at Harvard University between 1914 and 1915.

The occupiers had hoped to enlist Anesaki's aid in the formulation of religions policy, but Anesaki's failing health precluded his participation (he died in 1949).[50] Anesaki's son-in-law and eventual successor as chair of the University of Tokyo Religious Studies Department, Kishimoto Hideo, served as primary advisor to the occupiers in his father-in-law's stead. Anesaki's interpretations therefore held particular influence on Occupation religions policy both directly (in his English-language publications on Japanese religions) and indirectly through his protégé Kishimoto. In addition to enjoying Kishimoto's private tutelage, Bunce consulted Anesaki's *A History of Japanese Religions* (a compilation of his lectures at Harvard University in 1914–15 that Anesaki finished in 1928 and published in 1930) and *The Religious Life of the Japanese People* (published in 1936 and revised in 1938). However, Bunce creatively read—or simply ignored—some of Anesaki's points about the status of Shintō vis-à-vis the state.

Anesaki's primary contribution to the academic conversation on Shintō was his treatment of Shintō as Japan's indigenous religion and his claim that it was a unique religion distinct from Buddhism. The claim was significant. It functioned apologetically, using religious studies terminology to identify *as religion* a set of ritual practices that Europeans and Americans were likely to have described as "heathen." This portrayal would come to dominate scholarship on Japanese religions for many decades, with the apologetic aspect of the project trumping several inconvenient historical truths: imperial ritual, shrine rites, and veneration of terrestrial and heavenly deities (*jingi*) at local and regional scales did not necessarily constitute a comprehensive system that could be called "Shintō"; kami veneration had not existed separate from Buddhism for much of Japanese history; and the modern creation of Shintō as a religion distinct from Buddhism was intimately connected with nativist and nationalist political projects.[51]

Anesaki was obviously aware of some of these historical facts even if he confusingly portrayed Shintō as a timeless native religion. In his 1930 English-language book Anesaki claimed that Shintō, as Japan's diffuse indigenous religion, came closest to the national religion of the Japanese people in a cultural sense. However, he was careful to distinguish between Shintō as a shared set of cultural values and ritual practices, on the one hand, and periodic attempts to wed Shintō to the authority of the state on the other. He also indicated that Buddhism, more than Shintō, had actually served as an official state religion for large spans of Japanese history.[52]

Anesaki was pessimistic about the fate of essentially agrarian Shintō in a rapidly industrializing empire. By no means did he assume that Shintō was Japan's indissoluble state religion when he revised his Harvard lectures in 1928.[53] In that book, Anesaki concluded his analysis of Shintō by dividing it into what he called "the official cult of the State" and the "Shintō bodies furnished with church organizations" (the Shintō sects). The former emphasized "the sanctity of the Throne" and "making the local sanctuary the centre of communal life." While officials had tried to mobilize this official Shintō against "dangerous thoughts," such actions constituted blatantly instrumental uses of Shintō doctrines for narrow political gain by "men who are anything but religious" whose sincerity was "not unquestionable."[54]

Anesaki's evident suspicion of political leaders' motives in distinguishing "civic" from "religious" Shintō reflected his academic predilections as much as it reflected historical fact. As his critique of state officials' claims that shrine rites were not religious indicates, Anesaki brought to his project a normative conception about what constituted "real" religion. His scholarly expertise allowed him to make this judgment about the proper relationship between Shintō, state, and society from *a pretend outside* that could both accept and challenge bureaucratic-political and theological claims. He viewed the "Shintō as nonreligion" claim as antithetical to the very criteria that allowed Shintō to be "Japan's indigenous religion."

While Anesaki treated "Shintō" as essentially religious and followed the academic trends of the day in regarding it as Japan's indigenous religion, he also appealed to evidentiary historiography when he questioned the claim that Shintō had always been associated with Japanese statecraft or had consistently served as the "national religion" of the Japanese people. For example, in a chapter entitled "Shintō, the National and Ethnic Religion" that appeared in the 1938 reprint of his 1936 book, Anesaki rather perplexingly undermined his own chapter title by arguing that descriptions of Shintō as Japan's national religion were "misleading, if not erroneous."[55] He agreed with the official government position that shrines were state institutions more than they were religious institutions, but he also pointed out the ambiguous status of shrine priests, who were nominally state employees but were actually financially supported by donations for their "religious" ritual services. Anesaki ultimately described Shintō as an indigenous tradition that infused Japanese religiosity but did not have a strong "religious" character or discrete identity; he treated the state cult as a largely successful attempt to "secularize" formerly religious institutions.

By acknowledging shrine rites as secular but insisting on Shintō's essentially "religious" nature, Anesaki gingerly questioned contemporaneous claims about the nonreligious status of Shintō. As a scholar of religion, Anesaki positioned himself "outside" both religion and politics, arrogating to himself a superior vantage point from which he could register suspicion of politicians' claims. His treatment of Shintō as both indigenous and unambiguously religious would be crucial for Bunce's project.

As a final point of interest, in a footnote to the passage from his 1930 book cited above, Anesaki criticized contemporary thinkers who "try to give a new interpretation on this national cult . . . import[ing] too much their own new ideas, often borrowed from Occidental thought, and their interpretations are often far-fetched and artificial."[56] Anesaki may have been obliquely referring to his junior colleague at the University of Tokyo, Katō Genchi.

Shintō Is the Universalistic National Religion of Japan: Katō Genchi

Katō Genchi was born the scion of a prestigious Buddhist temple in Tokyo, but he exhibited an ornery streak from an early age, first by joining the antisacerdotalist Bukkyō Seito Dōshikai (Fellowship of Puritan Buddhists) and then by breaking ranks with that group over differences of opinion about the group's mission.[57] Although they were born in the same year, Genchi was three years junior to Anesaki at Tokyo Imperial University, and like Anesaki he was greatly indebted to Inoue Tetsujirō's foundational lectures on comparative religion.[58]

Unlike Anesaki, however, Genchi never had the opportunity to study abroad. He nevertheless seems to have had considerable facility in English, and published not only in that language but also in German and (I think) Esperanto.[59] While Anesaki chaired the Religious Studies Department at Tokyo Imperial University, Genchi gave lectures on Shintō there for about twenty years (he was never made full professor).[60] He also founded the Meiji Japan Society and served as a professor at Kokugakuin University before his purge as part of Occupation reforms in late 1945. Genchi lived his later life in obscurity, but he retained a group of devoted students and continued to offer monthly lectures at his suburban home until his death.[61] Despite his prestigious academic appointments, Genchi's idiosyncratic views seem to have placed him at the periphery of academic circles. Yet despite his somewhat marginal position, Genchi would come to wield incredible influence on understandings of Shintō through his American protégé, D. C. Holtom.[62]

Genchi was the creator of the academic category of State Shintō, although he did not use the term negatively. In his landmark 1926 English-language book *A Study of Shintō*, he argued that Shintō was not only a universal "world religion," but one that equaled—if not surpassed—individualistic religions such as Christianity and Buddhism because of its unshakeable basis in Japanese ethnicity. He suggested that although State Shintō (*kokkateki Shintō*) was a secular arm of the state that could be subdivided into civic ritual performed at shrines (*jinja Shintō*) and national morality taught in schools (*kokutai Shintō*), in actuality all of these collectively formed a religion that was part and parcel of Japanese nationhood from time immemorial. "The present writer . . . advances the view that Shintō—the State Shintō as well as the Sectarian Shintō—is in very truth a religion, *i.e.*, the original religion of the Japanese people, or, otherwise stated, the religion of the Japanese people from the very beginning down to the present time."[63]

Likewise, in a 1935 English-language handbook entitled *What Is Shintō?* that was published by the Japanese Government Railways Board of Tourist Industry as part of its "Tourist Library" series, Genchi defined Shintō as "faith in the . . . Divine Rule of the nation," but distinguished it from the state religions of Western countries that were merely adopted a posteriori for mere political ends: Shintō was "the religion *a priori* of the heart and life of every Japanese subject." Indeed, a Japanese "never ceases to be a Shintōist," even if he or she had embraced another faith. Shintō therefore had "an aspect of particularism or separatism or exclusionism like Judaism, but at the same time it [was] by no means devoid of a noble spirit of religious universalism."[64]

Genchi went on to draw a distinction between "theocratic" religions such as Christianity and "theanthropic" religions such as Shintō; the latter were, in his view, actually more tolerant than Judaism, Christianity, and Mohammedanism.[65] His apologetic statements about what he called *kokkateki Shintō* (Statist Shintō) served as part of his larger project of asserting the unique and superior character of Japanese Shintō through the language of comparative religion.[66] This positive view of State Shintō provided fodder for Bunce's memorandum not only by giving him a concept articulated by a local intellectual, but also by presenting State Shintō as thoroughly pervasive, politically demanding, and inextricably linked to Japanese national and ethnic identity.

State Shintō Is Dangerous: D. C. Holtom

Genchi greatly influenced the American missionary-scholar Daniel Clarence Holtom, and it is through the medium of Holtom's writings that his understanding of State Shintō came to wield such inordinate influence on Allied postsurrender policy.[67] While Holtom was generally sympathetic to the Japanese people and notably resistant to his compatriots' vitriolic anti-Japanese sentiment, he took an increasingly suspicious stance toward Shintō over the course of his academic career. Holtom had been asked to serve as an advisor or overseer of religious affairs in the Occupation military government, but he declined, citing his poor health.[68] It must be noted that Holtom was *the* authority on Shintō in the United States at the onset of the Occupation, and his previously obscure books were required reading for policy makers who had been preparing for Japan's defeat in 1945.[69] When Holtom demurred, Walter Nichols, who had grown up in the Kansai region as the son of an Episcopal bishop and had some facility with the Japanese language, took on the role of liaison with Shintō groups for the Religions Division.[70]

Holtom was a Baptist missionary who spent most of his adult life in Japan.[71] He moved to Japan to begin his missionary work in 1910, and during his time in the country he served as professor of modern languages at Tokyo Gakuin (1914–15), professor of church history at Japan Baptist Theological Seminary (1915–25), professor of history at Kantō Gakuin (1926–36), and dean of theology at Aoyama Gakuin (1936–40). At some point during this time, probably in the late 1910s or the very early 1920s, Holtom studied Shintō under Katō Genchi's supervision.[72] Although he had traveled back to the United States periodically for short lectureships during his long tenure in Japan, Holtom returned to the United States for good in 1941. From there he watched the developments of the Pacific War from afar while periodically offering his expertise on Shintō through contributions to government policies, academic journals, university lectures, radio programs, and missionary magazines. Holtom delivered Haskell Lectures at the University of Chicago in the summer of 1940 that were published in 1943 as a book entitled *Modern Japan and Shintō Nationalism*. That book, along with *The National Faith of Japan* (1938) and his doctoral dissertation, the *Political Philosophy of Modern*

Shintō (1922), were the main sources of information on Shintō for Bunce as he set Occupation disestablishment policy.[73]

While Holtom's early writings were hardly apologetic, they were somewhat sympathetic, and he was obviously at pains to show non-Japanese people how a "primitive" religion like Shintō could nevertheless exhibit great sophistication. He was, for example, distraught to find how poorly his American compatriots regarded Japan and how they viewed Shintō as "heathen."[74] However, if Katō Genchi had supplied Holtom with the category of State Shintō, Holtom's scholarship contributed significantly to an interpretation of the term that was decidedly more negative than that of his mentor.[75] Holtom borrowed this term and Genchi's focus on the "national psychology" of the Japanese people and used them to promote a view of the national cult as a shrewd ploy to eradicate all traces of liberalism, democracy, and freedom of religion from Japanese political life.[76] Genchi had described State Shintō in glowing terms as the fusion of religious ideals with national sentiment; Holtom turned this phrase into an imprecation.

From the time he published his doctoral dissertation in 1922 (*The Political Philosophy of Modern Shintō*), Holtom took a critical view of the official line that Shintō was not a religion. Focusing in particular on the 1900 separation of the Bureau of Shrines from the Bureau of Religions within the Home Ministry, Holtom suggested that this move was a rhetorical sleight of hand that allowed the government to falsely assert the suprareligious status of Shintō.[77] Holtom thereby turned Katō's assertion that Shintō was unambiguously religious in the opposite direction. Rather than arguing that Shintō was actually a religion and superior to other religions in its nationalistic aspect, Holtom suggested that Shintō was actually a religion but an outmoded one that had been manipulated for political use.[78]

Further refinement of this line of argumentation characterized Holtom's later works. In *The National Faith of Japan: A Study of Modern Shintō* (1938), Holtom clarified his position by showing that the nonreligious nature of Shintō was actually a matter of considerable domestic debate. Dismissing as unhelpful to the study of religion those legal theories that treated Shintō as nonreligious, Holtom suggested that State Shintō retained enough "religious" qualities to be treated as such. Moreover, in an age of scientific rationalism, it was incumbent upon government ideologues to acknowledge the irrational nature of the state cult. In this 1938 book, Holtom began to argue for the importance of universalistic principles over particularist ones.

The nationalism/universalism binary formed the core theme of *Modern Japan and Shintō Nationalism* (1943).[79] The book took a decidedly less sanguine view of Shintō than had been apparent in Holtom's earlier works. Whereas his earlier publications seemed to treat Shintō as a benign local tradition that had been co-opted by the state, in *Modern Japan and Shintō Nationalism* Holtom treated Japan as hopelessly mired in a chauvinistic nationalism more appropriate to a primitive age. Reflecting the wartime context in which it was written, this book in particular created the image of Japan as a nation of mindless drones who had been thoroughly indoctrinated with State Shintō ideology. Indeed, with the publication of *Modern Japan and Shintō Nationalism*, Holtom's tone shifted from that of a (mostly) disinterested academic observer of religious phenomena to that of an impassioned defender of American civilization. Holtom's foreword (dated 16 February 1942—just two months after the bombing of Pearl Harbor), for example, described Shintō as the driver of Japanese expansionism and as a threat to the "universalism of Christianity and Buddhism as well as to whatever liberalism may still be latent in Japanese national life."[80]

Of course, Holtom's status as a missionary concerned with Christians' abilities to practice their religion played a significant role in his portrayal. In a lecture delivered to missionaries sometime in 1941 or 1942, Holtom identified State Shintō as a great threat to Christianity in Japan.[81] At around the same time, Holtom published a series of articles in the mainline Protestant magazine the *Christian Century* detailing the challenges posed to Christianity by the Japanese state. His alarmist rhetoric in these publications indicated that he took his position as a representative of "all those . . . whose souls are yet free" seriously.[82] His 1942 Rauschenbusch Lectures at the Colgate-Rochester Divinity School featured a developing theme of "the foreign scapegoat," a concept that seems to have served double duty as Holtom's model for understanding Japanese chauvinism and as his way of making sense of his own departure from Japan in 1941.[83] Having been subjected to racist treatment, Holtom responded in kind.

Yet Holtom's fellow Christians pushed back against the pejorative nature of some of his claims, and Holtom had not entirely lost faith in the people of Japan.[84] In December of 1942, he participated in a lecture series titled "Permanent Values in Civilization" held at the University of California's Berkeley campus in which he spoke approvingly about latent democratic tendencies in contemporary Japanese society that he felt had unfortunately been suppressed.[85] Furthermore, as late as September 1944 Holtom participated in a *Reader's Digest* "Town Meeting of the Air" radio broadcast in which he took the position that Japan could be trusted to enter the ranks of democratic, peace-loving nations following its inevitable defeat in the

Pacific War. Even at that late date, Holtom was of the opinion that a prolonged military occupation of Japan would be unnecessary. He preferred to let the Japanese decide for themselves how to move forward after the war. He also cautioned that the US should not get mired in the inevitable internal strife that he expected would follow Japan's defeat.[86] In an article dated 14 February 1945, Holtom roundly excoriated the emperor system and State Shintō ideology, but suggested that excessive use of military force in destroying State Shintō institutions would backfire. After militarism had been stripped from the country, Holtom predicted that Japanese people would naturally dispense with the outmoded fictions that he associated with State Shintō.[87]

Holtom's thinking seems to have shifted rapidly after this article, however, and his criticism of Shintō took on a sharper edge. In an article published in late May 1945, he actively called for a thorough military drubbing to instigate a religious makeover for the country: "The primary step to be taken in the spiritual renovation of Japan is the administration of a thoroughgoing military defeat. The terrible truth is that nothing will clear the air and overturn false gods and false ideals like the winds of disaster in war that are already beginning to blow strongly across Nippon."[88]

It was this martial aspect of Holtom's oeuvre that seems to have had the greatest influence on American presurrender policy making. His skeptical vision of State Shintō received considerable attention as the US made preparations for Japan's surrender and the subsequent Occupation, and it is undoubtedly due to Holtom's influence that Vincent made his unexpected announcement on the NBC radio program that "National Shintō" would be eliminated. By 1945, Holtom's research was required reading for US policy makers.[89] Propaganda and policy alike treated Shintō as the source of Japanese militarism and portrayed the battle for the hearts and minds of the Japanese people as a struggle between democratic freedom and authoritarian theocracy.[90]

Unpublished documents among Holtom's collected papers suggest that he felt that Japan's defeat would bring about a terrible dilemma regarding official Allied policy on Shintō. He submitted and then retracted two drafts of an article to *Far Eastern Survey* to that effect, one immediately before and one immediately after the promulgation of the Shintō Directive of 15 December 1945.[91] In January 1946, Holtom finally posted a significantly revised version of his earlier article draft that praised the directive but cautioned that Shintō would not disappear overnight.[92] However, by the time this article had gone to press Holtom's influence on Occupation policy had already taken place, since both the memorandum and the Shintō Directive that followed it exhibited Bunce's heavy reliance on Holtom's earlier alarmist works. As the occupiers turned from the negative phase of disestablishing Shintō to the positive task of promoting religious freedom, Holtom could only watch from afar as a small group of inexpert personnel hastily cobbled together a religions policy based largely on his own research.[93]

THE RELATIONSHIP BETWEEN RELIGIOUS STUDIES AND POLICY MAKING

Generally speaking, scholars of religion create religious-secular distinctions by treating religion as a discrete aspect of social life.[94] By adopting a tone of academic authority and a nonconfessional stance, we place ourselves in a rhetorically powerful position that allows us to tolerate the particularist claims made by specific religions but simultaneously arrogates to us the prerogative to adjudicate the ultimate facticity of such claims. Similarly, political claims can be accepted at face value or treated as a product of "false consciousness" in which religious ideals appear as the deep motivators for behavior.

A nonconfessional stance is therefore not necessarily a doctrinally or politically neutral one, and scholarly assistance in states' policies about religion can occur in ways that favor certain modes of religious subjectivity (and certain modes of religious organization) over others.[95] While the ideal of nonconfessional neutrality is akin to—and perhaps dependent upon—secularist ideals such as the separation of religion and the state and latitudinarian conceptions of religious freedom, academic models may also describe certain religions as being more or less authentic, advanced, or malignant than others. Likewise, scholarship can identify particular types of religion-state relations and particular modes of secularism as illegitimate. The political and social consequences of such scholarly models can be immediate; they can also be long-lasting. They can rationalize violence. They can dictate religions' positions vis-à-vis the state. They can situate particular states as paragons of virtue, or as pariahs within the international community.

Bunce was probably drawn to academic accounts of the relationship between Shintō and the state because they represented a type of authority that could supersede mere political claims about the nature and scope of

Japanese secularism. Such accounts could authoritatively rank Shintō ideas and practices on a scale from "primitive" to "civilized." They could also reject specific doctrines, such as the concept of the divine emperor, as patently false. Bunce used these academic claims to buttress his bureaucratic project of strictly separating religious Shintō from governance. Academic claims could also distinguish Japan's "bad" religious governance from the Allies' "good" religious freedom. Following Holtom, Bunce turned the phrase "State Shintō" into an accusatory epithet. By juxtaposing governance with religion, the phrase highlighted an illegitimate form of religion-state relations, treating Japanese secularism as a heretical aberration and turning religious freedom into a universal norm.

But this pat solution engendered a new problem, because not everybody in the Occupation agreed about the nature or scope of that norm. Bunce's difficult task had just begun.

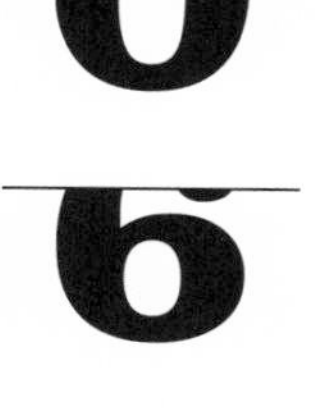

WHO WANTS RELIGIOUS FREEDOM?

> In the religious field where Occupation policies and the Japanese Constitution have guaranteed religious freedom to the Japanese people, the tie-up between religion and state has been severed, and laws restricting freedom to worship have been rescinded. State Shintō can no longer receive financial or other support from Government agencies. Manifestations of militarism and ultranationalism through religion have been prohibited. The Emperor has renounced his mythical divinity together with the idea that the Japanese are the "chosen" people destined to rule over the world. The Japanese people, for the first time in their long history, enjoy the blessings of freedom of conscience and thought. The spiritual and cultural reorientation of Japan has received a remarkable stimulus from the Occupation, and the effects on the minds and spirits of the people has been most encouraging.
>
> RELIGIONS DIVISION (1947)[1]

NEARLY TWO YEARS AFTER THE CESSATION of hostilities between Japan and the United States, a small bombshell dropped in the form of a 23 June 1947 *Richmond Times-Dispatch* article entitled "Rev. Mr. Hopkins Hits AMG [American Military Government] Policy in Japan, Citing Poor Job in Stressing Christianity." Recently returned from a May 1947 visit to missionary sites in Japan, US-controlled Okinawa, and Korea, this Garland Evans Hopkins (1913–65) publicly praised Supreme Commander of the Allied Powers Douglas MacArthur (1880–1964) as an earnest man of God.[2] Yet Hopkins dismissed the general's underlings in the Religions Division as incompetent bureaucrats operating under a "false philosophy of democracy" that was premised on the egalitarian treatment of all religions. Occupation policy therefore favored local religions and left Christianity at a disadvantage.

Given that America was a Christian nation, Hopkins argued, the military should reduce all restrictions on missionaries to allow Christianity to expand as rapidly as possible. "Any who think that the kingdom of God will be ushered into Japan through the beneficent rule of General MacArthur are sadly mistaken," Hopkins argued. "There will be no democracy in Japan, as there has never been in any country in the world, until the foundation for it is laid by the spread of the Christian faith."[3]

Hopkins's incendiary statements were not well received. Missionaries in Japan and senior church officials in the United States hastily dashed off letters to the Religions Division expressing their support for Occupation policy and emphasizing that Hopkins did not represent the official stance of the church. At least one church official also directly wrote to Hopkins to suggest that he was hurting, not helping, the Christian cause.[4] While Hopkins therefore appears as a particularly ardent outlier among those who hoped to spread Christianity in Japan in the wake of the war, the response his statements elicited from the head of the Religions Division, William K. Bunce (1907–2008), reveals a tension in Occupation policy between the ideals of latitudinarianism and Christian evangelism. The very definition of religious freedom was at stake.

With evident disdain for Hopkins's accusations, on 10 July 1947 Bunce wrote a letter to the Board of Missions and Church Extension of the Methodist Church that courteously but firmly stated that Hopkins's portrayal was inaccurate. Bunce argued that Hopkins's caricature was unfair to the fine missionaries currently serving in Japan who, along with Religions Division officials, had been targets of Hopkins's disparaging remarks. Not only that, Bunce wrote, but Hopkins's assessment also revealed an appalling lack of awareness about how religious freedom actually operated. The Religions Division chief suggested that after democracy itself, religious freedom was the most frequently cited principle guiding both Allied wartime objectives and the documents laying out postsurrender policy for Japan. Equal treatment of all religions before the neutral state was fundamental to this principle.

In actuality, the language of religious freedom that appeared in the policy documents Bunce cited was vague, and it was not always clear that the authors of presurrender policy were not simply using "religious freedom" as euphemistic language for Christian evangelism. Nevertheless, Bunce defended his egalitarian understanding of religious freedom by insisting that giving preference to Christianity, as Hopkins had suggested, would undermine the moral basis for the Occupation reforms. He pointed out that missionaries enjoyed preferential treatment in comparison to other nonmilitary personnel, writing that MacArthur's "deep interest in the adoption by the Japanese of Christian principles" was clear and that "everything legitimate under the principle of religious freedom [was] being done to encourage the missionary movement."[5]

Bunce invented this principle even as he appealed to it. Many members of the Religions Division were sympathetic to the Christian missionary project. Some of them had been missionaries themselves.[6] But just as the project of disestablishing "State Shintō" had served the larger purpose of clarifying the nature of the religious freedom that the occupiers hoped to promote, the principled act of resisting Christian missionary efforts served to disentangle religious freedom from particularist claims about the supposed causal relationship between Christianization and democratization. As author of the Shintō Directive, Bunce had resisted one type of particularism by decrying State Shintō as a threat to religious freedom. He now resisted another by decrying Christianizing rhetoric espoused by people like MacArthur and Hopkins as inimical to religious freedom as well. Bunce came to argue not only that Japanese people had misunderstood religious freedom, but also that the occupiers needed to learn how to embrace religious freedom as a universal, abstract principle rather than a clumsy tool that guaranteed rights for Christians alone.

Triumphalist postwar narratives have treated religious freedom as a principle that the occupiers introduced to Japan, but Bunce had to turn it into a "principle" in the first place. Bunce and his colleagues promoted this "principle" of religious freedom by interfacing with transdenominational and transsectarian religious organizations, ironically reproducing a dynamic that had characterized relationships between Japanese religions and the state in wartime.

FOSTERING A DESIRE FOR RELIGIOUS FREEDOM

As Bunce's reaction to Hopkins indicates, preferential treatment for Christians was particularly problematic because Christianization had a strong and vocal proponent in MacArthur and enjoyed tacit support from the highest echelons of the US government. The Religions Division leadership therefore wound up using their orders to foster "a desire for religious freedom" in the Japanese populace as a way of countering the Christian missionary view of religious freedom that was coming from above (in the figure of MacArthur), from below (many staff translators had evident Christian leanings), and from outside (in the case of non-Japanese missionaries like Hopkins). As helpful as it proved to be in countering Christian zeal, however, the project of fostering "a desire for religious freedom" in the Japanese people was difficult. How could the division make people *want* something? How could it convince people that the religious freedom they thought they already enjoyed was insufficient? Moreover, how could division members prove that they had actually established a desire for something?

Proving that the desire for religious freedom had stuck was ultimately impossible. So the Religions Division did the next best thing. Rather than promulgating religious freedom for all and then patting themselves on the back for a job well done, division members assiduously maintained contact with Japanese religious organizations to make sure that the message got through. They wanted religious groups to adopt a mildly antagonistic stance vis-à-vis the state. They wanted individuals to think of religious affiliation as a matter of personal choice. But because they could not interface with one group or another for fear of accusations of favoritism, Religions Division staff opted to interact with the transsectarian and transdenominational organizations that had been newly created or recently reformulated in the wake of Japan's defeat.

In so doing, the occupiers ironically reproduced a wartime dynamic. To govern religion and to protect religious freedom, bureaucrats and religious leaders alike needed some sort of formal interface that was immune to rank preferential treatment of one group or sect. Although Religions Division members critiqued the presurrender Japanese state for seeking to control religious groups through administered mass organizations, the division ultimately used transsectarian groups to keep tabs on developments in the religious world and to disseminate official interpretations of "real" religious freedom. Similar initiatives in the Religious Affairs Section of the Ministry of Education matched this effort, tying state and religion together even as legal changes technically pushed them apart.

This collaborative dynamic was functionally similar to the prewar and wartime status quo, but there were also important differences. As Bunce and his colleagues sought to explain religious freedom to Japanese religious leaders, they began to describe religious freedom in new terms that transcended national boundaries. This newly universalized version of religious freedom could not simply be granted to Japanese citizens by their state. Over the course of the Occupation, Bunce and his colleagues collaborated with their Japanese counterparts in reconfiguring religious freedom as an innate right that Japanese citizens needed to fight for, protect, and secure *from* the state.

This chapter traces how this new rhetoric about religious freedom developed as the Religions Division fought a pitched battle on multiple fronts: against the evangelistic tendencies of MacArthur, against the moral majoritarianism of Christian-leaning Occupation advisors brought in to consult on proposed educational reforms, and against the deeply ingrained tendency for Japanese religious groups to align themselves with political power as a way of gaining legitimacy. Disputes over preferential treatment for missionaries were one issue that forced the Religions Division to clarify policy, but debates over the place of religion in public school education and clerical concerns about the impacts of Occupation land reforms on shrine and temple finances also prompted new theorization about how religious freedom should work.

A GENERAL OVERVIEW OF OCCUPATION RELIGIONS POLICIES

The Occupation that formally began on 2 September 1945 was technically a multilateral endeavor on the part of the Allied nations, but it was undoubtedly an American project.[7] From the outset, Occupation policy was dictated by the State-War-Navy Coordinating Committee of the United States. The military government was dominated by American personnel. Occupation governance reflected specifically American interests in the areas of trade and national security, while the civilizing rhetoric adopted by prominent military government officials associated the United States with universal principles while treating Japan as backward and parochial. Occupation personnel included non-Americans and American people of color, but policy was racialized and religion-based, pitting "white" American civilization against "yellow" Japanese barbarism and "democratic" Christianity against "ultranationalist" Shintō.[8]

Inconsistencies and Ironies in the Occupation Project

Occupation policy was characterized by several ironies. In the name of promoting freedom of expression, the occupiers censored every publication produced in the country.[9] In the name of promoting religious freedom, they created circumstances that were particularly favorable for Christian missionaries and unfavorable for Shintō shrines and their priests; they also subjected some marginal religious movements to police surveillance and crackdowns.[10] In the name of promoting democracy, they reviewed a Japanese constitutional draft, scrapped it, and substituted it with one drawn up by a committee of American advisors who had supposedly been called in to guarantee that the new document truly represented the will of the Japanese people.[11]

These contradictions were not necessarily due to rank hypocrisy. Rather, they reflected competing bureaucratic visions about how to effect change in the occupied country and a certain degree of victors' hubris that confused military victory with ideological superiority. In some cases, different branches of the American military government pursued irreconcilable objectives.[12] In others, junior policy makers had to acquiesce to inflexible commands from the Occupation leadership or the US Department of State. Some of those commands were contradictory. Others were unexpected. This already complex situation was further complicated by the necessity of working closely with Japanese politicians, bureaucrats, policy advisors, and translators who all had their own political axes to grind. Many of these Japanese agents were not above using the aegis of the military government to lend legitimacy to their own pet projects.

Negative and Positive Objectives Related to Religion

In the area of religion, presurrender policy documents indicated that the occupiers were to encourage the Japanese people "to develop a desire for individual liberties and respect for fundamental human rights, particularly the freedom of religion, assembly, speech, and the press."[13] Freedom of religious worship was to be proclaimed at the outset of the Occupation, while "ultra-nationalistic and militaristic organizations and movements [would] not be permitted to hide behind the cloak of religion."[14] This distinction between "real religion" and spurious use of religious claims for nationalistic purposes matched similar distinctions then popular in the United States, where journalists and governmental agents often treated African Americans' religious freedom claims as "fraudulent, inauthentic, and overly political rather than as legitimately religious."[15]

At any rate, the Civil Information and Education Section (CIE) was established on 2 October 1945 in order to enact the aforementioned policies. Given the importance of its task, on 28 November 1945, the Religions Unit of this section became a separate division called the Religions and Cultural Resources Division (Religions Division for short). This administrative elevation of the unit responsible for handling religions policy was directly related to Bunce's project of defining and dismantling State Shintō described in chapter 5.

While Occupation policies regarding religion were complex and changed over time, they can be distilled down to two major objectives: one negative, one positive.[16] First, the occupiers were to proclaim religious freedom and arrange for the protection of civil liberties, including freedom of belief, expression, and conscience. This project necessitated eradication of the system that had been in place during the war. This process included the promulgation of the Civil Liberties Directive that guaranteed freedoms of speech and religion to Japanese citizens (4 October 1945); the formal elimination of militarism from public school education through the purge of teachers and censorship of school textbooks (22 and 30 October 1945); the research, drafting, and promulgation of the Shintō Directive that formally severed Shintō from all aspects of political life (15 December 1945); the promulgation of the Religious Corporations Ordinance that established new procedures for religious incorporation (28 December 1945); the abolition of courses in history, self-cultivation (*shūshin*), and geography in Japanese public schools (31 December 1945), and facilitating the emperor's famed renunciation of divinity on 1 January 1946. This negative phase was short. It lasted from the onset of the Occupation in the late summer of 1945 into the spring of 1946, when the occupiers turned their attention to drafting the new constitution and establishing the postwar educational system.[17]

The second objective related to religion was the directive to foster a desire for religious freedom among the Japanese people. This ambitious goal aimed to refashion Japanese society by reconstituting Japanese subjectivity. The concept of religion in its modern sense had been introduced to Japan in the middle of the nineteenth century, and over the course of the next several decades it came to be understood in Japan—as it was understood in the contemporaneous West—as a universal aspect of human experience with local variations such as "Hinduism," "Buddhism," and so forth.[18] While Protestant Christianity was undoubtedly the prototypical member of the category, the Protestant model of religion as a matter of private assent to propositional statements of belief did not map easily onto traditional Japanese practices.[19]

It would be erroneous to say that exclusivist approaches to religion did not exist in Japan, but Japanese people tended to have expansive notions of religious affiliation, and Japanese ritual practice had traditionally been determined by geography, family, or the annual calendar of ritual observances rather than by exclusive personal affiliation with one denomination or sect.[20] Accordingly, the occupiers had to bolster a sense of religious freedom that was inherently personal, elective, and exclusivist. To liberate Japan's religions, the occupiers needed to constrain them within the bounds of the personal and private.[21] One task for the occupiers, therefore, was to convince Japanese people that the religious freedom they thought they knew—the religious freedom they thought they already *had*—was false.[22] With no apparent sense of irony, officials representing an occupying military government averred that "the Japanese people, long accustomed to government paternalism . . . [required] indoctrination . . . in the understanding, appreciation, and proper exercise of their new religious liberties."[23]

The assumption that the Japanese people were ignorant about the importance of religious freedom matched a second, equally problematic, assumption about national characteristics. Policy makers initially thought that Occupation personnel would know, simply by virtue of being American citizens, what religious freedom was. This assumption was reflected in the fact that nobody bothered to define religious freedom until six months into the Occupation, in February 1946.[24] When policy makers did get around to defining the term, it was because they had belatedly realized that there was actually a wide variety of opinion among Occupation personnel regarding what it meant to institute religious freedom.[25] The concept would therefore have to be defined not only for Japanese religious leaders eager to ingratiate themselves with the new regime, but also for occupiers who sometimes had trouble distinguishing between elimination of preferential treatment for certain religions, promotion of Christianity to the detriment of other religions, and protection of all religions from excessive governmental oversight.

Specific Aims and Ongoing Projects

While the importance of religious reforms in Occupation policy was obvious, the specific objectives of the Religions Division were actually somewhat ambiguous for the first two months of its existence. It was only in February 1946 that the division was given a clear list of objectives separate from those given to the CIE. From that point on, the mission of the Religions Division was to

a. Expedite the establishment and preservation of religious freedom and encourage the Japanese people to develop a desire for religious freedom.
b. Prohibit Japanese Government sponsorship, support, perpetuation, control, and dissemination of Shintō.
c. Maintain vigilance to see that militaristic and ultra-nationalistic organizations and movements [did] not hide behind the cloak of religion.
d. Maintain liaison with religious organizations in order to insure their understanding and cooperation with the information and education objectives of the Supreme Commander.
e. Collaborate with the Arts and Monuments Division in making recommendations to the Supreme Commander on matters pertaining to the protection, preservation, restitution, salvage, or other disposition of religious articles and religious buildings.
f. Formulate policies relating to the return of Christian missionaries to Japan and Korea.[26]

While this coherent list was not established until six months into the Occupation, some of the objectives were clear from the moment the Religions Division was created. In particular, points (b) and (c) occupied the Religions Division in the first month of its existence. With the promulgation of the Religious Corporations Ordinance on 28 December 1945, the division soon found itself fielding questions from leaders of religious organizations who were eager to forestall schism or who wanted to incorporate as newly recognized groups (d). Occupation land reforms prompted significant anxieties that the Religions Division and the Japanese Religious Affairs Section were hard-pressed to address, and the Religions Division and Education Division were deeply divided on the contentious issue of religion's proper role in public school education.

Although it was listed first, the policy (a) of "[expediting] the establishment and preservation of religious freedom and encourag[ing] the Japanese people to develop a desire for religious freedom" was quite difficult to implement as its intangible outcomes were not easily measured. As a result, once the basic legal instruments for guaranteeing religious freedom to all were in place, the Religions Division could only "encourage the Japanese people to develop a desire for religious freedom" indirectly through informal interactions with religious leaders and, especially, through contacts with transdenominational and transsectarian organizations.[27] Whereas the wartime Japanese state had expected such religious organizations to cultivate spiritual sentiment in the service of nation-building and waging total war, the American military government called upon them to spread the ideal of a personalized, elective form of religious freedom that presumed mildly antagonistic relationships between religions and the state. But for some members of the Occupation such as General Douglas MacArthur, there was really only one religion to choose.

RELIGIOUS FREEDOM AS CHRISTIANIZATION

At a meeting of the Allied Council for Japan that took place on the morning of 26 November 1947, chair of the Committee on the Establishment of Religious Freedom in Japan, William J. Sebald (1901–80), opened his report with the following statement:

> The importance of spiritual concepts in the reorientation of the Japanese nation was clearly stated by the Supreme Commander [General Douglas MacArthur] when he declared following the formal surrender on September 2, 1945: "The problem basically is theological and involves a spiritual recrudescence and improvement of human character. . . . It must be of the spirit if we are to save the flesh."
>
> From its inception, the occupation has proceeded with minimum display of Allied force. While its course has been firmly charted toward the achievement of political objectives, progress has rested largely upon the application of those guiding tenets of our Christian faith—justice, tolerance, understanding—which, without yielding firmness, have underwritten all Allied policy.[28]

Such a transparently evangelical pronouncement from the bureaucrat singularly responsible for promoting religious freedom in Japan may seem incongruent. However, Sebald's remarks represent a strain of thought that exerted significant influence on Occupation policy even if it was never formally incorporated into Occupation objectives.[29] In this line of thinking, the purpose of the Occupation was to promote a mass conversion of the Japanese populace. Christianity would guide Occupation initiatives, and as the foundation for democracy, it would serve as a bulwark against both militarist recidivism and communism.[30] Yet as Bunce pointed out time and again, there was simply no provision in the documents laying out the objectives of the Occupation that suggested specifically that Christianity should be promoted in Japan.[31]

Japanese people and Occupation personnel alike must be forgiven for thinking otherwise. Supreme Commander General Douglas MacArthur interpreted his authority rather liberally, injecting his own project of spiritual rehabilitation into the political and economic reforms that dominated prewar and immediate postwar State Department policies.[32] This conceit led him to unilaterally inform the State Department via telegram on 29 December 1945 that he planned to facilitate the return of Christian missionaries to Japan.[33] Once missionaries were in the country, he offered some of them signed letters, easily misinterpreted by locals as direct orders from the supreme commander, as a way of granting them access to otherwise impenetrable areas.[34]

From the moment of Japan's surrender, MacArthur described the Occupation in evangelistic rhetoric and frequently portrayed the Occupation as a Christianizing mission.[35] He also used communication with church leaders and legislators at home to reinforce the notion that the Occupation was a Christian effort. For example, in a radio address to the US Congress given on 24 February 1947, he wildly overestimated the success of the Christianization of Japan when he claimed that more than two million people had "moved to embrace the Christian faith as a means to fill the spiritual vacuum left in Japanese life by the collapse of their past faith." Japan's example would also provide spiritual strength to the "hundreds of millions of backward peoples" in the Far East, he claimed, thereby helping to prevent future war.[36]

The US Department of State did not deign to correct the general's evangelizing rhetoric, implicitly sanctioning the idea that Christianity would counter the spread of communism in East Asia. While MacArthur would eventually run afoul of US president Harry Truman (1884–1972) due to his propensity for insubordination, on the subject of Japan's Christianization MacArthur received support from the highest echelons of the US government, including statements from Truman himself suggesting that the president agreed with MacArthur's assessment that the problem with Japan was "basically theological."[37] This reflected a tendency in the Truman administration to equate Christian proselytizing and the spread of religious freedom with the defeat of communism.[38] As former Religions Division researcher William P. Woodard drily noted in 1972: "Commendable as this motive may have been, this was a stark reminder that the Japanese extremists did not have any monopoly when it came to using religion, including Christianity, for the achievement of political ends."[39]

MacArthur enjoyed tacit support from his political superiors, but subordinates who were directly in charge of religions policy chafed at the supreme commander's evangelism. They were the ones who had to deal directly with disgruntled local religious leaders, so they were more likely to recognize that MacArthur's estimation of Christianity's prospects in Japan were greatly overblown. As foot soldiers on the front lines of the religious freedom campaign, they were also more likely to see the detrimental effects of MacArthur's statements, many of which directly undermined the egalitarian vision of religious freedom they aimed to implement.

In this regard it is crucial to point to the influence of division chief William K. Bunce, whose attitudes not only affected everything the Religions Division did, but who also spearheaded the momentous process of redefining religious freedom in terms that could be applied transnationally and across denominations.[40] As the opening exchange with Hopkins showed, Bunce fiercely resisted Christian missionaries' attempts to co-opt the Occupation. He also tried, albeit with limited success, to get MacArthur to tone down his missionary rhetoric.[41]

Prior scholarship has treated Bunce's resistance to MacArthur's evangelism as a triumph for civil liberties and a check on abuses of American power.[42] However, Religions Division documents reveal that MacArthur was not alone in his hope that Japan would become Christian under Occupation influence, and it must be stressed that Bunce was inventing new understandings of religious freedom as he went along. Bunce strictly promoted egalitarian, latitudinarian interpretations of religious freedom, but he was sympathetic with MacArthur's ultimate aims even if he disagreed with his methods.[43] Publicly, Bunce sought to distance the Religions Division from the appearance of giving undue preference to Christian organizations. Privately, he was interested in promoting religious freedom precisely because it would provide the best circumstances for Christianity to flourish in Japan in the long term.

For example, in his response to Hopkins's provocative comments addressed to the Board of Missions of the Methodist Church, Bunce wrote as follows:

> There has always been a state religion in Japan, and even yet [in July 1947] the requirements of religious freedom are not completely understood. It

> would be a betrayal of the purpose for which we are occupying Japan if in our enthusiasm for Christianity we should further becloud the issue. I believe that Christianity now faces its greatest opportunity in the history of Japan. The people are receptive and the government friendly. But I also believe that the greatest service the Occupation can in the long run perform for Christianity and all other minority religions is to establish respect for the principle of religious freedom so firmly that years after the Occupation is ended no Japanese official will desire to return to the old policy of favoritism and discrimination. Only on such a basis can Christianity look forward to a hopeful future in Japan.[44]

While I can only speculate as to how much these private statements to missionaries were intended as conciliatory platitudes rather than heartfelt sentiments, I suspect that Bunce was actually quite invested in the long-term success of the Christian church.[45] Indeed, he wrote in similar terms on multiple occasions, although his attempts to placate disgruntled missionaries usually doubled as teachable moments for him to remind them that religious freedom was not necessarily just the freedom to be Christian.

This was a difficult tone to strike. For example, responding to a complaint from a missionary named Elizabeth Whewell (d.u.) that Occupation policy did not allow Christians to hold meetings in public school buildings, on 2 October 1947 a Religions Division official (almost certainly Bunce) wrote that the Occupation had been fundamentally "guided by the Christian principles of justice, tolerance, and understanding" before gently reminding Whewell that Christian missionaries actually already enjoyed preferential treatment under the military government's rule. Nevertheless, because the principle of religious freedom was "universally accepted as basic to democracy" and required "that all religious faiths be given an equal opportunity to practice and to propagate their beliefs," further favoring Christians, as Whewell requested, would "do violence to the principle of religious freedom and in the long run would be detrimental to the Christian cause."[46]

Bunce regularly pushed back against Christians' requests for further preferential treatment, but observers of Religions Division reports astutely noted that much of the research conducted by the division reflected a missionary outlook.[47] This tendency was likely a by-product of the early training and personal experiences of Religions Division staff. Researcher William P. Woodard had served as a missionary in Japan prior to the war, for example, and Shintō liaison officer Walter Nichols had grown up in Japan as the son of the Episcopal bishop of Kyoto.[48] Several of the Japanese staff members were also professed Christians, and their prescriptive statements appeared in staff translations and routine reports. Some of these junior staff wanted to encourage religious organizations to develop in favorable ways by clearing out deadwood among the leadership, for example, or by facilitating increased Christian cooperation with other religious organizations because they assumed that Christians could have a salutary influence on such groups.[49]

As I examined Religions Division documents, my initial instinct was to suspiciously read these behind-the-scenes dynamics as evidence of a nefarious plot to smuggle Christianity into Japan through the language of religious freedom. There was historical precedent, of course, and supercilious attitudes regarding the putative superiority of Christianity over other religions appeared with considerable frequency in Religions Division memos, translations, and reports. However, even though many of the staff were clearly personally invested in the long-term success of Christianity in Japan, I came to realize that Bunce and his colleagues were aiming for something quite different. The Religions Division promoted religious freedom not because Japanese people would therefore be finally free to practice Christianity. Legally, they had been able to do so for decades. Rather, members of the Religions Division seem to have understood what they called a "desire for religious freedom" as an entirely new paradigm, still foreign to Japan, in which religion was understood as formal affiliation with one denomination based on private, individual assent to propositional statements of belief. Bunce and his colleagues wanted Japanese citizens to choose their religious affiliations without the state getting in the way. They also wanted to make sure that no religious denomination would be given excessive sway over public life. This commitment came to the fore in disputes with the Education Division concerning understandings of religious education.

CIE's Internal Battles over "Religious Education"

As the author of the Shintō Directive, Bunce was deeply committed to the project of disaggregating religion from all aspects of politics and public life. After the promulgation of the directive on 15 December 1945, he followed up with several memos directing the Japanese government to strip any and all reminders of Shintō-centric education from public schools. On 22 April 1946, for example, Bunce wrote a brief memorandum to his superior in the CIE on the subject of mass bowing to the imperial palace in Japanese public schools. Although the Japanese Ministry of Education had instructed schools that ceremonial bowing to Shintō shrines was now prohibited on 22

December 1945, students were still reportedly bowing in the direction of the imperial palace. Bunce recommended that the ministry be instructed that "ceremonial bowing toward the Imperial Palace is not deemed in keeping with the educational objectives of the occupation."[50]

Even as Bunce assiduously worked to strip schools of religious practices, a group of American educators brought to Japan to survey the educational system was suggesting that schools still needed to foster pupils' spiritual development.[51] Their influential 30 March 1946 report and the March 1947 passage of the Japanese Fundamental Law on Education set the stage for a showdown between the Religions Division and Education Division on the subject of religious education. A November 1947 flurry of correspondence between officials in the two divisions and their superior officers in the CIE revealed that several questions remained unanswered about the relationship between religious freedom and religious education.[52] On the one hand, Bunce took a hardline stance against any incorporation of any type of religious instruction in schools, fearing that even ambiguous language of "education about religion" or "religious toleration" might be used to revivify State Shintō. On the other, Education Division chief Mark T. Orr (1914–2010) saw room in Japanese public education for nonsectarian "religious education." He argued that it was impossible to inculcate religious freedom without talking with students about religious difference. While both men agreed that sectarian education had no place in Japan's public schools, they differed over narrow (Orr) and broad (Bunce) definitions of "religious education." Their intrasection memoranda abandoned civility for hostility, revealing one of the major fault lines that characterized Occupation policy making.

The details of this dispute are fascinating enough to deserve separate treatment, but the simple point here is that Bunce consistently tried in his capacity as head of the Religions Division to advance a notion of religious freedom that was relatively strict in comparison to the attitudes adopted by many of his American contemporaries. He feared that introducing any sort of language about religion into public settings like schools might give teachers the opportunity to proselytize or discriminate. By contrast, Orr represented the view, then popular in America, that while schools must not engage in sectarian education, they *should* foster spiritual growth. The impasse between the two stances reached an ambiguous standoff with yet another ironic outcome. At home, Americans were vigorously experimenting with various ways of bringing religion *into* public schools, especially as the anticommunist rhetoric of the early Cold War pitted religiosity against "godless communism."[53] Abroad, Bunce's strict secularizing vision stripped Japanese schools of religious accoutrements and discontinued all practices that had even the faintest whiff of religion.[54] This tension between domestic and foreign policy would become even more pronounced a few years after the Occupation ended, when American legislators incorporated the words "under God" into the Pledge of Allegiance recited by American schoolchildren (1954) and when they made the national motto "In God we trust," adding the phrase to American paper currency in 1956.[55]

TRANSSECTARIAN GROUPS AND THE STATE

As the objective of encouraging the Japanese people to "develop a desire for religious freedom" suggests, members of the Religions Division needed Japanese people to convert. Changing educational practices was one way to foster new forms of subjectivity in Japanese youth. But it was not feasible for Bunce and his staff to go door-to-door encouraging adult citizens to embrace the one true faith of religious freedom. Instead, they chose to liaise with transdenominational organizations, effecting the epistemological change they envisioned from the top down.

Even as the Religions Division team treated transdenominational organizations as intermediaries that would help to promote the religious freedom ideal, Japanese religious groups in turn banded together to ensure that the occupiers' policies would protect their customary rights and political interests.[56] This complementary dynamic reveals a stunning point of continuity between the Meiji constitutional regime and the Occupation military government. In both cases, governing religion as a potentially deleterious force and harnessing religion in service of the public good meant that officials had to interface with representatives of religious groups without giving the impression of preferential treatment. In both cases, securing rights for religions necessitated overcoming sectarian differences in pursuit of shared political goals. If during the war these transdenominational and transsectarian groups had ensured that member organizations contributed to the war effort, in the postwar period such groups ensured that member organizations understood and embraced the new paradigm of religious freedom represented by the occupiers. While both the wartime Japanese government and the American military government maintained the pretense of leaving doctrine up to religious leaders, each in its own way established parameters for acceptable doctrine and practice through censorship, surveillance, reprimands, bureaucratic advice, and occasional police crackdowns.[57]

The occupiers regularly critiqued wartime Japanese religions for their sycophantic orientation toward the state, but during the Occupation Japanese transdenominational organizations came to rely on contact with Religions Division officials to confirm that they were conducting their affairs in a manner appropriate to the new regime.[58] These groups quickly learned that the occupiers' vision of religious freedom rewarded those who made their claims by appealing to liberal principles like freedom from state intervention rather than by citing historical precedent and asserting customary rights. The groups that did so first and loudest tended to subtly influence how Occupation policy makers understood and regulated local religions, and those that could render customary rights claims in the powerful idiom of religious freedom talk had greater success in securing resources and legitimacy.

Specific Transdenominational Organizations and Their Objectives

Many religious leaders responded to the circumstances of the Occupation with a combination of dread, curiosity, and opportunism. For the so-called new religious movements, the postwar regime change provided fertile ground for claiming a new religious dispensation (see chapter 8). For shrine and temple priests, the future looked bleak as the economic and legal structures that had undergirded the religious world of the past came tumbling down. Occupation reforms uprooted long-standing sources of financial support, facilitated a wave of schisms, and allowed previously marginalized groups to flourish.[59] The religious world was rife with confusion, and one way to navigate the uncertain seas of change was to use transdenominational and transsectarian groups to acquire and disseminate information about the expectations of the new regime.

In the immediate aftermath of the war, the transdenominational and transsectarian religious organizations that had served as intermediaries between religious groups and the wartime state quickly reorganized in anticipation of (or in response to) Occupation reforms.[60] In some cases, new organizations like the Jinja Honchō (National Association of Shrines) lobbied for member organizations' interests in the potentially inhospitable context of the new regime. In other cases, marginal religious movements that lacked political clout sought strength and protection in numbers. Many of these new transdenominational groups wound up serving as vehicles for the dissemination of the occupiers' messages about the importance of religious freedom, even if some of the groups in question had good reason to be suspicious of the Occupation project.

The Jinja Honchō was established on 3 February 1946 through an amalgamation of the preexisting Kōten Kōkyūsho (Institute for the Teaching and Investigation of the Imperial Classics), the Dai Nihon Jingi Kai (Greater Japan Deities Association), and the Jingū Hōsai Kai (Association for the Veneration of [Ise] Shrine).[61] By its own account, the new organization was developed specifically to resist the effects of the 15 December 1945 Shintō Directive.[62] Given this objective, the association's interactions with SCAP were naturally mildly combative. It was no secret that shrines suffered more than other religious groups due to the Occupation reforms, but interactions between the Jinja Honchō and Religions Division were not purely antagonistic. In at least one case, the Jinja Honchō invited a member of the Religions Division to deliver a speech for the benefit of shrines who were struggling to understand and meet the demands of the new regime.[63] The Jinja Honchō also appealed to the Religions Division to make shrines the beneficiaries of the 28 December 1945 Religious Corporations Ordinance.[64] Thus, even though the Jinja Honchō served as a way to protect Shintō interests from overzealous Occupation reforms, the denizens of the shrine world recognized that they could do so best by familiarizing themselves with the requirements of the new status quo and by using the occupiers' own policies to their advantage. For their part, members of the Religions Division seized on opportunities presented by the formation of the new organization to disseminate their ideas about how "real Shintō" could be disaggregated from State Shintō.[65]

The Japanese Buddhist Federation carried over with minimal changes after the war.[66] Various transsectarian Buddhist groups had been in existence in some form or another since the late nineteenth century, and over the course of the Meiji constitutional period they had served as political lobbies that could exert pressure on democratically elected politicians and as administered mass organizations that could contribute materially and ideologically to the war effort. With the passage of the 1939 Religious Organizations Law, the number of Buddhist sects was halved, from fifty-six to twenty-eight, and some administrators aimed to overcome sectarian differences entirely by collapsing Buddhism into a single unified sect.[67] Although these top-down measures seem draconian in retrospect, Buddhist organizations generally embraced the changes. They also avidly contributed to the war effort by making donations for the purchase of fighter planes and tanks.[68]

In the postwar period, these Buddhist organizations appeared eager to determine how exactly they were supposed to imagine themselves vis-à-vis the new regime, in part because they wanted to ensure that policy makers considered Buddhist interests when addressing controversial decisions such as land reform.[69] Many sect leaders also viewed the new rules for religious incorporation with alarm because factional defections presaged erosion of their parishioner bases. They sought reassurance from Religions Division leaders that their customary rights would be taken into account as the division considered matters of schism, temple property, and the threatening rise of new religious movements.[70]

The Churches of Christ in Japan (often referred to simply as the Kyōdan) had been created on a federal model in 1940 and then consolidated into one unified body in November 1942 after most non-Japanese Christian missionaries had fled the country.[71] This historical background presented a unique situation in the wake of the war. Because Japanese Christians had seized autonomy during the war and had distanced themselves from the influence of foreign missionaries, during the Occupation non-Japanese missionaries found their former positions of authority as the bearers of "real" Christianity to have been destabilized. This meant that despite shared theological commitments, a sense of uncertainty prevailed regarding who exactly was to direct the future of Christian organizations in Japan: Japanese Christians themselves or the foreign missionaries? This uncertainty was exacerbated by the fact that the first missionaries to arrive in Japan in the fall of 1945 did so as members of the Occupation, giving them a tactically superior position through alignment with contemporary political authority.[72] MacArthur's evangelism contributed to the confusion. While Japanese Christians enjoyed the preferential treatment given their religion, it was unclear whether they would be allowed to conduct their own affairs.

In sum, the Jinja Honchō was in a position of tension with the Occupation because Shintō shrines had been explicitly targeted for surveillance by the Shintō Directive. Member organizations of the Church of Christ of Japan were uncertain about their future because they had finally come into their own during the course of the war and were loath to lose their newfound domestic authority over doctrine and church policy with the sudden postwar influx of foreign missionaries. While the Buddhist Federation and the Sect Shintō Federation escaped some of the dilemmas that their Christian counterparts faced, like all religious organizations they were anxious about procedures for incorporation, secession, and taxation under the new regime.

Against this background, religious leaders collaborated in reconstituting the Greater Japan Wartime Religions Patriotic Association as the Japanese Religions Association (Nippon Shūkyō Kai) in the fall of 1945. Thereafter it served as an umbrella organization encompassing the aforementioned Buddhist, Shintō, and Christian transdenominational organizations and lobbying for their collective interests.[73] The group passed through a tenuous phase in the spring of 1946 when it seemed that some member organizations would secede over insurmountable differences of opinion, but a meeting held on 23 May 1946 confirmed that the organization would survive.[74] It took the new name the Japanese Religions Federation (Nippon Shūkyō Renmei) on 2 June 1946, and the umbrella organization encompassed four transsectarian bodies: the Jinja Honchō, the Sect Shintō Federation, the Buddhist Federation, and the Christian Kyōdan.[75]

While leaders of the organization were at great pains to distinguish it from the Greater Japan Wartime Patriotic Religious Association, functionally it was remarkably similar to the wartime group in that it provided an interface between bureaucrats and religious leaders. This is not to suggest that salient differences did not exist between the two. For example, the wartime organization had been headed by the Japanese minister of education and the group had received a sizable annual sum from the government (around 300,000 yen) in support of its spiritual mobilization efforts. Immediately after the war, the minister of education and the vice minister of education resigned from the organization and the government terminated financial support. However, institutional memory continued because Andō Masazumi (1876–1955) moved from his wartime position of vice president into the position of chairperson of the new federation.[76]

Andō's eminent stature in both the Buddhist and political worlds during the course of the Pacific War is indisputable. Sometime before December of 1941, Andō became chairperson of the Greater Japan Buddhist Youth Association League (Dai Nippon Bukkyō Seinen Kai Renmei).[77] The 1 October 1942 issue of *Seikyō shinron* listed Andō alongside Tokyo Imperial University professors Anesaki Masaharu (1873–1949) and Takakusu Junjirō (1866–1945) and six other politicians and bureaucrats who had been confirmed as "advisers" (*komon*) to the Greater Japan Buddhist Association (Dai Nippon Bukkyō Kai) on 30 August 1942.[78] Andō was also listed as the chairman of the East Asia Buddhist Cooperation Association (Tōa Bukkyō Kyōwa Kai) in a 10 April 1944 issue of that group's organ, *Wagō no chikara* (*Power of Harmony*).[79]

Andō's diaries also suggest that he served in a prominent liaison capacity between the Ministry of Education and the Greater Japan Buddhist Association in discussions of how to create a central transsectarian Buddhist university; he also served on a committee established in March 1944 that was investigating how to better use religion for social edification efforts.[80] As a synecdoche for the transsectarian and transdenominational organizations operating during and immediately after the war, Andō represents one way in which continuities in religion-state relations existed across the prewar, wartime, and postwar contexts. As the face of the postwar Religions Federation, Andō strove to ensure that religious interests would be protected under the new regime much in the same way that he had as a leader in various wartime transsectarian Buddhist organizations.

Difficulties for New Religions

While Religions Division personnel tried to eliminate any hints of favoritism in their dealings with Japanese religions, naturally they were drawn to large transsectarian groups like Andō's because they served as convenient interfaces for explaining Occupation religions policy and taking the pulse of the domestic religious situation. One side effect of this state of affairs was that independent religious groups that were not members of any of the four transsectarian organizations (the Jinja Honchō, the Sect Shintō Federation, the Buddhist Federation, and the Christian Kyōdan) were at a political disadvantage in their relationships with the Occupation government and the Japanese state. This was especially true in cases where negative press reportage made these newly arisen religions targets for surveillance and suppression as threats to peace and order.[81]

Very late in the Occupation, on 17 October 1951, several of these new religions established a new transsectarian organization that could lobby for their interests; the Japanese Religions Federation begrudgingly welcomed the new group shortly thereafter. A 1963 retrospective study produced by this new Japanese Federation of New Religious Organizations recalled that the initiative to create the organization happened at the suggestion of Religions Division researcher William P. Woodard.[82] By the federation's account, Woodard had argued that the group would be able to counter negative press coverage, unjust police surveillance, and social marginalization by combining their efforts and exerting pressure on the Japanese government. While Woodard made no corroborating mention of this interaction in his 1972 memoir, he did state that members of the Religions Division were overwhelmed with the sudden explosion of new religious organizations during the Occupation.[83] Presumably, Religions Division staff would have welcomed the existence of an umbrella organization to help them keep tabs on the new groups. Woodard had also personally overseen attempts to ensure that the Religious Juridical Persons Law of 3 April 1951 would reflect the interests of mainstream and marginal religious movements alike, so it is unsurprising that he might have made the suggestion to representatives of the new movements to band together in defense of their collective interests.

A Symbiotic Relationship

Overall, the relationship between the Religions Division and Japanese transsectarian groups was cordial, conciliatory, and collaborative. Religions Division records included careful documentation about transsectarian groups, including records of their internal affairs and summaries of their monthly meetings with the division.[84] Division researchers also placed some leaders of transdenominational organizations such as Andō Masazumi alongside academic specialists in religion such as Kishimoto Hideo (1903–64) and historians such as Ienaga Saburō (1913–2002) in their lists of trustworthy human resources who could provide policy makers with authoritative information about religions.[85] For their part, transsectarian groups publicized their interactions with the Religions Division and regularly invited division members to participate in their events.[86] Division members' actual attendance at such conferences and lecture meetings seems to have been somewhat rare, but when it did occur it lent an air of official approval to the proceedings.

This pattern of interaction developed in part because the Occupation aim of establishing religious freedom invited confusion on the part of Japanese religious leaders, many of whom felt that religious freedom had already been guaranteed in the Meiji Constitution and that the legal principle had been generally upheld by the prewar Japanese state.[87] Woodard later recalled that one of the prime responsibilities of the Religions Division was to assure religious leaders that a policy of strict separation of religions from the state amounted to an attitude of respect for religions rather than a denigration of their status. Indeed, many religious leaders suspected the occupiers of aiming to abolish religion in Japan altogether, while the occupiers struggled to encourage religions to "sit in judgment on the state" rather than operating in close relationship with it.[88]

In meetings with religious organizations, division personnel refrained from offering support that could be perceived as favoring a particular religion, but they did encourage the groups to submit petitions to protest, for example, General MacArthur's statements about the superiority of Christianity or elected officials' inappropriate actions as far as religion was concerned.[89] They also encouraged groups to band together to influence Japanese policy makers. For example, in a 22 September 1949 meeting with leaders of the Japanese Buddhist Federation, Religions Division advisor Walter Nichols (d.u.) advised the group to create a "central Buddhist organ" that could disseminate information to the various sects while also exerting political pressure on the state.[90]

The symbiotic relationship between the Religions Division and Japanese religious groups is particularly evident in the passage of the aforementioned 3 April 1951 Religious Juridical Persons Law. Members of the Religions Division viewed the new law as a victory for their vision of religious freedom insofar as the legislation was a largely homegrown effort on the part of the Japanese Religions Federation to replace the occupier-drafted Religious Corporations Ordinance (28 December 1945) with legislation that was more conducive to Japanese religions' interests. Under the rules of the Occupation, the new legislation was actually drafted in the Religious Affairs Section of the Japanese Ministry of Education, but Woodard was skeptical of draft legislation that he saw as a thinly veiled attempt to reinstate the abrogated Religious Organizations Law of 1939. He ensured that members of Japan's various religious organizations would have a say in the matter by inviting them to weigh in on the ministry's drafts.[91] The legislation that resulted represented compromise on all sides, but it enshrined a vision of religious freedom in Japanese law that defined the right to religious freedom as inalienable while simultaneously establishing limits so that charlatans could not use religious liberty as an excuse to infringe on public welfare. It therefore addressed concerns shared by mainstream religious leaders, Japanese government officials, and Occupation officials who feared cynical abuses of religious freedom language.[92]

THE JAPANESE GOVERNMENT'S ROLE

Just as the Religions Division tried to foster a "desire for religious freedom" by interfacing with transdenominational organizations, the Japanese Religious Affairs Section (Shūmuka) housed in the Ministry of Education also tried to refashion Japanese religiosity by providing guidance to religious organizations through its monthly periodical *Shūkyō jihō* (*Religion Times*). Established in the summer of 1947 just two months after the new "Peace Constitution" went into effect, *Religion Times* served as a one-stop source of information about religions policy. According to Shūmuka head Fukuda Shigeru (1910–97), the journal's mission was to bridge the gaps that had arisen between policy makers and clerics in the wake of the war.[93]

On the first page of the inaugural issue, Fukuda wrote a short introductory message suggesting that while religious liberty had been thoroughly guaranteed in the new constitution, several religious leaders were engaging in "anachronistic" (that is, retrogressive) behavior and many evidently misunderstood the meaning of separation of religion from the state. Fukuda admitted that this unfortunate situation was largely the fault of the bureaucrats themselves for not being sufficiently clear about the nature of the various new laws and regulations. In this context, *Religion Times* would serve as a helpful mediator between the clerical and administrative worlds.[94]

Fukuda's emphasis on the necessity for better collaboration between bureaucrats and religious leaders was no doubt intended to assuage religious leaders' concern that separation of religion from the state was a diminution of religions' status.[95] Fukuda also averred that religious freedom was prone to misunderstanding and abuse, a statement that placated clerical concerns about upstart new religions even as it established guidelines for appropriate behavior. While Fukuda did not mention specific examples of abuses of religious freedom, *Religion Times* provided religious leaders with a prescriptive administrative vision characterized by detailed explanations of how to meet the reporting and taxation demands of the new regime. Many pages of each issue featured a question-and-answer column that gave religious leaders a chance to inquire about how to navigate the new system. A "materials explained" column provided a detailed explication of various requirements for clerics who may have been confused about the changes introduced by the occupiers' Religious Corporations Ordinance (28 December 1945).

These guides to paperwork and reporting procedures sat alongside editorials and serialized articles about the proper postwar development of

Japanese religions and religion-state relations. For example, the inaugural issue included another article by Fukuda that somewhat condescendingly explained that the new constitution was not an onerous imposition on religions' traditional privileges, as some clerics evidently feared, but was in fact a latitudinarian document that provided religions with greater freedom than they had hitherto experienced. While Fukuda admitted that some Japanese citizens had unfortunately interpreted the constitution's strict separation of religion from the state as reason to scorn and avoid religion altogether in the wake of the war, overall the new constitution actually enhanced the status of religions.[96]

Religion Times served a crucial function by explaining the new dynamic in which religions were distant from the state rather than close to it. It also interpreted the expectations of the new regime for worried Japanese clerics who saw their customary rights eroding and their financial support dwindling. The issue of land reform and the restitution of shrine and temple property was a particularly charged topic for clerics, and indeed one of the main purposes served by the question-and-answer column in *Religion Times* was to normalize new understandings of religious juridical persons, their land, and their relationships with the state.[97]

This property issue was challenging. As part of a rural land reform designed to abolish "feudal" tenancy arrangements (see figure 7), the occupiers stripped many shrines and temples of land that had been granted to them in bequests from patrons, placing them in dire economic straits.[98] (The occupiers ironically used a version of the shrine and temple land law that had passed in conjunction with the 1939 Religious Organizations Law to conduct their land reform project.)[99] Furthermore, in an echo of an issue that had caused serious consternation in previous decades, a great deal of land managed by shrines and temples technically belonged to the government, with shrines and temples simply managing such tracts in "custodial" relationships.

Such customary financial arrangements complicated the project of separating religion from the state. The occupiers tried to get in front of the problem by encouraging the Japanese government to achieve a speedy settlement of the shrine and temple precincts and custodial forests issue before the new constitution was promulgated in November 1946. As a 31 October 1946 CIE memo stated, the principle of separation of religion and the state "render[ed] undesirable the continued possession by the government of title to land used for religious purposes" and that "freedom of religion would seem to require that religious institutions be given control over areas necessary to their religious functions and in which they have more than a mere possessory interest." However, the memo also clarified that religious institutions should not obtain so much land from the state that they could operate without popular economic support.[100]

The land reform issue is one situation (there were many) where competing branches of the Occupation worked at cross-purposes. The Natural Resources Section single-mindedly pursued the land reform policy over the protestations of religious groups and the Religious Affairs Section of the Japanese government. As William Woodard recalled, many religious organizations saw land that had been donated to them as entirely different from "unconsecrated land," meaning that it should not be subject to the official policy of breaking up large parcels of land into smaller units of 2.5 acres that could be cultivated for personal use.[101] When *Religion Times* began publication in July 1947, the question-and-answer column was filled with anxious questions about how the state would dispose of particular tracts of land based on their customary use and in consideration of the relationship between the local community and the religious institution.

For example, in the November 1947 issue of *Religion Times*, one Takagi (Chūryū?; d.u.) of "Chō [illegible]" Temple in Tokushima Prefecture wrote in with the details of the deed for his temple to ask whether the property would be subject to the new law regarding the disposition of state-owned land. The documentation he provided from 1906 amounted to a terse note about land tax, another single line indicating approval of a transfer of the property to the Home Ministry and a laconic note suggesting that the property was tax exempt.[102] The response Takagi received from the Religious Affairs Section was hardly reassuring: "With this small amount of material it is difficult to quickly make an assessment, but you can assume that about 80 to 90 percent [of the land in question] might be subject [to return to the state]. This is because the reason for the transferal of ownership to the Home Ministry in 1906 is not clarified."[103]

While the *Religion Times* question-and-answer column was directed primarily to clerics with similar questions about land law and property rights, the column also fielded questions from laypeople who were apparently having trouble getting a handle on basic terminology. One person wrote, for example, "Recently we often hear 'religion, religion,' but please tell me its true meaning. Also, what exactly are kami and buddhas?"[104]

The author of the column responded gently with a recommendation to seek out religious training at the person's local shrine, temple, or church. However, the nature of the question itself suggests that some of the basic terms that authorities took for granted did not translate easily for Japanese audiences. No less than the Religions Division, the Religious Affairs Section had to teach people what religion was and how to freely choose it. It is telling that although the *Religion Times* response demurred from offering a definition of religion, by lining up "shrine, temple, and church" as options, the editors turned religious affiliation into a matter of personal choice.

RELIGIOUS FREEDOM AS CONVERSION

The Occupation policy of fostering "a desire for religious freedom" was essentially an attempt to change the way that Japanese people understood their own religion-state relations. Religions Division members anticipated a diminution of sacerdotal authority, increased suspicion of state initiatives, a new emphasis on the ability of the individual to directly connect with deities without clerical mediation, and the expansion of a new model in which sectarian affiliation was determined less by the circumstances of birth and location than by individual choice.

Despite the individualistic focus of this vision of religious freedom, Religions Division members promoted it by interfacing with transsectarian and transdenominational groups. Superficially, this transsectarian and transdenominational organizing was simply a convenient way to bolster member organizations' ability to lobby the Japanese government by using the power of numbers to press for their interests, but it also provided bureaucrats with convenient intermediaries who could report on religions' activities and disseminate information and directives to member organizations. While the political context was quite different, these postwar transsectarian organizations were functionally quite similar to their wartime counterparts. The Occupation therefore exhibited continuity at least as much as it was characterized by rupture.[105]

The Occupation also marked a historical break, but not because the Americans introduced religious freedom where it was previously absent. The main change was that the circumstances of the Occupation—a situation in which governance nominally resided with the sovereign Japanese state but was monitored and often directly dictated by the Occupation government—created the necessity for treating rights and liberties as universal principles that transcended the jurisdiction of one particular state and eschewed customary privileges for any given religion. While rights and liberties had been discussed in universalistic terms prior to and during the war, during the Occupation the need to transform that universalism from rhetoric to reality became immediately apparent. Religious freedom could no longer be treated as merely a civil liberty granted to Japanese citizens by their state, because the occupiers feared that the Japanese state might get it wrong. Religious freedom had to change so that it was both innate (inherent in individuals regardless of their citizenship) and transcendent (superseding the authority of any single government). Religious freedom had to become a human right.

7

UNIVERSAL RIGHTS, UNIQUE CIRCUMSTANCES

> Although a maximum of freedom on the part of individuals to select and practice a creed of their own choice has been provided, and though all religions and creeds are now entitled to precisely the same opportunities and protection, time will be required before the Japanese people, long accustomed to government paternalism and police scrutiny, can understand the true meaning of religious freedom. The activities of the Religions and Cultural Resources Division in this field, therefore, are now directed towards indoctrination of the Japanese people in the understanding, appreciation, and proper exercise of their new religious liberties.
>
> "Mission and Accomplishments of the Occupation in the Civil Information and Education Fields" (1950)[1]

IN MAY OF 1951, RECENTLY RESIGNED chair of the Japanese Federation of Religious Organizations and elder statesman Andō Masazumi (1876–1955) published a collection of essays under the title *Kōwa o mae ni shite: Tsuketari, tsuihō no hakusho* (*Confronting the Peace, with A White Paper on [My] Purge [from Office]*).[2] Collectively, the essays in the book advanced Andō's vision about how Japan's defeat, while painful, could serve as an opportunity for the country to thrive in the new postwar spirit of peace and cooperation.

Confronting the Peace offered an extended meditation on the role of religious freedom in postwar Japan. While the Andō retained some of his long-standing evolutionary rhetoric about the historical development of religion-state systems, he took a different tack by adopting new language when it came to the specific topic of religious freedom. No longer was the legal institution of religious freedom a desideratum just because it could serve as an index of Japan's level of "civilization" in the eyes of the international community. No longer was protection of religious freedom necessary merely as a means for ensuring that ecclesial organizations were best positioned to support nation-building at home or connections with people abroad. Such considerations remained as important for Andō in the postwar context as they had been prior to and during the war, but in his 1951 book he suggested that religious freedom needed protection for another reason.

Andō argued that religious freedom derived from a universal human religiosity. That religiosity formed the foundation of healthy political intercourse, because all humans were collectively bound up in what he termed a shared "moral existence" (*dōtokuteki jitsuzai*).[3] "Essentially," Andō wrote, "freedom of religious belief is among the most fundamental of the rights that citizens should enjoy. That is because [religious] belief is an innate human right."[4]

This was a striking statement of the sort that Andō would not have made just a few years prior.[5] He probably *could not* have made it because it would have been literally unthinkable.[6] During the war, Andō had consistently understood religious freedom to come from the state rather than from any innate source.[7] Yet by the end of the Occupation, Andō's conception of religious freedom had clearly changed. Religious freedom was now a human right.

THE NEW HUMAN RIGHTS

So what makes a human right, and when exactly did human rights emerge? Critical histories of human rights have pursued these intertwined questions with verve. Scholars have mobilized evidentiary historiography to critique narratives that plot the development of human rights on a straight line from early modern European political philosophy to the present; they have similarly questioned triumphalist accounts that see the consolidation of human rights as a final victory of reason over the devastatingly irrational totalitarianism of World War II.[8]

A summary of the basic points of this recent historiography might run as follows: If the defining feature of human rights is that they are innate (and therefore devolve upon individuals as opposed to groups), universal (and therefore culturally odorless), and superior to state sovereignty (and therefore enforceable by a vigilant international community), then the emergence of human rights must be traced to a historical point when each of these distinguishing features became evident. Agreeing on these basic features but differing on the types of historical evidence they prefer, researchers have placed the origins of "human rights" at different points in history. Some have seen feasible efforts to promote and protect human rights emerging as early as the 1930s as part of European Christians' strategic deployment of the concept of human dignity.[9] Others have looked to the recuperative postwar geopolitics of the late 1940s as the origins of human rights proper.[10] Still others have preferred to place the rise of human rights in the watershed moment of the late 1970s, when nongovernmental organizations like Amnesty International began successfully and very publicly exerting international political pressure on repressive states.[11] These interpretive decisions largely depend on how each scholar understands the scope of human rights. They also reflect the extent to which each sees realistic means of enforcement as an integral part of human rights as such.[12]

However, distortions inevitably arise in historiographic narratives that seek out origins or that draw straight, stark lines from specific points in the past to the present.[13] Two simple maneuvers correct for these distortions. First, human rights can be disaggregated. Certain of these rights came to be understood as innate, universal, and in need of international protection earlier than others, meaning that focusing on the emergence of a designated *grouping* of rights (for example, those outlined in the 1948 Universal Declaration of Human Rights) can be a distraction from understanding the historical reconfiguration of specific rights as "human rights." A logical second step is to examine the moments when these specific rights became topics of discussion, protection, and legal enforcement in international contexts.[14] This focus highlights those moments of transition when rights or privileges that were previously understood as civil liberties or customary rights acquired a new stature antecedent to citizenship (becoming innate) and transcending the regulatory purview of the state (becoming universal).

In this chapter I focus on a specific right—religious freedom—and I focus on a particular historical moment.[15] I show that the Allied Occupation of Japan was a unique situation in which policy makers were required to not only pay lip service to the postwar ideal of religious freedom as a human right, but also to explicitly define and actively enforce that right.[16] This necessity derived from the inherently transnational nature of the Occupation, the importance that religious freedom had been given in Occupation policy from its inception, and the occupiers' need to clarify the exigency, scope, and fairness of the Occupation reforms while distinguishing their project from that of the wartime Japanese state.

The occupiers were supposed to teach the Japanese people how to understand religious freedom, but in the unique environment of the Occupation the occupiers themselves came to understand religious freedom in a new way. Up until the Occupation, religious freedom had served as a rhetorical placeholder that justified the Pacific War and sublimated its racism. In addition to the irony that the Americans aimed to teach the Japanese how to enjoy their new civil liberties even at a time when the United States' own record with civil liberties was ambiguous at best, the fact that the occupiers were working with policy documents that used the language of human rights demanded that they formulate what exactly was being protected and which institutions could guarantee it.[17] The context of the Occupation transformed human rights from a flowery propagandistic phrase into a full-fledged legal concept, even if the protocols for securing and enforcing human rights remained inchoate.

The occupiers were not the only ones who felt the need to define religious freedom as a human right. Japanese scholars, politicians, policy makers, and religious leaders collaborated with the occupiers in making the language of religious-freedom-as-human-right intelligible, meaningful, and enforceable. The concept of religious-freedom-as-human-right that emerged during the Occupation was therefore not simply a product of American tinkering with existing propagandistic vocabulary as they transmitted the ideal of religious freedom to a passive Japanese population. Rather, religious freedom became a human right as a result of a robust multilateral interaction in which all parties involved learned from each other and in which all parties exerted pressure on operative definitions of religion and freedom.

This cross-cultural discussion reflected the specific understandings of religion that undergirded Occupation reforms. "Bad religion"—what the occupiers had somewhat hastily labeled "State Shintō" in their need to define the religious freedom they were ordered to promote—was an exigent problem in need of an immediate fix. Because Japanese militarism had been diagnosed as a symptom of this "bad religion," the cure was to eliminate any sense that religion supported statecraft or even that religion and governance were (in the classic Buddhist phrasing) "like two wheels of a cart." Religion had to be repositioned as unquestionably superior to the state, while religiosity had to be positioned as irrefragably antecedent to citizenship. Moreover, because the state could not be trusted to protect citizens' freedom of conscience or their right to free expression of their belief, religious freedom needed to be vigilantly protected by an international community that kept tabs on state policies and documented possible infringements. Religious freedom became a human right during the Allied Occupation not because religious people were in danger of persecution simply for being religious (the problem that spurred talk of religious-freedom-as-human-right in Europe), but because of fears that the state might once again impose the *wrong kind of religion* on its citizens.[18]

This is not to say that the threat of atheist (or "secularist") communism that drove roughly contemporaneous religious freedom claims in Europe did not feature in the Occupation. In fact, the negative link between religious freedom and communist atheism surfaced late in the Occupation as the American occupiers turned their gaze to political developments and military conflicts on the Asian mainland and used the recently demilitarized Japanese archipelago as a factory for manufacturing military matériel to support the war on the Korean peninsula. Having successfully transplanted "real" religious freedom to Japan, the Americans made the international promotion of religious freedom a central point of their foreign policy.

Like the military equipment that was shipped to the Korean peninsula to support the fight against communism there in the closing years of the Occupation, religious-freedom-as-human-right was made in Japan and then exported for American foreign policy use.[19] As a human right, religious freedom could only have been constructed in a unique transnational moment in which the ultimate source of rights was ambiguous and the fundamental nature of "religion" undergoing rapid semantic reconfiguration. Religious freedom became a human right because the circumstances of the Occupation demanded that religiosity be understood as innate and universal, states understood as problems rather than solutions, and freedom understood as something that the international community safeguarded for vulnerable individuals.

OCCUPATIONAL POLICY AIMS AND OUTREACH

Although the aim of establishing religious freedom in Japan was included in presurrender policy documents, and although the inculcation of a desire for religious freedom was a prime Occupation objective, the vagueness of this directive made it difficult for the members of the Religions Division to enact.[20] It was also nearly impossible to test whether such efforts had been successful. Behind this problem lay the simple fact that the presurrender planning documents had not clarified what religious freedom would mean in the context of the Occupation. Religions Division policy memos, press releases, and outreach lectures reveal that the occupiers were in the process of learning about the significance of religious freedom just as much as the Japanese were. Through these documents, it is possible to trace a trend in which wartime propaganda rhetoric about religious freedom as a "human right" gradually became a reality.

Policy Memos

Despite the central role it played in Occupation planning, the concept of religious freedom was not systematically defined until Religions Division chief William K. Bunce (1907–2008) authored a formal document on the subject six months after the formal start of the Occupation, on 21 February 1946. It stated:

> Religious freedom is a juridical principle concerned with the external relations of individuals and groups. It involves three aspects: (1) Individual autonomy in the choice of creed, (2) Group autonomy in the pursuit of religious activities, and (3) Legal equality of religious groups before the state . . . . . . [*sic*] Religious freedom is violated by an ecclesiastical institution only when it attempts to enforce its intolerant prescriptions by invoking the sanctions of civil power. Religious freedom involves not only the right on the part of the individual to choose for himself but to be safeguarded against potential coercion. Accordingly, it must embrace two factors: (1) A maximum of freedom to believe in and practice the creed of their choice on the part of individuals and groups, and (2) A minimum of propagation, restraint, and interference on the part of the government.[21]

As a policy statement this was clear enough, but the fact that it was announced six months into the Occupation (after all of the major directives related to religion had been promulgated) suggests that it was only in hindsight that Religions Division personnel realized that the concept of religious freedom was open to interpretation. Furthermore, the fact that Occupation personnel had to be repeatedly reminded that their job was not to propagate Christianity suggests that the vision of religious freedom officially favored by the Religions Division was not transparent, nor does it seem to have been widely held.

For example, a 25 March 1946 draft of a Religions Division document entitled "~~Instructions to~~ Information for Agencies of the Occupation Forces in the Field of Japanese Religions" concluded with a paragraph saying that "while the sympathies of occupational personnel are undoubtedly behind the Christian movement in Japan, the propagation of Christianity is not one of the objectives of the [O]ccupation. Occupation personnel should, therefore, leave the propagation of Christianity among the Japanese people to missionaries and to Japanese Christians."[22] This statement clearly demarcated the division between permissible and impermissible behaviors for the rank and file. A similar 29 August 1946 memorandum directed to all Civil Information and Education Section personnel stated that "freedom of religion . . . does not imply freedom on the part of agents of the civil authority to propagate the religion of their choice."[23] The repetitive nature of the second memo suggests that some occupiers needed to be reminded repeatedly that promotion of religious freedom was not promulgation of Christianity.

Press Releases

While the majority of the directives related to religions policy and religious freedom were promulgated in autumn 1945, the clearest theoretical expressions of religious freedom were articulated after the fact, in 1946.[24] In addition to the February 1946 internal policy statement authored by Bunce and various memos outlining appropriate behavior for occupation personnel, the Civil Information and Education Section authored a 4 October 1946 press release on the subject of religious freedom. Symbolically timed to coincide with the first anniversary of the Civil Liberties Directive that had abolished the 1939 Religious Organizations Law, this document laid out a vision of religious freedom that would supersede alternate visions of religious freedom that may have existed (either among the Japanese or among the occupiers).

The first page of the five-page press release repeated the basic components of Bunce's internal memo about religious freedom, stating that religious freedom had been universally acclaimed and emphasizing that religious freedom was a juridical principle designed to manage the external relations of religious organizations. (Here the press release ironically reproduced the logic advanced by proponents of the 1939 Religious Organizations Law; see chapter 4.) Although evangelical religions by their nature resisted egalitarian policies, the press release argued, such attitudes violated religious freedom only when such groups tried to conscript civil power in the service of their missionary ends.

The second page of the document turned to the factors that had led to the historical development of the concept and practice of religious freedom. In a single sweeping paragraph, it suggested that religious freedom had developed as a natural outcome of religious wars and persecution, but also out of growing awareness on the part of religious groups that their own freedom from state control could be secured by ensuring that other groups also enjoyed such freedom. Meanwhile, liberal political thinkers who were concerned with "broad humanitarian principles" rather than theology had determined that "individual liberty was impossible without freedom of religion." Even those religious groups that had traditionally enjoyed political favor had ultimately discovered that state protection came at the price of enduring restrictions.

The document went on to argue that for most of Japanese history religious intolerance had not been an issue because religious conflict had been ameliorated by the inherently irenic qualities of Buddhism. Yet despite this, Japanese people had never truly enjoyed real religious freedom. Citing the Tokugawa period (1603–1868) bans on Christianity and the Meiji era (1868–1912) principle of unity of rites and rule, the press release suggested that Japanese religions had always been expected to conform to the state, and that only a "pretense" of religious liberty had been maintained through the fiction that Shrine Shintō was not a religion. The necessity of establishing religious freedom was obvious because Japan, like the model nation the United States, was a pluralistic society featuring many different religious groups.

After a brief recapitulation of the various directives promulgated in autumn 1945 and their intended outcomes (removal of restrictions on incorporation, more freedom from administrative oversight), the press release suggested that the new directives preserved and protected religious freedom because they had been vetted by various Japanese religious organizations and had even been praised by the Japanese Religions Federation. While confusion had unfortunately erupted as a number of schisms and secessions occurred in response to the new laws, this merely represented the growing pains of the new system and eventually the various groups would realign themselves in a mutually beneficial fashion.

So, the document continued, while some may harbor trepidation at the sudden emergence of previously obscure or new religious movements, calls for state suppression of such movements were unwarranted.[25] The various civil laws would suffice for managing any unlawful behavior, and in time those groups that shrewdly incorporated as religions for tax evasion purposes would be caught. For those who were concerned about the flourishing of superstition, the press release stressed that what was "religion" to one person might be "superstition" to another, and that for still others all religion was nothing more than superstition. It closed on an ambiguous note, suggesting that religious freedom would ultimately serve as a prophylactic against "unwholesome" movements: "Undoubtedly, unworthy religious movements will gain adherents[,] and quacks will for a time be able to pose as religionists. But this is the price that has to be paid to guarantee freedom to all. Quackery flourishes in ignorance. The remedy lies not in governmental paternalism, but in education and time."[26]

Aside from the somewhat tone-deaf critique of "governmental paternalism" from an occupying military power, several features of this document deserve close attention. First, the press release problematically assumed that the boundaries between "religious" and "civil" authority (or "internal" and "external" aspects of religion, for that matter) were transparent and self-evident. Second, it offered platitudes about the desirableness of religious freedom, but little clarity on how exactly the postwar versions of religious freedom differed from the type that had been encapsulated in the Meiji Constitution. It was also vague when discussing the history of religious freedom outside of Japan: Religious freedom was widely lauded, anonymous thinkers praised it as the foundation of liberty, and nameless religious organizations had recognized that tolerating others was better than receiving political favor.

In the crucible of the Occupation, the people directly responsible for creating religions policy were hard-pressed to construct a vision of religious freedom that derived its authority from transcultural principles. The vagueness of the history the press release proffered was, of course, partially reflective of the fact that press releases speak in sound bites and catchphrases. But it was also vague because the occupiers needed to articulate religious freedom in a way that would be simultaneously coercive and culturally odorless. Policy makers had to deny that Japan had ever enjoyed "real" religious freedom in order to justify their drastic interventions such as the abolition of preexisting religions legislation and the creation of a new constitution (the occupier-drafted constitution was promulgated one month after the press release, in November 1946). At the same time, they had to downplay the idea that religious freedom was the unique province of the West. Such an argument would have undermined the idea that religious freedom was a universal principle that could and should be adopted in Japan.

Lectures and Speeches

In addition to promulgating press releases for a general Japanese audience, Religions Division members also used invitations to speak at gatherings sponsored by transsectarian groups and religious universities to push their interpretations of religious freedom. Such appearances had to conform to the basic criterion that they not be seen as lending support to any particular religious group, but they formed prime opportunities for Religions Division bureaucrats to hammer home the point that Japanese religious leaders had mistaken the prewar status quo for genuine liberty and that local religious leaders needed to reeducate themselves in the true significance of religious freedom.

For example, an undated speech given by an anonymous Religions Division member to the Jinja Honchō (National Association of Shrines) shows that at least some Religions Division representatives readily told religious organizations which aspects of their own doctrines were more or less acceptable under the new regime. The speech, probably delivered in 1946 when the Jinja Honchō was newly formed and trying to clarify Occupation policy vis-à-vis shrines, adopted a generous if somewhat supercilious approach. The orator flatly stated that the closure of some shrines would probably be unavoidable in the context of the Occupation and that some shrines might face unprecedented economic difficulties. However, he argued, the trees that marked shrine properties should be protected as "the most distinctive and attractive feature of the Japanese landscape" and as physical evidence of long-standing Shintō tradition rather than being felled to make a quick profit. Similarly, while the attrition among parishioners was no doubt a matter of grave concern, by no means should potential or actual parishioners be coerced into supporting shrines.

Turning from economic matters to the politically problematic nature of Shintō doctrine, the Religions Division representative took the opportunity to lecture the assembly about those aspects of Shintō doctrine that had not been overly tainted by earlier political affiliation and therefore "prevented . . . from developing religious ethics of a very high order." Despite the existence of a few minor martial deities, imperial deities such as Amaterasu were actually more interested in peaceful pursuits such as agriculture and weaving. By tying Amaterasu to pacifism, the official implied that Shintō was essentially peaceful and that militarists had corrupted Shintō doctrine during the war years.

The Religions Division representative also argued that despite Shintō's linkages with narratives of racial superiority, eminent scholar of Shintō Katō Genchi (1873–1965) had indicated that the religion had redeemable ethical qualities. Such qualities could and should be developed and nurtured in recognition of the "inherent equality" of all people. The official concluded the speech by saying that it was "to be hoped that Shintō leaders will be able to draw out of their own tradition a philosophy and a practice which while preserving the best of the Japanese heritage will be ethically consistent with advancement in a modern world."[27]

The lectures and speeches Religions Division officials gave as part of their outreach efforts encapsulated a major epistemic shift that was then underway regarding how religious freedom could be tied to broader humanistic ideals. The vague nature of the "higher ethical principles" that they advocated reflected the similarly ambiguous language of human rights that had recently come into vogue. During the war, human rights had served as flowery rhetoric justifying American participation in the war more than they had served as a substantive facet of international law or diplomacy.[28] In the context of the Occupation, however, officials were forced to articulate what precisely this meant. One step of this process, exemplified by the speech delivered to the Jinja Honchō, was to effectively redefine religion so that "real" religions were understood to link themselves to universalistic ideals rather than to particularist sentiments (such as nationalism, in the case of Shintō). The second step was to associate religious freedom with universalism and to invite religious leaders to treat religious freedom as the most fundamental and precious among all other rights and liberties.[29] This was part of the process of affixing religious freedom to an innate religiosity shared by all humans, a project that required Japanese interpreters to construct new histories, legal theories, and visions of the human.

JAPANESE NIGHTMARES

The concept of religious-freedom-as-human-right gestated in wartime propaganda and was born in the policy initiatives of the Allied Occupation. However, as had been the case with the policy of eradicating "National Shintō," theoretical interpretations that could support and justify the policy of promoting religious-freedom-as-human-right came after the fact. Just as Occupation officials hastily concocted rationales for the promotion of religious freedom once they realized that they had not formally defined the term, there was a parallel move on the part of influential Japanese interpreters such as political theorists, constitutional scholars, and scholars of religion to construct new theories of religious freedom with the start of the Occupation and particularly with the promulgation of the new constitution on 3 November 1946.[30]

The promulgation of the new constitution prompted scholars of constitutional law to identify how the new religious freedom clause (Article 20) and a clause about restrictions on state financing of religious institutions (Article 89) differed from the stipulations in Article 28 of the 1889 Meiji Constitution, which had offered an explicit guarantee of religious freedom. For the most part, these attempts focused on showing why Japan had previously gotten religious freedom wrong, but in these early stages, they also revealed considerable confusion as to what it meant to treat religious freedom as a human right.

This meant that a degree of theorization was necessary to make the language of innate, universal rights intelligible as a facet of constitutional law. Japanese scholars of constitutional law, government bureaucrats, and scholars of religion engaged in a campaign to promote popular and clerical understanding of religious-freedom-as-human-right by treating religiosity as a universal human attribute, but one that had "true" and "false" manifestations. "Real religion" was supposed to be internal, private, and psychologically beneficial; "false religion" was magical, public, and for the material benefit of clerics or the political benefit of the state.[31] The humanism these new interpretations of religion shared performed triple duty: it countered sacerdotalism, statism, and "superstition" all at once.

This humanist emphasis would become increasingly important in theoretical justifications of the new human rights paradigm. As a human right in a world characterized by religious pluralism, religious freedom could not come from a transcendent source that was affixed to any particular religious worldview (rights could not be "god-given"), nor could it flow from states to their citizens (because states, like wartime Japan, might get it "wrong"). The sole remaining alternative was to have religious freedom well up from within humans themselves. This necessitated the construction of a religious anthropology: a worldview that saw religion as an essential and irreducible component of human life.

Legal Interpretations of Articles 20 and 89 of the New Constitution

One of the most notable of the many ironies that characterized the Occupation was that in the name of promoting democracy the American occupiers scrapped a painstakingly crafted Japanese constitutional draft and replaced it with one written by a committee of American "advisors."[32] Given the strong policy emphasis on eradicating Japan's "bad religion" of State Shintō, it is no surprise that Article 20 of the new constitution offered a particularly thorough separation of religion from the state. The text of Article 20 read:

> 1) Religious freedom is guaranteed to all. No religious organizations shall receive special privileges from the state, nor exercise any political authority.
>
> 2) No person may be forced to participate in any religious acts, celebration, rites, or practice.
>
> 3) The state and its organs shall refrain from religious education or any other religious activity.

While clearly the new constitution was not of Japanese creation, it is not the case that it simply bestowed unprecedented religious freedom on the Japanese people. From the moment the constitution was promulgated in November 1946, Japanese people were proactive interpreters of the religious freedom guarantee. Numerous books and pamphlets explaining the significance of the new regime were published immediately after the so-called Peace Constitution was promulgated. These books were usually written in a plain, unadorned style; some were illustrated (figure 8).[33] The sheer volume of such texts suggests that they enjoyed an avid readership, although it may also have been the case that savvy authors recognized a lucrative opportunity to capitalize on a timely topic.[34] At any rate, these relatively affordable explanatory tracts exhibited considerable creativity in parsing the role of religious freedom in the new document.

One of these handbooks was published by a group called the Tokyo New Japan Group and edited by one Nagasawa Hitoshi (d.u.). The book went by the title *The New Constitution Reader: All Articles and Clauses Explained* and featured a picture of the National Diet Building on its cover.[35] The accessible primer began with a general introduction by an anonymous author (probably the editor Nagasawa) and then an opening chapter by

Kanamori Tokujirō (1886–1959) that laid out the "Characteristic Features of the Revised Constitution—Awareness of Noble Ideals, Respect for Universal Human Principles." Kanamori enumerated these principles in his subheadings: "(1) Lack of Specificity"; "(2) Thoroughgoing Rationality"; "(3) Respect for the Individual"; "(4) Popular Sovereignty"; "(5) Imperial System"; and "(6) Upholding World Peace." The first of these sections referred to the fact that the constitution did not advance any particularist claims about the uniqueness of Japan vis-à-vis other nations, but rather based the legal document on universal human principles.[36] The second section laid out a secularist argument in the sense that Kanamori praised the diminution of empirically unverifiable claims in politics. He argued that Japan's prewar constitution had included a provision of religious freedom, but had failed to adopt a truly rationalist spirit (presumably in its designation of the emperor as "sacred and inviolable"). This was because the prewar regime had based political governance on irrational mythology and because it had adopted a system of "officially recognized religions" that reserved privileges for Buddhist and Shintō sects with established pedigrees while reserving for some Shintō shrines and ideas a position beyond the pale of garden-variety "religion."[37] The remaining sections of Kanamori's opening chapter explained the principles of "democracy," "freedom," and "peace" that were enshrined in the new constitution.

The next section of the text, "The New Constitution and Interpretation," featured the text of the constitution followed by terse explanatory prose. In the section explaining the religious freedom clause (Article 20), the author described religious freedom as being an essential component of human rights discourse, but identified the motive for the introduction of a religious freedom clause as being primarily about eradicating State Shintō.[38] At this early stage (the text was published in 1946), the link between human rights and religious freedom existed primarily at a rhetorical level. Despite Kanamori's claims about the new constitution being premised on "universal principles," in the text's explanation of the religious freedom clause the true motive for the inclusion of the clause was primarily negative (abolishing State Shintō) rather than positive (safeguarding a universal right). The author claimed that State Shintō had infringed on religious-freedom-as-human-right but did not clarify how; the source of religious-freedom-as-human-right was also unclear. The author sidestepped the issue by vaguely gesturing to the intellectual history of human rights without citing any sources. (This move was strikingly similar to the vague intellectual history offered in the Occupation press release cited above.)

Minobe Tatsukichi (1873–1948), the former Tokyo Imperial University law professor who had been forced to resign his post in 1935 for his theory that the emperor was merely an "organ of the state" rather than superior to it, also published a constitutional primer in 1947. Minobe had contributed directly to the construction of new constitutional drafts as a local legal adviser during the first two years of the Occupation; his opinions seem to have been trusted by the occupiers, no doubt because they viewed him as a hero who had sacrificed his career to resist "emperor worship." Minobe's 1947 text *An Overview of the New Constitution* can therefore be seen as a treatment of the main provisions of the constitution by an intellectual who was esteemed for his knowledge of constitutional law and intimately familiar with the new legal regime.[39]

Minobe's book covered the constitution methodically, laying out the rationale for its promulgation and comparing it with the constitutions of other countries. Like the book previously cited, later sections of Minobe's book covered each constitutional provision, providing the text of the clause and then following it up with an explanation. Under the heading for Article 20 of the new constitution, Minobe argued that the 1889 Meiji Constitution had acknowledged religious freedom but had subjected it to numerous restrictions, meaning that religious freedom itself had not been thoroughly actualized. As evidence, Minobe pointed to the prewar treatment of Shintō as Japan's national religion, state support of shrines and priests, the compulsory participation of schoolchildren in rites at public schools, the obligatory participation of bureaucrats and citizens in shrine rites, and differential treatment of the thirteen "Shintō sects" and Buddhist schools in comparison to Shrine Shintō. While Minobe's accusations were accurate in terms of the mandatory participation in shrine rites, technically his claim that the prewar constitution made Shintō Japan's national religion was inaccurate. The Meiji Constitution specifically avoided making any such claim, and throughout the Meiji constitutional period (1890–1945), administrators, legal scholars, and clerics had tied themselves in knots trying to fit compulsory shrine rites into the legal framework provided by the constitution. (Indeed, as I showed in chapter 1, Minobe was one of them.)

Moving from the Meiji Constitution to the new "Peace Constitution," Minobe argued that the 15 December 1945 Shintō Directive had been promulgated in order to eliminate the unsavory legal practices of the past and inaugurate *true* religious freedom. According to the constitutional scholar, Article 20 of the new constitution had been based on this Occupation directive. In this way, he averred, genuine religious freedom would be guaranteed to all. Strikingly, Minobe did not argue that religious freedom derived from any ultimate source, but rather from a directive issued by a military occupying power.

Minobe's concluding move on the topic of religious freedom was equally noteworthy. Although he had criticized the Meiji Constitution for imposing untoward limits on religious freedom, he suggested—quite against the letter of the religious freedom clause in the postwar constitution—that religious freedom had natural limits in the case of "pseudo-religions." While it might be difficult to draw the line between "true" and "false" religions, he argued, despite the expansive scope of the new constitution it was obvious that people who disingenuously adopted the "mask of religion" and disturbed peace and order by disseminating "absurdly false teachings" should be stopped by the state. "Real religions" were genuine because they had historically been recognized as such, according to Minobe, while "false religions" claimed a divine mandate in order to deceive gullible people.[40] How newly arisen religions could acquire the status of "real religion" over time was not a problem that Minobe's tract addressed.

The Influence of Religious Studies on Universalistic Conceptions of Religious Freedom

Even as legal experts tried to explain how a national constitution could guarantee universal rights that transcended the jurisdiction of the state, scholars of religion took to the pages of newspapers to offer to clerics and laity alike their normative claims about what had been wrong with Japanese religions in the prewar period and how Japanese religions should develop in the new postwar era. While their attitudes were not necessarily cynical or nakedly opportunistic, the Occupation gave scholars of religion a chance to underscore the importance of their relatively young field.[41] To policy makers and bureaucrats, they were a source of expertise about the religious world; to ecclesiastical authorities, they were a source of authoritative information about the expectations of the new regime.[42]

This unique position of simultaneous interpretation allowed religious studies scholars to not only provide the terms through which Occupation policy was formulated, but also to frame the very parameters of "acceptable" and "unacceptable" religion.[43] University of Tokyo scholars Oguchi Iichi (1910–86) and Kishimoto Hideo (1903–64) and Religions Division researcher William P. Woodard (1896–1973) all tried to advance prescriptive understandings of religion from their positions of academic authority. If the interpreters of the new constitution had been inconsistent in the ways that they understood the origins and import of religious freedom, the scholars of religion offered a normative framework that affixed religious freedom to a universal, innate religiosity even as they maintained subtle distinctions between "true" and "false" religion.

Scholars of religion were quick to advertise the value of their unique type of expertise at the onset of the Occupation. For example, in an article published in the religious journal *Shūkyō kōron* (*Religion Forum*) on 15 December 1945, scholar of religious studies Oguchi argued that greater awareness of religious studies would not only have prevented the problems of the past, but could also help to guide Japan toward a better future: To the uninitiated, he wrote, religious studies probably seemed to be a field reserved for those of "antiquarian and eccentric taste." However, in reflecting on Japan's recent defeat, Oguchi speculated that the factors that led to Japanese religious nationalism (concepts of the divine nation, a chosen people, emperor worship) could have been avoided if intellectuals and administrators had been better versed in religious studies. Indeed, with the benefit of historical hindsight, religious studies seemed to be not the province of armchair academics, but rather *the* academic field of cultured individuals. Moreover, given that the recent abolition of the 1939 Religious Organizations Law would likely result in the efflorescence of any number of unsavory marginal religious movements, now more than ever the expertise of scholars of religion was necessary. Here Oguchi insinuated that religious studies could provide otherwise gullible Japanese citizens with the requisite intellectual tools for distinguishing genuine religion from state ideology and spurious superstition alike.[44]

Oguchi staked out a position for religious studies that was clearly based on wishful thinking. However, his description was a surprisingly accurate representation of the influential role played by scholars of religion in negotiating postwar religion-state relations. In December 1945 Oguchi could only speak in vague, aspirational terms about what this would look like. However, on the same day that he published his reflections on the edifying power of religious studies, the occupiers promulgated the Shintō Directive that officially separated Shintō from the state. That directive bore the fingerprints of Oguchi's University of Tokyo colleague Kishimoto Hideo.[45]

The Occupation directive to "encourage the Japanese people to develop a desire for religious freedom" was difficult to accomplish. To the extent that it was a success, it was greatly aided by Kishimoto, a cosmopolitan scholar who blended a politically progressive commitment to latitudinarian religions policy with a technocratic approach that aimed to thoroughly redefine the capacities of religion and state in postwar society. Top officials in the Japanese Ministry of Education turned to Kishimoto, then a relatively junior assistant professor in the Department of Religious Studies at Tokyo Imperial University, to serve as a mediator between the ministry and its parallel branch in the occupying military government.[46] In his capacity as an informal advisor to the Religions Division and private tutor to author of the Shintō Directive William K. Bunce, Kishimoto greatly influenced Occupation policy. He simultaneously served as a consultant for the Religious Affairs Section (Shūmuka) of the Ministry of Education and as an expert witness in hearings on the prospect of post-Occupation constitutional revision.[47] In addition to influencing policy on both the Japanese and American sides, Kishimoto met regularly with transsectarian groups and published prolifically in religious journals and mainstream newspapers.

Although the mobilization of religious studies expertise during the Occupation was clearly intended to provide an objective, academic standpoint regarding Japanese religion-state relations, Kishimoto readily made prescriptive statements about how Japanese religions should behave in the context of the new regime.[48] He used the anodyne tone of academe to speak authoritatively about religious doctrine and history when interacting with Occupation policy makers and Japanese governmental officials, but when talking to religious groups Kishimoto cultivated an air of intellectual superiority to superciliously draw distinctions between "genuine" and "false" religion. While I do not want to overstate his influence, the academic authority that Kishimoto represented exerted considerable influence on operative definitions of "religion" and "freedom," both during the Occupation and afterward. Indeed, in listing up his contributions as advisor to the occupiers, Kishimoto's former assistant Takagi Kiyoko (1918–2011) argued that he persuaded the Japanese to establish "religious freedom in the true sense."[49]

Takagi's encomium was not an unbiased assessment, and her conception of "religious freedom in the true sense" is one I fundamentally reject. That said, the evidence suggests that Kishimoto advanced a particular vision of religion-state relations that diagnosed the problems with the religious world, prescribed antidotes for the various reactionary tendencies he saw as impediments to progress, and offered a long-term prognosis for the continued viability of some religions while anticipating desuetude or death for others. Kishimoto's humanistic understanding of religion provided theoretical support for the new religious-freedom-as-human-right.

For example, in a March 1947 article entitled "The Modern Religious

Spirit and Shrine Shintō" serialized in *Jinja shinpō* (*Shrine News*), Kishimoto argued that Shrine Shintō faced two types of problems.[50] The first was immediate and was directly related to the Occupation reforms. Specifically, it concerned how shrines could embrace the principle of religious freedom, eliminate militarism, and eradicate ultranationalistic thought. The second was both long-term and fundamental. "In a word," Kishimoto wrote, "it is a problem of how much Shrine Shintō can persevere in the face of the modern spirit of criticism and of finding elements within Shintō that can transcend the age and continue indefinitely."[51]

Looking at the broader arc of his outreach articles, what Kishimoto apparently meant was that "real" religion cultivated exalted inner states, while inferior religious practices were based on magic, crass pursuit of material benefits, or the melding of religion with politics. That is, Kishimoto's academic approach privatized religion in the sense that it drew a sharp distinction between personal religious sentiment and public life. This attitude frequently verged on the paternalistic, as when Kishimoto prefaced an article serialized in the Shintō newspaper *Jinja shinpō* in July 1947 with the potentially incendiary claim that Shintō priests were ignorant of the "true character of religion."[52]

In addition to publishing hortatory articles in religious journals read primarily by clerics, Kishimoto also used the public forum of the newspaper opinion column to outline prescriptive measures for religions' postwar development. For example, in a serialized article entitled "Expectations for the Religious World at the Start of the Year" that appeared in the mainstream newspaper *Tokyo Daily News* (*Tokyo Nichinichi Shinbun*) over five days in early January 1948, Kishimoto began by reiterating his claim that the age of religion being solely for the gods was long past and that the age of religion existing for the sake of humans had arrived.[53] With this functionalist understanding of religion established, Kishimoto laid out his expectations for Shrine Shintō, Buddhism, Christianity, the groups formerly designated as the Shintō sects (*shoha shūkyō*), the upstart "new religions" (*shinkō shūkyō*), the political administration of religion, public education, and journalism. These expectations were not merely predictions about the challenges that each of these fields would face; they were "expectations" in the sense that Kishimoto advocated prescriptive measures about how to construct ideal religion-state relations.

Kishimoto's treatment of the problems of religious administration in this article is of particular note. He argued that while the line between religion and the state had been clearly drawn in the immediate postwar period, the reasons for drawing that line were still poorly understood. Separation was not important because religion was now irrelevant (as some Japanese clerics apparently feared), but rather because the principle of separation *respected* religion and guaranteed citizens' freedom of belief. While Kishimoto argued that separation of religion from the state was the basic requirement of religious freedom because it kept the state from protecting or persecuting specific religions, the rest of his article made clear that certain religious practices—particularly those of the "new religions" and Shintō shrines—needed refinement.

Kishimoto's Occupation-era articles collectively presented his humanist understanding of religion as an essential part of the "modern critical spirit," but they created that idealized religiosity as much as they described an existing suite of modern dispositions. He presented religion as socially influential in a way that could be both positive (promoting democracy, fulfilling emotional needs) and negative (misleading the people through vulgar practices, counteracting postwar cosmopolitanism with revanchist ultranationalism). His outreach publications encouraged clerics and laypeople alike to embrace religion as a conduit for democratization and a font of emotional fulfillment while jettisoning past practices and attitudes as so much magic and superstition. This moralizing quality of his work was hardly subtle.[54]

Kishimoto's influence was bolstered in part because of his prestigious academic appointment at the University of Tokyo, his eventual position as chairperson of the Japanese Association for Religious Studies, and his connections with both the Ministry of Education and the Religions Division of the Occupation. In addition to his close ties to Religion and Cultural Resources Division chief Bunce, Kishimoto had a close partner in Religions Division research specialist William P. Woodard. Woodard's duties were primarily focused on gathering information rather than setting policy, but by the latter half of the Occupation he was regularly engaging in outreach projects that turned his previous missionary training to the task of promoting religious freedom.[55]

For example, in a 4 November 1949 speech given at Taishō University (a transsectarian Buddhist seminary) on the subject of "Religious Education in Social Studies," Woodard argued that the most pressing task for a young university in the wake of the war was to investigate the principle of religious freedom, particularly religious freedom as a fundamental aspect of a democratic society.[56] Precisely because a Buddhist university such as Taishō was unencumbered by the stipulations regarding religious education that faced public institutions, it was in a unique position to take the lead in clarifying the importance of religious freedom and the (limited) role that religion could play in education. Woodard recommended that Taishō establish a seminar on the topic of religious freedom and separation of religion and the state as a way of staking out a position of authority in this topical field. Although freedom of religion might seem to be a simple matter of elective liberty in terms of religious affiliation, in fact the situation was far more complicated and demanded strict scrutiny. "A university which wishes to prepare religious leaders who understand the modern situation," he argued, "should provide ample opportunity for the study of religious freedom so as to make it plain to the leaders of all sects concerned that there can be no freedom in an authoritarian state."[57]

Although Woodard was somewhat patronizing in his outreach lectures, it would be a mistake to assume that he assumed the superiority of American civilization to Japanese. In fact, Woodard's memoir and his collected papers housed at the University of Oregon suggest that he firmly resisted the chauvinistic attitudes many of his compatriots and fellow occupiers exhibited.[58] But for many Americans of the day, the Occupation simply confirmed the superiority of American political practices. The concept of "real" religious freedom that the Americans were supposedly offering to Japan was a new construction that was developed for the specific propagandistic and policy purposes of the Occupation, but inevitably it was linked to the nascent, still inchoate, language of human rights. The paradoxical relationship between this American particularism and the universalism of human rights claims was never fully resolved during the Occupation, but the pivot to fighting communism provided a framework in which these seemingly oppositional impulses could be partially harmonized.

AMERICAN DREAMS

The American promotion of religious liberty in Japan not only spurred new Japanese understandings about how to properly parse faith and freedom, but also fostered new American understandings of the same issues. The vision of a liberal democracy premised on America's unique relationship with religious freedom was just emerging at around the time of the Pacific War (1941–45). It was an invented tradition that discovered new liberal heroes (e.g., Locke) and posited the origin of modern liberalism in a theological position (the quest for religious freedom among the early American colonists). It also advocated a type of latitudinarian religions policy that nevertheless assumed primacy of place for Christianity.[59]

As the negative image of the Japanese foe changed over the course of the Occupation, the ineluctable recognition of non-Christian religiosity as valid forced a reconfiguration of the recently invented American tradition of religious freedom. Emphasis on the universal human right to religious freedom superseded the particularist claim about America's manifest destiny. Similarly, the evident successes of Japan's fledgling postwar democracy called into question the causal connection some Americans were wont to posit between Christianity and democracy.

This shift was already apparent in the ways American propaganda discussed the Japanese in war and peace. For example, whereas wartime propaganda films like *Know Your Enemy: Japan* drew a contrast between "good" and "bad" religion by comparing the falsely apotheosized Japanese emperor with "our own Son of God," the Occupation training film *Our Job in Japan* argued that the problem of rehabilitating Japan lay in reconfiguring "the Japanese brain."[60] The former film drew an implicit contrast between indistinguishable Japanese soldiers who were like "prints off of the same negative" and fully enfranchised American individuals capable of thinking for themselves, but the latter film was more magnanimous. The Japanese brain was "just like any other brain," but it had unfortunately been "hopped up" by militarists who had shrewdly used the "tired old religion of Shintō" in their plan for world domination.

Our Job in Japan was written by Theodor Geisel, better known as children's book author Dr. Seuss, and featured the famous author's characteristically rhythmic cadences in the narration. Its message exemplified the attitude that would come to dominate the later Occupation period: The Japanese people were human just like "us," but not all religious ideas were created equal. The film explicitly contrasted "good ideas" (a shot of a venerable Buddhist priest) with "mumbo-jumbo" (long shots from effervescent Shintō festivals accompanied by a soundtrack that would have sounded alien to American ears). The right to choose one's religion had to be preserved, but *Our Job in Japan* made clear that the occupiers were to help the Japanese make "better choices."

An American Export Made in Japan

Our Job in Japan may have been targeted to American military personnel headed to Japan, but its message was also designed to resonate with audiences at home. American articles and editorials from the later Occupation period show that Americans loosely kept tabs on the progress of the Occupation but generally paid little attention to Japan now that the nation was no longer considered an existential threat. To the extent that the home audience did pay attention, however, reportage on Japanese religion tended to reinforce distinctions between "real" and "false" religions even as reports tended to emphasize the high-mindedness of American policy and the pacific outcomes of American-style latitudinarianism.

A 4 February 1947 dispatch from Tokyo entitled "Shintō Spreading throughout Japan: Hundreds of Sects Spring Up—Faith Healing and Spirit Possession Are Dominant" by *New York Times* reporter Burton Crane (1901–63) shows how reporting on Japan could advance normative claims about "real religion" and the proper position of religions vis-à-vis society and the state.[61] Even as it breathlessly discussed the efflorescence of marginal religious movements with roots in Shintō traditions, Crane's article functioned to reassure readers that Occupation reforms had worked and that Shintō had been thoroughly demilitarized.[62]

"Shintō, Japan's religion of blood and iron before the war, is the focus for extreme nationalism's reverting toward the crude superstitions from which it sprang," Crane's article began. Offering a vivid image of devotees of a Shintō-derived new religion gathered in a small room engaged in rhythmic chanting and "enveloped in religious fervor," Crane implicitly drew a distinction between "proper" (staid) and "improper" (fervent) religious practice. Mildly disparaging references to multiple deities also subtly highlighted a distinction between "real" monotheistic religion and "false" polytheism. By mobilizing phrases like "crude superstition" and by highlighting the criminal records of some of the leaders of the new groups, Crane implied that the new sects—and, by extension, Shintō—were "false religions." Yet his article was also reassuring in that these primitive practices were apparently innocuous. The new groups were purportedly seeking peace, not war. The Occupation introduction of religious freedom had worked in that these peculiar groups, however wacky, had been allowed to flourish.

This magnanimous attitude reflected an expanding tolerance of previously repugnant modes of religious being.[63] Ongoing interactions with the formerly dehumanized enemy exerted influence on American conceptions of religion and religious freedom, building upon a corresponding domestic trend. For the previous several decades, American understandings of authentic "religion" had already been expanding beyond mainline Protestantism to include evangelical, Catholic, and Jewish perspectives.[64] Against this background, the practical need to extend religious freedom to Buddhists and Shintō adherents in Japan demanded even greater expansion of the religious freedom concept.[65] When paired with the wartime rhetoric of human rights and the exigent need to make the language of human rights intelligible, religious freedom came to be premised on the existence of a universal, innate religiosity that needed to be protected at all costs. In other words, the Japanese case offered confirmation of the idea that America's unique relationship with religious freedom was exportable.

This effort to universalize religious freedom took place in a somewhat bizarre fashion. One of the many ironies of the Occupation period is that even as the occupiers encouraged the Japanese to disaggregate religion from politics and reject theories of Japanese uniqueness, the Americans were in the process of attempting to bring religion into a stronger, more central position in American public life and foreign policy. The Americans had criticized the Japanese for subsuming sectarian differences under the overarching goal of nation-building prior to and during the war, but US president Harry S. Truman (1884–1972) was similarly invested in getting religious leaders to set aside their sectarian differences in the service of uniting Americans—and the world—in combating communism.[66] American promotion of religious freedom abroad took on a new urgency in the incipient Cold War, becoming the centerpiece of what William Inboden has called "America's diplomatic theology."[67]

This was not merely an executive branch project. For example, the *New York Times* reported on 15 February 1949 that a new "Committee for Protection of Religious Freedom throughout the World" had been established in Brooklyn the day before. According to the article, the group intended to combat communism's "unprovoked and unrestricted attack on all religions."[68] A few months later, the *New York Times* editorial page advocated the global promotion of religious freedom by arguing that petty sectarianism had no place in the face of the threat posed by "those who would deny freedom of religion." While sectarian differences would remain, the editors admitted, all religious communities were united in opposition to tyranny and in favor of freedom.[69]

In making this claim, the *New York Times* editorial posited the existence of a universal religiosity that both informed and demanded human dignity and freedom. This sort of language had matured in the context of the Occupation as the democratizing project was extended to social imaginaries and modes of religious being that were not necessarily Western or Christian.

While the Occupation did not result in the wholesale Christianization of Japan that many Americans anticipated, it did provide Americans with a model for promoting religious freedom abroad: Religious freedom had been America's gift to Japan; it could be America's gift to the world.

But was it actually American? With the benefit of historical hindsight, it is clear that the concept of religious-freedom-as-human-right was actually the result of collaborative conversations between American policy makers and their Japanese counterparts, not the unidirectional transfer of an American tradition of "real freedom" to the Japanese. Indeed, the vaunted architecture of American religious freedom was still under construction when the Occupation began, and arguably the construction of an "American" tradition of religious freedom had required the existence of a foil in a dehumanized, ostensibly theocratic enemy like Japan.[70]

The language of human rights that featured in the Occupation may have originally come from wartime propaganda on the Allied side, and it was undoubtedly reinforced by postwar international initiatives that culminated in the 1948 Universal Declaration of Human Rights. However, human rights talk only acquired real substance as the American occupiers tried to create a model in which the state could not easily infringe on citizens' rights and in which the international community vigilantly surveilled states in order to safeguard those rights. That model may have been a convenient tool in American efforts to combat communism globally as the world entered the 1950s, but its origins in the Occupation of Japan should not go overlooked.

THE INHERENT WEAKNESS OF THE NEW HUMAN RIGHTS REGIME

The American project of making the world safe for religion through appeals to protecting religious freedom as a human right was, of course, not as magnanimous as its proponents averred. While President Truman (a Baptist) and Occupation supreme commander General MacArthur (an Episcopalian) were evidently willing to collaborate with Catholics in pursuing their foreign policy ends, in American diplomacy and outreach Protestantism remained the model for religion, and the right to religious freedom that Americans were willing to fight to protect was a right that was premised on religion looking familiar enough that it could be recognized as valid.[71] This represented a triumph of Protestant models of religiosity in international relations insofar as operative conceptions of religious freedom were premised on prioritizing freedom of conscience (private assent to propositional statements of belief).

Nevertheless, the language of human rights and the associated conception of a universal religious anthropology also expanded the range of tolerable beliefs to include modes of religious being and belonging that were not part of the transatlantic cultural heritage. The incorporation of a religious freedom clause in the 1948 Universal Declaration of Human Rights, for example, referred to religion in vague, nondenominational terms that went far beyond the Rooseveltian "freedom to worship God in [one's] own way." The new declaration declared that "everyone has the right to freedom of thought, conscience and religion; this right includes freedom to change his religion or belief, and freedom, either alone or in community with others and in public or private, to manifest his religion or belief in teaching, practice, worship and observance."[72]

Policy makers were already aware at the time of the promulgation of the declaration that the concept of human rights was vague. It was easily liable to misinterpretation or excessively broad application.[73] In 1948 there was still no reliable mechanism for enforcement, no way of determining when and how international observers could and should intervene in domestic politics in order to protect "human rights." There was also no way of guaranteeing that all *homo sapiens* would be regarded as "people" deserving of equal rights. As seen in Minobe's aforementioned interpretation of the religious freedom clause of the postwar constitution, there was additionally the lingering problem that influential interpreters might circumscribe rights based on what they thought of as commonsense distinctions between good and bad religions.

Arguments about the necessity of promoting religious freedom worldwide were furthermore complicated by fundamental contradictions within the concept of religious freedom itself.[74] Religious freedom was simultaneously understood as a freedom *from* religion that reduced the excessive impact of religious actors and ideas on politics and public life, the liberty *to* choose whatever religion one wanted without fear of violent reprisal or the threat of disenfranchisement, and a right *born out of* a particular civilizational complex that was frequently associated with Protestant Christianity (but was sometimes more expansively labeled "Judeo-Christian").[75]

So religious freedom was not universalized overnight simply by including it in a list of "human rights" drawn up by the new United Nations organization. The world still needed a scheme that would position all religions in a comprehensive theoretical framework that showed how religious freedom could apply equally to all people everywhere. Equally necessary was a way to ensure that religious freedom was not mistaken for unfettered license. Healthy restrictions would serve as prophylactics against statist suppression of religion. Religious freedom was good as long as it was not inimical to common sense, peace, and order.

Ultimately, the perennial questions about how liberty might be balanced with security were not made any easier by treating religious freedom as both innate and universal. Treatment of religious freedom as a human right naturally and inevitably gave rise to another set of questions. How could a "human right" that transcended the purview of the state and preceded national citizenship be enforced? Who could police a state? What supervisory body existed to ensure that states provided unqualified religious freedom to their citizens? What agent could define "religion" and "freedom" in a way that could preserve the logic of religious-freedom-as-human-right while simultaneously policing states for potential violations of that right?

While international humanitarian organizations would ultimately step in to fill this watchdog role, in the immediate postwar period a crucial part was played by scholars of religion, who could ostensibly stand "outside" both religion and politics. From their privileged position of academic authority, scholars of religion could designate certain religions legitimate or illegitimate, certain political practices oppressive or emancipatory. The next chapter traces how this process played out in the postwar scholarly study of Japanese religions. However, the exercise was not merely academic, and its effects were not limited to Japan. "State Shintō" provided the postwar world with a paradigmatic model of the political abuse of religious ideas. "Buddhist war responsibility" offered a stereotype of derelict clerics abandoning their duty to protect religious freedom. Finally, the category of "new religions" provided the postwar world with an anodyne term for marginal movements that had previously been saddled with pejorative language like "superstitions," "cults," and "sects."

This was the world that religious studies in (and of) Japan made. When scholars and policy makers today discuss religious freedom as a human right that deserves protection, they begin from the common presupposition that a universal religious anthropology exists. They assume that all humans are predisposed to religiosity even if they are not religious. But this linkage between universal religiosity and human rights only emerged because formerly dehumanized enemies had to be humanized, because radically different religiosities had to be synthesized under a new system of rights and liberties that crossed national boundaries and cultural barriers, and because a wartime propaganda catchphrase had to be turned into reality.

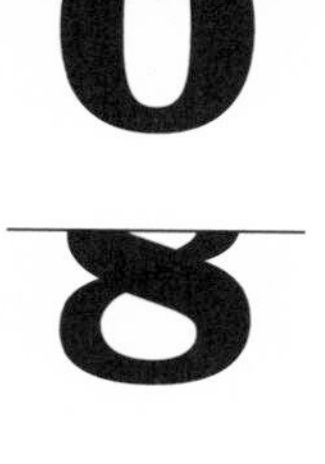

OUT OF THE SPIRITUAL VACUUM

> The establishment of religious freedom was experienced as a distinct shock by the religious world of Japan. Then gradually there came a glimmer of what freedom meant or what it could mean. Many Buddhist temples and Shintō shrines are still floundering in bewilderment, not knowing how to adjust themselves to the current situation. Yet there seems to be evidence that the old sense of dependence on the government is weakening. . . . Inevitably, the establishment of religious freedom releases great stores of social energy. Whether shrines and temples can and will adjust themselves permanently to the ways of a free society or will move in the direction of the revival of the authoritarian system, I cannot prophesy. But as the situation stands today, it will be their choice, and there are many who wish to move forward in accordance with their new freedom.
>
> WILLIAM P. WOODARD (1954)[1]

I BEGIN THIS CHAPTER WITH AN admittedly impossible task. I want to draw attention to a dynamic in postwar scholarship on Japanese religions by talking about something that I distinctly remember reading but initially could not easily trace in the secondary literature. It was precisely because I could not remember exactly *how* I first encountered the phrase that I was able to recognize the significance of the conceptual problem it harbored.

It goes like this. With military defeat and the eradication of State Shintō during the Allied Occupation, Japan in the postwar period was a "spiritual vacuum." The phrase caught my attention because I vaguely recalled that more than one scholar had used it; for years it also nagged at my conscience because the metaphor does powerful rhetorical work. Nature abhors a vacuum. A vacuum is the space into which things rush. If Japan was characterized by a "spiritual vacuum" in the wake of its utter defeat in 1945, something needed to sweep in to fill the void.

When I began investigating the history of this idea of postwar Japan as a "spiritual vacuum," I expected to find it first in the early scholarship trying to explain the postwar efflorescence of "new religions." However, this seemingly reasonable explanation turned out to be wholly incorrect. In fact, the phrase "spiritual vacuum" first emerged in a 1945 plea made by General Douglas MacArthur to Protestant leaders to deliver one thousand missionaries to Japan; he later repeated the phrase in a radio address delivered to the American Congress on 24 February 1947.[2] It is possible that I had first encountered the phrase in Helen Hardacre's brief mention of MacArthur's usage in her 1989 book on Shintō and the state, but I could not shake the feeling that I had encountered the "spiritual vacuum" elsewhere.[3]

A search for "spiritual vacuum" on the Google Books N-gram viewer suggested that MacArthur's turn of phrase was avidly adopted in Christian publications as missionaries sought to turn Japan's temporary state of shock into an opportunity to acquire new converts.[4] However, I also saw that variations on the phrase ("moral vacuum," for example) began to appear in scholarship generated by both Japanese and American academics over the ensuing decades. As I had initially suspected, some of this scholarship used the idea of spiritual vacuity to explain the efflorescence of new religious movements that had taken place in the wake of the war and the Occupation reforms.[5]

When I broadened my search beyond the precise wording "spiritual vacuum," I found the idea reproduced time and again, if not the phrase itself. Historians described postsurrender Japan as a tabula rasa.[6] Scholars portrayed Japanese Buddhist sects in the postwar period as in dire straits due to the loss of traditional political authority and the concomitant suspicion targeted toward ecclesial organizations that had provided ideological and material support for the war. Perhaps the most common assessment was that with the disestablishment of State Shintō and the disintegration of emperor worship, the Japanese people had lost their shared moral compass.[7]

The opportunistic evangelism seen in MacArthur's 1947 speech clearly differs from the more cautious assessments offered by historians and scholars of Japanese religions. Nevertheless, the imagery of the phrase has done considerable rhetorical work for scholars and missionaries alike: a wartime Japanese populace captive to one type of religious ideology (State Shintō) was suddenly wiped clean by military defeat and deprogrammed by Occupation reforms. In the process, the formerly brainwashed Japanese populace became susceptible to a different sort of religious allure (new religions) or ripe for conversion (Christianity).

Many scholars of religion have now critiqued this portrayal because historical facts have gotten in the way of the pat narrative. Christianity never took off in Japan, for example, and eventually scholars of religion pointed out that most of the "new" religions had their historical origins in the prewar period rather than in postwar circumstances.[8] Yet despite these crucial correctives, it is still common to encounter narratives depicting the postwar efflorescence of new religions as a side effect of Occupation legal reforms and the collapse of mainstream religious authority. We repeat it because we know it to be true. We know it to be true because we have read it somewhere. To offer just one example of how tenacious the narrative has been, in a 2006 book chapter on "new religions," Trevor Astley argued that analyses attributing the postwar explosion of new religions to the postwar introduction of religious freedom were misleading, only to contradict himself two pages later and attribute the postwar efflorescence of new religious movements to the Occupation legal reforms.[9]

In sum, the concept of Japan's postwar "spiritual vacuum"—a term initially coined by a megalomaniacal Episcopalian evangelist who happened to sport five stars on his epaulets—has fundamentally structured the study of Japanese religions for the last seventy-odd years. While the phrase "spiritual vacuum" has largely faded from our scholarly conversation, echoes of it reverberate in the truism that the Occupation brought religious freedom to Japan and that the inauguration of religious freedom in Japan elicited a paradigm shift in Japanese religiosity.

DISCIPLINING JAPAN, DISCIPLINING RELIGION

The purpose of this chapter is to make explicit two of the disciplining functions that have structured the postwar study of Japanese religions, with the ultimate aim of showing how the global legal horizons of religious freedom have been partially shaped by academic theorization about religion and rights that initially took place in Japan. On the one hand, I demonstrate that politics and policy objectives informing the postwar academic study of Japanese religions have created and reproduced doctrinal presuppositions about "good" and "bad" religion that have informed conceptual distinctions and working definitions that directly affect which groups are deserving of legal protection and which are not.[10] On the other hand, I intend to show that divorcing the study of Japan from the study of Japan's place in the world has the unfortunate result of downplaying the clear influence of the Occupation on postwar global understandings of religious freedom. By understanding the Occupation's role in constructing religious freedom as a global legal norm (and by elucidating how postwar scholarship reinforced that norm), we can see not only how religious freedom came to be understood as a universal human right at a certain point in history (as I showed in chapter 7), but also why efforts to protect that right often reflect a set of internally inconsistent presuppositions about how religious people should be and behave.

I begin my analysis by tracing how two scholars collaborated in constructing the infrastructure of the academic study of religion during and immediately after the Occupation. Having established the historical origins of the field, I then turn to three topics that have dominated the postwar study of Japanese religions: 1) the aforementioned efflorescence of "new religions" during the Occupation; 2) the rise, disestablishment, and putative postwar resurgence of "State Shintō"; and 3) the moral imperative for Buddhists to confront their "war responsibility." In what should be an obvious pairing with my discussion of scholarly models of resistance and complicity in chapter 4, I show that each of these topics is problematically premised on value judgments about "real religion" being either apolitical or politically progressive. Finally, I show how the study of Japanese religions has had a hitherto unexplored influence on global narratives about religious-freedom-as-human-right. Simply put, the occupiers did not bring religious freedom to Japan on behalf of the world. Rather, Occupation-era Japan happened to be one place and situation (and there were certainly others) where universalistic understandings of religious freedom were born. Scholarship on religion played a crucial role in that process.

KISHIMOTO HIDEO, WILLIAM P. WOODARD, AND POSTWAR RELIGIOUS STUDIES IN JAPAN

The nonconfessional academic study of religion developed relatively early in Japan. Early lectures by Inoue Tetsujirō (1855–1944) at Tokyo Imperial University in the late 1890s eventually turned into a formal lecture series (*kōza*) in 1905; the university established a full-fledged department in 1918.[11] True to that university's mandate of providing cutting-edge scholarship that could support state initiatives, members of the department contributed to policy making by making public statements about religious toleration, negotiating collaborations between religious leaders and policy makers, and sitting on exploratory committees investigating potential religions legislation.[12] While these activities never garnered religious studies scholars the same clout as, say, historians, religious studies expertise captured the attention of American policy makers who were engaged in postsurrender planning (see chapter 5). Since the occupiers had diagnosed Japanese militarism as a fundamentally theological problem, the field of religious studies offered powerful explanatory tools for understanding Japan's wartime missteps.[13] The occupiers' reliance on University of Tokyo assistant professor of religious studies Kishimoto Hideo (1903–64) as a mediator between the Religions Division and the Religious Affairs Office in the Ministry of Education is telling in this regard.[14]

Kishimoto worked closely with members of the Occupation Religions Division and was undoubtedly their primary source of information about Japanese religions. Like his father-in-law and mentor Anesaki Masaharu (1873–1949), Kishimoto had spent time at Harvard and was intimately familiar with American scholarship on religion. He favored a psychologized approach to religion and tended to think about religion primarily in functionalist, humanistic terms. As I showed in the previous chapter, Kishimoto was not at all hesitant to make normative statements about how religions should be or behave, and his willingness to do so made him both a valuable asset and an occasional nuisance for members of the Religions Division.[15]

Kishimoto was a man of international stature and considerable influence in the postwar religious studies world, a position no doubt created in part by his work with the occupiers. He served as president of the Japanese Association for Religious Studies twice (1950–54 and 1960–62), delivered Haskell Lectures at the University of Chicago (1954), held visiting professorships at Stanford (1953–54) and Princeton (autumn 1962), and served as head of the Afro-Asian Secretariat of the International Association for the History of Religions (1958–?).[16] In addition to his aforementioned publications that unstintingly offered normative assessments about how religions should develop, Kishimoto published a slim textbook called *Religious Studies* (*Shūkyōgaku*) in 1961 that outlined the history of the field and laid out a programmatic statement for how the discipline should change in the coming decades.[17]

Like Kishimoto, Religions Division researcher William P. Woodard used his position to influence religious groups. Although he was a junior researcher and was primarily responsible for overseeing the translation work of the Japanese-speaking staff, he had originally trained as a missionary and seems to have turned that early training toward the project of spreading the gospel of religious freedom. In the postwar years, he gave numerous public speeches and lectures on the subject.[18] Woodard also personally facilitated the passage of the Religious Juridical Persons Law of 3 April 1951, which Takemae Eiji later described as "an exercise in democratic self-regulation that exemplified the best of the postwar reforms."[19]

Woodard's departure for the United States at the close of the Occupation in 1952 marked a hiatus in, rather than a cessation of, his academic activities in Japan. During the last years of the Occupation Woodard had already begun discussions with local academics and religious leaders about the possibility of establishing a new research institute dedicated to the academic study of Japanese religions. While such an institute would serve first and foremost as a bilingual clearinghouse for timely information on developments in the Japanese religious world, it would also continue the important task of investigating religious freedom and determining how this most lofty of principles could be continually applied to, and perfected in, the Japanese context.[20]

This planning eventually bore fruit. Woodard returned to Japan in late 1953 to collaborate with Kishimoto in the establishment of this International Institute for the Study of Religions.[21] In his capacity as director of research at the new institute, Woodard organized roundtable conferences on topical issues in the Japanese religious world and solicited translations of cutting-edge Japanese research in the anglophone journal *Contemporary Religions in Japan* (published 1960–70).[22] Woodard used every opportunity to promote religious freedom as he understood it. For example, in a fragmentary draft of a speech on the subject of religious freedom given at Dōshisha University sometime after the establishment of the aforementioned institute (probably around 1960), Woodard exhorted his Christian audience to thoroughly investigate religious freedom in its philosophical and practical aspects, referring to the experiences of people in other countries but firmly basing such investigations in Japanese culture and history. Even as he did so, Woodard implored his audience to keep his comments secret, as they might be misconstrued as his attempt to influence contemporary political decisions or as the official stance of the International Institute for the Study of Religions.[23]

Woodard was responsible not only for editing *Contemporary Religions in Japan* (the predecessor of the contemporary flagship *Japanese Journal of*

Religious Studies), but also for much of the journal's content: by my count he authored or coauthored forty editorials, book reviews, and obituaries for the journal; he also wrote short editorial notes clarifying or critiquing aspects of articles that appeared in the journal. He also published a steady stream of Religions Division documents from his personal records collected during his time in the Religions Division to fructify postwar studies of the Occupation.[24] This research—part memoir, part critical appraisal of Occupation religions policy—was published in 1972 as *The Allied Occupation of Japan, 1945–1952, and Japanese Religions*. While decidedly biased as an insider's account, Woodard's book remains one of the single best sources on Occupation religions policy available to this day. Among other things, Woodard's postwar assessment helped to create the image of Religions and Cultural Resources Division chief William K. Bunce (1907–2008) as a principled hero who introduced the idea of strict separation of religion from the state to Japan through his authorship of the Shintō Directive. This sanguine assessment of Bunce's role deserves revision for reasons traced in previous chapters, but it was tremendously influential on later scholarship.[25]

Woodard also singlehandedly framed how anglophone readers understood the past, present, and future of Japanese religions. Several of the earliest postwar anglophone monographs on Japanese religions featured forewords by Woodard that highlighted the expertise of the authors and indicated the importance of the content.[26] As a general rule, Woodard's forewords positioned a contemporary Japan adjusting to the new reality of religious freedom while rejecting an authoritarian past characterized by its total absence. This twist on MacArthur's "spiritual vacuum" idea would fundamentally shape subsequent scholarship on Japanese religions.

VISIONS OF RELIGIOUS FREEDOM IN THREE POSTWAR SCHOLARLY TRENDS

Even if the postwar study of religions in Japan was not totally monopolized by people in Kishimoto and Woodard's ambit, it would not be inaccurate to say that virtually all postwar nonsectarian scholarship on Japanese religions has been influenced in some way or another by the institutions and journals they established.[27] This was a legacy of the Occupation not only in the sense that the two men initially met through their ongoing interactions at Religions Division headquarters, but also in the sense that both wholeheartedly embraced the Occupation project of instilling a "desire for religious freedom in the Japanese people."[28] For each of them, to study religion from an academic standpoint *was* to promote and protect religious freedom (although Kishimoto had already begun to modify his commitment to strict separation of religion from the state in a series of essays on the subject published from the late 1940s and through the 1950s).[29]

The circumstances of the Occupation had created a new understanding of religious freedom as a human right, but in the absence of an international legal system that could safeguard "human rights" (as opposed to "civil rights" granted to citizens by their states), it was unclear how such rights would be protected. Scholarship stepped in to fill this legal void by highlighting the ideal of latitudinarianism, designating specific ideas and practices as illegitimate, and creating normative expectations for religions' historical development and social engagement. Religious studies discourse pushed religion into the private sphere, rendered potentially unruly religions docile, and protected some marginal religions from persecution. These discussions filtered out of Japan to other areas, providing the contemporaneously expanding global religious studies community with useful terms and concepts. Postwar Japanese exports ultimately included not only the cars and electronics for which the nation is justifiably famous, but also crucial categories that continue to shape the global governance of religions today.

The postwar use of religious studies to promote prescriptive religious freedom norms happened in at least three ways. Scholars transformed marginal religious movements from targets of suspicion into recipients of protection by creating the academic-apologetic category of "new religions" and exporting that category to the anglophone scholarly community. Other scholars elaborated on the category of State Shintō as a model for both "bad religion" and "bad secularism," anticipating and facilitating later uses of terms like "Islamism" in the geopolitical context of the twenty-first century.[30] Still others constructed the popular narrative that Buddhist clerics had been derelict in their duty to protect rights and freedoms, suggesting that clerics had abandoned the politically progressive tendencies supposedly inherent in Buddhist doctrine.

"New Religions"

It is not the case that the Occupation spurred an efflorescence in new religions so much as it is true that the circumstances of the Occupation rendered marginal religions visible in a new way. Indeed, while human history has been periodically punctuated by the emergence of novel religious movements, the scholarly category of "new religions" is of very recent provenance and can be traced directly to the Occupation period.[31] In his "Overview" in the 2004 *Oxford Handbook of New Religious Movements*, James R. Lewis argued that the phrase was actually introduced to anglophone scholarship via studies that were generated in response to the spurt of schisms and incorporations of religious juridical persons that occurred in early postwar Japan.[32] Those studies used the term "new religions" (*shinshūkyō*) as a result of a modestly successful apologetic campaign on the part of the Japanese Federation of New Religious Organizations to change the terminology bureaucrats and academics used to discuss member groups.[33]

As discussed briefly in chapter 6, the establishment of the Federation of Japanese New Religious Organizations (Shin Nihon Shūkyō Dantai Rengō Kai, commonly known by its Japanese acronym, Shinshūren) on 17 October 1951 took place because leaders of new movements such as Risshō Kōsei Kai and PL Kyōdan recognized that they did not benefit from the lobbying power wielded by the recently formed Japanese Federation of Religious Organizations. These groups were politically marginalized even if they boasted numerous adherents; the federation they formed was specifically designed to ensure that emergent groups would not suffer due to any legal revisions that favored the clerical establishment or that otherwise intruded upon their religious liberties. Simply put, the emergent groups organized their own transsectarian lobby because they had been shunned by the clerical establishment and initially could not find a voice in the Japanese Religions Federation.

By Shinshūren's own account, it was Religions Division researcher William P. Woodard who urged the leaders of the various marginal movements to organize in this way.[34] Although Woodard later criticized the lax rules for religious incorporation included in the 28 December 1945 Religious Corporations Ordinance and was overtly skeptical of some of the new religious movements, he was nevertheless concerned that marginal movements might suffer discrimination under the Occupation.[35] Woodard's encouragement of the new religious organizations to organize their own transsectarian group suggests that he recognized that they would have better success legally and socially if they could link their objectives with religious freedom, both as a juridical principle and as a humanist ideal. His influence on Shinshūren can be seen in the group's intense preoccupation with religious freedom, its anticlericalism, and its professed disdain for "authority worship." The diverse religious organizations that comprised the group took three principles as their shared objectives, namely: 1) to protect the freedom of religious belief; 2) to promote religious cooperation; and 3) to contribute to world peace.[36] These objectives were sufficiently banal as to overcome any significant doctrinal differences between member groups, but they also reflect the premium placed on religious freedom in the wake of the war.

For religious movements that had suffered persecution during the war or had formally incorporated after it, embracing the version of religious freedom promulgated by the occupiers also served an apologetic purpose by aligning these groups with the new status quo while associating mainstream temple Buddhism and Shrine Shintō with the discredited wartime regime.[37] It is therefore significant that Shinshūren's founders settled on the name "Shin Nihon Shūkyō Dantai Rengō Kai." Although usually translated as the "Japanese Federation of New Religious Organizations," when translated word for word, this could read "League Association of Religious Organizations *for the New Japan*."[38]

Consistent with this ambiguous phrasing, the federation regularly depicted the clerical establishments of Buddhism and Shintō as hopelessly out of touch and mired in a sycophantic relationship with the state. Shinshūren member organizations vehemently fought for respectful treatment in journalism and scholarship and consistently called for latitudinarian governmental policies that would take their needs and perspectives into account.[39] The organization turned to scholarship in pursuit of this apologetic project. For example, a 1963 decennial retrospective published by the research division mobilized all the accoutrements of an academic publication such as an authoritative tone, documentary evidence in the form of charts and photographs, and interviews with leading authorities on religion including Kishimoto and Religions Division chief William K. Bunce. However, a polemical streak appeared throughout, implying that only the new religions could properly understand religious freedom.[40]

Shinshūren's member organizations had little to lose by promoting religious freedom so vigorously. Unlike their counterparts in the temple Buddhist and Shrine Shintō worlds, most of them had no traditionally close relationship with the state to preserve. Aside from tax exemption, most of them also had no financial incentives to align themselves with state initiatives (as I showed in chapter 6, shrines and temples were desperate to keep property, or to regain land lost, as a result of Occupation land reforms). This relative economic freedom allowed them to identify themselves as the religious groups best suited to the new postwar context. In the aforementioned 1963 retrospective, for example, the research unit for the organization argued that freedom of religion was "still unripe" and had not yet "been rooted in Japanese soil" nearly twenty years after the occupiers transplanted religious liberty to Japan. Bureaucrats aimed to control religions, the group opined, while even mainstream Buddhist and Shintō clerics did not yet recognize that "freedom of religion is the source of all freedoms and forms the foundation of human rights."[41]

Formerly marginalized religious groups were thus able to make appeals to religious-freedom-as-human-right the mark of an enlightened stance. As the use of a scholarly publication to make these claims suggests, the new religions were not only quick to embrace the legitimizing language of religious freedom. They also recognized the importance of granting themselves legitimacy through academic enterprise. For some time the federation even made regular attendance at a *scholarly* meeting the sole requirement for membership in the organization. (No doubt the academic format allowed the federation to guarantee a doctrinally neutral meeting ground for its member organizations.)

More importantly, while it would take some time for the change to take effect, prominent members of the federation such as executive director Ōishi Shūten (1903–96) successfully pushed academics to adopt the nomenclature *shinshūkyō* (new religions) over the mildly pejorative *shinkō shūkyō* (new fad religions).[42] As a result of this PR campaign, local scholars began using the new terminology in their publications, and non-Japanese people also began using the term when writing for anglophone academic audiences. Woodard, for example, consistently used Shinshūren's preferred terminology in his own publications and in his forewords to other publications on Japanese religions.[43]

The category of "new religions" appeared in Japan in the wake of World War II to serve the apologetic purposes of the groups represented by the nascent Shinshūren. Influential academics like Woodard adopted it and exported it to the rest of the world as a substitute for regnant pejorative terminology.[44] Translating the Japanese term *shinshūkyō* as "new religions," scholars introduced to the American and European academy an alternative nomenclature for groups that had previously been described as marginal "sects" or morally pernicious "cults."[45]

This process happened in fits and starts, and I do not mean to suggest that all scholarship on "new religions" uncritically accepted the apologetic or even triumphalist attitudes adopted by the new movements themselves. In fact, the first wave of anglophone academic work on Japanese new religions somewhat simplistically saw the new religions as stepping-stones to Christian conversion. Because the new religious movements readily embraced the legitimizing rhetoric of religion as a matter of private choice and elective affiliation, some Western scholars spoke approvingly of the new groups and seemed particularly enamored of the new religions' open borrowing of Christian organizational models. One notable example is Harry Thomsen's (d.u.) *The New Religions of Japan*, which includes a laudatory preface by Olaf Hansen (d.u.) applauding its usefulness for the missionary headed to Japan to convert "the Buddhists."[46] Even scholars who conscientiously avoided explicitly Christian missiological language regarded the new religions as convenient vehicles for smuggling Christianity into the country.[47]

A roughly contemporaneous strain of scholarship was less missiological, situating the rise of the new religions within prevailing sociological models of modernization and secularization. Japanese scholars of religion like Oguchi Iichi (1910–86) tried to figure out how to situate Japan's new religions within the Weberian "Protestant ethic" framework while historians like Ienaga Saburō (1913–2002) attempted to do the same with Marxian models of religious innovation as an epiphenomenal marker of material distress.[48] Murakami Shigeyoshi (1928–91), a pioneer in the historical study of new religious movements and an early analyst of State Shintō, also treated emergent religions as a symptom of economic unease or social crisis.[49] The American scholar H. Neill McFarland (1923–?) similarly popularized the crisis model in a series of influential English-language publications on Japan's new religions.[50]

Members of the University of Tokyo Department of Religious Studies also produced a slew of articles, dissertations, and books on Japanese new religions in the decades after the war. Although methodological debates arose among members and graduates of this influential department about whether to take a strictly quantitative approach to these movements or to include qualitative studies regarding adherents' worldviews, the terminology of "new religions" became fixed even as the Japanese academy divided into camps favoring sociological and phenomenological methods.[51] Debates continue today among Japanese scholars as to how the term should be applied and refined—the rise of "spirituality studies" and the challenges presented by the violent activities of Aum Shinrikyō have been topics of heated discussion—but until very recently scholars have rarely questioned the naturalness of the category itself.[52]

The establishment of an academic infrastructure devoted exclusively to the study of alternative and emergent movements happened in the United States slightly later than it had in Japan. When it did, American scholars used the originally Japanese terminology ("new religions") as a corrective for preexisting terms such as "cult."[53] This linguistic shift seems to have been partially motivated by attempts to make sense of religious innovation more generally, but also by scholars' attempts to provide critical yet sympathetic responses to the infamous Jonestown incident of November 1978, in which nearly nine hundred members of the Peoples Temple died in a highly publicized murder-suicide.[54]

The marginal position of new religious movement studies initially matched the peripheral position of the groups the nascent subfield took as its object of analysis. The founding of the New Religious Movements Group of the American Academy of Religion in the early 1980s marked the formal birth of the subfield; the launch of the journal *Nova Religio* in 1997 marked its coming of age. Today the category of "new religions" enjoys currency throughout the anglophone academy, although debates continue as to how it should best be applied and taught.[55] The flagship journal devoted to the study of these groups, *Nova Religio*, exhibits the eclectic nature of the field in its subtitle, "The Journal of Alternative and Emergent Religions."[56] Debates within the pages of this publication reflect profound disagreements about how, when, and why the categories of "new religion," "new religious movement," or "alternative religious movement" should be applied to specific groups.[57] Nevertheless, the "new religions/new religious movements" terminology seems to be firmly established.

Behind these debates over how to apply "new religions" lies a set of lingering issues that led to the creation of the terminology in the first place. The study of "new religions" (as opposed to "cults") was designed to take the theological claims and ritual practices of marginal and emergent movements seriously, but ethical problems related to psychological abuse, sanctified violence, and state crackdowns on marginal movements have influenced the field. For example, incidents such as the group suicides of the Peoples Temple in 1978 and Heaven's Gate in 1997, the confrontation between the Branch Davidians and the US government in 1993, and the Aum Shinrikyō sarin gas attack on the Tokyo subway in 1995 have presented scholars with the conundrum of whether our job is to operate as critics or caretakers of marginal movements.[58] Concerns about whether it is feasible and desirable for governments to mobilize scholarly expertise on marginal movements in order to forestall or defuse future violent incidents further complicate the issue.[59] A number of scholars of new religions have tried to protect the "good religion" of marginal movements they see as benign and misunderstood from misguided state suppression.[60] At the same time, governments surveil the "bad religion" of violent groups like Aum Shinrikyō, sometimes enlisting scholars for their intelligence gathering purposes.[61]

In this regard, it is crucial to note that the "good religion/bad religion" distinction was present even at the early stages during the Occupation when the academic-apologetic category "new religions" was just coming into being. For example, even as he sympathetically defended the new religions from unreasonable attacks by the religious mainstream, William Woodard saw legal restrictions on religious incorporation as an indispensable mechanism for deterring untoward abuses of religious juridical person status.[62] The mainstream Japanese Religions Federation reluctantly considered including marginal movements in its ranks only because it would serve as a way to distinguish "real" from "false" religions.[63] Even Shinshūren, the group that had pushed scholars and bureaucrats to adopt the category of "new religions" in the first place, regarded some nonmember minority groups with suspicion. The aforementioned 1963 retrospective offered a bleak assessment of religious freedom by highlighting how Buddhist clerics and Shintō priests remained ignorant of the concept, but the organization further policed the boundaries of "real religion" by highlighting the rapid postwar growth of the nonmember organization Sōka Gakkai and decrying Gakkai entry into electoral politics in the last paragraph of the document.[64] Clearly, while Shinshūren promoted the terminology of "new religions" as a way of protecting members' interests, the organization was not opposed to designating specific marginal movements as in need of state control.[65]

To be clear, highlighting the historical origins of a now commonplace academic term is different from disputing the obviously important analytic role that the term plays. I would not suggest that we return to the pejorative language of "cults" or "upstart religions" (*shinkō shūkyō*). But I do think that the category of "new religions" can cut in more than one way, and it may not always protect the most marginalized. The example of the Shinshūren critiques of Sōka Gakkai shows that "new religions" have their own conceptions of orthodoxy and heresy and will readily use academic forums like research publications to police those boundaries. We miss something if we ignore the ways that the academic category of "new religions" can function apologetically to exclude some groups and practices from the realm of "real religion."

State Shintō

The case of new religious movement studies shows that an apologetic project of extending religious freedom to marginal groups in postwar Japan created terminology that scholars subsequently exported for use beyond Japan's borders. While the category of State Shintō has also been useful to both Japanese and non-Japanese scholars of religion, the category has generally only been applied to Japan and its colonial territories. Yet State Shintō has had a broader impact in the sense that it has become a paradigmatic model for a sort of perverted relationship between religion and the state. This idea of a "perversion of faith" has been particularly powerful in the context of the twenty-first century "War on Terror."[66]

Foremost among the studies offering this view was a slim 1970 volume in Japanese by Murakami Shigeyoshi that depicted State Shintō as a totalizing system that ensnared the hearts and minds of the Japanese people between 1868 and 1945.[67] While Murakami's erudition was considerable, his historical investigations were based on an a priori assumption that something identifiable as State Shintō actually existed in the sense described in William Bunce's "Staff Memorandum on State Shintō" and the alarmist scholarship on which Bunce's study relied. This interpretive decision reflected Murakami's political ideology at least as much as it reflected historical fact. For Murakami, State Shintō was an oppressive system used by a coterie of elites to enthrall the Japanese masses; the Japanese people were in turn psychologically predisposed to accept such a system without complaint. This reading echoed the occupiers' claim that State Shintō had impeded Japan's supposedly natural progression toward democracy.

Murakami's thesis enjoyed considerable prestige in the years following its publication in 1970, and subsequent analyses of State Shintō have necessarily responded to it.[68] Many studies on the relationship of Shintō and the state reproduced the Murakami thesis verbatim, adding to it Kuroda Toshio's later observation that the Shintō tradition was effectively invented in the early Meiji era.[69] Kuroda unabashedly argued that State Shintō was a political co-optation of what he saw as an originally pure "popular religion"; he also saw the rise of the modern Japanese state as a major factor in the decline of the "religion of the people."[70]

In her 1989 book *Shintō and the State, 1868–1988*, Kuroda's student Helen Hardacre reproduced Murakami's periodization and mildly modified his expansive definition of State Shintō while drawing on Kuroda's claim that Shintō was a modern political invention.[71] Hardacre also argued at length that religious freedom had not been truly guaranteed under the Meiji Constitution.[72] Hardacre's claims about religious freedom were based on her selective reading of a series of articles by Abe Yoshiya (1937–2003) that reproduced his argument that religious leaders in the prewar period were "ignorant" of the principle of religious freedom. Unfortunately, Hardacre seems to have overlooked Abe's more basic point that democratic, not authoritarian, processes characterized the legislative battles over religious legislation in what I call the Meiji constitutional period.[73]

This criticism does not diminish the important contribution made by Hardacre's book, which for a long time was the single best monograph on the subject and continues to be cited extensively by people within and outside the field of Japanese studies (including, it should be noted, numerous citations by scholars writing on the political effects of the modern category of religion).[74] The point here is that the category State Shintō has influenced scholarly analysis to such an extent that even the most diligent researchers have tended to view the history of modern Japan through the filter of that problematic concept. Their work then informs the work of others who are less familiar with the Japanese historical context.[75] The tendency to view State Shintō as a coherent national religion that existed with minimal change between 1868 and 1945 interferes with the ability to see how the Meiji Constitution actually created a secularist system (a point that recent scholarship has stressed and that Hardacre herself has come to embrace).[76]

Scholars of religious studies have been prone to interpret the Meiji constitutional period as dominated by a single state religion in part because we are primed by our training to see religion at work where others see economics or politics. This stance, for example, is evident in Shimazono Susumu's recent work, which tweaks Murakami's periodization and treats State Shintō as an aspect of daily life prior to Japan's defeat that continues today in the postwar emperor system and conservative attempts to revise Japan's constitution.[77] While Shimazono critiques analyses that give undue influence to shrine priests without considering how other agents such as schools may have also contributed to the dissemination of State Shintō ideology, his project is illustrative of how scholars of religion can reinforce the interpretation of State Shintō as a pervasive national religion even as scholars in other fields (particularly historians) seek to elucidate the complex and multifarious factors behind the special treatment of shrines.[78]

Scholarly "religion-making from outside" *can* identify the political practices of the Meiji constitutional period as essentially religious, but that is not the only way to view the history. If the legacy of phenomenology or the promise of a "lived religion" approach for religious studies is to take others' worldviews and practices seriously on their own terms, then we owe it to the Japanese people of the past to not simply assume that what we now call State Shintō was religion masquerading as politics or politicians co-opting an originally "pure" religion.[79] As some people of the time claimed, perhaps shrine rites were simply expressions of Japanese national identity. To make this observation is not to condone Japanese militarism, nor is it to deny the coerciveness of the Meiji constitutional regime. We can disaggregate the normative political claim (Japanese militarism was bad and Japanese governance oppressive) from reductive or essentialist claims about religions (state actors distorted "pure" religious ideas to rationalize violence; Japanese people failed to "properly" separate religion from the state).

This observation is not new, nor is it mine alone. Against the view of State Shintō as Japan's de facto national religion, a small body of Japanese historical scholarship that began to be published in the late 1980s sharply questioned the historiographical applicability of the category of State Shintō and advocated circumscribing its use.[80] In particular, several historians affiliated with Kokugakuin and Kōgakkan Universities began to question Murakami's claim that State Shintō was a unified, monolithic system that held all Japanese subjects in its thrall from the time of the Meiji Restoration of 1868 until the promulgation of the Shintō Directive in 1945. These scholars highlighted the fact that Buddhists—not Shintō priests or the Japanese government—were initially responsible for the argument that Shintō was not a religion.[81] They have also argued that State Shintō only came into existence through major administrative distinctions made in 1900 and 1913, when jurisdiction over shrines was separated from jurisdiction over "religious" institutions.[82] The more apologetic branch of this scholarship has also identified hypocrisies in Occupation policy, pointing to inconsistencies in the expectations for separation of religion and the state in the Shintō Directive as compared to contemporary expectations in American civic and political life.[83]

To date, however, these historical and comparative correctives for Occupation-era excesses have failed to gain significant traction in anglophone scholarship. Historians writing in English have rightly questioned the top-down model of State Shintō and have recognized it as a product of the peculiar context of the Occupation, but they have tended to correct that model not so much by relativizing the position of the United States (as the Shintō apologists have done) but rather by highlighting the diverse, bottom-up pressures that supported state projects. In such accounts, what seemed to be a top-down project from the perspective of the occupiers was actually made possible by the activist efforts of various interest groups and civil society organizations.[84]

Recently, some Japanese scholars have also engaged in similar projects mobilizing hitherto untapped documents, showing that rural Shintō priests tried to shore up their authority and protect their parochial interests by linking shrine rites to national mobilization, for example, or showing how State Shintō could only exist through the assent and support of people who had been indoctrinated with the ideas of imperial divine descent, the divine nation, and so forth.[85] Both Japanese and non-Japanese scholars have also highlighted the continued postwar existence of practices reminiscent of the wartime regime as a way of challenging the Occupation-era claim that the Shintō Directive successfully eradicated a national religion.[86]

Scholarly discussions of State Shintō have thereby served a political purpose by operating as a check on ongoing attempts by Japanese politicians and shrine groups to align shrines with public policy or to bring Shintō-derived ideals into public school education.[87] State Shintō has also served as a negative example for contemporary discussions of ideal Japanese religion-state relations, operating as the foil against which "real" religious freedom is measured. In this sense, scholars and journalists have carefully documented and vociferously criticized politicians' use of the legitimizing language of religion, such as the outcry over former Tokyo governor Ishihara Shintarō's claim that the 11 March 2011 earthquake and tsunami were "divine retribution" for Japan's sins. Critics have also decried the pageantry of religious ritual such as public visits to the controversial Yasukuni Shrine by former prime minister Koizumi Jun'ichirō and Prime Minister Abe Shinzō's controversial decision to hold a May 2016 G7 meeting at Ise-Shima including a public visit to the Ise Shrine by world leaders.[88] An academic majority claiming to protect religious freedom attacks the "bad religion" of a putatively renascent State Shintō.[89] An academic minority claiming that Shintō has been misunderstood fiercely protects the secularism of "Japan-style religion-state relations," arguing that the category of State Shintō itself is a product of hypocritical, overbearing American imperialism that held Japan to an unfair double standard in matters of religious freedom.[90] Both positions are somewhat extreme, but together they reinforce my contention that the modern history of Shintō provides a useful framework for considering the religion/not-religion distinction that lies at the heart of secularist governance (see chapter 1).[91]

Buddhist "War Responsibility"

Finally, the topic of Buddhist war responsibility has also been an arena for scholarly and clerical discussions about the importance of religious freedom. For example, in an article entitled "Japan's Modernization and Buddhism," published in English in the journal *Contemporary Religions in Japan* in 1965, historian of Buddhism Ienaga Saburō (1913–2002) argued that Japanese Buddhists had missed a golden opportunity provided by the 1868 Meiji revolution to overcome the "indolence" that had characterized the Tokugawa period (1603–1868).[92] Although Buddhists reacted to the attacks of the *haibutsu kishaku* ("destroy the buddhas, expel Śākyamuni") movement by appealing to their long-standing rights vis-à-vis the state, in Ienaga's estimation this appeal was not based (as he clearly thought it should have been), on any commitment to the separation of religion and state.[93]

Ienaga suggested that Buddhists aimed to survive under the new Meiji regime by ingratiating themselves with the state, working assiduously to identify the threat posed by growing numbers of Japanese Christians. Not only did Buddhists denounce Christians who made freedom of conscience claims in the 1890s (such as Uchimura Kanzō, 1861–1930), but they also actively resisted "democratic trends from below," meaning that they were unable to develop any alternative path outside of merely following state authority.[94] Ienaga argued that even reformers such as Shimaji Mokurai (1838–1911), who had famously advocated separation of religion and the state in the 1870s, fell into the trap of misconstruing freedom of religion by adopting an apologetic stance that sought favor with the state through persecution of Christians.[95] In Ienaga's account, the Meiji Constitution failed to provide genuine religious freedom while religious leaders failed to do their democratic duty in securing that freedom. These failures derived from the "feudal" attitudes that Ienaga (a somewhat doctrinaire Marxist) felt Buddhists were never able to fully shed. The implication, of course, was that "real religious leaders" would necessarily resist state power. To behave otherwise was to betray oneself as a victim of false consciousness.

In what seems to have been an attempt to correct the interpretive excesses of earlier studies like Ienaga's, Abe Yoshiya published a six-part essay series entitled "Religious Freedom under the Meiji Constitution" in the journal *Contemporary Religions in Japan* between 1968 and 1970. Somewhat surprisingly, Abe rejected his predecessors' presupposition that religious freedom had been entirely absent under the Meiji Constitution. Against the view that Shintō became Japan's state religion with the Meiji political transition of 1868 and remained so until the end of the war, Abe argued that the status of Shintō changed significantly over the course of modern Japanese history, suggesting preferential governmental treatment of Shintō only began around 1900. This special treatment was not solidified until 1913 when the administrative apparatus for managing shrines was shifted to a department different from the one in charge of managing religions.[96]

According to Abe, religious freedom existed in a legal sense during the Meiji constitutional period, but clerics were too myopically focused on jostling for position vis-à-vis the state to notice that their rights were steadily eroding.[97] In his narrative, the burden of responsibility for the loss of religious freedom lay as much with religious leaders who failed to challenge governmental initiatives as it did with state bureaucrats who concocted statist interpretations of religious freedom that placed the state in a position of ultimate authority. Abe suggested that Buddhist clerics in particular were obstacles to the development of religious freedom in Japan because they were ignorant of the principles that were at stake. This narrative matched Ienaga's disparaging assessment of parochial Buddhist clerics as myopically focused on preserving traditional privileges.

A variant of Abe's critique also circulated in postwar clerical circles as Buddhist priests confronted sectarian complicity in Japan's war efforts. It was obvious that most Japanese Buddhist sects had actively contributed to the war effort, particularly in the early 1940s as total mobilization engulfed Japan. In the context of the postwar regime, then, one of the great challenges for Buddhists was to find tools within Buddhist doctrine to support the postwar ideals of human rights, egalitarianism, and strict separation of religion from the state.

For example, Ichikawa Hakugen (1902–86) engaged in a protracted critique of Buddhist ethics, particularly in his 1970 piece *Bukkyōsha no sensō sekinin* (*Buddhists' War Responsibility*).[98] This critique informed subsequent scholarship criticizing the relationships between Zen and nationalism such as Brian Daizen Victoria's influential, albeit controversial, 1997 monograph *Zen at War*.[99] Similar research by non-Japanese scholars has investigated the role of the Kyoto school in legitimating nationalism and war, the role of Japanese militarism in undermining ostensibly universal Buddhist tenets such as nonviolence and compassion, and the long-standing history of Buddhism being used as a tool of statecraft (or of Buddhist law and temporal kingly law as being mutually dependent).[100]

Such critiques from within and outside the Buddhist community have continued up to the present. The "Critical Buddhism" (*hihan Bukkyō*) movement centered on the work of the Sōtō Zen cleric-scholars Hakamaya Noriaki and Matsumoto Shirō argued that the culture of Japanese imperialism derived from distortions of original Buddhist teaching.[101] These scholars argued that immanentist Mahāyāna Buddhist doctrines of universal buddha-nature problematically provided theoretical rationales for Buddhist warmongering and the social oppression of minority groups. In responding to high-profile controversies concerning Buddhist oppression of outcaste groups, Matsumoto and Hakamaya came to articulate a broader critique of Buddhism that questioned aspects of the Japanese Buddhist tradition that seemed to stray from what they saw as the core, irreducible doctrines of co-dependent origination and no-self. These scholars began from a position of ethical best practices and attempted to philosophically reevaluate the Buddhist tradition through a fundamentalist approach that hearkened back to what the authors perceived as the doctrinal heart of the Buddhist tradition. In their view, Japanese Buddhist participation in the war was premised on a misinterpretation of Buddhist truth. While this assessment caused a considerable stir in the clerical and academic worlds, it overlooked the simple historical fact that Buddhists throughout history have molded doctrine to suit their particular political ends.[102]

Today, Buddhist guilt over war complicity and concern about state intervention in religious affairs continues to generate a prodigious research literature. For example, a 2008 two-volume set entitled *Kokka to shūkyō* (*State and Religion*), published by the Kyoto Buddhist Association, opened with a preface written by chairman Arima Raitei that lamented Buddhists' slow recognition of the importance of religious freedom.[103] His contrite tone is emblematic of some recent insider scholarship about religion-state relations and Buddhist political life, but it has been matched by religious studies scholarship that has valorized liberal "resistance" and castigated Buddhist support for militarism. For example, James Mark Shields has used the figure of Seno'o Girō (1889–1961) as an example of a Buddhist who resisted imperialism and militarism out of commitment to a socialist Buddhism that was consistent with Marxian principles.[104] Similarly, Paul Swanson has recently published a chapter celebrating the short life of Buddhist socialist Takagi Kenmyō (1864–1914), whom he describes as "a Meiji misfit and martyr."[105] Fabio Rambelli's slim volume translating the "egalitarian dharma" of activist Buddhist cleric Uchiyama Gudō (1874–1911) also repeated this pattern of celebrating Buddhist martyrdom, and Richard K. Payne's foreword to that work drew an explicit contrast between the ideas of Buddhist "complicity" and "resistance" that I problematized in chapter 4.[106]

In summary, a great deal of postwar scholarship has presented Buddhist engagement with wartime projects as a mistaken interpretation of basic Buddhist doctrines or as a craven subsumption of Buddhist moral authority to that of the state. In this narrative, insufficient awareness of religious freedom is a fundamental political problem for Buddhists to overcome, while promotion and protection of religious freedom in the future has become intrinsic to the scholarly understanding of "good Buddhism." This stance reflects the profound influence of transnational Buddhist modernist discourse, which has frequently portrayed Buddhist doctrine as intrinsically advancing a progressive political project or, conversely, has mobilized Buddhist doctrine in support of such projects.[107] But there is nothing in Buddhist doctrine *as such* that promotes progressive politics. Rather, Buddhists and the scholars who study them today read progressive political objectives (environmental conservation, feminist liberation, rectification of long-standing racial injustice) into Buddhist doctrine and retroject their contemporary concerns and value judgments back onto the Buddhists of the past.[108]

THE PIKE AND SHIELD OF RELIGIOUS FREEDOM

The word for "paradox" in the Japanese language is *mujun*, or "pike and shield." In the postwar period, scholarly appeals to the principle of religious freedom have operated as a pike, puncturing the veil of political ideology masquerading as religion. Simultaneously, scholars' religious freedom talk has acted as a shield, protecting marginalized groups from persecution. Not infrequently, the impenetrability of the shield and the acuity of the pike have been evenly matched but inconsistently wielded. I have argued in this chapter that scholars' decisions about which groups to protect and which practices to critique have often reflected tenacious Occupation-era distinctions between "good" and "bad" religion.[109] As the three cases I outlined above suggest, prescriptive visions created during and immediately after the Occupation through close working relationships between policy makers, scholars of religion, and religious apologists have affected not only state management of religions in Japan, but also the governance of religions worldwide. Academic terminology like "new religious movements," "State Shintō," and "Buddhist war responsibility" provided stakeholders with new ways to imagine the beneficiaries of the religious freedom guarantee. We must therefore critically reassess the interpretive proclivities of the nonconfessional academic study of religion with an awareness of how terms commonly used today reflect the politically fraught circumstances that birthed them.

The academic study of religion as it exists today reflects imperial encounters with cultural difference, sublimated Protestant supersessionism, anticommunist Cold War politics, and tenacious cryptotheological attempts to posit a transhistorical, universal human religiosity.[110] In the postwar academy, nonconfessional and re-descriptive studies of religion have occupied a narrow intellectual space between the confessional practice of theology and the positivist disciplines of history, anthropology, sociology, political science, and psychology. This intellectual distribution of labor has had political effects.[111] For decades, the existence of religious studies departments allowed social scientists to regard religion as a relatively unimportant variable, meaning that they were unprepared to address the obvious impacts of "religion" on social and political life.[112] The pervasive influence of modernization theory on mainstream historiography also rendered religion as either epiphenomenal or atavistic, and teleological theories of secularization long interfered with researchers' abilities to see that activities and institutions commonly coded as "religion" have had (and continue to have) demonstrable effects on politics, law, and public discourse.[113]

But just as social scientists finally got religion, humanists were giving it up.[114] Thanks to the insights of critical theorists of religion, religious studies scholars came to recognize the field's indebtedness to Eurocentric models in which Protestantism appeared as the prototypical member of the category, not to mention a widespread presupposition that "religion" is a discrete thing in the first place.[115] Critical religion theorists also revealed that the phenomenological method of "bracketing," long favored by religious studies scholars as a way of guaranteeing theological neutrality, has often obscured serious epistemological differences by collapsing diverse embodied practices, intellectual dispositions, and social institutions under the overarching but internally inconsistent rubric of "religion."[116] The conventional organization of religious studies departments around a "world religions" model furthermore reinforced the intertwined and contradictory notions that *religion* is a transhistorical, culturally universal phenomenon and that *religions* are discrete civilizational units that can be categorized according to their distinctive doctrines, institutions, and practices.[117] In sum, just as social scientists began turning to humanist scholars of religion for information on how to sensitively treat religion as an analyzable variable, we replied by saying that we were not sure that "religion" was ever a thing at all.

This uncertainty reflects long-standing tensions between essentialist, functionalist, and constructivist approaches in the field: Is our job to describe what religion really *is*, what ideological work religion *does*, or who *makes* religion by arbitrarily defining some cultural practices as religious, others as not?[118] In this book I have favored constructivist approaches because I think they help us understand how religion can be artificial but can nevertheless have real political effects as a "socially dependent fact."[119] Indeed, I chose the subject of religious freedom in part because religious freedom talk is one place where the always-constructed category of religion becomes "really real" in policy and public life.

But I also recognize my own complicity in the legal and political problems I have been trying to describe. Because its very existence depends on the intellectual move of making religion from an imagined "outside," the nonconfessional academic study of religion must render some activities and ideas as "religious," others as something else. Scholars of religion *have* to draw a line between religion and not-religion in order to do our work, but by drawing that line we run the risk of excluding some ideas and practices from religious freedom guarantees.[120]

We can never fully escape this dilemma, but I think that most of us in the field would agree that as long as there are people in the world who reflexively describe themselves as "religious" (and as long as there are those who would say that others lack "real religion") then we have a responsibility to analyze such claims re-descriptively and nonreductively, without adopting the theological prescriptions or essentialist assumptions on which they depend.[121] I would also submit that until scholars of religion fully attend to historical moments like the Allied Occupation of Japan when policy makers operationalized "neutral" religious studies expertise in pursuit of political objectives that were decidedly *not* neutral, we run the risk of letting received terms dictate our thinking. Our ability to be re-descriptive without being reductive can be short-circuited by the terminology we use.

This is a problem that scholars of religion generated for ourselves, but it is not just *our* problem. When scholars, policy makers, and activists treat religious freedom as a corrective for oppressive religio-political systems today, they reproduce narratives that scholars of religion and policy makers constructed in occupied Japan for the express purpose of designating some modes of religiosity as fundamentally better than others. The distinctions born during that period not only justified the establishment of American military hegemony in the Pacific; they also rationalized domestic "civilizing" missions pursued by Japanese elites like Kishimoto Hideo.

Occupation-era revisions of the concepts of "freedom" and "religion" contributed to a series of changes that continue to reverberate globally today in scholarship, human rights activism, and international law. The echoes exist in the form of operative metaphors (the "spiritual vacuum"), catchphrases ("State Shintō"), revisionist doctrine ("Buddhist war responsibility"), and academic jargon ("new religious movements"). These words structure scholars' expectations when we speak to informants. They have already done their work long before we even step into archives. They dictate what we see, and they determine what we say about it. They allow governments and nongovernmental organizations to position their policies as beyond reproach.[122] They help various stakeholders render some modes of religiosity as genuine, others as fake or flawed. But if these concepts emerged from the legal morass and ethical quandary that was the Occupation, then the emancipatory capacity of the religious freedom they imagine is always-already compromised.

CONCLUSION

The Bellicose Pacifism of Religious Freedom

> This is not just a matter of what any new constitution says. Democracy is not only a way of voting. It is a way of thinking. People have to feel equal, not just be regarded by the law as such. Such religious tolerance has to be taught and argued for. Those who oppose it have to be taken on and defeated not only by arms but by ideas.
>
> TONY BLAIR (2014)[1]

ANYTIME A PERSON INVOKES FREEDOM, SHE also implicitly calls to mind its opposite. By this I do not simply mean that the language of freedom calls to mind the unfortunate existence of oppression. Rather, I mean that calls for freedom are themselves appeals for a type of constraint. Paradoxically, freedom works thanks to the power of the law to constrain behavior. Those who are free to be free are designated as such through the coercive capacities of legislation and jurisprudence. Frequently and tragically, the ranks of the free are separated from the ranks of the dead through the split-second decisions of law enforcement officers and military personnel.

This inherently contradictory quality of freedom is rarely acknowledged in popular discourse celebrating liberty. Even in the staid halls of academe and the somber chambers of the judiciary, stakeholders grant freedom a magical status akin to that enjoyed by unicorns and rainbows. Academics, journalists, politicians, and that pontificating patriot perched next to you at the pub are all quite likely to understand freedom as an apolitical objective or as an ahistorical principle.

It is not.

Legislative action, judiciary decisions, and law enforcement all highlight the grubby politics of freedom. Quasi-legal activities (such as lobbying) and extralegal contributions to public discourse (such as journalism) are inherently political activities. Their visions of freedom can have violent effects. Calls for freedom mobilize the punitive machinery of the state. They demand compliance. Perversely and counterintuitively, appeals to freedom operate by requiring those who hear them to submit. To invoke freedom is to demand submission of the personal will to an abstract, ambiguous, often mercurial ideal.

Freedom is amorphous. One person's right to free expression is bounded by another's right to avoid calumny. One person's right to worship infringes upon another's sense of propriety. The definition of orthodoxy held by a police officer or a judge affects a group's right to assemble or even to exist. To free religion, one must tie it up in legalese. To free religion, one must make sharp distinctions between religion and not-religion. Some aspects of social life must be put behind bars for others to survive and thrive. Religion is free only insofar as some stuff is not. The perennial question thus remains paramount and unanswerable: Just what is *religion*, anyway?

CLARIFYING THE QUESTION

My method in the foregoing chapters has been more or less historiographic and my scholarly curiosity focused squarely on the problem of who gets to define religion and what she means when she does so. Just what *is* religious freedom? Is religious freedom an indisputably good thing when it can so obviously be used in the service of discrimination? Is religious freedom a human right? If so, what do we mean when we say that it is, and what visions of religion and humanity are we advancing? How can we reconcile religious freedom claims with equally valid concerns about maintaining peace and order?

As the conclusion to the previous chapter suggests, a set of questions related to scholarly method has also informed this book. Do scholars of religion bear any particular responsibility for promoting religious freedom or policing infractions thereof? If so, why? If so, what are the best practices for engaging with our students and the public? Is the objective of religious studies to foster religious literacy, as some claim? Do we aim to foster tolerance of ideas that our students initially find abhorrent? Is that how we define "cultural sensitivity," a catchphrase that so many of us use when rationalizing our existence in the academy? As scholars of religion, do we *want* policy makers, legislators, and journalists to listen to us? If so, what messages do we want them to hear? How can American scholars of religion talk about religious freedom in an intelligible, rational way when the operative terms "religion" and "freedom" so frequently go unexamined in American popular discourse? How can those of us who specialize in non-American countries responsibly talk about religious freedom when the geopolitics of religious freedom are so obviously uneven?

I do not have answers to all of these questions. Many of them are inherently unanswerable, and some are so grand in scope that no individual can answer them alone. In conclusion, I limit myself to offering brief reflections on the position of religious freedom in our post-9/11 historical moment before outlining some ways forward for religious studies and Japan studies alike.

INGENIOUS SOLUTION OR PART OF THE PROBLEM?

Religious freedom is everywhere. Since 9/11, major newspapers such as the *New York Times*, the *Washington Post*, and the *Guardian* have repeatedly quoted prominent policy makers and pundits who have identified religious freedom as an ingenious solution to the ongoing military conflicts that have embroiled much of the world. Behind these superficially reasonable assessments lies a problematic set of assumptions about the relationship between religion and violence. Secularist demagogues argue that religion makes otherwise good people do bad things. Policy makers argue that religion is inherently benign even as they claim that some bad people distort the religious good in pursuit of violent ends. Politicians make sweeping statements that depict entire religions as intrinsically oppressive. Human rights campaigners criticize cultural practices as inherently religious and inescapably barbaric. If only those people enjoyed more freedom. If only they had more choice.

This counterfactual way of thinking about religious freedom as the antidote to violence and oppression is so commonplace that it is easy to forget that it is essentially an article of faith, not fact. There is a sort of imaginative sleight of hand that allows us to associate the spread of religious freedom with the diminution of repression, to see a direct and causal relationship between freedom and peace. It cannot possibly be so simple, and yet the problematic association of religious freedom with peace is pervasive. This association is not exclusively a journalistic trope. It extends to the highest levels of government. It reaches into the academy. It spills over into the realm of international aid work. It pervades global governance structures.

An example. On 25 January 2014, former British prime minister Tony Blair published an opinion piece in the *Guardian* newspaper under the eye-catching title "Religious Difference, Not Ideology, Will Fuel This Century's Epic Battles." While Blair almost certainly did not determine the title for the article, the content matched the headline. The piece laid out a vision in which religion served as the fundamental motivator for armed conflicts and terrorist attacks around the globe. Through the language of "perversion of faith" and "abuse of religion," Blair's article advanced an argument that suggested that religion is primarily about *belief*, that belief motivates violent behavior, and that such beliefs and motivations are "bad religion."[2] The tacit corollary of Blair's claims was that *real* religion is pacifist and nonsectarian.

Blair's article was an ideological salvo in the ongoing "War on Terror."[3] The curious logic of this ceaseless conflict designates through the word "terror" the violent actions of specific nonstate actors as anathema while treating the violent actions of states and their militaries as just.[4] This rhetorical move perversely rationalizes the use of illiberal governance techniques such as extrajudicial capital punishment, indefinite incarceration, pervasive and intrusive surveillance, and torture. It makes religious freedom an ideological appurtenance of the military-industrial complex. It prompts the generation of policy papers that deem certain types of religion "bad" and in need of correction.[5] The global governance of religion becomes the global antiterror project. Academic inquiry rallies in support.

The post-9/11 interest in religion as a prime motivator of violence and international conflict has motivated intelligence agencies, think tanks, nongovernmental organizations, and academic funding agencies to make deep financial investments in understanding religion as a facet of international relations.[6] Many of these agencies laud religious freedom as a panacea for armed conflict and intolerance.[7] Lobbies with explicitly evangelical Christian missions such as the Institute for Global Engagement have cultivated strong ties with policy makers and have created new academic periodicals to promote their ideas.[8] Other academic initiatives such as the Religious Freedom Project hosted by the Berkley Center at Georgetown University take a superficially neutral stance even as they advocate spreading religious freedom worldwide.[9]

There is nothing politically neutral in this. It is not theologically neutral either. The lobbying and legislative endeavors of these groups advance prescriptive notions about how religious people should be and how they should behave.[10] They prioritize the views of religious constituencies who work very hard to make themselves legible to academic and governmental authority. Lobbies and think tanks generate an enormous amount of text supporting the notion that religious freedom is a cure for the ills of a world riven by religious strife.

Think tanks' efforts to promote religious freedom in foreign policy have spurred matching initiatives at the highest levels of government in the United States. Then US president Barack Obama gave a speech at the annual National Prayer Breakfast in February 2014 in which he noted that promotion of religious freedom around the world was a central pillar of US foreign policy. "History shows that nations that uphold the rights of their people, including the freedom of religion, are ultimately more just and more peaceful and more successful," Obama averred. "Nations that do not uphold these rights sow the bitter seeds of instability and violence and extremism. So freedom of religion matters to our national security."[11]

In a subsequent move lauded by some members of the scholarly community as a vindication of the value of religious studies, John Kerry argued in *America* magazine in September 2015 that the academic study of religion is important because some bad apples advocate violence and destruction "in the guise of religion."[12] In so doing, Kerry reproduced a long-standing conceit in American foreign policy circles that religion serves as camouflage for violent impulses and oppressive ideology. A corollary of this idea is that global promotion of religious freedom serves as a prophylactic against terror and repression, a claim repeated by former US ambassador-at-large for religious freedom David Saperstein in an October 2015 press conference accompanying the rollout of the 2014 International Religious Freedom Report.[13]

The motivations behind this post-9/11 spate of scholarship, academic philanthropy, activism, journalism, and foreign policy are presumably noble, but many of these initiatives have outlined simplistic visions of "good" and "bad" religion even as they have claimed to embrace religious diversity.[14]

They are premised on the twin presuppositions that religion is essentially pacifist (it is not) and that religious ideas in particular serve as motivators of violent behavior (they do not).[15] These conjoined presuppositions contradict one another, creating an incoherent position that is repeated time and again: religion is bad because it is intrinsically parochial and therefore fosters conflict, but religion is good because it is essentially benevolent and therefore lays the groundwork for peace. Commonplace words like "cult," "sect," and "heresy" identify some types of religion as genuine and others as false. Appending the suffix "-ism" to otherwise neutral terms turns them into pejorative epithets ("Islamism"), just as affixing the word "State" to "Shintō" in the wake of the Pacific War rendered Japanese governance as a heretical secularism (chapter 5).

The common assumption that tolerant policies mitigate the religious conflict that arises from competing beliefs is not only based on a problematic understanding of religion.[16] It is also based on a flawed history. It either overestimates the historical effectiveness of secularist political systems in equitably managing religious difference, or it anticipates a near-future utopia by presuming that religious liberty is a uniquely Western (sometimes "Christian" or "Judeo-Christian") product that must be adopted by the entire global population despite—or for some parties precisely because of—its culturally specific origins.[17] Like the aforementioned problem regarding perceptions of religion, stakeholders such as policy makers, clerics, journalists, academics, and laypeople espouse these mutually incompatible positions in the same breath. The result is that religious freedom appears in public discourse as a panacea for conflict. Academic expertise then becomes enrolled in helping people "get religious freedom right."

Scholarly knowing is half the battle in the crusade against religious violence, even if policy makers enlist scholarly expertise on religion in the service of making reductive claims of the sort that many of us who study religion critically would be inclined to resist.[18] Kerry's aforementioned article in *America* magazine anticipated the critiques of prominent academic gadflies like Elizabeth Shakman Hurd by denying that the global promotion of religious freedom was about designating certain religions as "good and "bad." The then secretary of state went on in the same paragraph to decry those who use religion to wage war, effectively advancing an image of "bad religion." Kerry was probably trying to thread a fine line by simultaneously appealing to the interests of multiple demographics, but the upshot was that Hurd's stunning critique of religious freedom promotion policies was lost.[19]

Policy makers and journalists frequently raise religious freedom as a panacea for "religious violence," but the fact that religious freedom can have repressive effects is curiously absent from these commonsensical elocutions. Meanwhile, behind this incautious celebration of religious liberty as an unmitigated public good and global desideratum lies a conundrum regarding enforcement. At the national scale, states inevitably give greater credence to majoritarian claims in constitutionalization, legislation, jurisprudence, policy making, and law enforcement, and their mandate to protect public order lets them vilify, criminalize, and oppress minority religions.[20] This problem is not unique to totalitarian states, nor is it particular to states with Muslim majorities or communist politics, as some have claimed. It is fundamental to religion-state separation and inherent to guarantees of religious freedom, where legislators, judges, and law enforcement officers get to determine what counts as religion and which groups are deserving of freedom.[21]

Domestic policies theoretically guarantee religious *freedom*, but in actuality they frequently simply *tolerate* diverse religious positions. As Wendy Brown has persuasively argued, to tolerate something is to, first, acknowledge its fundamental abhorrence and, second, to co-opt or neuter it through generous treatment.[22] Toleration operates by subsuming religious difference under overarching regimes. This often happens by giving priority to the claims of the state and political authorities over the claims of religious groups and individuals.[23] In this context, politically influential ecclesial authorities often dictate for policy makers and legislators the parameters of "real religion." Not infrequently, these theologically motivated distinctions between genuine and ersatz religion arbitrarily deny protected status to minority groups while further solidifying the political privilege of the religious mainstream.[24] Even when religious groups successfully negotiate for separation of religion from the state or for greater freedom from political intervention in their affairs, they often do so by redrawing the boundaries of both political and religious orthodoxy: "good" religions fit neatly into the religion/not-religion framework preferred by the state (itself reflective of dominant ecclesial authority); "bad" religions now appear as "cults," "superstitions," or threats to common decency and peace and order.[25] No wonder some scholars have argued that guaranteeing religious freedom is fundamentally impossible.[26]

Indeed, concerns about the feasibility of promoting or protecting religious freedom have recently received considerable scholarly attention. However, this scholarly conversation also reflects the always-political allocation of economic resources. Organizations like the Mellon Foundation and the US Department of State commit funds to better understanding religion as a source of global conflict. The Tony Blair Faith Foundation partners with esteemed institutions of higher education like Yale to promote scholarship that begins from the premise that "those who oppose [religious tolerance] have to be taken on and defeated not only by arms but by ideas."[27] This bellicose rhetoric of intolerant tolerance—and the academic infrastructure it creates and is sustained by in turn—neatly encapsulates the complicated relationship between religious freedom, academic inquiry, politics, and policy making that I have described above.

THE WAY FORWARD

What do we do? Is there no way to write and speak about religious freedom without retreating into problematic normative claims? Is there no way to speak prescriptively in a way that allows for the eradication of injustice in the present, even if it may turn out that our attempts might have unintended, even illiberal, consequences?

When I started researching this book, I had a naive expectation that I would conclude with a definitive statement about the "right way" to do religious freedom. Over the course of the research, however, I found myself developing an allergy to prescriptive claims of all sorts. Benefiting from the hindsight that the historical method provides, I now know that efforts at prediction are so obviously doomed to failure and efforts at prescription are so transparently shortsighted that I find myself loath to conclude with any definitive statement about how to conduct American foreign policy. I am similarly not prepared to say that there are ideal ways to guarantee religious freedom at home, although I admire those who try.[28] I admit that I am dismayed that American lawmakers and business owners would use religious freedom claims to justify what seems to me to be rank discrimination, but I also recognize that this is just the way religious freedom works. Majoritarian claims quash minority groups. Minorities use religious freedom talk to push back against the majority. Different interest groups define religious freedom so that it is capacious enough to suit their own interests but narrow enough to exclude the other team. With this in mind, I cannot in good conscience close this book with any prescriptions about doing religious freedom right. But I do feel a responsibility to comment on scholarly method.

Disentangling Religious Freedom Claims from the Nation

Aside from the pervasive and problematic perception that religion is actually a thing that can be freed, the single greatest problem in the material I have examined in this book is the assumption that national characteristics foster specific dispositions regarding religion or religious freedom. Japanese debates about religious freedom during the Meiji constitutional period were vociferous and contentious. Those debates inevitably revolved around questions of whether a given religion fit or did not fit with Japan's national character (*kokutai*). For example, apologetic attempts to link a specific religion with the state by making it a state religion or "officially recognized religion" invariably used fit with national character as a rationale. Critical attempts to eradicate "superstitions" depicted them as inappropriate for Japanese modernity, often contrasting such marginal movements with mainstream religions like Buddhism. Political attempts to construct and maintain what Jason Josephson calls the "Shintō secular" took place by linking shrine rites to patriotic duty. On investigation, all of the apparent infringements on religious freedom that occurred during the Meiji constitutional period took place because some interest group or individual decided that a particular religious organization or ritual practice was not Japanese, or was not Japanese enough.

The occupiers' claim that Japan had distorted the universal principle of religious freedom was downright false. Japan's constitution guaranteed religious freedom, and many different interest groups showed themselves to be deeply concerned with protecting it. They did so through inherently democratic means like free speech, parliamentary debate, and public protest. But the occupiers assumed that Japan lacked religious freedom because they treated *Japan* as the problem and religious freedom as the solution. Setting aside for the moment the obvious corollary that the United States therefore appeared to have a monopoly on "real religious freedom," this narrative created the binary expectations that religious freedom was something that nations enacted or did not enact, got right or got wrong. It conveniently elided America's own troubled history with rights, race, and religion.[29]

Even with the efflorescence of universalistic human rights language during the Occupation, this nation-centric narrative remained intact and is one of the legacies that the transnational Occupation experience bequeathed to later generations. It performed a sort of sleight of hand in which the problematic nature of religious freedom was allowed to go unquestioned while countries like Japan could still be faulted for failing to properly provide it. It is no accident that the narratives thereby generated tended to favor the victors and the powerful, nor is it an accident that religious freedom has served as a potent ideological weapon in American foreign policy since.[30] Today, the annual reports generated by the US Commission on International Religious Freedom ignore Japan. The previously terrifying country only appears in the annual report as a junior partner that can help exert pressure on "countries of particular concern" like China and North Korea. Today, the United States and its Japanese ally "have" religious freedom; ideologically distant and overtly hostile states apparently do not.

This is particularly perplexing because Japan is not bereft of religious freedom disputes. Despite what I said about the problems of prediction above, the political backlash to the occupiers' reforms on the Japanese side could have been easily anticipated even during the Occupation. Led by the Jinja Honchō and supported by political pressure groups such as the Shintō Seiji Renmei (Shintō Association for Spiritual Leadership) and Nippon Kaigi (the Japan Council), a number of conservative academics, policy makers, and politicians have argued for decades now that the occupiers fundamentally misunderstood Japan's unique relationship between religions and the state. This claim serves as the basis for lamentations about the materially rich yet spiritually bereft state of postwar Japanese society. It also serves as a rationale for advancing the causes of constitutional revision, state support of the controversial Yasukuni Shrine, and calls for a more direct political role for the symbolic emperor.[31]

While some academic commentators are inclined to see these initiatives as renascent State Shintō and a threat to Japan's hard-won postwar religious liberty, the common denominator undergirding these diverse political objectives is a claim about national character (*kunigara*), not religion. Conservative pet projects related to public school education, the emperor, and Yasukuni Shrine all *can* be seen as attempts to roll back the religious freedom enshrined in the American-drafted postwar constitution, and there is plenty of scholarship and journalism decrying these moves as exactly that.[32] But strikingly, the advocates of these changes mostly ignore the issue of religious freedom in favor of making claims about Japaneseness. Schoolchildren need to be given good moral guidance and need to learn to be proud of Japan. The imperial house needs to be accorded proper respect and its traditions upheld as the essence of Japanese identity. Japan's glorious yet pitiable war dead deserve proper veneration from the nation as a whole. None of these claims is specifically about religion, and yet each impinges upon religious freedom. We cannot understand prominent postwar religious freedom issues in Japan if we do not pay due attention to the problem of how overemphasizing Japan's putative uniqueness distracts us from the definitional issues intrinsic to religious freedom itself.

The postwar dilemmas and controversies regarding Yasukuni Shrine, constitutional revision, public school education, and the imperial institution must ultimately be resolved by Japanese citizens who are facing rapid population decline, the prolonged effects of devastating natural and artificial disasters, significant changes in the traditional structures of the family and the workforce, and real and perceived security threats from Asian neighbors. What they do with religious freedom is up to them, but the solution to Japan's ongoing problems with religious freedom probably does not lie in any theory of Japanese uniqueness. The issue for postwar Japan is decidedly *not* that a unique "Japan-style relationship between religion and the state" was misunderstood by the American occupiers, nor is it that Japanese people fundamentally misunderstood the transcendent "principle" of religious freedom. The definition of religion itself is at stake, and there are always those who would draw the boundaries around that category a little too neatly for the comfort of others.

While I cannot agree with those who would paper over Japan's history of aggressive imperialism by highlighting Japan's subordinate status vis-à-vis the United States as global hegemon, I do have new sympathy for the incredibly awkward postwar Japanese position regarding democracy, religion, and freedom that is one legacy of the Occupation. My study should not give comfort to those who see contemporary Japan as in need of something resembling the glorious wartime past, but neither should it reassure those who see the work of freeing religion as finished. The project of freeing religion is ongoing. It must be continually subjected to scrutiny if it is to work at all. That includes paying attention to the historical factors that have led us to assume that Japan got religious freedom wrong, that the Allies introduced religious freedom to a place where it was absent, and that postwar conservatives are launching coordinated assaults on a universal human right. Every one of these assumptions is flawed.

For Americans and our Japanese counterparts, there is no workable religious freedom that exists without coming to terms with our intertwined histories. As Americans, we need to think long and hard about how our well-intentioned emancipatory project put our Japanese brothers and sisters in a terribly awkward place. If we truly take the project of democracy seriously, then we must acknowledge that they have every right to change their constitution. They have every right to collectively decide whom the emperor represents and how his (or *her*) responsibilities as the high priest of Shintō fit into that role. They have every right to decide when and how they will remember their dead. Personally, I hope that they make such decisions together, through respectful and open debate, and without simply acquiescing to the whims of the powerful. But what Japanese people do with religious freedom is ultimately up to them. Meanwhile, we Americans have little right to proclaim our nation an unambiguous bastion of freedom when that freedom has obviously come at the expense of the dispossessed indigenous person, the enslaved laborer, the vilified immigrant, the disenfranchised woman, the LGBT+ target of discrimination, the surveilled religious minority.

Our shared history suggests that we cannot stand upon the decks of aircraft carriers and declare mission accomplished. We cannot stand upon the decks of battleships and proclaim the "fundamentally theological" problem of militarism solved simply because the combatants have signed an instrument of peace. Peace treaties and commissions on international religious freedom do not *solve* the problems of religious freedom. If anything, they ossify religious difference.

If we truly want to promote and protect religious freedom, then we must recognize that religious freedom is never just one thing. "It" is not enshrined in constitutions. "It" is not protected by police. *Religious freedoms* are owned and interpreted by many different groups. Religious freedom claims may mobilize the language of nationhood and national character, but viewing religious freedom as something that states have or lack will always fall short.

By the same token, treating religious freedom as a perennial, universal principle that exists out there in the ether will never accord with reality. Religious freedom does not exist until somebody makes a claim about it for a specific set of political reasons. Religious freedom does not exist until particular human bodies are made to suffer, or are freed from suffering, in contexts that are always-already local. We must pay attention to these microclimates of religious freedom if we are to understand this problematic concept at all.

EPILOGUE

Songs of Freedom

There's a land that I see where the children are free
And I say it ain't far to this land from where we are
Take my hand, come with me, where the children are free
Come with me, take my hand, and we'll live
In a land where the river runs free
In a land through the green country
In a land to a shining sea
And you and me are free to be you and me

THE NEW SEEKERS (1972)[1]

BEFORE MY COUSIN TONY INTRODUCED ME to the Michael Jackson albums *Off the Wall* and *Thriller*, the defining soundtrack of my childhood was an album by Marlo Thomas and Friends called *Free to Be You and Me*.[2] The album promoted an idyllic vision of a near-future land characterized by gender equality, honesty, and emotional sensitivity through a collection of uplifting songs, humorous dialogue, and inspiring anecdotes. Its profound influence on my young mind must have been considerable. Freedom became something of an intellectual obsession for me from an early age. The vision of liberty presented in *Free to Be* was also a perfect snapshot of that particular historical moment. Though the Cold War was still raging, the palpable effects of the civil rights movement and marginally successful feminist interventions in American public life were encapsulated in the album's starry-eyed idealism.

That my die-hard liberal parents provided such an album for my edification and entertainment was no accident. My white mother was the daughter of a laconic Midwestern minister known for his advocacy of civil rights, on the one hand, and a Scot who had been raised in northeast China as the daughter of missionaries, on the other. A small-town Iowan through and through, she nevertheless grew up with a cosmopolitan outlook and a penchant for social justice. My black father narrowly escaped the endemic poverty and deeply institutionalized racism that characterized South Side Chicago to attend a small college in rural Iowa. Shortly after he met my mother at Grinnell, his activities as cofounder of a campus organization called Concerned Black Students placed him on an FBI watch list. His FBI file, which I have seen, turned the innocuous details of an innocent man's life into a devastating indictment of seditious intent. While my father remained unfailingly optimistic about democratic process and the power of the state to grant liberties to its disenfranchised citizens, the humiliating experience of being labeled a potential enemy of the state also left him understandably cynical about the United States' promise of freedom. Even as he encouraged us to embody and express our freedom and dignity in ways that he never could have in his own childhood, he also taught my brother and me to be suspicious of authority and keenly aware of the double standard that all black men face in America. Later run-ins with cops would repeatedly prove him right.

As my parents' ethnically ambiguous firstborn child growing up in the predominantly white city of Des Moines in the 1980s, I had many opportunities to reflect on the American ideal of freedom. Coming up with inventive ways to respond to the blatantly racist question "What are you?" was a defining feature of my childhood, and it prompted a great deal of thinking at a very early age about "one drop" rules, about being three-fifths human, about the very ability to be "free to be." In my angsty adolescence, these meditations elicited despair more than they did hope. I settled into a long fugue, trying to reconcile the American theme of freedom with my own contrapuntal experience. Clearly some were more free than others.

As Janis Joplin warbled in her rendition of Kris Kristofferson's tune, "freedom" was just another word bandied about in the debates about political correctness and multiculturalism that smoldered, rather than raged, for most of my high school and college years, when I spent more time listening to my parents' vinyl than they did. It took on a new register during my postbaccalaureate semester of student teaching, when hijackers flew planes into iconic American buildings on 11 September 2001. The tragedy was terrible.

At the risk of sounding insensitive, the flag-waving jingoism and extreme xenophobia that ensued felt almost worse. Disappointed with my compatriots' nationalistic response to the atrocity, I capriciously decided to leave the United States and move to Japan just a few months after 9/11. My first stint living in Japan (2002–4) coincided almost perfectly with the onset of the wars in Afghanistan and then Iraq.

In a sense, my professional career as a student of Japan emerged out of the ashes of the collapsed buildings. The Bushian refrain of vaguely defined terrorist enemies hating America for its freedoms was ridiculous and offensive, but the more time I spent abroad, the more I found myself defending American freedom.[3] This was true even as I took every opportunity to lambaste American foreign and military policy. Through conversation with Japanese friends and expatriates from all over the globe, I came to a new understanding of how powerful the experiences of slavery, Jim Crow, and the Civil Rights Movement had been in shaping American sensibilities. These historical experiences, I realized, were far from universal. American sensitivity to issues of freedom came from a real historical place, even if domestic rhetoric about a unique American relationship with freedom was frequently exaggerated.

Racial profiling was officially a matter of routine police procedure during my longest stints in Japan (2002–4 and 2005–7). As a brown man with dreadlocks, I had to devise a number of stratagems to allay the suspicions of patrolling Tokyo police officers and to anticipate their frequent demands that I produce proper documentation. The reggae and hip-hop soundtrack I favored for my commute would quietly play songs of freedom from earphones dangling around my neck as I did my best to fend off officers' importunate requests with humor, gamely provided my documentation, or—all other stratagems failing—submitted to their invasive searches of my belongings. Similar profiling procedures greeted me at American airports on trips home, where those of us who were subject to "random" screenings somehow all happened to have brown skin.

When I returned to Japan in 2012 to conduct research for this book, the dreadlocks were gone and police policies regarding foreigners had been significantly relaxed. However, the Tokyo Metropolitan Police had a new project of stamping out many of the Tokyo nightclubs that had been my stomping grounds off and on over the previous decade. The law used to crack down on these "liberated zones" (as my Japanese friends cheekily called them: *kaihōku*) dated from the Allied Occupation of Japan (1945–52). The law had been originally designed to minimize unseemly fraternization between local

Japanese people and American service members by restricting dance halls to a type of large, open space that is rarely found in Tokyo. Nearly seventy years later, social conservatives repurposed the same Occupation-era law to crack down on Japan's relatively tame clubs for fear that they were hotbeds of iniquity.[4] Over the course of my research year, one beloved music venue after another folded due to police harassment. The club where I spent the first few hours of 2013 surrounded by gregarious Tokyoites freely slurping sake from communal tubs had closed its doors for good by May of that year.

Back home once again, the writing of this book took place against the backdrop of heightened American awareness of the quotidian murder of black people by police, the school-to-prison pipeline, and the necessity of vocally and repeatedly affirming that, yes indeed, Black Lives Matter. I put D'Angelo's jeremiad *Black Messiah* on repeat.[5] I wore the grooves down on my roots reggae LPs. I wrestled internally with how my academic inquiry into the politics of religious freedom could fit with the ongoing project of perfecting liberty in America.

As the seemingly ceaseless wave of news stories rolled in now that America was paying attention, they confirmed what black and brown people have known all along. That our bodies are twice as likely to be surveilled, slapped, stunned, or shot by police. That we are always guilty until proven innocent. That any encounter with law enforcement, no matter how superficially innocuous, is a brush with death. That for every highly publicized incident in which a bystander with a phone and a conscience captured a cop killing an unarmed black person, there were countless other stories that did not make the news. The incidents were literally innumerable, as law enforcement agencies realized that they did not actually keep accurate statistics about their killings of citizens. When journalists at the *Guardian* and the *Washington Post* began keeping count, the numbers were sickening.[6] They matched equally disturbing numbers about the racial makeup of America's prisons. About the fact that prisoners are excluded from unemployment statistics, meaning that the unemployment rates for black and brown men are much higher than the official numbers would suggest. About the fact that prison labor perpetuates the system of bonded servitude that besmirches our national history. About the fact that prison populations artificially inflate the representative votes allocated to rural, predominantly white districts even though felons themselves are denied the vote, and even though the absence of their black and brown bodies diminishes the voting power of their urban homes.[7] All this in the land of the free.

The chilling domestic statistics documenting American double standards matched grim reports from watchdog organizations monitoring American intelligence and military operations overseas.[8] Drone strikes in other nations' sovereign territory obliterated black and brown bodies with such regularity that it ceased to be news. Drone pilots confused wedding processions for military convoys.[9] Ugly euphemisms likened extrajudicial executions to exterminating vermin ("bug splats") or winning the lottery ("jackpots").[10] Military analysts counted dead boys as "enemies killed in action" to artificially lower the collateral damage body count.[11] Being free in America meant incarcerating enemy combatants offshore at an unconstitutional prison, extracting confessions through "enhanced interrogation," shooting first and asking questions later.

Yes, we can. The logic that undergirded the Obama administration's drone war and illegal incarcerations was continuous with the logic of the Bush administration that preceded it, even if the rhetoric was different. Protecting freedom for us at home meant denying it to foreign others abroad. But on the home front, the paradoxes of freedom remained intertwined with race and religion. Journalists and politicians described domestic mass killings as unfortunate tragedies, but not as terrorist acts. (Unless, of course, the perpetrators were Muslims.)[12] The gun lobby doubled down on the need for more weapons and called for the loosening of restrictions on their sale. The "good guy with a gun" was all too obviously the one who got to determine the parameters of freedom. He took the law into his own hands. He *was* the law. The "bad guy with a gun"? Well, we know him when we see him. We know him because we label him an extremist. He is not a protester. He is a hoodlum. He is not a champion of freedom. He is inhuman. Good guys with guns walked through public spaces with hands on their holstered weapons and long guns slung over their shoulders, intimidating others with aggressive demonstrations of their Second Amendment rights.[13] Bad guys with guns were children playing in city parks.[14] Bad guys with guns were Walmart shoppers holding unpackaged merchandise while chatting on the phone.[15]

On reflection, these incidents were all too familiar to me. I even had my own moment of having been the bad guy with a gun. I was seventeen. I was riding shotgun in a car with two blond-haired kids from the wealthy suburbs. Apparently some do-gooder citizen thought that my friends were in danger when she saw the *Star Wars* blaster in my hand. Maybe I thought for a moment that I was just like Billy Dee Williams's dashing space scoundrel Lando Calrissian. Maybe she thought I had hijacked that nice white boy's Honda. When we were pulled over by a phalanx of police vehicles and swarmed by a hostile group of armed good guys, the cop who dragged me from the car and threw me to the ground pressed his gun hard against my skull and threatened to fucking kill me unless I showed him the fucking weapon. (Had I pulled the blaster from my pocket at that moment, there is no doubt that I would now be dead.) Finding the toy in the car, the cops laughed the whole incident off. But just to prove the point in case I had missed it, they treated the white kids deferentially. They left me standing alone on the side of the road with a cop holding a shotgun pointed directly at my chest for the better part of an hour. There was no question about who was in charge. There was no question about the hierarchies in operation. There was no ambiguity about who the good guys and bad guys were. It was 1996, and I was a couple of weeks shy of adulthood. The cops threatened to charge me with terrorism. That word did not yet have the meaning it does today, but its function was clear. A person like me would never get to be the good guy. A person like me would never be simply free to be.

In retrospect, it seems only natural that my abiding fascination with freedom as it relates to race and American foreign policy would manifest itself in my academic work on religion. This book has shown how religious freedom operated in competing legal, political, bureaucratic, ecclesiastical, and academic discourses during the democratically draconian Meiji constitutional period and the short period of authoritarian democratization that was the Allied Occupation of Japan. But it also obliquely offered an autobiographical account of how my long-standing curiosity about rights, freedom, and America's protean definitions of personhood dovetailed with my enduring professional fascination with the conundrum of how the categories of "religion" and "not-religion" have operated and continue to operate in modern Japan and elsewhere. Between the lines of text, it shared a personal journey in which I came to understand "religion" and "freedom" in new ways, coming to what I feel is a far more nuanced approach to the topic. But that is not to say that I know religious freedom when I see it. If anything, I am more confused than ever about what religious freedom is and how it might be perfected. The idealist in me celebrates religious freedom as a cherished progressive ideal. The cynic wonders if it will ever be feasible to juxtapose the words "religious" and "freedom" in a way that makes any sense.

My modest proposal is neither to jettison the category of religion nor to conclude that pursuit of freedom and justice is meaningless. My proposal is instead to suggest that we abandon once and for all the politely rude question "What are you?" This question dehumanizes. It asks for a "what" and not a "who." It confuses personhood for religion and hue. It demands that people position themselves in relationship to an identity politics that can never be of their own choosing.[16] "What are you?" is the implicit question in religious freedom talk. What it really asks is, "Are you like me?" The very act of asking the question answers it, and in the negative. The more humane question is, "What do you need?"

This brings me to human rights. It is common to see paeans to human rights today, even as academic observers and former practitioner-advocates recognize just how fraught the category is.[17] Human rights language seems to solve the problems of inequity and injustice by highlighting our fundamental commonality. But the solidarity described and imagined by human rights discourse is subject to the fluid definitions of who counts as human, and the humanity of others evaporates all too easily when the observer confronts religious and racial difference. One need only look at how the accusation of "terrorism" supersedes whatever human rights might be enjoyed by freedom fighters in southwestern and central Asia. Mere suspicion of ties to the "bad religion" of Islamism is enough to make one target of a Hellfire missile. Religious difference is weaponized.

In the world of human rights this should not happen. But the world of human rights is still a world that discriminates between people who are deemed more and less human. In a sense, the racist propaganda that characterized the conflict between the United States and Japan has never really left us. It lingers in the everyday words we use: Terrorist. Militant. Extremist.

We can sing paeans about religious freedom, and we can uphold it as an inalienable human right. But if we do, then we must ensure that our definitions of "religion" and "the human" are capacious enough to allow our songs of freedom to be characterized by contrapuntal melodies and the blue notes of discord at least as much as they feature mellifluous harmony.

ACKNOWLEDGMENTS

SCHOLARLY CONVENTION USUALLY SAVES the most personal for last when it comes to acknowledgments, but this book would not exist except for an ongoing conversation with Kimberley Thomas about what we have come to call "the problem with solutions." Our daily workshop about scholarly method informs every word of this text. Kim's hands gave me countless gentle reminders to stop turtling over my computer screen. She reminded me to go for a run when I was cranky and to eat when light-headedness interfered with productivity. She took me to Bangladesh and Vietnam, forever changing my outlook and my gastrointestinal tract in equal measure. She encouraged me to cook, to sleep, to host, to play games, to buy records. She asked precisely the right question when I needed to break out of a rut, and she patiently listened as I tried to work through ideas. When I needed intellectual distractions, she taught me about the population genetics of pelagic marine organisms, gave me pop quizzes about evolution on isolated Pacific islands, and solicited my editorial help on her own research projects on the politics of water governance and the justice of climate finance schemes in South and Southeast Asia. It was thanks to Kim that I began thinking about how the politics of religious freedom operate at different scales, and it was due to her research that I was able to think about how legal instruments engender as many problems as they solve. While the project is indisputably mine in that it reflects my intellectual interests in Japan and religion, in a very real sense the book should bear both of our names on its cover. One day a different book doubtless will. Anyway, I dedicate this one to Kim, and I thank her for being my most inspiring teacher, day after day after day.

This book is far better for Jackie Stone's characteristically thorough comments on numerous chapter drafts. Buzzy Teiser, Jonathan Gold, Dave Leheny, Shel Garon, Amy Borovoy, Jeff Stout, Eddie Glaude, Wallace Best, Judith Weisenfield and David Howell helped tremendously in the early phases of this project. Fujiwara Satoko hosted me for a research year at the University of Tokyo and pushed me to think about how Japanese audiences would take my claims, and Sarah Thal provided excellent feedback during my postdoc year at the University of Wisconsin–Madison. I developed my interest in the politics of Japanese Buddhism in a reading course with Michel Mohr at the University of Hawai'i, and my interest in the politics of Shintō in seminars with Shimazono Susumu at the University of Tokyo. George Tanabe helped me disaggregate my previous research on manga and anime from inchoate ideas that formed the kernel of this one, and a timely conversation with Henry Rietz at a bar in Honolulu helped me confirm that parts 1 and 2 really do belong together in one book. Incisive comments from Jason Josephson-Storm, Tisa Wenger, and an anonymous reader for the University of Chicago Press greatly improved the final product.

I presented parts of this work at Dartmouth College (2018), the Pennsylvania State University (2018), the Japanese Association for Religious Studies (2016), the American Academy of Religion (2014, 2013), the Association for Asian Studies (2016, 2015, 2011), Asian Studies Conference Japan (2010), a Global Secularisms conference held at New York University in 2014, the American Anthropological Association (2011), and at workshops at Western Michigan University (2015), the University of Wisconsin Center for the Humanities (2014–15), the Modern Japan History Workshop at Waseda University (2013), the University of Tokyo religious studies colloquium (2013), the University of Chicago human rights workshop (2014), Duke University (2013), the University of Pennsylvania (2014), Nanzan University (2013), the University of Hawai'i at Mānoa (2009), and Old Dominion University (2014). I thank audiences and discussants at these events for their feedback.

Winni Sullivan, Beth Hurd, Mark Mullins, Helen Hardacre, Jim Ketelaar, Ben Dorman, Mark Rowe, Barb Ambros, Steve Covell, Tim Graf, Levi McLaughlin, Chika Watanabe, Kawahashi Noriko, Hayashi Makoto, Okuyama Michiaki, Yoshinaga Shin'ichi, Ōmi Toshihiro, Hoshino Seiji, Yijiang Zhong, John Person, Cameron Penwell, Helen Findley, Orion Klautau, James Dobbins, Ōtani Eiichi, Bryan Lowe, Jeff Schroeder, Shimizu Toshiki, Rick Shweder, Usha Menon, John Borneman, Kristen Ghodsee, Darryl Wilkinson, Darien Lamen, Daegan Miller, Elaine Fisher, Ben Schonthal, Tom Ginsburg, Paul Copp, Dan Arnold, Anne Hansen, Mark Bradley, Margaret Mitchell, Matthew Kapstein, Lael Weinberger, Takashi Miura, John Breen, Mark Teeuwen, Aike Rots, Kate Wildman Nakai, Ross Bender, Kanahara Noriko, Jessie Starling, Matt McMullen, Matt Mitchell, Terasawa Kunihiko, April Hughes, Steve Poland, Erin Brightwell, Erik Schicketanz, Justin

Stein, Ryan Ward, Yuma Totani, Bob Huey, Chiba Shin, Date Kiyonobu, Satō Seiko, Kondō Mitsuhiro, and Anna Su were excellent conversation partners at panels, workshops, and casual venues.

Colleagues at the University of Pennsylvania provided excellent feedback on late drafts of this project, especially Hsiao-wen Cheng, Adam Smith, David Spafford, and Brian Vivier. Ayako Kano, Frank and Linda Chance, Fred Dickinson, Eric Feldman, Chris Atwood, and Eiichirō Azuma were influential interlocutors, as were Justin McDaniel, Jamal Elias, Anthea Butler, Steve Weitzman, Donovan Schaefer, Megan Robb, Tim Powell, and Eve Troutt Powell. As I worked on revisions, I learned a ton from discussions with members of the Andrea Mitchell Center for the Study of Democracy "States of Religious Freedom" planning committee and regular workshop attendees: Heather Sharkey, Sally Barringer Gordon, Melissa Wilde, Jeff Green, Rogers Smith, Ram Cnaan, Michele Margolis, William Schultz, and Ronit Stahl. Conversations with students in my courses "The Politics of Shintō," "Sects and Violence in East Asia," "Japanese History and Civilization," "Asian Religions in the Global Imagination," and "Violence, Tolerance, and Freedom" deeply influenced my thinking. Grad students Mark Bookman, John Grisafi, Tianran Hang, and Kaitlyn Ugoretz were particularly adept at pushing me in new directions.

Iwata Fumiaki and Ōmi Toshihiro generously provided access to unpublished materials on Chikazumi Jōkan. Yoshinaga Shin'ichi, Hoshino Seiji, and Bryan Lowe gave me access to documents on the Fellowship of New Buddhists. Ōsawa Kōji tracked down the minutes of the Religions Systems Investigation Committee, and Inoue Nobutaka and Hirafuji Kikuko gave me access to D. C. Holtom's library of Japanese-language materials at Kokugakuin University. Staff at the Claremont Colleges and the University of Oregon helped me locate and photocopy the papers of D. C. Holtom and William P. Woodard, respectively. Archivists at the National Diet Library Government Documents Room provided access to Andō Masazumi's collected papers. Staff at the University of Maryland Prange Collection and the US National Archives helped me gather more material related to the Allied Occupation than I could possibly use. Archivists at the University of Tokyo Modern Newspaper and Magazine Archive and the Risshō Kōseikai Library helped me locate some rare magazines cited here. Charlotte Nunes and Paul Miller helped me get images from the East Asian Images Collection maintained by Paul Barclay at Lafayette College, Robbie Sittel and Jace Klepper helped me get high-quality images from the University of North Texas digital collections, and Kana Jenkins helped me get a high-quality image from the Prange Collection. Deborah Shamoon, Julie Nelson Davis, Molly des Jardin, Maki Kaneko, and Kawata Akihisa provided assistance with image permissions. Katelyn Stoler learned how to send a fax.

While I did not wind up citing any of the interview material directly, Jim and Yoshie Tanabe have my deep thanks for facilitating a whirlwind series of interviews in Hawaiʻi with former translators and clerical staff who served in the Occupation. I thank all of these interlocutors for their time and for the invaluable insight they provided on the cultural dynamics of the Occupation.

Katie Lofton and John Modern have my thanks for the invitation to contribute to the Class 200 series, and Alan Thomas and Kyle Wagner my gratitude for shepherding the book through to completion. Randolph Petilos took care of the important paperwork. Mark Reschke provided exemplary copyediting, and John Grisafi helped me prepare the index.

Several organizations financially supported the research that went into writing this book. I received grants, fellowships, research funds, and subvention support from the University of Pennsylvania, Princeton University, the University of Maryland, the Association for Asian Studies, Fulbright-IIE, the Whiting Foundation, and the Mellon Foundation. I also benefited immensely from workshops conducted by the Nanzan University Institute for Religion and Culture, the Op-Ed Project, the US-Japan Network for the Future, and the Institute for Research in the Humanities at the University of Wisconsin–Madison. The *Asian Journal of Law and Society* gave permission to reuse material that appears in chapter 2.

Finally, my parents and my in-laws slogged through drafts and talked shop with me over meals, and many friends and family members helped me frame the ideas in ways that I hope are more engaging and accessible than they otherwise might have been. To all of you who asked me what I was working on at barbecues, in bars, and on the beach: Thank you.

ABBREVIATIONS

ARCHIVES AND COLLECTIONS

AM Andō Masazumi kankei bunsho (Modern Japanese Political History Materials Room, National Diet Library of Japan)

CJP Chikazumi Jōkan Papers (CJP; Kyūdō Kaikan Archives)

DCH D. C. Holtom Papers (Claremont Colleges Honnold/Mudd Library Special Collections)

FRUS Foreign Relations of the United States (FRUS; University of Wisconsin Libraries: https://uwdc.library.wisc.edu/collections/FRUS/)

FDR Franklin Delano Roosevelt Papers (http://www.fdrlibrary.marist.edu/archives/collections/franklin/)

KHS Kishimoto Hideo shū (Wakimoto Tsuneya and Yanagawa Keiichi, eds. 1975–76. *Kishimoto Hideo shū*. 5 vols. Tokyo: Keiseisha.)

KGSR Kizokuin giji sokki roku (National Diet Library of Japan)

MTZ Makiguchi Tsunesaburō zenshū (Makiguchi Tsunesaburō. (1981) 1987. *Makiguchi Tsunesaburō zenshū*. Tokyo: Daisan Bunmeisha.)

Prange Prange Collection (University of Maryland at College Park)

RCR Records of Allied Operational and Occupation Headquarters, Religion and Cultural Resources Division (US National Archives II, College Park, Maryland)

SBRS Shin Bukkyō ronsetsu shū (Futaba Kenkō, supervising director; Akamatsu Tesshin and Fukushima Hirotaka, eds. 1979–82. *"Shin Bukkyō" ronsetsu shū*. Vols. 1–4. Kyoto: Nagata Bunshōdō.)

SMDKES Shōda Monbu Daijin kunji enzetsu shū (Monbusho (Ministry of Education), ed. 1929. *Shōda [Kazue] Monbu Daijin kunji enzetsu shū*. Tokyo: Monbushonai Insatsu Shitsu.)

SGSR Shūgiin giji sokki roku (National Diet Library of Japan)

SSCK Shūkyō seido chōsa kai (Japanese Agency of Culture Records)

USDS US Department of State Records on Japanese Internal Affairs (Central File: Decimal File 894.404, Internal Affairs of States, Social Matters, Japan, Religion, Church, February 13, 1932–July 12, 1939; Records of the Department of State Relating to the Internal Affairs of Japan, 1930–39; US National Archives)

WPW William P. Woodard Papers (Coll. 153, Special Collections and University Archives, University of Oregon Libraries, Eugene)

PERIODICALS

B *Bukkyō*

CLJ *Central Law Journal*

TCP *The China Press*

TCR *The Chinese Recorder*

CC *Christian Century*

CSM *Christian Science Monitor*

CL *Current Literature*

D *Daihōrin*

TF *The Friend* (Hawai'i Evangelical Association newspaper)

JTW *Japan Times Weekly*

LAT *Los Angeles Times*

MS *Meikyō shinshi*

NJ *Nippu jiji*

NCH *North China Herald and Supreme Court and Consular Gazette*

SJ *Seikyō jihō*

SS *Seikyō shinron*

SB *Shin Bukkyō*

ShJ *Shūkyō jihō*

SK *Shūkyō kōron*

TG *Tokkō geppō*

U *Uchū*

NOTES

PROLOGUE

1 US president George W. Bush, in a 20 September 2001 speech to Congress.
2 Dower 2003.
3 Dower 1999.

INTRODUCTION

1 Prominent scholar of Japan August Karl Reischauer (1879–1971), in a 1 December 1927 article in *The Chinese Recorder* (emphasis in the original).
2 Maruyama Masao (1914–96), "Theory and Psychology of Japanese Ultra-nationalism," a May 1946 essay published in *Sekai* (*The World*). Reproduced in Maruyama 1969.
3 Lavigne 2013.
4 Juaregui 2012; Canepari and Cooper 2015; Lah 2010.
5 Sherriff 2015.
6 Roemer 2009.
7 Reader and Tanabe 1998.
8 Fitzgerald 2000.
9 Maruyama 1969.
10 Swanson 2014; Shields 2012.
11 Garon 1997.
12 In English, O'Brien and Ohkoshi 1996. In Japanese, Nakano 2003.
13 See Hardacre 1989b, especially chapter 6.
14 For examples from Japan, Breen 2010a. For theoretical approaches, Mahmood 2016, 1–28.
15 Sullivan 2005; Mahmood 2016.
16 Mahmood and Danchin 2014b; Sullivan, Yelle, and Taussig-Rubbo 2011; Hunter 2014.

17 In addition to Sullivan 2005, see Mahmood and Danchin 2014a; Hurd and Sullivan 2014; Hurd 2015; and Sullivan, Hurd, Mahmood, and Danchin 2015.

18 Mahmood (2016) uses the case of Egypt to make a similar observation.

19 Maxey 2014. Krämer (2015) persuasively points out that something akin to the modern religion/not-religion distinction existed prior to the solidification of *shūkyō* as a translation for the English "religion" in the mid-nineteenth century, but defining religion in order to free it was a late nineteenth-century project.

20 Sullivan 2005.

21 Indeed, others have been. See Wenger 2017; Su 2016; Curtis 2016; Mahmood 2016; and Hurd 2015 for a few examples.

22 See, respectively, Hardacre 1989b; Nakano 2003; and Mullins 2012b.

23 Su 2016.

24 Hurd 2015.

25 See Johnson and Weitzman 2017 on the FBI and religion.

26 Wedemeyer 2013.

27 The idea of a "Japan-style separation of religion and the state" first appeared in Yasumaru 1979; it was addressed in more detail in Inoue and Sakamoto 1987.

28 In recent years, two scholars have represented these views. Shimazono Susumu (2010) has vehemently critiqued State Shintō, while his protégé Isomae Jun'ichi has advanced a postcolonial argument of Japanese victimhood (Isomae 2013; Isomae 2014).

29 See Totani 2008 for a thorough treatment of the War Crimes Tribunal. Larsson 2017 covers some high-profile court cases about the place of religion in constitutional law.

30 This is what Schonthal (2016) calls "constitutional microhistory."

31 See Scheid 2013 and Zhong 2016.

32 See Krämer 2015.

33 For an overview of recent scholarship on State Shintō, see Okuyama 2011. Also see Thomas 2017b.

34 Hurd 2015.

35 Curtis 2016; Wenger 2017.

36 Dressler and Mandair 2011.

37 See Josephson 2012; van der Veer 2014; and Josephson-Storm 2017.

38 Garon 1986, 274.

CHAPTER ONE

1 Andō Masazumi, from a summer 1942 op-ed in the *Yomiuri Shinbun* arguing against the adoption of Shintō as Japan's national religion. Andō Masazumi, "Nihon rekishi no kaiko to dentō no Bukkyō," *D* 11, no. 1 (1 January 1944), 8 (AM Reel #11, Item #155).

2 Mori 1872, 3.

3 Mori 1872, 9.

4 This understanding was only just beginning to emerge in Japan, although some im-

portant precursors had existed for centuries. See Isomae 2003, 2014; Josephson 2012; Maxey 2014; Krämer 2015.

5 Howland 2002.

6 Itō (1889) 1906, 58–61.

7 For a comparison of the Meiji Constitution to other contemporaneous constitutions, see Josephson 2012.

8 O'Brien and Ohkoshi 1996, 40.

9 Inoue T. 1893; Sueki 2004a, 62–85.

10 Dorman 2012a, 24–44; Garon 1997, 60–87.

11 See, for example, Maruyama Masao's 1946 essay "Theory and Psychology of Japanese Ultranationalism" in Maruyama 1969.

12 See, for example, "Review of Religions in Japan," iii–iv, RCR Box #5787, Folder #13.

13 To offer just one example, see Shimoma Kūkyō's ninety-five-page treatise on religious law published as part of a ten-volume set on social policy by Daitō Press in December 1927. Shimoma (1927) 2002.

14 As Jason Ānanda Josephson (2012) has argued, stakeholders sequestered "religion" not only from the category of the secular, but also from related terms like "superstition" and "morality."

15 Curtis 2016, 2–3.

16 Scheid 2013, 20–21.

17 Zhong 2016, 15.

18 Josephson 2012. As Agrama (2012) has shown, maintaining public order is an essential feature of secularist states.

19 Japanologists tend to periodize by using either imperial reign dates (e.g., the Meiji era, 1868–1912) or the concept of "modern Japan" (1868–?).

20 Maxey 2014.

21 Hayashi 2006; see also the special issue of *Japanese Religions* guest edited by Orion Klautau in 2014. Hoshino (2012), Josephson (2012), Maxey (2014), and Zhong (2016) have all told stories about the religion/not-religion distinction that more or less ended in the Meiji era, although Zhong gestured toward postwar scholarship in his conclusion.

22 The claim is factually inaccurate because Shintō was never designated a national religion in law. For one example of the claim, see Murakami 1970. For a critique, see Sakamoto 2000. Helen Hardacre adopted Murakami's periodization in her 1989 book *Shintō and the State*, but judiciously revised it in her magisterial 2017 survey *Shintō: A History*.

23 See Maxey 2014 on five significant shifts in governmental understandings of religion in the Meiji era alone.

24 Ketelaar 1990; Maxey 2014.

25 Zhong 2016.

26 Ketelaar 1990; Collcutt (1986) 2014.

27 Jaffe 2001. The legal change was part of a broader effort on the part of the Meiji state to eliminate the status and occupation system that had characterized the Tokugawa period (1603–1868) in favor of a new system of "flat" national citizenship. See Howell 2005.

28 Bernstein 2006, 114–17.

29 On the historical development of Shintō, see Kuroda 1981 and Teeuwen 2002, as well as Havens 2006 and Breen and Teeuwen 2010. On tensions between Buddhism and Shintō in the early Meiji era, see Ketelaar 1990. On the introduction of "religion" to Japan, see Isomae 2003; Hoshino 2012; Josephson 2012; Maxey 2014; Isomae 2014; Krämer 2015.

30 Ikeda 1976.

31 Maxey 2014, 159–60; Krämer 2017.

32 See Maxey 2014, 140–82.

33 Zhong 2016; Teeuwen and Breen 2017.

34 See Josephson 2012; the timeline included in Scheid 2013; Maxey 2014; and Zhong 2016.

35 See Anonymous, "The Emperor of Japan," *North-China Herald and Supreme Court & Consular Gazette*, 4 November 1910, 253.

36 Bernstein 2006, 91–98; Maxey 2014, esp. 93–139.

37 The constitution was promulgated in 1889 and enacted in 1890. It was formally suspended with Japan's official surrender on 2 September 1945. Until the Allied-drafted "Peace Constitution" was promulgated in November 1946 and enacted in May 1947, the main oversight of religious matters and religious liberties happened through the Civil Liberties Directive promulgated by SCAP on 4 October 1945, the Shintō Directive of 15 December 1945, and the Religious Corporations Ordinance of 28 December 1945. See part 2.

38 Krämer 2017.

39 Asad 2003; Josephson 2012. On secularism in Japan, see Rots and Teeuwen 2017. Mahmood (2016) calls this "political secularism."

40 See Mahmood 2016, drawing on Asad 2003.

41 Here my project departs from Josephson (2012), who focuses on the historical emergence of what he calls "the Shintō secular."

42 Mahmood 2016, 2.

43 See Mahmood and Danchin 2014a and Calhoun, Juergensmeyer, and van Antwerpen 2011, 16.

44 Dressler and Mandair 2011.

45 Here I am slightly reformulating Saba Mahmood's (2016) distinction between political secularism and secularity. Whereas Mahmood makes a functionalist argument about governance, I am interested in making a constructivist argument about who asks and answers the "what is religion" question at the heart of secularist arrangements. See Agrama 2012.

46 Shimazono Susumu (2010) has pointed out this ambiguous imperial role.

47 See Rots 2017 for a convincing discussion of how "sacred space" may be set aside as special without necessarily being made "religious."

48 Agrama 2012, 28–29. Also see Mahmood 2016, 4.

49 Schonthal 2016, 12. Schonthal terms this "pyrrhic constitutionalism."

50 Curtis 2016, 2.

51 For one example of suppression, see Takeda 1991. Journalists singled out the rise of Renmonkyō as a *result* of the new policy of religious freedom in their calls for its suppression (Takeda 1991, 40).

52 Josephson 2012, 132–63; Krämer 2017.

53 See Mahmood 2012 and Josephson 2012, 71–93.

54 Maxey 2014. "Sect Shintō" designated a certain group of confraternities and groups founded by charismatic leaders that venerated at specific Japanese shrines or took specific kami to be their main objects of veneration. See Inoue N. 2002.

55 Chamberlain 1912, 27. Chamberlain's short pamphlet was published by an association of "freethinkers" and was widely cited in the global press of the day; it seems to have been largely responsible for popularizing the notion of emperor worship. See chapters 3 and 5.

56 Jason Josephson (2012), Trent Maxey (2014), and Helen Hardacre (2017) have all made arguments that support my claim here.

57 See Asad 2003, esp. 181–201. On tolerance as governmentality, see Brown 2006.

58 Josephson 2012, 226–36.

59 On imperial pageantry, see Fujitani 1996.

60 On Ise as an imperial mausoleum, see Teeuwen and Breen 2017. On the spread of Yasukuni belief in the period around the Russo-Japanese War, see Takenaka 2015. On the establishment of Meiji Shrine, see Imaizumi 2013.

61 For an overview of these initiatives, see Inoue E. 1972.

62 Bellah 1967. Civil religion might be described as an amalgam of broadly shared nonsectarian theological commitments, ritual practices, and political ideals that inform a nation's public life.

63 This sui generis understanding of religion has come in for serious and deserved critique by a number of scholars and does not require extensive elaboration here. See especially McCutcheon 1997.

64 Isomae 2003; Maxey 2014; Zhong 2016.

65 The fact that Bellah had a long-standing interest in Japan is crucial. In an aside on page 12 of the 1967 *Daedalus* article in which he first laid out his idea of "America's civil religion," Bellah clarified that critics of what he had termed "America's civil religion" were wont to describe it pejoratively as an "American Shintō." Bellah did not name those responsible for this claim, but given his own interest in the sociology of Japanese religion it seems that Bellah's idea of "civil religion" was constructed with Shintō in mind perhaps a little more than he was inclined to admit in his 1967 piece. See Borovoy 2016.

66 Bellah 1967, 8. Those familiar with Talal Asad's searing critique of Clifford Geertz's 1966 essay "Religion as a Cultural System" will recognize the problems inherent in this portrayal. See Asad 1993, 27–54.

67 Borovoy (2016) suggests that Bellah built the concept of civil religion in response to the collection of Japanese practices commonly called State Shintō.

68 See the review articles by Okuyama (2011) and myself (2017) on the question of State Shintō.

69 State Shintō in this sense appeared in the first few months of the Occupation (see chapter 5), but it was solidified in Murakami Shigeyoshi's 1970 paperback *Kokka Shintō*.

70 On lay interest groups' complicity in state ideology, for example, see Gluck 1985 and Garon 1997. More recent bottom-up approaches include Shimazono 2009 and 2010 and Azegami 2009 and 2012.

71 Although he focuses on intellectuals, this is one point made by Skya (2009) in a perplexing book on what he calls "radical Shintō ultranationalism."

72 Gluck 1985; Garon 1997; Kushner 2006.

73 Dower 1993, 101–54.

74 See Nitta 1999a, 1999b; Sakamoto 1994, 2006.

75 See Nitta 2000.

76 Inoue and Sakamoto 1987. The idea of a "Japan-style relationship between religion and politics" first appeared in Yasumaru 1979.

77 Jakobsen and Pellegrini 2008; Warner, van Antwerpen, and Calhoun. 2010.

78 Ōhara 1989; Sakamoto 1989.

79 Asad 2003, 14. I'm thinking specifically of Isomae Jun'ichi's writings on the development of religion and the secular in Japan, which consistently present Japan as a misunderstood victim of Western epistemological violence. See Isomae 2003, 2013, 2015, and my review of the last (Thomas 2016a).

80 Sakamoto 1994, 2006.

81 Sakamoto 2000.

82 Shimazono 2009, 2010.

83 Mullins 2012b; Guthmann 2017.

84 Hardacre 2017; Larsson 2017.

85 Agrama 2012; Dressler and Mandair 2011.

86 This dynamic is emblematic of what Schonthal (2016) calls "pyrrhic constitutionalism." On "third terms," see Josephson-Storm 2017.

87 As Saba Mahmood has argued, secularism is a modern political form with global reach; it adopts local modalities while retaining homogenizing tendencies. Mahmood 2016, 10.

88 I take inspiration here from Cavanaugh 2014, 491–92, and Arnal and McCutcheon 2013, 17–30. Both texts draw distinctions between substantivist (= essentialist), functionalist, and constructivist approaches to "religion." See also Curtis 2016.

89 Again, this is Schonthal's "pyrrhic constitutionalism."

90 See Holtom 1927 for a contemporaneous critical take.

91 Shimazono 2009, 103; Nakai 2013. The debates about obligatory obeisance became particularly pronounced in the 1920s and 1930s.

92 Henry 2014.

93 In a 7 January 1942 article in the mainline Protestant magazine the *Christian Century*, missionary-scholar D. C. Holtom described obligatory school shrine visits as largely pro forma affairs, but he nevertheless suggested that they were indisputably a part of a national religion that he called "State Shintō." D. C. Holtom, "Japanese Christianity and Shintō Nationalism I: Christian Participation in Shintō Shrine Ceremonies," *CC*, 7 January 1942: 11–13, DCH Box #1, Folder #45.

94 For more on Minobe, see Skya 2009, 82–111.

95 Joseph C. Grew, February 1933 missive to State Department, in USDS (Religions in Japan), 4–5 (my pagination).

96 Nakai 2013, 2017.

97 Prefect Peter Cardinal Fumasoni-Biondi and Secretary Celsus Constantini, Titular

Archbishop of Theodosia, "Sacred Congregation of Propaganda Fide: Instructions," 1, DCH Box #2, Folder #36: "Roman Catholic Church & Shrine Problem."

98 "Sacred Congregation of Propaganda Fide: Instructions," 2.

99 "Sacred Congregation of Propaganda Fide: Instructions," 3–4.

100 Krämer 2011.

101 See D. C. Holtom's string of articles on the issue in the mainline Protestant publication the *Christian Century*, DCH Box #1, Folder #45.

102 Kōno 1938, 57–58.

103 Andō 1941. A version of this text was serialized in *Chūgai nippō* in twelve installments from 23 July 1941 under the title "Nihon Bukkyō zenshin no kōryō" ("A Platform for Advancing Japanese Buddhism"). See AM Reel #10, Item #133. The version cited here is available in its entirety online: http://kindai.ndl.go.jp/info:ndljp/pid/1464236.

104 Andō was probably thinking of Anesaki Masaharu (1873–1949) and Katō Genchi (1873–1965). See chapter 5.

105 On imperial pageantry, Fujitani 1996 and Shimazono 2009.

106 Isomae 2013.

107 See Brown 2006 on toleration.

108 Asad 2003.

109 Mahmood 2005 and Vásquez 2011 are examples.

110 Shimazono 2009.

111 This was Bellah's observation, cited above. Bellah 1967. On American currency, see Kruse 2015, 111–125.

112 Shimazono 2009.

113 Josephson (2012, 136) refers to these as "higher-order ideographs."

114 However, nationalism can and should be distinguished from religion. See Schilbrack 2013b.

115 See Mahmood and Danchin 2014b; Mahmood 2016.

116 Garon 1997, 60–87. Also see Agrama 2012.

CHAPTER TWO

1 "Shinkyō no jiyū no gokai," unsigned editorial probably written by Chikazumi Jōkan in *Seikyō jihō* (*State and Religion Times*), 29 December 1899.

2 KGSR 9: 92.

3 In addition to the legislative record (KGSR 9), see *MS* 4395 (16 December 1899), 4–7.

4 A more detailed play-by-play account of the deliberations can be found in Abe 1970a.

5 KGSR 17: 607.

6 Briefly, many of these transsectarian groups were designed to lobby for Buddhist legal and political interests; they tended to coalesce around new journals such as *Meikyō shinshi* (*Meiji Religious News*, published 1875–1901 by laicized priest, reformer, and activist Ōuchi Seiran [1845–1918]).

7 Maxey 2014, 227.

8 Tōgō Ryōchō, in Kitamura, ed. 1898, 1.

9 The fact that most Japanese people identified (or, more accurately, were identified as) Buddhist derives from a Tokugawa period mandate that all Japanese subjects register with local Buddhist temples as a way of proving they were not potentially seditious Christians. See Hur 2007.

10 Nagaoka 2010, 47n31. Also see Miyoshi 1967.

11 Tōgō made this argument more explicitly in the second part of his speech on 20 November 1898.

12 Ōsawa 2009, 17. Of roughly 1,900 inmates, only 30 were Christians. The vote passed by a slim margin: 102 were in favor while 91 were opposed.

13 On the Sugamo Prison chaplain affair, see Thelle 1987, 158–59; Ōsawa 2009, 17; and Nagaoka 2010, 43–44.

14 Tan 1897; Inoue 1897. Also see Katō T. 1899 for another example of this Buddhist discourse on mixed residence.

15 Fujishima 1899.

16 Fujishima was referring to American legal disputes with the Mormon Church concerning plural marriage.

17 For an overview of French law regarding minority religions, particularly Islam, see Date 2015. Fujishima's depiction seems to have been accurate.

18 One example of contemporaneous publications on the issue is Ashihara 1898.

19 On this "Buddhist youth culture," see Ōtani 2009; 2012a.

20 Ketelaar 1990.

21 Shields 2017.

22 See Hoshino 2009 and 2012 on the representative figure of Nakanishi Ushirō (1859–1930).

23 On the concept of lay centrality, see Hardacre 1989a.

24 On these changes, see Stone 1990; Ōtani 2012a; Hoshino 2012; and Yoshinaga 2012a.

25 Suzuki Daisetsu is one famous example of this trend; he wrote his first book, *Shin shūkyō ron* (*On the New Religion*) in 1896.

26 This attitude was primarily evident among state bureaucrats, but some Buddhists also accepted it as natural. For example, in a short letter to the editor of the Buddhist journal *Meikyō shinshi*, Katō Totsudō (1870–1949) argued for the statist vision of religious freedom advocated by the Yamagata cabinet. See *MS* 4395 (16 December 1899), 3.

27 The text of Article 28 of the Constitution of the Empire of Japan read, "Japanese subjects shall, within limits not prejudicial to peace and order, and not antagonistic to their duties as subjects, enjoy freedom of religious belief." Itō (1889) 1906. Josephson (2012, 226–36) has indicated that this religious freedom clause was actually relatively liberal in comparison with most contemporary European constitutions, some of which singled out certain religions as "state religions" (Catholicism, in Spain) or identified certain religious groups (Jews, in the case of Norway's constitution) as having fewer rights.

28 Uchimura Kanzō (1861–1930) was a Christian schoolteacher who made political waves by refusing to bow before the imperial portrait (*goshin'ei*) at a school ceremony in 1891. Uchimura was forced to resign, but the incident prompted a flurry of debate about the relationships between religious freedom and public duty that was encapsulated in

the title of Inoue Tetsujirō's 1893 book, *The Clash of Education and Religion* (*Kyōiku to shūkyō no shōtotsu*). See Inoue T. 1893.

29 Accounts of this persecution include Sawada 2004, 236–58, and Dorman 2012a, 24–44.

30 Sueki 2004a, 62–85; Hoshino 2012, 152–68.

31 Abe 1970a, 31–37.

32 "Shūkyō hōan," Clause 1, KGSR 9: 89.

33 KGSR 9: 89–90.

34 KGSR 9: 90.

35 KGSR 9: 90.

36 The stringent revisions of the stipulations required for achieving religious juridical person status under the Religious Corporations Law (Shūkyō hōjin hō) that followed the 1995 Aum Shinrikyō affair are one example of "public interest" superseding religions' rights. See Hardacre 2003 and Baffelli and Reader 2012, 7–11.

37 KGSR 9: 90–92, esp. 91–92.

38 See, for example, KGSR 17: 575.

39 This particular interpretation dominated the postwar Occupation. See the 1955 research volume *Religions in Japan*, which was attributed to William K. Bunce (1907–2008) but was actually the product of the collective efforts of the Religions and Cultural Resources Division, Civil Information and Education Section, SCAP. The book was based on a Religions Division report completed in 1948.

40 *MS* 4395 (16 December 1899), 3.

41 Maxey 2014, 227.

42 By "customary right," I mean a perquisite traditionally granted to an individual or group based on precedent or a long-standing claim (i.e., claim to property or position). In the case of Japanese religions, customary rights featured most prominently in clerics' ability to wear special garb (clerical robes), their right to tax exemption and exemption from the corvée, and temples' rights to serve as landholders.

43 Bernstein 2006, 114–17.

44 This "Japanese-style relationship between religion and the state" was first advanced by Yasumaru Yoshio in 1979; the idea was picked up in Inoue and Sakamoto 1987 and occasionally resurfaces in contemporary scholarship.

45 On the Japanese constitution vis-à-vis contemporary European constitutions, see Josephson 2012, 226–36. For example, Ashihara Ringen (d.u.) published a tract in November 1898 that outlined the *kōninkyō* systems in various countries such as England, the Austrian Empire, France, the countries of the German Empire, Italy, Belgium, and the United States.

46 The fact that Buddhism and Christianity were even recognized as two similar species of the genus "religion" is striking. In different ways, Isomae Jun'ichi (2003, 2014), Hoshino Seiji (2012), Jason Josephson (2012), and Trent Maxey (2014) have each highlighted the adventitious process whereby this conceptualization became possible.

47 *MS* 4395 (16 December 1899), 1–3.

48 The fits and starts whereby Shintō came to be recognized as transcending the category of religion have been ably described by Josephson 2012; Maxey 2014; Krämer 2015; Zhong 2016; and Hardacre 2017.

49 I have relied on the pioneering scholarship of Iwata Fumiaki and his research circle in constructing this overview of Chikazumi's life, particularly Iwata 2014; Ōmi 2009, 2014; Chikazumi 2009; and Ōsawa 2009.

50 Kiyozawa was a famed Shinshū reformer. He and Chikazumi remained close after Chikazumi left for Tokyo, and when Chikazumi left on a tour of Europe, Kiyozawa occupied Chikazumi's residence, forming his private study circle the Kōkōdō there.

51 Chikazumi began the equivalent of a graduate degree, but his political activism interfered with his studies. Iwata Fumiaki (2014, 34) suggests that Chikazumi may have been pushed out of his graduate program because his remonstrations with the government were not appropriate for a student at Japan's elite national university.

52 Ōsawa 2009, 17.

53 The leadership of the movement is attributed in some contemporary sources to Chikazumi, and in others to Shinshū cleric Ishikawa Shuntai (1842–1931). I suspect that Ishikawa pioneered the resistance to the Sugamo decision but left the day-to-day operation of the journal *Seikyō jihō* largely to the younger Chikazumi. Clearly Ishikawa was a vocal critic of the Sugamo decision; he wrote several letters to prominent politicians and bureaucrats (the prime minister, the chiefs of the army and navy, members of the House of Peers and House of Commons) protesting the decision in 1898. See Kitamura, ed. 1898, 4–5, 12–14.

54 Ōsawa 2009, 15–16.

55 Iwata 2014, 45.

56 Anonymous, "Shinkyō no jiyū no gokai," *SJ* 24 (29 December 1899).

57 On French treatment of Algerian Muslims, see Date 2015.

58 Dai Nippon Bukkyōto Dōmei Kai 1900.

59 The founders of the Bukkyō Seito Dōshikai were explicitly indebted to Puritan ideals; the neologism "Seito" was their attempt to translate the word "Puritan" (now translated into Japanese as *seikyōto*). See [Sakaino] Kōyō, "Shin Bukkyō yōnen jidai," *SB* 6 (4), in SBRS 1:42–43. In previous publications I have referred to this group as a "Fraternity," but I prefer James Mark Shields's translation of "Fellowship." See Shields 2017.

60 Sakaino 1910, 1–2. Also see Thelle 1987, 207; Davis 1992, 167; Moriya 2005, 286. The Hanseikai journal *Hansei zasshi* went on to become the liberal journal *Chūō kōron*, still in publication today.

61 Yoshinaga 2012b, 33–34.

62 Yoshinaga 2012b, 34.

63 Watanabe Kaikyoku (1872–1933) and Sugimura Jūō (1872–1945) joined the original four as founding members sometime in 1899.

64 Takashima, "Shin Bukkyō jindai shi," SBRS 2:1056–57. See Anonymous, "Bukkyō Seito Dōshikai no soshiki naru," *B* 148 (15 March 1899), 101–3.

65 See "Wagato no sengen," *SB* 1, no. 1 (July 1900): 4–5.

66 [Sakaino] Kōyō, "Shin Bukkyō yōnen jidai," SBRS 2:42.

67 Takashima Beihō, "Shin Bukkyō jindai shi," *SB* 11, no 7. (1910), SBRS 2:1056–67. Also see Sakaino 1910, 1.

68 The founders initially rejected the applications of the prominent Buddhist ecumenist

Murakami Senshō (1851–1929) and the Christian advocate of comparative religion Kishimoto Nobuta (1866–1928; Kishimoto's son Hideo features prominently in part 2 of this book). See Takashima, "Shin Bukkyō jindai shi," SBRS 2:1060.

69 Takashima, "Shin Bukkyō jindai shi," SBRS 2:1056–67. An anonymous *Bukkyō* article announcing the group's existence promised to not disclose members' identities. *B* 148 (15 March 1899), 103.

70 Takashima, "Shin Bukkyō jindai shi," SBRS 2:1063–64; Yoshinaga 2012b, 34.

71 Adapted from Anonymous, "Kōninkyō ni kan suru iken," *B* 148 (15 March 1899), 103–9.

72 Such distinctions had already been drawn by Nakanishi Ushirō in 1889. See Ōtani 2012a, 45–47. For an extended examination of Nakanishi's work, see Hoshino 2012.

73 Anonymous, "Bukkyō Seito Dōshikai no sōshiki naru," *B* 148 (15 March 1899), 101–2.

74 Jiyūshugi Bukkyōto Dōmei Kai, "Shūkyō hōan ni tai suru iken," *B* 158 (24 January 1900), 34.

75 Sakaino Kōyō, "Shin Bukkyō yōnen jidai," *SB* 6, no. 4, SBRS 1:42.

76 In addition to retrospectives published by these authors in *Shin Bukkyō* in 1901, 1905, 1906, 1907, and 1910, see also Takashima's postwar retrospective published in the trans-sectarian Buddhist magazine *Daihōrin*. Takashima 1946a, 1946b (*D* April 1946: 34–37; *D* May 1946: 29–33).

77 Kōyō Shō (Humble [Sakaino] Kōyō), "Kaiko nisoku," *SB* 7, no. 1; SBRS 2:173–75.

78 Akamatsu, "Kaisetsu: Shin Bukkyō undō ni tsuite," SBRS 1:1121–29; Ikeda 1976, esp. 264–305; Thelle 1987, esp. 194–213. More nuanced recent treatments include Yoshinaga 2012a; Ōtani 2009, 2012a, 2014; and Shields 2017. On the political tendencies of Buddhist studies scholars, see Hayashi 2009.

79 On the New Buddhists' criticism of emergent and heterodox groups, see Garon 1997, 80.

80 Thomas 2014b. Shields 2017, 128–31.

CHAPTER THREE

1 Anonymous teacher, cited in P. P. Claxton et al., "A Survey of Education in Hawai'i," *US Department of the Interior Bureau of Education Bulletin* 16 (15 July 1920), 132.

2 McCarthy [as McCarty] 1921.

3 McCarthy 1921.

4 McCarthy 1921, 40.

5 MacCaughey 1919, 101–2.

6 Asato 2010, 56–57.

7 Asato 2010, 57.

8 Claxton et al. 1920, 134.

9 "An Act Relating to Foreign Language Schools and Teachers Thereof," S.B. No. 32. Signed by Governor of the Territory of Hawai'i Charles J. McCarthy.

10 These changes were the result of recommendations by the Joint Committee on Re-

vision of Japanese Textbooks, submitted to MacCaughey on 28 July 1922. See "Language School Progress," *TF*, August 1922, 173–74. MacCaughey was apparently chased out of office in Spring 1923 (E.V.W., "Aloha to Mr. MacCaughey," *TF*, May 1923, 104).

11 Following scholarly precedent, I transliterate Imamura's given name as Yemyō rather than Emyō. On Imamura, see Moriya 2008.

12 Wenger 2017, esp. 188–231 on African Americans.

13 Sehat 2011; Wenger 2017; Curtis 2016.

14 Sehat 2011, 4–7.

15 S. Smith 2014.

16 Taylor 2007 focuses on the "North Atlantic world" at the expense of examining the crucial role of American and European encounters with religious difference through empire. The result is a flawed account of the rise of secularity in modern times. See Mahmood 2010.

17 Su 2016, 11–35; Wenger 2017, 15–100.

18 Wenger 2017.

19 Su 2016.

20 Lum 2018.

21 Mahmood (2012) discusses similar mobilization of religious freedom in the construction of the notion of the "religious minority" in the Middle East.

22 Josephson 2012, 71–93.

23 On the role of religious freedom in the American takeover of Hawai'i, see Weingarten 1946, 7. A religious freedom clause was included as Article XI of the amity treaty between the Kingdom of Hawai'i and the United States that was signed on 20 December 1849 and ratified on 19 August 1850. http://hawaiiankingdom.org/pdf/United_States_Treaty.pdf. For a strident history of the annexation of Hawai'i that critiques the assemblages of race, religion, and empire diagnosed by Tisa Wenger (2017), see Silva 2004. On Japanese diplomats' ability to quickly learn the rules of the game of international law, see Dudden 2005.

24 Shimizu 1998; Burnidge 2016, 94–101.

25 Hawai'i was still a sovereign kingdom when Japanese immigration began, but it was forcibly annexed by the United States in 1898 at the behest of white sugar-plantation owners. Hawai'i became a formal American territory in 1900.

26 Borup 2013, 24; Williams and Moriya argue that a successful Japanese immigrant push for territorial government acknowledgment of the validity of marriages conducted by Buddhist and Shintō priests marked an early accomplishment in Japanese American religious freedom claims. See Williams and Moriya 2010, xiv. Apparently "picture brides" were not subject to the immigration restrictions established by the 1907 "Gentlemen's Agreement." In a House of Representatives Committee on Immigration and Naturalization hearing held on 25 June 1921, statistician Charles F. Weeber (d.u.) reported that 10,617 picture brides arrived in Hawai'i in the decade between 1910 and 1920.

27 Silva 2004, 48–51.

28 On Japanese marriage patterns, see Gulick 1918, 226–28.

29 Reflecting on a chance encounter he had with a girl born to Japanese parents shortly after his arrival on the islands, Japanese Christian Okumura Takie recalled that he could not understand the girl's response to a simple question because her response (in Hawaiian plantation laborer's pidgin) incorporated words from three distinct languages (Japanese, Hawaiian, and English). Okumura 1917, 163–64.

30 Williams and Moriya 2010, xi. Recall from chapter 2 that prominent Japanese Buddhists weighing in on Japan's own immigration debate in the late 1890s had turned the "mixed residence" issue on its head by advocating the propagation of Buddhism overseas.

31 Asato 2006.

32 Borup 2013.

33 Shimada 2008, 154–55.

34 Asato 2010, 54–56.

35 Gulick 1918, 240–41.

36 Chamberlain 1912. The Rationalist Press Association was founded as a forum for freethinkers, humanists, and others critical of religion. See https://newhumanist.org.uk/history. It appears that Chamberlain's pamphlet was actually a collection of articles previously published. See "Japan's Efforts to Create a New Religion," *CL*, July 1912, 76.

37 Chamberlain 1912, 5–6.

38 Chamberlain 1912, 14–15.

39 Chamberlain 1912, 7–9.

40 Chamberlain 1912, 17.

41 "Japan's Efforts to Create a New Religion," *CL*, 75.

42 The "Three Religions Conference" was heavily criticized by members of the Fellowship of New Buddhists and Chikazumi Jōkan (see chapter 2). However, it also provided the impetus for a new, mutually beneficial relationship between these critics of state power and bureaucrats. See Thomas 2014b, 44–46.

43 "Japan's Efforts to Create a New Religion," *CL*, 76–77.

44 "Japan's New Epoch," 29 August 1912, *CSM*, 16.

45 "Japan's New Epoch," *CSM*.

46 Griffis 1915, v. Griffis had been awarded the Order of the Rising Sun, Gold Rays with Rosette, in 1907. He was not an unbiased observer.

47 Asato 2006.

48 Shimizu 1998.

49 Gulick 1918, 14–29.

50 Gulick 1914, 27.

51 Gulick 1914, 6, 19–21.

52 Professor Nagai (given name unknown), in Gulick 1914, 16.

53 Wenger 2017.

54 Miyaoka 1918, 299.

55 "Constitution of Japan Reviewed: Mr. Miyaioka [*sic*] of Tokyo Declares before American Bar Association Religious Freedom Is a Fundamental in His Country," *CSM*, 31 August 1918, 5.

56 Miyaoka 1918, 302.

57 Burnidge 2016, 94–101.

58 On Japan's ability to successfully manipulate international law and norms to justify its annexation of Korea, see Dudden 2005.

59 For a play-by-play account of the deliberations, see Shimizu 1998, 13–37.

60 Quoted in Landman 1919, 117.

61 "Reforms by Japan in Korean Schools: New Administration Has Already Instituted Changes Which Are Said to Embody a Degree of Religious Freedom," *CSM*, 16 June 1920.

62 Henry 2014, 62–91, 168–203.

63 Interviews with an anonymous teacher, citing a conversation with a student in Claxton et al. 1920, 133.

64 MacCaughey 1919, 102.

65 Imamura 1918, 5.

66 Imamura 1918, 8–9.

67 MacCaughey 1918, 26.

68 Krämer 2015, 2017.

69 Claxton et al. 1920, 111.

70 Asato 2006, 32–33, 127n25, 2010, 55–56.

71 Shimada 2008; Takagi-Kitayama 2008.

72 Asato 2006, 32.

73 In the English-language section of the 7 November 1919 *Nippu jiji*, editor Yasutaro Sōga (d.u.) suggested that the language schools divest from the Buddhist missions as part of a broader message about the importance of assimilation. Y. Sōga, "Japanese Language School Question to the Fore Again," *NJ*, 7 November 1919, 8.

74 Shimada 2008, 151–55.

75 Asato 2006, 27. For an example of how the Japanese-language press reported on the issue, see "Nihongo gakkō no bokumetsu ron o kōchō: Torento shi kageki naru benron o nasu," *NJ*, 6 November 1919, 2.

76 Asato 2006, 24–25; Takagi-Kitayama 2008.

77 On the divide-and-rule strategies of the planting class, see Weingarten 1946, 19–22.

78 "Nihonjin rōdō renmei naru," *NJ*, 5 December 1919, 1.

79 Quoted in Weingarten 1946, 25.

80 Shimada 2008, 154. Weingarten gives the official date of the Japanese participation in the strike as 23 January, the day after Imamura's open letter. See Weingarten 1946, 25.

81 Weingarten 1946, 27.

82 Shimada 2008, 155.

83 Claxton et al. 1920, 131.

84 Claxton et al. 1920, 133. Consciously or unconsciously, the language the teacher used echoed the language of the 1890 Imperial Rescript on Education.

85 Testimony of Walter F. Dillingham, 21 June 1921, in US House of Representatives 1921, 215.

86 Testimony of Wallace Farrington, 22 June 1921, in US House of Representatives 1921, 257.

87 Testimony of Royal D. Mead, 22 June 1921, in US House of Representatives 1921, 277.

88 US House of Representatives 1921, 299–301.

89 Testimony of royal D. Mead, 23 June 1921, in US House of Representatives 1921, 299.

90 Imamura 1921, 2. These words from the preface were dated March 1920, so Imamura wrote at the height of the labor strike.

91 Shimada 2008.

92 For background on the debates between the two men, see Asato 2006, 1–41; also Shimada 2008.

93 Imamura 1921, 15.

94 Imamura 1921, 12.

95 Imamura 1921, 15.

96 Imamura 1921, 20–21.

97 Imamura 1921, 36.

98 Cited without a date in Imamura 1921, 39.

99 Imamura 1921, 43–44.

100 Imamura 1921, 44.

101 Imamura 1921, 46–47.

102 Shimada, 2008, 164–65.

103 Takagi-Kityama 2008, 223–25.

104 Takagi-Kitayama 2008, 227–28.

105 Takagi-Kitayama 2008, 227.

106 Wenger 2017.

107 Imamura 1921, 30.

108 Wenger 2017.

109 Wenger 2017 143–231; Curtis 2016.

110 Curtis 2016. Both Sehat 2011 and S. Smith 2014 point to the importance of Supreme Court jurisprudence in shifting conceptions of religious freedom and the First Amendment, particularly in the middle twentieth century. However, Sarah Imhoff (2016) has persuasively suggested that many of these landmark decisions followed cultural trends rather than precipitating them.

111 Blankenship 2014 makes brief mention of religious freedom in a discussion of Japanese internment.

112 Williams 2006, 63.

113 Blankenship 2014, 318; Williams 2006, 66.

114 Blankenship 2014, 321; Williams 2006, 67–68.

115 Azuma 2009.

116 Fujitani 2011, 155–56. My own conversations with some former Occupation staff translators living in Hawai'i suggest that these young Americans were in a double bind: subject to suspicion but unable to prove that they were "real Americans." Thanks to Jim Tanabe for arranging a series of interviews with informants on O'ahu in 2010, and thanks to the many former Occupation translators who shared their stories with me.

117 A. K. Reischauer, "The Development of Religious Liberty in Modern Japan," *TCR* 1 December 1927.

118 "Law Regulating All Religions Urged in Japan," *TCP*, 16 June 1926.

119 "Religious Freedom in Japan: Laws Revised and Amended for Restraint of Religious Politicians," *NCH*, 19 June 1926.

120 "Japan Christians Protest Bill of Religions," *TCR*, 1 March 1927; "Japan's New 'Religions Bill,'" *CSM*, 11 November 1927.

121 Joseph C. Grew, letter to US Secretary of State, 1 March 1939, USDS.

CHAPTER FOUR

1 Brian Victoria, *Zen at War* (1997), 78. Victoria cites Ketelaar 1990, 215.

2 Ives 2009.

3 Garon 1986, 1997, 60–87.

4 See, for example, the speeches by Hiranuma Kiichirō (1867–1952), Shōda Kazue (1869–1948), and Andō Masazumi (1876–1955) in the deliberations of the Religions System Investigative Committee: SSCK, 10 January 1929, 1–12.

5 See, for example, Shōda Kazue's remarks in a briefing (*shōtai kaiseki*) for ruling party members held on 27 December 1928 about the proposed religious organizations bill. SMDKES, 213–18.

6 Takase Kōji, writing for the Zenkoku Bukkyōto Shūkyō Hōan Hantai Renmei (League of Japanese Buddhists Opposing the Religions Bill), *Shūkyō hōan hantai riyū*, CJP, "Shūkyō hōan" Folder #3. The undated document is probably from early 1927.

7 Hardacre 1989b, 114–32.

8 Abe 1970a.

9 This assumption appears most strikingly in Brian Daizen Victoria's work (e.g., Victoria 1997), but it is widespread. See, for example, Payne in Rambelli 2013. A more nuanced take that retains palpable progressive commitments is Shields 2017.

10 This chapter takes inspiration from Saba Mahmood's stimulating 2005 exhortation to extricate scholarly analysis from progressive politics and Rick Shweder's equally inspiring 2009 call to resist what he calls "imperial liberalism."

11 For one example, see Terasawa 2012.

12 For an example of this view, see Richard K. Payne's foreword in Rambelli 2013. The view also appears, albeit with a bit more nuance, in Shields 2017.

13 While my conclusions differ somewhat, I take inspiration from Berry 1998 in this regard.

14 As Stone (1999, 182–83) has indicated, doctrine is ideologically undetermined; specific political and ideological readings of religious doctrine are applied in historical context.

15 Garon (1997, 60–87) has also pointed out that religious leaders sometimes downplayed the importance of tolerance in favor of protecting their own parochial interests.

16 Andō 1943, 163–84. Indeed, it was Andō who introduced several of the revisions that made passage of the bill possible, and Andō himself gave a rousing speech on the floor of the House of Commons urging its passage. SGSR 30 (24 March 1939), 692–94.

17 See, for example, O'Brien and Ohkoshi 1996.

18 *TG*, August 1943, 152. Shimazono (2006) has also discussed the case in some detail, but my points differ from his in a few important respects described below.

19 SSCK, 10 January 1929, 1–12. Hiranuma would later become prime minister and would oversee the passage of the 1939 Religious Organizations Law.

20 I deal with this customary rights issue regarding temple lands in more detail below. For a brief treatment, see Garon 1986, 276–85.

21 See Takashima 1946b. *D* May 1946, 30.

22 This narrative initially emerged as part of Religions Divisions reports. See the memorandum "Religion in War Time," 25 June 1947, RCR Box #5800, Folder #2.

23 One notable exception is Krämer 2011.

24 Two excellent sources on Chikazumi's career and influence are Iwata 2014 and Ōmi 2014.

25 During Chikazumi's absence Kiyozawa Manshi (1863–1903) sublet his lodgings near Tokyo Imperial University and used them as the basis for his Kōkōdō study circle.

26 Ōmi 2012b.

27 Chikazumi's Kyūdō Kaikan served as a physical monument to the inspiration he had gained from Christianity: the interior resembled a Christian church and the culture reflected Chikazumi's admiration of the Young Men's Christian Association. See Washington 2013. Also see Ōmi 2012a, 2012b.

28 Ōsawa 2009, 20–21.

29 I discussed the response to this event in the anglophone press briefly in chapter 3.

30 Yoshinaga 2012b, 40. See the editorial in *Kyūdō* 9 (1), 1 February 1912, 1–6.

31 Chikazumi Jōkan, *Shūkyō hōan hantai raireki*, CJP 1.

32 The bill was first debated in the House of Peers on the afternoon of 15 February 1929; after a long discussion, the measure was sent to a committee of fifteen members for further review (one of the members was Okada Ryōhei, namesake of the failed legislation from two years prior). KGSR 15: 321–40. A separate measure regarding the discharge of national property on shrine and temple lands was brought up on the same day, and after some debate the legislators determined that it should be entrusted to the committee investigating the Shōda bill.

33 It is unclear how Chikazumi first got wind of the proposed legislation, but religious journals began discussing the rumored legislation at least as early as 1 December 1928. The journal *Uchū* (glossed in some issues as *Kosmos*) featured a series of five short articles about the proposed legislation in its December issue of 1928. *U* 3 (12), 1 December 1928, 16–20. Abe Yoshiya (1970a, 66) suggested that Shōda intentionally leaked information about the legislation in hopes that it would garner popular support.

34 Chikazumi Jōkan, "Sankyō kakuitsu wa futettei seisaku nari" (2 March 1929), CJP 1.

35 The colophon indicates that this pamphlet was published on 29 January 1929.

36 Garon 1986, 283.

37 An undated, handwritten pamphlet entitled "A Clause by Clause Comparative Critique of the Okada [Religions] Bill and the Religious Organizations Bill," published by the Buddhist Alliance against the Religious Organizations Bill, argued that the change in nomenclature masked the fact that the bill was essentially the same as the Okada legislation. CJP 1, "Okada an/shūkyō dantai hō an chikujō hikaku hihan."

38 Andō 1943 includes the politician's recollection that Chikazumi repeatedly called on him and asked him to change his mind about the legislation.

39 For a general biography of Andō, see Takahashi 2012.

40 Chikazumi Jōkan also participated. According to Takahashi Hara (2012), Andō and Chikazumi were allies in their efforts to resist legislation that would have provided greater statutory oversight over religions, but their relationship soured after the failed attempt to introduce a religions bill in 1929. A database of Chikazumi's letters maintained by Iwata Fumiaki lists at least eighteen separate pieces of correspondence between Chikazumi and Andō between the years 1903 and 1939.

41 By 1942 *Seikyō shinron* served as the official organ for the Greater Japan Buddhist Association (Dai Nippon Bukkyō Kai).

42 Andō's departure from the clergy seems to have been a calculated move to allow him to enter politics, since clerics were banned from holding political office until 1925. See Ives 2009, 25–26. Andō critiqued the policy in his 1923 book *Seiji to shūkyō to no kankei.*

43 Andō served as vice president for the Japan League of Religions; he also served as chair of the Greater Japan Buddhist Youth Association League, advisor to the Greater Japan Buddhist Association, and chair of the East Asia Buddhist Cooperation Association.

44 Andō published a treatise on religion-state relations in 1923 under the title *Seiji to shūkyō to no kankei.*

45 Andō 1926, 641.

46 Andō 1943, 163–73.

47 The Alliance was listed on the cover of this pamphlet as having the same address in Hongō Ward as the Kyūdō Kaikan, and Chikazumi was listed as the group's representative (*daihyō*). Chikazumi signed the pamphlet and dated it 22 January 1929.

48 Chikazumi, *Shūkyō dantai hōan hantai riyū*, 2 (CJP 1).

49 KGSR 15: 336–40.

50 KGSR 15: 338–40.

51 See Abe 1970a for a recapitulation of Shirakawa's questions.

52 Abe 1970a outlines the legal debates that occurred in contemporary newspapers.

53 Shūkyō Dantai Hōan Hantai Bukkyōto Dōmei, 22 February 1929.

54 Sakami Chūsei, "Shūkyō dantai hōan keidaichi kanpu mondai hayawakari" ("Quick Guide to the Shrine and Temple Land Restitution Problem in the Religious Organizations Bill"), CJP 1.

55 See the section beginning on 5.

56 Bernstein 2006, 114–17; Collcutt (1986) 2014, 162–63.

57 "Sankyō kakuitsu wa futettei naru shūkyō seisaku nari," 2 (CJP 1).

58 Kubutsu Shōnin was evidently a terrible administrator who wasted valuable sectarian resources, but he was also tremendously popular. Ward 2009, 27–29.

59 On *Shinkai kengen*, see Ward 2009.

60 The bill was taken up in the House of Peers on 24 January 1939 and sent to a special investigative committee of eighteen members the same day; it was formally promulgated on 8 April 1939 and went into effect on 1 April 1940.

61 The one clue that I have about Chikazumi's response is a document included in the collection of materials recovered during the restoration of the Kyūdō Kaikan, a press release by one Tōge Nobuo (d.u.). Although the text of this carefully handwritten docu-

ment is less rhetorically sophisticated than Chikazumi's own bombastic writing style, in terms of content it hewed closely to Chikazumi's arguments in critiquing the legislation. Tōge Nobuo, "Shūkyō dantai hōan hantai iken sho," CJP 2.

62 "Shūkyō dantai hō mondai: Sanjūnana nenkan no enkaku to yo no iken narabi ni sono kankei," *U* 10 (11), 1 November 1935 (AM Reel #9, Item #122). *Uchū* featured the subtitle *Kōdō hatsuyō; shūkyō senpu* (*Invigorate the Imperial Way and Promulgate Religion*). It was edited by law professor Yamaoka Mannosuke (1876–1968) and apparently affiliated with a transsectarian group initially called the Nihon Shūkyō Kyōkan (Japan Religions Teaching Hall; see *U* 2 [2], 64). By 1928, the group was called the Nihon Shūkyo Kai (Japanese Religion Association; see *U* 3 [4], 89).

63 A similar retrospective was published in Andō's 1943 volume *Seikai o ayumi tsutsu* under the title "Shūkyō dantai hō no konjaku" ("The Past and Present of the Religious Organizations Law").

64 For a historical overview of the Religions Bureau, see Ōsawa 2013.

65 This is the sort of claim that Sakami Chūsei (cited above) disputed in his pamphlet.

66 SSCK I (10 January 1929), 5–12.

67 Andō 1943, 163–73.

68 AM Reel #9, Item #122, 24.

69 KGSR 4: 38.

70 KGSR 4: 38.

71 SGSR 30 (24 March 1939), 692–94.

72 For the Religions Division view, see "Religion in War Time," 25 June 1947, RCR Box #5800, Folder #2. For the view of the American legation to Japan, see Eugene H. Dooman, letter to US Secretary of State, 23 May 1939, USDS. Hans-Martin Krämer (2011) has argued that positive Christian responses to the legislation have been largely overlooked.

73 Anonymous (under "Notes and Comments"), "Religious Legislation," *JTW* 2 (14): 446.

74 Stuart Lillico, "Christians and the Japanese Caesar," *CC*, 24 May 1939, reproduced in the *China Weekly Review*, 24 June 1939, 106.

75 Joseph C. Grew, letter to US Secretary of State, 1 March 1939, USDS.

76 I am not the only one to make this observation. See Shimazono 2006 and Victoria 2014.

77 Recently, for example, scholars have celebrated Seno'o Girō (1889–1961) and his Youth League for the Revitalization of Buddhism as an example of a principled martyr who fiercely resisted the state out of commitment to his socialist ideals. See Victoria 1997, 66–73; Ōtani 2008, 2012a, esp. 71–92 and 252–80; Shields 2012 and 2017.

78 Shimazono 2006, 241.

79 In his interrogation, Makiguchi clarified that the group that used this terminology was actually Honmon Butsuryū Kō, not the Sōka Kyōiku Gakkai. However, the spirit underlying the practice of destroying and discarding religious materials other than the *honzon* (primary object of worship) of Nichiren Shōshū was the same. *TG*, August 1943, 158–59; MTZ 10, 210–11.

80 For a critical take on this rhetoric, see Victoria 2014.

81 Makiguchi likely saw himself as confronting hostile government forces in much the

same way that Nichiren (1222–82) himself had; the very fact of governmental persecution was confirmation of one's personal righteousness and proof (according to the *Lotus sūtra*) that one's Buddhahood would be assured. See Stone 2014.

82 *TG*, August 1943, 161; MTZ 10, 212–13.

83 Seno'o was also a Nichiren Buddhist; he recanted while in prison. See Victoria 1997, 66–73; Ōtani 2008; and Shields 2012, 2017.

84 Makiguchi used the language of *honji suijaku*, referring to the Meiji Constitution as the *suijaku*, or trace, of the original teaching of the *Lotus sūtra*. *TG*, August 1943, 153–54; MTZ 10, 204–5.

85 *TG*, August 1943, 152; MTŽ 10, 202–3. There are fruitful comparisons to be made here between American religious freedom jurisprudence and the sometimes flamboyant exercise of religious righteousness. See Weiner 2014 (esp. 79–138) and Gordon 2010 (esp. 15–55).

86 It is possible that Makiguchi was trying to protect his followers from incarceration (Shimazono 2006, 245). But as Jacqueline Stone has pointed out (2014), it is also the case that remonstrating with political authority could serve in the Nichiren tradition as ultimate proof of one's promise of Buddhahood.

87 This reveals the tension in majoritarian and minority claims inherent in religious freedom practices. See Mahmood and Danchin 2014b.

88 See Shields 2017 on socialist and progressive Buddhist movements.

89 "Re: A Petition for Cancellation of Memorandum for Public Office Purge Directive" (letter from Andō Masazumi directed to Prime Minister Yoshida Shigeru), RCR Box #5787, Folder #18.

90 On Nichiren exclusivism, see Stone 1994.

91 Kushner 2006; Orbaugh 2015.

92 *SS* 29, no. 10 (1 October 1942): 19.

CHAPTER FIVE

1 Robert Oleson Ballou, from the October 1945 foreword to *Shintō: The Unconquered Enemy*.

2 FDR, 6 January 1941, State of the Union address (the "Four Freedoms Speech"), reading copy, 22.

3 Moyn 2010.

4 On the emergence of the term "Judeo-Christian" in the years immediately prior to the Pacific War, see Sehat 2010. See Dower 1986 on American and Japanese propaganda during the war.

5 Dower 1986, especially chapter 3, "War Hates and War Crimes." More recently, Selden 2014.

6 Potsdam Declaration, 1945.

7 Moore 2011; Woodard 1972.

8 SCAPIN (Supreme Commander of the Allied Powers Instruction Note) 93, "Removal of Restrictions on Political, Civil, and Religious Liberties," promulgated 4 October 1945.

9 "History of the Non-Military Aspects" (WPW Box #13, Folder #3), 6. For a detailed account of presurrender planning on Shintō, see Nakano 1993 and 2003. Crucial planning documents are included in FRUS, particularly FRUS 1943, 1944, and 1945.

10 *New York Times, "Progress in Japan,"* 1945.

11 William P. Woodard, "The Disestablishment of Shintō: The Shintō Directive and the Kokutai Cult," WPW Box #8, Folder #3, 1–6. The change in tone reflected a personnel change in the State Department, marking the departure of former ambassador and undersecretary of state Joseph Grew and other "Japan hands" who had taken a conciliatory approach to Shintō and the imperial system. On Grew and his policy stances, see Nakamura 1992.

12 Woodard 1972, 197–98.

13 He was later awarded the Legion of Merit for his work. Woodard 1972, 25, 362.

14 This 3 December 1945 document is also called the "Staff Study." Various versions exist in print, including in Woodard 1972. The version I cite here is twenty-five pages long, followed by a seven-page appendix (providing various data about the disposition of religions in Japan in late 1945 and background information about the contemporary Japanese legal framework) and the seven-page text of the Shintō Directive itself. *Contemporary Religions in Japan* 7, no. 4 (1966): 321–60. The file is available online at http://nirc.nanzan-u.ac.jp/nfile/3176.

15 Takagi 1993; Okuyama 2009.

16 Woodard 1972, 197–98; Anonymous, "Constitution," Part I, 103–6.

17 Bunce's attitudes toward Shintō are ably described by Mark Mullins (2010). For Kishimoto's reflections on Bunce's attitudes, see Kishimoto 1963, "Arashi no naka no Jinja Shintō." KHS 5, 3–87.

18 Woodard (1972, 186–87) indicated that Bunce even resisted Kishimoto's own attempts to inject his normative ideas into Occupation policy.

19 The State-War-Navy Coordinating Committee (SWNCC) was the American organization directly responsible for determining Occupation policy on behalf of the Allied powers. It was created in late 1944; thereafter, its decisions served as official policy given directly to the military Far East command through the Joint Chiefs of Staff; the other Allied powers subsequently approved this official policy. Thus, US State Department and US military and foreign policy objectives formed the basis for both pre- and post-surrender policy.

20 Woodard 1972, 9–10.

21 Woodard 1972, 10–13.

22 Dower 1986.

23 On the tautological definition of State Shintō, see Ōhara 1989 and Sakamoto 2005, esp. 152–78.

24 "Memorandum," 321. The last sentence included a citation referring to two directives given to SCAP by the SWNCC (SWNCC Paper 150/4, 21 September 1945) and the Department of State (State Serial 23 [Byrnes], 13 October 1945).

25 Several studies exist on the creation of the Shintō Directive. General overviews include Woodard 1972; Nakano 1993, 2003. Kishimoto Hideo recalled his first-person perspective on the drafting of the Directive in Kishimoto 1963, although more recently Okuyama Michiaki (2009) has used Kishimoto's diary entries to offer a more nuanced view.

26 Anonymous, "International: Shintō after Bunce," *Time* 24 December 1945, 1 (my pagination).

27 I address human rights discourse in more detail in chapter 7.

28 Helen Hardacre (2017) has also made this point. See Josephson 2012, 226–36, for a comparative discussion of Japan's 1889 constitution and those of several European countries.

29 Nakano 1993.

30 William J. Sebald, chair of the Committee on the Establishment of Religious Freedom in Japan, in an oral report given at the Forty-Sixth Meeting of the Allied Council for Japan (either 26 November or 10 December 1945, citing a postsurrender statement made by MacArthur on 2 September 1945), RCR Box #5773, Folder #7.

31 Dressler and Mandair 2011.

32 As Hollinger (2017) has pointed out, missionaries were often more cosmopolitan and less racist than their counterparts at home, but they were still limited by the horizons of their own perceptions.

33 Preston 2012 diagnoses the origins of this seemingly contradictory position in a long-standing American tradition of fusing Christian majoritarianism with American foreign policy.

34 On the Meiji constitutional regime as a secular system, see chapter 1.

35 As I showed in chapter 3, American observers in the interwar period were far more likely to use the vague term "Mikadoism," but they were also likely to equate this emperor worship with Buddhism much more than they were to identify it with Shintō.

36 Josephson 2012, 24, 29–38.

37 For a more recent take on this trinary, see Josephson-Storm 2017.

38 Masuzawa 2005. The understanding of evolution that undergirded such accounts was flawed in that it was teleological (progressing toward a predetermined goal) rather than adventitious (accidents of environment and random mutation spurring adaptation and speciation).

39 Dyke [Bunce] (1945) 1966," 328.

40 Holtom (1938) 1995, 3.

41 Aston 1905, 376–77.

42 Dyke [Bunce] (1945) 1966, 322.

43 Chamberlain 1912.

44 One satirical tract on the potential threat posed by Japan is Mills 1905. A relatively recent attempt at a more nuanced approach to Chamberlain's basic project is Fujitani 1996.

45 Chamberlain 1912, 27.

46 Dyke [Bunce] (1945) 1966, 324.

47 On religious studies in Japan, see Hayashi and Isomae 2008.

48 See Isomae 2003 and Takahashi 2008. In English, see Isomae 2014.

49 Josephson (2012) has shown that Japanese intellectuals wielded influence on Western understandings of Japanese religions from basically the moment that the words "Japanese" and "religion" were juxtaposed.

50 Woodard 1972, 26.

51 See Kuroda 1981; Teeuwen 2002; Havens 2006; Breen and Teeuwen 2010; Hardacre 2017.

52 Anesaki (1930) 1963, 9–10.

53 Anesaki (1930) 1963, 7.

54 Anesaki (1930) 1963, 407–8.

55 Anesaki 1938, 15.

56 Anesaki (1930) 1963, 408.

57 I use Katō Genchi's given name here to distinguish him from his contemporary Katō Totsudō, who appeared in chapter 2. I have written about Katō Totsudō in more detail elsewhere. See Thomas 2014b.

58 Isomae 2003.

59 The online archive of article titles maintained by the Meiji Japan Society gives an indication of the breadth of Katō's interests (as well as a sense of his coterie). See the list at http://www.mkc.gr.jp/seitoku/vol.1–20.htm. Katō's personal correspondence with D. C. Holtom indicates that his facility with English was considerable. DCH, Box #1, Folder #4.

60 The short-lived chair in Shintō studies was established after his retirement in 1933, although Shintō lectures were established by 1920 and a separate department of Shintō studies was established in 1923. The language of "Shintō studies" (*Shintōgaku*) was inaugurated in 1924. See Isomae 2003, 199–221, esp. 212–19. Also see Takahashi 2008.

61 See Hylkema-Vos 1990 and the biography compiled by Shimazono Susumu, Maekawa Michiko, and Hara Takashi in KGS, volume 9 (2004). In a letter to D. C. Holtom dated 7 June 1950, Katō complained of his inability to conduct research due to his failing eyesight, the loss of his personal library during the firebombing of Tokyo, and his retirement to Gotenba following his purge (DCH Box #1, Folder #4).

62 Miyamoto 2006.

63 Katō G. 1926, 3.

64 Katō G. 1935, 64–65.

65 Katō G. 1935, 65–66.

66 Miyamoto 2006.

67 The mutual affection and respect between the two men is apparent in their correspondence, but Holtom did not accept all of Katō's ideas at face value. See Holtom 1927, 445–46.

68 Woodard 1972, 26.

69 Takemae 2002; Bisson 1944, 20n14. Religions Division researcher William P. Woodard recorded in a diary entry that Religions Division chief Ken R. Dyke was far too influenced by D. C. Holtom's interpretations of Shintō. William P. Woodard diary entry, 4 January [no year, but it must have been 1946], WPW Box #10a.

70 Dorman 2012a, 92.

71 For Holtom's biography, see Haring 1963.

72 Shimazono et al. 2004, 29. Katō's influence is quite evident in the series of articles that

Holtom published on "The Meaning of Kami" in *Monumenta Nipponica* in 1940 and 1941, especially in the second installment.

73 Woodard 1972; Sakamoto 2005, 168.

74 Throughout his career Holtom resisted chauvinism, both American and Japanese. See Haring 1963, 892.

75 Holtom used the phrase "official Shintō" in his 1922 book and a subsequent 1927 article, but by 1938 had started to use the phrase "State Shintō." Kato's aforementioned book was published in 1926.

76 See Holtom's six-part article series, "Japanese Christianity and Shintō Nationalism," *CC*, January–February 1942 (DCH Box #1, Folder #45). Also see his Rauschenbusch Lectures given at the Colgate-Rochester Divinity School in spring 1942 (DCH Box #1, Folders #27–28).

77 Holtom 1922, chapter 1. Also see Holtom 1927.

78 See especially his concluding argument: Holtom 1922, 299–308.

79 I refer here to the original, not the 1947 reprint. The reprint included two additional chapters that were apparently based upon lectures that Holtom gave at around the time the original version had gone to press. These included his Berkeley lecture "Some Permanent Values in Japanese Civilization" (14 December 1942) and what appears to be his Rauschenbusch Lectures given at Colgate-Rochester Divinity School in spring of 1942, DCH Box #1, Folder #21; Box #1, Folders #27–29.

80 Holtom 1943, vii.

81 Holtom, "Christianity and National Religion" (undated lecture fragment), DCH Box #3, Folder #43.

82 "Japanese Christianity and Shintō Nationalism," *CC* (six-part article series, January–February 1942), DCH Box #1, Folder #45.

83 See Holtom's Rauschenbusch Lectures (DCH Box #1, Folders #27–28).

84 See Walter McS. Buchanan, "From a Veteran Missionary," *CC*, 11 March 1942, DCH Box #1, Folder #45.

85 Holtom, "Some Permanent Values in Japanese Civilization," lecture delivered 14 December 1942 at Berkeley, DCH Box #1, Folder #21.

86 Holtom, "Affirmative Response to the Question: 'Can We Trust Japan to Keep the Peace without Prolonged Military Occupation?,'" during "America's Town Meeting of the Air" radio broadcast sponsored by *Reader's Digest*, 14 September 1944 (DCH Box #1, Folder #22).

87 Holtom 1945b.

88 Holtom 1945a, 743.

89 Takemae 2002; Bisson 1944.

90 Holtom's influence can be seen in the Office of War Information films *Know Your Enemy—Japan* and *Our Job in Japan*.

91 Holtom, "The Shintō Dilemma," DCH, Box #2, Folder #43. Holtom's uneasiness about the Occupation proved to be prescient: the vexatious issues regarding the maintenance of the emperor system and the controversial Yasukuni Shrine not only outlasted the Occupation, but have remained topics of heated debate to the present day. On the emperor system and the possibility of trying the emperor as a war criminal, see Nakamura

1992; Dower 1999; Bix 2000; and Totani 2008. For a recent take on the subject of Yasukuni, see Mullins 2010.

92 Holtom 1946.

93 On the lack of expertise in religions among Religions Division personnel, see Woodard 1972. As Takemae (2002) and Nakano (2003) have pointed out, it is not exactly true that all Occupation personnel were lacking in specialized training. However, there was nobody in the Religions Division that had training in the nontheological academic study of religion; if anything, most RCR members had Christian missionary or seminary backgrounds (see RCR Box #5774, Folder #22).

94 Dressler and Mandair 2011.

95 Maekawa 2015; Hurd 2015.

CHAPTER SIX

1 Religions Division report for the "TIE Orientation Bulletin," 10 February 1947, RCR Box #5773, Folder #23.

2 The biographical dates given here are from a WorldCat entry on one Garland Evans Hopkins who apparently authored a book of sermons on the biblical book of Genesis. I suspect that the author of the sermons and the missionary are the same person.

3 See RCR Box #5773, Folder #23 (Miscellaneous Correspondence).

4 RCR Box #5773, Folder #23 (Miscellaneous Correspondence), letters from Rowland Cross to W. K. Bunce (29 July 1947, with addendum of R. Cross to G. E. Hopkins, dated 23 June 1947) and John Cobb to R. E. Diffendorfer (11 July 1947).

5 William K. Bunce, 10 July 1947, Letter to Board of Missions and Church Extension of the Methodist Church (in response to article from *Richmond Times-Dispatch* dated 23 June 1947), 2, RCR Box #5773, Folder #20.

6 See Hollinger 2017 on the prevalence of missionaries in American intelligence and foreign service.

7 Overviews of the Occupation include Dower 1999 and Takemae 2002.

8 On the association of the Occupation with whiteness, see SWNCC 65/2, "Establishment of a Far Eastern Advisory Commission, Appendix B: Discussion" (30 April 1945), FRUS 1945, 534.

9 All of these censored publications are housed in the Prange Collection at the University of Maryland, College Park.

10 Moore 2011; Dorman 2004.

11 Dower 1999, 346–73.

12 Dorman 2004 provides one example.

13 "History of the Non-Military Aspects of the Allied Occupation of Japan, Volume: Freedom of Religion, 2 September 1945–1 September 1946" (WPW Box #13, Folder #3), 2.

14 Notably, the document laying out this policy (6 September 1945 directive SWNCC 150/4, publicly announced by the White House on 22 September 1945) did not subject the freedom of religion clause to the caveat (applied to the other freedoms of assembly,

speech, and press) that it would be "subject to the necessity for maintaining the security of the occupying forces."

15 Wenger 2017, 191. Also see Johnson 2017. Both authors highlight how black Americans were subjected to surveillance on suspicion of being Japanese sympathizers during the war years.

16 Previous scholarship specifically on the religious policies of the Occupation includes Woodard 1972; Ikado 1993; Nakano 2003; Moore 2011; Dorman 2012a; and Thomas 2014c.

17 Woodard (1972, 28) recalled in retrospect this shift in Religions Division policy. Also see "Mission and Accomplishments of the Occupation in the Civil Information and Education Fields" (RCR Box #5785, Folder #7, 1 January 1950) and the foreword to the "Semi-Annual Report of Stateside Activities Supporting the Reorientation Program in Japan and the Ryukyu Islands" (RCR Box #5774, Folder #1, January 1951).

18 Masuzawa 2005.

19 Josephson 2012. Isomae (2003, 2014) has argued that "religion" was a foreign imposition that is still alien to Japanese sensibilities.

20 One exception to this inclusivist attitude is Nichiren Buddhist exclusivism, documented by Stone (1994).

21 This paradox has been ably described, in different ways, by Agrama (2012) and Mahmood (2016).

22 Woodard 1972, 49–50, 182–83.

23 "Mission and Accomplishments of the Occupation in the Civil Information and Education Fields" (RCR Box #5785, Folder #7, 1 January 1950), 22–23.

24 "History of the Non-Military Aspects of the Allied Occupation of Japan, Volume: Freedom of Religion, 2 September 1945–1 September 1946" (WPW Box #13, Folder #3), 6–7, citing Supreme Commander of the Allied Powers Civil Information and Education Section (SCAP CI&E) statement of 21 February 1946, "Notes on Religious Freedom."

25 See "Instructions to Agencies of the Occupation Forces in the Field of Japanese Religions," 25 March 1946, RCR Box #5787, Folder #14.

26 See "History of the Non-Military Aspects of the Allied Occupation of Japan: Volume: Freedom of Religion" (WPW Box #13, Folder #3), 3–4, citing 1 February 1946 Checksheet from SCAP CI&E to chief of staff, "Mission and Functions of the Religions Division."

27 Woodard 1972, 178.

28 William J. Sebald, chair of the Committee on the Establishment of Religious Freedom in Japan, in an oral report given at the Forty-Sixth Meeting of the Allied Council for Japan, RCR Box #5773, Folder #7.

29 Both paragraphs paraphrased statements made by Supreme Commander Douglas MacArthur. The second paragraph loosely quoted a statement MacArthur made to one Dr. Lewis C. Newton, president of the American Baptist Convention, in a letter reported in the military newspaper *Stars and Stripes* on 13 December 1946. See Woodard 1972, appendix G:4, 355.

30 Moore 2011; Woodard 1972, 241–46.

31 Woodard 1972, 210. A fantastic overview of the presurrender policies and their initial

implementation in the fall of 1945 is Nakano 1993. As Andrew Preston (2012) has argued, while American foreign policy has consistently reflected America's indisputable Christian heritage, competing interest groups have had different ideas about how to implement religious ideals in policy.

32 Moore 2011, 32–34; 56; Takemae 2002, 377–79.

33 Moore 2011, 61–63.

34 Woodard 1972, 210–13, 243–45.

35 A collection of MacArthur's quotations about the goal of spreading Christianity in Japan can be found in Woodard 1972, appendix G:4, 355–59.

36 Douglas MacArthur, 24 February 1947, radio address to Congress, reproduced in Woodard 1972, 356.

37 See Inboden 2008 and Moore 2011, 31, 139–40.

38 Inboden 2008; Preston 2012.

39 Woodard 1972, 245.

40 Woodard 1972, 188–89; Nakano 1993, 66–67.

41 Woodard 1972, 241–48.

42 Nakano 1993, 66.

43 Moore 2011, 68–73.

44 10 July 1947, Letter to Board of Missions, Methodist Church (RCR Box #5773, Folder #20), 3.

45 On the subject of Christianity facing "its greatest opportunity in the history of Japan," it bears mentioning that among the correspondence directed toward the Religions Division, an inordinate number of letters stressed the writers' convictions that Japan should adopt Christianity as its national religion. RCR Box #5773, Folder #6.

46 Anonymous [almost certainly W. K. Bunce], 2 October 1947, letter to Elizabeth A. Whewell in response to a 21 July letter complaining about the inability of missionaries to use public schools for Christian meetings. RCR Box #5773, Folder #20.

47 News clipping from *CC*, 7 July 1948, RCR Box #5791, Folder #11.

48 On Woodard, see Clark 2006, 2–3 (my pagination); on Nichols, see Dorman 2012a, 92.

49 T. S. Kotani, "Draft Memorandum: Religions League, Reasons for the Weakness of," 22 November 1948. Also see T. S. Kotani, "Religious League," 19 November 1948. Both in RCR Box #5787, Folder #18. Also see Moore 2011.

50 Bunce, "Memorandum [on Bowing toward the Imperial Palace]" (22 April 1946), RCR Box #5791, Folder #12.

51 Report of the US Education Mission to Japan, 30 March 1946, translated by Akira Watanabe, xii–xiv. Version found in the Daniel Clarence Holtom papers held at Kokugakuin University.

52 See collected documents in WPW Box #23, Folder #2.

53 Kishimoto Hideo, "Shūkyō to kyōiku to no sokan," KHS 5, 279–90. Two historical takes on education and religion in this period are Gordon 2010, 24–95, and Kruse 2015, 95–125.

54 See "Memorandum for the Japanese Government on Religions and Public Education," RCR Box #5802, Folder #9.

55 Kruse 2015, 95–125.

56 For example, religious leaders successfully put pressure on the occupiers to promulgate the Religious Corporations Ordinance on 28 December 1945 for fear that the abrogation of the Religious Organizations Law would put them at a disadvantage when interfacing with the Japanese state. See Bunce, "Japanese Religious Laws," 25 January 1946, RCR Box #5785, Folder #23.

57 Dorman 2004.

58 See, for example, RCR Box #5774, Folder #33, which includes digests of the periodic meetings between Religions Division officials and members of the Buddhist Federation. RCR Box #5787, Folder #17 includes reports on the activities of the Religious League of Japan, including many short news clippings on attempts by the league to clarify or protect religious freedom and human rights.

59 Takemae 2002, 379–80; Thomas 2014c.

60 Leaders' eagerness to prove to the Religions Division that they were now different from their wartime counterparts can be seen in a series of interviews conducted in early 1947. See RCR Box #5787, Folder #21.

61 Recently, John Breen and Mark Teeuwen (2010) have replaced the traditional acronym with a less unfortunate one, referring to the Jinja Honchō as the "National Association of Shrines."

62 This is the Occupation directive, described in the previous chapter, that formally disaggregated Shintō from the state and eradicated Shintō-derived ideals from public school education. See the Jinja Honchō website: http://www.jinjahoncho.or.jp/honcho/index.html.

63 RCR Box #5774, Folder #35, "Speeches by Religions Division Personnel."

64 WPW Box #9, Folder #1, "The Religious Juridical Persons Law," 4 (my pagination).

65 RCR Box #5744, Folder #35, "Speeches by Religions Division Personnel."

66 For example, the Buddhist Federation was formally reconstituted in its postwar form at a conference held on 20–21 May 1946. See the handwritten document "Interview Report with Mr. Tatsuo Satomi, Standing Director (Jōnin Riji) of the Buddhist Confederation," RCR Box #5773, Folder #32. The document is dated 21 April with no year, but it could not have been compiled any earlier than 1947.

67 Andō 1941.

68 See, for example, *SS* 29, no. 10 (1 October 1942): 25.

69 Covell 2005, 30–31.

70 RCR Box #5774, Folder #33.

71 Krämer 2011.

72 Moore 2011, 15–19.

73 The group successfully pushed for the continuation of the Religious Organizations Law until the occupiers had prepared the 28 December 1945 Religious Corporations Ordinance. See WPW Box #9, Folder #1, "The Religious Juridical Persons Law," 3 (my pagination).

74 RCR Box #5787, Folder #19, "History of Religions League."

75 The various officers and member organizations of the new umbrella group are listed in a 3 September 1946 Civil Information and Education Section, Analysis and Research Division (Religions) Staff Translation on the subject of the "Union of Federation of

Religions Headquarters and Affiliated Organizations" that was current as of 19 June 1946.

76 In an interview with Religions Division staff conducted on 15 April 1946, the general affairs officer of the Buddhism section of the postwar Japan Religions League, Hori Sadao (d.u.), indicated that Andō had served as vice president and chief councillor for the Japan League of Religions that was established around October of 1942 (or 1943, according to some sources) to support the war effort. Hori indicated that the wartime Japan League of Religions was directly managed by the minister of education. RCR Box #5787, Folder #21.

77 As indicated on the title page of Andō 1941.

78 *SS* 29, no. 10 (1 October 1942): 19.

79 *Wagō no chikara* 8 (4), 10 April 1944 (AM Reel #11, Item #157).

80 AM Reel #2, Items #10-1 and 10-2.

81 Dorman 2004. However, leaders of some marginal movements, such as Kitamura Sayo, made a point of taking the initiative to visit the Religions Division regularly to ensure that they were in the good graces of the Occupation officials in charge of religious affairs. See Dorman 2012a, esp. 180–83.

82 Shinshūren Chōsa Shitsu 1963, 173–75.

83 Woodard 1972, 209. Also see WPW Box #9, Folder #1: "New Religions and the Religious Juridical Persons Law" for Woodard's thoughts on marginal religions.

84 RCR Box #5787 includes several folders with documents related to the postwar Japanese Federation of Religions, the Buddhist Federation, and other religious associations. Also see RCR Box #5774, Folder #13, which includes summaries of monthly meetings held in autumn 1949.

85 T. S. Kotani, "A Tentative List of Scholars and Religionists Who May Be Consulted on Various Religious Subjects," 23 April 1949 (RCR Box #5788, Folder #10).

86 RCR Box #5787, Folder #18 ("Activities of Religions League").

87 Woodard 1972, 49–50.

88 Woodard 1972, 182–83.

89 See "Buddhist Federation Meeting with SCAP," 22 September 1949 (RCR Box #5824, Folder #7).

90 "Buddhist Federation Meeting with SCAP," 22 September 1949 (RCR Box #5824, Folder #7). Other documents suggest that the Buddhist organizations had been planning to construct a central Buddhist hall in Tokyo. Draft translation: "The Representatives Conference of the All Japan Buddhist Association [held 29 June 1949]," 26 July 1949 (RCR Box #5824, Folder #5).

91 Woodard, "The Religious Juridical Persons Law," 6, WPW Box #9, Folder #1.

92 Woodard, "The Religious Juridical Persons Law," 17–18, WPW Box #9, Folder #1.

93 Fukuda served as chief of the Religious Affairs Section from 11 May 1946 to 24 July 1948. See *Shūmu jihō* 116, 88. By his own account, he was one of the few "witnesses" to the intricate workings of the reciprocal and mutually beneficial relationship between the Religions Division and the Religious Affairs Section. See Fukuda 1993, 522.

94 *ShJ* 1, no. 1 (July 1947), 1.

95 As an editorial included in the October 1947 issue claimed, the journal's purpose was to

unite the "center and periphery" (that is, the government and religious organizations), which were like the two wheels of a car. See Anonymous, "Honshi no shimei," *ShJ* 1, no. 4 (October 1947), i (my pagination).

96 Fukuda, "Shin kenpō to shūkyō," *ShJ* 1, no. 1 (July 1947), 8–9.

97 See Bernstein 2008 for a fantastic study of how competing interest groups laid claim to the peak of Mount Fuji in the wake of Occupation reforms.

98 Woodard 1972, 227–28.

99 Bernstein 2008, 67–76. Also see Takemura 1993.

100 "Memorandum for the Chief of Staff (CIE): Disposition of State-Owned Land Used by Religious Institutions," 31 October 1946 (RCR Box #5773, Folder #21).

101 Woodard 1972, 230.

102 The version available to me is largely illegible due to poor printing (probably partially a result of the widespread use of cheap paper during the Occupation), so my reading here is not particularly confident.

103 *ShJ* 1, no. 4 (November 1947), 39.

104 *ShJ* 1, no. 4 (November 1947), 33.

105 This distinguishes my project from Nakano Tsuyoshi's earlier studies (1993; 2003) of the premises that guided US Occupation policy. While critical of US policy making, Nakano (1993, 66–67) nevertheless reproduces the triumphalist narrative of the Occupation as a desirable and drastic liberal intervention that irrevocably changed Japanese religions policy.

CHAPTER SEVEN

1 "Mission and Accomplishments of the Occupation in the Civil Information and Education Fields," 1 January 1950, RCR Box #5785, Folder #7.

2 Andō 1951.

3 Andō 1951, 195–96.

4 Andō 1951, 202. The citation is from a chapter entitled "Kokka to shūkyō to no kankei" ("The Relationship between the State and Religion") dated January 1951.

5 Indeed, very few people in the wartime period (in Japan, the United States, or elsewhere) thought of rights and liberties in both universalistic and individual terms; nations remained the fundamental units of analysis for discussions of rights. Goldstone, cited in Cohen 2012, 67.

6 The Japanese word *jinken* (human rights) did exist from the mid-nineteenth century, but its semantic range was ambiguous and its usage contested. For the most part, even if the concept of "natural rights" was used to exert pressure on the state, there was no idea that an external party could force the state to guarantee "human rights." See Howland 2002, 122–52.

7 Andō 1943, 163–84.

8 Moyn 2010; Hoffmann 2011a; Mazower 2011; Iriye, Goedde, and Hitchcock 2012; Weitz 2013 (reviewing Moyn 2010); Bradley 2016; Lindkvist 2017.

9 Moyn 2015.

10 Bradley (2016) highlights important precursors in the 1940s but agrees with Moyn (2010) and Hoffmann (2011b) that the 1970s were the high mark of human rights discourse.

11 Moyn 2010; Hoffmann 2011b.

12 Weitz 2013.

13 Wedemeyer 2013, citing Hayden White. Also see Weitz 2013 on human rights specifically.

14 Here I am in line with Bradley (2012), who suggests we examine moments of rupture or transition in trying to find the origins of human rights. Also see Lindkvist 2017, esp. 12–16.

15 Another take on religious freedom as a human right is Lindkvist 2017.

16 Focusing on developments in Japan in the late 1940s is a way of expanding on the existing historiography of human rights, which has been curiously focused primarily on developments in Europe. This is especially true in the case of religious freedom, which Moyn (2010, 2014) has suggested became understood as a "human right" in transatlantic efforts to protect Christian conscience from communist persecution.

17 Bradley 2016, 86–91.

18 See Moyn 2010, 2014, and 2015 for discussions of the development of human rights talk related to the communist threat to Christian religious liberty.

19 On the American exportation of religious freedom across the twentieth century, see Su 2016.

20 Woodard 1972, 178.

21 "History of the Non-Military Aspects of the Allied Occupation of Japan, Volume: Freedom of Religion, 2 September 1945–1 September 1946" (WPW Box #13, Folder #3), 6–7, citing SCAP CI&E Section statement of 21 February 1946, "Notes on Religious Freedom."

22 "~~Instructions to~~ Information for Agencies of the Occupation Forces in the Field of Japanese Religions," 25 March 1946, Religions Division Box #5787, Folder #14 (General: Comments on Religion in Japan by Occupation Personnel). The strikethrough in the title here reproduces a penciled change added to the document. The final version of the document omitted the caution against proselytizing, probably as a way of appeasing MacArthur. See "Information for Agencies of the Occupation Forces in the Field of Japanese Religions," 15 April 1946, Religions Division Box #5787, Folder #14 (General: Comments on Religion in Japan by Occupation Personnel). Bunce's efforts to establish policies that would tone down MacArthur's evangelistic rhetoric were quietly quashed by Colonel Donald Nugent (head of CI&E from Spring 1946). See Woodard 1972, 352–53; Moore 2011, 69–72.

23 "Memorandum to All CIE Personnel: Participation in the Religious Life of the Japanese People," Religions Division Box #5802, Folder #9.

24 The autumn 1945 directives included the promulgation of the Civil Liberties Directive on 4 October (abolishing the Religious Organizations Law and proclaiming religious freedom for all), the promulgation of the Shintō Directive on 15 December, and the promulgation of the Religious Corporations Ordinance on 28 December.

25 Many new movements emerged in the wake of the war, and some attracted considerable sensationalist press. See Dorman 2012a.

26 General Headquarters, Supreme Commander for the Allied Powers, Civil Information and Education Section Press Release dated 4 October 1946, 11:00 hours (Religions Division Box #5787, Folder #14).

27 Undated speech by Religions Division staff to Jinja Honchō, Religions Division Box #5774, Folder #35.

28 Moyn 2010.

29 Religions Division researcher William P. Woodard, for example, frequently referred to religious freedom as the "most precious and fundamental of all freedoms." WPW Box #9, Folder #1, "Religious Freedom in Postwar Japan," 1.

30 The constitution was enacted six months later, on 3 May 1947.

31 This trend matched a contemporaneous trend in the United States. See Orsi 1998.

32 The occupiers' decision to scrap the Japanese draft and replace it with a hastily compiled American one has been thoroughly documented (Dower 1999, 346–404).

33 See, for example, Yomiuri Shinbunsha 1946 (which featured the text of the new constitution followed by short explanatory paragraphs) and Kitaura 1947 (which used the same model and accompanied the text with pictures). Both books courtesy of the Prange Collection.

34 Dower 1999, 346–404 (esp. 402–4).

35 Nagasawa 1946. Courtesy of the Prange Collection.

36 Kanamori, in Nagasawa 1946, 4–5.

37 Kanamori, in Nagasawa 1946, 5–6.

38 Nagasawa 1946, 25–26.

39 Minobe 1947, included in the Prange Collection.

40 Minobe 1947, 106–7.

41 Takagi 1993, 428.

42 See Takemae 2002, 375.

43 Takagi 1993, 428. Again, see Orsi 1998 on comparable trends in the US.

44 Oguchi, "Kyōyō to shite no shūkyōgaku," *SK* 14, no. 11 (December 1945), 4.

45 Kishimoto 1963 (included in Shinshūren Chōsa Shitsu 1963 and KHS 5). For a critical study based on Kishimoto's diaries, see Okuyama 2009.

46 Takagi 1993, 424–27.

47 Advice on the prospect of constitutional revision began during the Occupation but continued after it. One such debate occurred in 1959–60; see Constitution Investigation Council 1962a, 1962b, 1962c, 1963a, 1963b.

48 Religions and Cultural Resources Division (Religions Division) researcher William P. Woodard (1972, 186–87) later recalled that Kishimoto frequently tried to inject his normative ideals into Occupation policy. Bunce apparently resisted many of these efforts, to Kishimoto's documented chagrin. See Kishimoto 1963.

49 Takagi 1993, 433–34.

50 Kishimoto preferred to use the term "Shrine Shintō" rather than "State Shintō"; he registered his displeasure with the occupiers' preferred term in Kishimoto 1963 (see KHS 5, 14–16), suggesting that the occupiers confused Shintō nationalism with Shrine Shintō.

51 KHS 5, 92–93.

52 Kishimoto, "Jinja Shintō no ikiru michi [The Path for the Survival of Shrine Shintō]," KHS 5, 100.

53 See Kishimoto, "Nentō: shūkyō kai ni nozomu," KHS 5, 200–212. Originally serialized in the *Tokyo Nichinichi Shinbun*, 4–9 January 1948. Even before the war Kishimoto's scholarship had this prescriptive tone. For example, in a 1934 article entitled "The Task of Buddhism," Kishimoto argued that Japanese Buddhists needed to modernize their religion to make it more palatable globally.

54 Orsi 1998.

55 Woodard's duties were outlined in Religions Division Box #5774, Folder #22, in a memo from one A. N. Nelson dated 11 May 1946. Also see Woodard 1972.

56 WPW Box #10, Folder #6, "Religious Education in Social Studies."

57 "Religious Education in Social Studies" (WPW Box #10, Folder #6), 5–6.

58 See Woodard 1972.

59 See Bell 2014 on the contextual history of discourses about liberalism. See Sehat 2011 on what he terms the "myth of American religious freedom."

60 Capra 1945; US War Department, Information and Education Division, 1945.

61 Crane 1947.

62 A dispatch on 8 January 1949 by Crane's *New York Times* colleague Lindesay Parrott suggested that Shintō was not, however, fading away as some had predicted. Parrott's article emphasized the growing numbers of Japanese people patronizing major shrines during the New Year season. Parrott 1949.

63 Brown 2006.

64 Wenger 2017.

65 Nakano 2003.

66 *New York Times* 1951.

67 Inboden 2008, location 390 of 5298 (last page of the introduction). Also see Preston 2012.

68 *New York Times* 1949a.

69 *New York Times* 1949b.

70 See Sehat 2011 for a historical account of when the United States developed a tradition of "religious freedom" in the sense that it is used today.

71 Mahmood 2006.

72 United Nations Universal Declaration of Human Rights, Article 18, http://www.un.org/en/documents/udhr/.

73 Mazower 2004; Moyn 2010.

74 There is a robust literature on the contradictions inherent in religious freedom. See Sullivan 2005; Mahmood 2006, 2010, 2016; Hurd 2013; Mahmood and Danchin 2014b; Hurd and Sullivan, eds. 2014; Hurd 2015; and Sullivan, Hurd, Mahmood, and Danchin 2015.

75 Hurd 2008. Bell (2014) has shown that understandings of "liberalism" were greatly transformed during the war period, with postwar political theory embracing liberal democracy as an antidote to "totalitarianism." While he focuses on the specter of communism, during the war it was the Japanese (and German) enemy that served as the

totalitarian foil for American liberty. Here it is also important to highlight the fact that the Holocaust was apparently less crucial for the postwar formulation of "human rights" talk than has commonly been supposed. See Cohen 2012.

CHAPTER EIGHT

1 William P. Woodard, director of the International Institute for the Study of Religion, in a 15 November 1954 foreword to W. K. Bunce, *Religions in Japan* (1955), vii.
2 Woodard 1972, 243–44.
3 Hardacre 1989b, 135.
4 "Spiritual vacuum" on the Google Books N-gram, https://books.google.com/ngrams/graph?content=spiritual+vacuum&year_start=1940&year_end=2000&corpus=15&moothing=3&share=&direct_url=t1%3B%2Cspiritual%20vacuum%3B%2Cc0. Last searched 14 March 2015. Use of the phrase peaked in 1958.
5 One example is Kishimoto 1960b, 14.
6 Dower 1999.
7 Takayama 1993 is one example.
8 See, as one example, Shimazono (1992) 2006, 45. This point was actually also made by William P. Woodard in a speech on new religions delivered sometime after the Occupation ended. See William P. Woodard, "New Religions and the RJPL," 2, WPW Box #9, Folder #1. Christians only constitute about 1 percent of the Japanese population.
9 Astley 2006, 99, 101–2.
10 On the good/bad religion paradigm, see Hurd 2015.
11 Isomae 2003; Takahashi 2008.
12 A couple of examples include founding professor Anesaki Masaharu's role in coordinating the "Three Religions Conference" of 1912 and his position as an academic authority on the Shūkyō Seido Chōsakai (Religions Systems Investigation Committee) in the late 1920s. More generally, see Maekawa 2015.
13 On linkages between postwar geopolitical considerations and religious studies, see McCutcheon 2004 and Imhoff 2016.
14 See Kishimoto's reflections on his role in Shinshūren Chōsa Shitsu 1963 and KHS 5. Also see Okuyama 2009.
15 Woodard 1972, 186–87.
16 Kitagawa 1964. Also see the encomium by Ishizu (1965).
17 Kishimoto 1961.
18 See, for example, a fragmentary draft of a speech on the subject of religious freedom Woodard gave at Dōshisha University sometime after the establishment of the aforementioned institute (probably around 1960): Woodard, "Religious Freedom—Dōshisha," WPW Box #10, Folder #5.
19 Takemae 2002, 381.
20 In correspondence between Royal H. Fisher and D. C. Holtom, Fisher wrote that Woodard had gone back to "help the Japanese Govt, at their request, on the involve-

ments of keeping religion and Govt 'separate.'" R. H. Fisher to D. C. Holtom, 25 February 1954 (DCH Box #1, Folder #4).

21 Woodard, "The International Institute for the Study of Religions: A Report of the First Decade (1954–1964)," *Contemporary Religions in Japan* 5 (1964). For an overview of the efforts of these men, see 243–45 of *Gendai shūkyō 2008* (Tokyo: Akiyama Shoten, 2008). Also see Kishimoto Hideo, "From the Editorial Board," and William P. Woodard, "From the Editor," *Contemporary Religions in Japan* 1, no. 1 (1960): 3–6. Also see the IISR webpage: http://www.iisr.jp/about_us/history/.

22 The journal *Japanese Religions* was actually founded a year before *Contemporary Religions in Japan* (in 1959), but initially its target audience was missionaries. By contrast, Woodard and Kishimoto adopted a nontheological, nonmissiological tone for their journal. The editorship of the *Japanese Journal of Religious Studies* eventually moved to the Nanzan Institute for Religion and Culture in Nagoya in 1981.

23 Woodard, "Religious Freedom—Dōshisha," WPW Box #10, Folder #5.

24 See http://nirc.nanzan-u.ac.jp/en/publications/crj/.

25 See, for example, Nakano 2003.

26 In addition to the epigraph above, see Ono Sōkyō's 1962 book on Shintō: *Shintō: The Kami Way*.

27 See Takagi 1993.

28 As an indication of the close relationship between the two men, Kishimoto's diary is included in the Woodard's collected papers housed at the University of Oregon. See Okuyama 2009.

29 See KHS 5, 253–305.

30 See Hurd 2015 for more on the good/bad religion paradigm. The language of "perversion of faith" can be found in the 2016 report generated by the Tony Blair Institute for Global Change, "Struggle over Scripture." See Skya 2009 for an explicit comparison of State Shintō with Islamism.

31 However, the phrase *shinshūkyō* in Japanese was used in the late nineteenth and early twentieth centuries as part of a normative project of constructing a "new religion" that fit with Japan's newfound modernity.

32 Lewis 2004, 3.

33 Ōishi 1963, 47–48.

34 Shin Nihon Shūkyō Dantai Rengō Kai Research Division 1966c; Shinshūren Chōsa Shitsu 1963, 173–75. Woodard makes no corroborating claim in his 1972 memoir, but given his high hopes for the institution of what he perceived as healthy religious freedom it is likely that he played such a role.

35 Woodard 1972, 209.

36 See the group's webpage: http://www.shinshuren.or.jp/.

37 See Shinshūren Chōsa Shitsu 1963 for a retrospective account of the Occupation years that strongly reinforces this view from the perspective of the collected new religious movements. A serialized English translation is Shin Nihon Shūkyō Dantai Rengō Kai Research Division 1965a, 1965b, 1966a, 1966b, 1966c.

38 Emphasis added.

39 Shin Nihon Shūkyō Dantai Rengō Kai Research Division 1966c, 268–73. See McLaugh-

lin 2012 on the long-standing pejorative treatment of marginal movements, and Sōka Gakkai in particular.

40 Shin Nihon Shūkyō Dantai Rengō Kai Research Division 1965a, 202–3. This section corresponds to *Sengo shūkyō kaiso roku*, 78–79.

41 Shin Nihon Shūkyō Dantai Rengō Kai Research Division 1966c, 267–68.

42 Ōishi 1964, 47–49. Also see McFarland 1960a, 37. Ōishi also aimed to change journalistic practices, but scholars of religion were more inclined to adopt the new terminology. As Dorman (2012) has shown, journalists tended to prefer sensationalist terms that made for better headlines. The same is true today.

43 Woodard, "Foreword," in Bunce 1955.

44 Lewis 2004, 3.

45 An earlier overview of this history can be found in Dorman 2012b.

46 Hansen 1963. See also Thomsen 1963.

47 McFarland 1960c, 68–69.

48 Hayashi and Yamanaka 1993. Talcott Parsons's (1902–79) student Robert Bellah (1927–2013) attempted to apply the Weberian thesis to Japan by examining ways in which the Shingaku movement had contributed to the development of proto-modernity during Japan's Tokugawa period (1603–1868); the book was translated into Japanese and eagerly consumed by the Japanese intelligentsia. See Bellah 1957. Also see Ienaga 1965, which disparaged the Buddhist "feudal" mindset.

49 See Murakami (1982) 2006 and especially the explanatory comments by Shimazono Susumu, 253–59; also see H. Byron Earhart, "Translator's Introduction," in Murakami (1968) 1980, xiii–xiv. Many American social scientists of the same period were also beholden to the model of economic base and epiphenomenal, ideological superstructure. See Robbins 2000, 515.

50 See McFarland 1958, 1960a, 1960b, 1960c, and 1967. For a critique of the crisis model, see Hardacre 1984, esp. 30–31.

51 Dorman 2012b, 167–71.

52 See, for example, Inoue N. 1991, 1992; Shimazono (1992) 2006. One overview of the field is Astley 2006. As of 2018 a working group of Japanese scholars has begun a project on revisiting and revising the category.

53 Lewis 2004, 3–7.

54 Chidester 1988 is one monograph on the subject of the Jonestown incident. A chapter-length seminal treatment is J. Z. Smith 1983, 102–20.

55 The publication of the 2004 *Oxford Handbook for the Study of New Religious Movements* is one marker of the degree to which new religious movements studies have moved from the margin to the mainstream of the American Academy of Religion (the Oxford handbooks are published by the AAR in conjunction with Oxford University Press).

56 Lucas 1997, 2008.

57 Melton 2004a, 2004b; Barker 2004; Bromley 2004; Robbins 2005; Reader 2005; Gallagher 2007. These debates reveal a fundamental split between social scientists who focus primarily on the social function of religion or typologies of religious movements (e.g., Stark and Bainbridge 1979) and humanists who focus more on the cultural or historical ramifications of doctrinal or ritual innovation.

58 Dorman 2012b; Strenski 1993; Wessinger 2009.

59 Weitzman 2017.

60 Agne and Tracy 2001; Agne 2007; Gallagher 2007; and Wessinger 2009.

61 Reader 2012; Dorman 2012b.

62 WPW Box #9, Folder #1, "The Religious Juridical Persons Law" and "New Religions and the RJPL."

63 "Conference between Directors of Religions League and Researchers of RCR," RCR Box #5787, Folder #18. The 18 October 1949 report details a meeting held on 17 October.

64 Shinshūren Chōsa Shitsu 1963, 272–73.

65 McLaughlin 2012.

66 Hurd 2015, esp. 22–36.

67 Murakami 1970, i.

68 Yamaguchi (1999) 2005, 4–5; Okuyama 2011, 123–24. Scholars who have been indebted to Murakami include Helen Hardacre (who reproduced his periodization and massaged his definition of State Shintō in her seminal 1989 study *Shintō and the State, 1868–1988*) and Shimazono Susumu, who expanded upon Murakami's thesis and nuanced his periodization in his own 2010 *shinsho* volume, *Kokka Shintō to Nihonjin*.

69 Kuroda 1981. More recent scholarship has criticized Kuroda's sweeping claims by showing that a loose amalgamation of ideas, rites, and spaces existed distinct from Buddhism in earlier periods. See Havens 2006 and Breen and Teeuwen 2010, as well as Teeuwen 2002. Shimazono (2009) is most explicit in reproducing Murakami's periodization.

70 Kuroda 1996.

71 For Murakami's reading as a "broad definition," see Nitta 1999a and 1999b. Hardacre acknowledges her debt to Kuroda in her 2017 magnum opus, but also suggests that he may have been too successful in convincing a generation of scholars that Shintō was a modern construct.

72 Hardacre 1989b, esp. 114–32. Kuroda also claimed that Japanese people had no epistemological basis for truly comprehending religious freedom. See Kuroda 1996, 349.

73 Abe 1968, 1969a, 1969b, 1970a, 1970b, 1970c.

74 See, for example, Nongbri 2013, chapter 6.

75 For example, two books on religious freedom: Sullivan 1994 and O'Brien and Ohkoshi 1996.

76 See Josephson 2012; Maxey 2014; and Zhong 2014 as well as Hardacre 2011, 2017.

77 Shimazono 2009, 2010.

78 See Shimazono 2009, 96–98; Scheid 2013. Also see the discussion of this issue in chapter 1.

79 Scheid 2013, 20–21.

80 Okuyama 2011 is a lucid overview of this scholarship.

81 Nitta 2000.

82 Sakamoto 2000. Sakamoto and his protégés have contributed historically nuanced studies of primary sources in several books and edited volumes that have argued that the Murakami thesis is untenable. See, for example, Sakamoto, ed. 2006.

83 See, for example, Ōhara, Momochi, and Sakamoto 1989.

84 Two examples are Gluck 1985 and Garon 1997.

85 On shrine priests, see Azegami 2009, which appeared in a condensed English translation as Azegami 2012. On bottom-up support for the ideas of State Shintō, see Shimazono 2010.

86 Hardacre (1989b) highlighted several high-profile court cases related to the controversial Yasukuni Shrine and groundbreaking ceremonies (*jichinsai*), a project also seen in O'Brien and Ohkoshi 1996. Nakamura (1992) and Dower (1999) both addressed the controversial decision to keep the Shōwa emperor on the throne during the Occupation. More recently, Breen and Teeuwen (2010) skeptically regarded the postwar activities of the Jinja Honchō (National Association of Shrines) as problematic; I also mentioned Shimazono Susumu's (2010) arguments on this score. Mark Mullins (2012a, 2012b) has also been engaged in an ongoing research project tracing recidivist tendencies among Japanese right-wing political groups and their supporters in the shrine world. Also see Guthmann 2017.

87 McNeill 2013.

88 On Abe's decision, see McCurry 2016. More generally, see Larsson 2017.

89 O'Brien and Ohkoshi 1996; Shimazono 2010; Breen and Teeuwen 2010 (esp. chapter 6); Mullins 2012a, 2012b; and Guthmann 2017 all register suspicion about the postwar survival of State Shintō.

90 This scholarship is almost entirely in Japanese. These studies tend to focus on "State Shintō in the narrow sense" as described by Nitta Hitoshi (1999a, 1999b). For examples of how these scholars react to controversial legal cases, see Breen 2010c; Breen and Teeuwen 2010.

91 Thomas 2017.

92 Ienaga's essay first appeared in Japanese in 1961. His claim reproduced a tendency in modern Japanese Buddhist scholarship to characterize Edo period Buddhism as decadent. See Klautau 2008.

93 Ienaga 1965, 11.

94 Ienaga 1965, 14, 17.

95 Ienaga 1965, 22.

96 Abe 1968, 285.

97 Abe 1970a, 49, 53.

98 Ichikawa 1970; Ives 2009.

99 Sharf 1995; Victoria 1997.

100 Heisig and Maraldo 1994; Ives 2009.

101 See Hubbard and Swanson 1997 and, more recently, Shields 2011.

102 Stone 1999, 183–84.

103 Arima, in Arai and Tanaka 2008.

104 See Shields 2017 and Thomas 2018.

105 Swanson 2014.

106 Rambelli 2013.

107 See McMahan 2008 on Buddhist modernism in general; also see Queen and King, eds. 1996 for examples. A particularly salient example using the case of Tibetan appeals to environmentalism is provided in Huber 1997.

108 Thomas 2018, reviewing Shields 2017.
109 Hurd 2015.
110 On imperialism and comparative religion, Masuzawa 2005. On linkages between postwar geopolitical considerations and religious studies, see McCutcheon 2004 and Imhoff 2016.
111 Arnal and McCutcheon 2013.
112 See C. Smith et al. 2013; Desch and Philpott, eds. 2013; Dawson 2013.
113 Jakobsen and Pellegrini 2008, 4–17.
114 See Schilbrack 2011 on critical religion theorists and "abolitionist" and "retentionist" responses to critiques.
115 Asad 1993; McCutcheon 1997; Fitzgerald 2000.
116 McCutcheon 2001, Nongbri 2013, Schilbrack 2013b.
117 Masuzawa 2005; Owen 2011; Cotter and Robertson 2016.
118 Cavanaugh 2014.
119 Schilbrack 2011; Schilbrack 2013a; Dressler and Mandair 2011.
120 Dressler and Mandair 2011; also see Hurd 2015 on "expert," "lived," and "governed" religion. Also see Sullivan 2005 for a reflection on scholarly expertise in American courts.
121 Schilbrack 2011.
122 Hurd 2015.

CONCLUSION

1 Former British prime minister Tony Blair, writing an op-ed in the *Guardian* newspaper on 25 January 2014 in his capacity as head of the Tony Blair Faith Foundation (now the Tony Blair Institute for Global Change)
2 These claims have been systematically debunked by Cavanaugh (2009).
3 See the Tony Blair Faith Foundation website: http://www.tonyblairfaithfoundation.org.
4 See Cavanaugh 2009, 2014.
5 Comerford and Bryson 2017.
6 See Desch 2013.
7 For example, Shah et al. 2012.
8 See the IGE website: http://globalengage.org. The IGE quarterly the *Review of Faith and International Affairs* is exclusively devoted to studies of religious freedom. Notably, head of IGE Chris Seiple topped a list of nominees for the vacant US ambassador-at-large for religious freedom position in a *Religion News Service* article that was republished by the *Washington Post* on 15 January 2014. See Markoe 2014. Seiple's father previously served in the post when it was inaugurated in 1998. See Melani McAlister's (2013) contribution to "Engaging Religion at the Department of State" at *The Immanent Frame*: http://blogs.ssrc.org/tif/2013/07/30/engaging-religion-at-the-department-of-state/.
9 See http://berkleycenter.georgetown.edu/rfp.
10 Hurd 2015.

11 The speech took place less than two weeks after the publication of Blair's aforementioned op-ed. See Baker 2014, 1 (my pagination). http://www.nytimes.com/2014/02/07/us/politics/obama-denounces-religious-repression.html?_r=0.

12 Kerry 2015.

13 http://www.humanrights.gov/dyn/2015/10/ambassador-saperstein-at-the-release-of-the-2014-report-on-international-religious-freedom/.

14 Altman 2013; Hurd 2013, 2015.

15 Cavanaugh 2009.

16 See Laborde 2014 for a clear overview of the various critiques of the problematic category of "religion." Laborde highlights the work done by Talal Asad (1993, 2003) and Saba Mahmood (2005, 2006) in highlighting the anthropology of religion assumed by certain state policies and popular perceptions.

17 Cavanaugh 2009; Hurd 2015; Mahmood 2016.

18 Weitzman 2017.

19 See Sullivan 2014; Hurd 2015; Mahmood 2016; and Hurd, Sullivan, Mahmood, and Danchin 2015 for examples.

20 Mahmood and Danchin 2014b, 2014c; Sullivan 2005.

21 Asad 2003; Mahmood 2016.

22 Brown 2006.

23 Asad 2003.

24 McGarry 2013.

25 Examples from the Japanese case can be found in Garon 1997 and Josephson 2006 and 2012.

26 Sullivan 2005.

27 Blair 2014, 3 (my pagination). The foundation is now called the Tony Blair Institute for Global Change.

28 See, for example, Tebbe 2017.

29 Wenger 2017. Also see Johnson and Weitzman 2017 on the FBI and religion.

30 Su 2016.

31 These claims all appear, for example, on the website of the aforementioned Shintō Seiji Renmei: http://www.sinseiren.org/shinseirentoha/shinseirenntoha.htm.

32 Mullins 2012b; McNeill 2013; Adelstein and Yamamoto 2016; Guthmann 2017.

EPILOGUE

1 The New Seekers, "Free to Be You And Me," from the 1972 album *Free to Be You And Me*.

2 Jackson 1979, 1982; Thomas 1972.

3 Bush 2001.

4 Hartley 2015.

5 D'Angelo 2014–15.

6 The Counted is the *Guardian*'s database: http://www.theguardian.com/us-news/ng-interactive/2015/jun/01/the-counted-police-killings-us-database.
7 On all of the foregoing, Alexander (2010) 2012.
8 International Human Rights and Conflict Resolution Clinic (Stanford Law School) and Global Justice Clinic (NYU School of Law), 2012.
9 Haj 2013.
10 On the term "bug splat," Hastings 2012. On "jackpot" and other terminology, see Begley 2015.
11 Begley 2015.
12 Mazzetti and Schmitt 2016.
13 *Dallas Morning News* 2014.
14 Dewan and Oppel 2015.
15 Swaine 2014.
16 See Hurd 2015.
17 Moyn 2010; Hopgood 2013.

REFERENCES

Abe Yoshiya. 1968. "Religious Freedom under the Meiji Constitution: Part I." *Contemporary Religions in Japan* 9 (4): 268–338. http://nirc.nanzan-u.ac.jp/nfile/3204.

———. 1969a. "Religious Freedom under the Meiji Constitution: Part II." *Contemporary Religions in Japan* 10 (1–2): 57–97. http://nirc.nanzan-u.ac.jp/nfile/3208.

———. 1969b. "Religious Freedom under the Meiji Constitution: Part III." *Contemporary Religions in Japan* 10 (3–4): 181–203. http://nirc.nanzan-u.ac.jp/nfile/3222.

———. 1970a. "Religious Freedom under the Meiji Constitution: Parts IV and V." *Contemporary Religions in Japan* 11 (1–2): 27–79. http://nirc.nanzan-u.ac.jp/nfile/3228.

———. 1970b. "Religious Freedom under the Meiji Constitution: Part VI." *Contemporary Religions in Japan* 11 (3–4): 223–66. http://nirc.nanzan-u.ac.jp/nfile/3238.

———. 1970c. "Religious Freedom under the Meiji Constitution: Appendixes and Bibliography." *Contemporary Religions in Japan* 11 (3–4): 267–96. http://nirc.nanzan-u.ac.jp/nfile/3239.

———. 1989. *Seikyō bunri: Nihon to Amerika ni miru shūkyō no seijisei*. Tokyo: Simul Press.

Adelstein, Jake, and Mari Yamamoto. 2016. "The Religious Cult Secretly Running Japan." *Daily Beast*, 10 July 2016. https://www.thedailybeast.com/the-religious-cult-secretly-running-japan.

Agne, Robert. 2007. "Reframing Practices in Moral Conflict: Interaction Problems in the Negotiation Standoff at Waco." *Discourse & Society* 18 (5): 549–78. doi: 10.1177/0957926507079634.

Agne, Robert, and Karen Tracy. 2001. "'Bible Babble': Naming the Interactional Trouble at Waco." *Discourse Studies* 3 (3): 269–94. doi: 10.1177/1461445601003003002.

Agrama, Hussein Ali. 2012. *Questioning Secularism: Islam, Sovereignty, and the Rule of Law in Modern Egypt*. Chicago: University of Chicago Press.

Alexander, Michelle. (2010) 2012. *The New Jim Crow: Mass Incarceration in the Age of Colorblindness*. New York: New Press.

Altman, Michael. 2013. "Why the U.S. State Department Should Take My Introduction to Religious Studies Course (or At Least Read the Syllabus)." *Medium*, 8 August 2013. https://medium.com/sacred-and-profane/47f83e4564f6.

Andō Masazumi. 1923. *Seiji to shūkyō to no kankei*. Tokyo: Kaneo Bun'endō.

———. 1926. "Rōdō seisaku oyobi shūkyō to seiji." In *Seiji kōza*, edited by Rikken Seiyūkai. Tokyo: Nihon Seiji Gakkai.

———. 1941. *Kessen taisei to Nihon Bukkyō: Zen'itsu Bukkyō no teishō*. Tokyo: Bōōkaku.

———. 1943. *Seikai o ayumi tsutsu*. Tokyo: Daichi Shobō.

———. 1951. *Kōwa o mae ni shite, tsuketari, tsuihō no hakusho*. Tokyo: Keizai Ōraisha.

Anesaki Masaharu. (1930) 1963. *A History of Japanese Religion*. Rutland, VT: Charles E. Tuttle Company.

———. 1938. *The Religious Life of the Japanese People*. 2nd ed. Tokyo: Kokusai Bunka Shinkokai.

Arai Ken and Tanaka Shigeru, eds. 2008. *Kokka to shūkyō: Shūkyō kara miru kingendai Nihon*. 2 vols. Kyoto: Hōzōkan.

Arnal, William E., and Russell T. McCutcheon. 2013. *The Sacred Is the Profane: The Political Nature of "Religion."* Oxford and New York: Oxford University Press.

Asad, Talal. 1993. *Genealogies of Religion: Discipline and Reasons of Power in Christianity and Islam*. Baltimore: Johns Hopkins University Press.

———. 2003. *Formations of the Secular: Christianity, Islam, Modernity*. Palo Alto, CA: Stanford University Press.

Asato, Noriko. 2006. *Teaching Mikadoism: The Attack on Japanese Language Schools in Hawaii, California, and Washington, 1919–1927*. Honolulu: University of Hawai'i Press.

———. 2010. "The Japanese Language School Controversy in Hawaii." In *Issei Buddhism in the Americas*, edited by Duncan Ryūken Williams and Tomoe Moriya, 45–64. Urbana, Chicago, and Springfield: University of Illinois Press.

Ashihara Ringen. 1898. *Kakkoku kōninkyō yōryaku*. Tokyo: Shūeisha.

Astley, Trevor. 2006. "New Religions." In *The Nanzan Guide to Japanese Religions*, edited by Clark Chilson and Paul L. Swanson, 91–114. Honolulu: University of Hawai'i Press.

Aston, William George. 1905. *Shintō: The Way of the Gods*. London: Longmans, Green, and Co.

Azegami Naoki. 2009. *"Mura no chinju" to senzen Nihon: "Kokka Shintō" no chiiki shakaishi*. Tokyo: Yūshisha.

———. 2012. "Local Shrines and the Creation of 'State Shintō.'" *Religion* 42 (1): 63–85. doi: 10.1080/0048721X.2012.641806.

Azuma, Eiichirō. 2009. "Brokering Race, Culture, and Citizenship: Japanese Americans in Occupied Japan and Postwar National Inclusion." *Journal of American-East Asian Relations* 16 (3): 183–211.

Baffelli, Erica, and Ian Reader. 2012. "Editors' Introduction: Impact and Ramifications: The Aftermath of the Aum Affair in the Japanese Religious Context." *Japanese Journal of Religious Studies* 39 (1): 1–28. http://nirc.nanzan-u.ac.jp/nfile/4081.

Baker, Peter. 2014. "Religious Freedom Is a Tenet of Foreign Policy, Obama Says." *New York Times*, 6 February. http://www.nytimes.com/2014/02/07/us/politics/obama-denounces-religious-repression.html.

Ballou, Robert Oleson. 1945. *Shintō: The Unconquered Enemy*. New York: Viking Press.

Barker, Eileen. 2004. "Perspective: What Are We Studying? A Sociological Case for Keeping the '*Nova*.'" *Nova Religio* 8 (1): 88–102. doi: 10.1525/nr.2004.8.1.88.

Begley, Joshua. 2015. "A Visual Glossary: Decoding the Language of Covert Warfare." *The Intercept, The Drone Papers*. 15 October. https://theintercept.com/drone-papers/a-visual-glossary/.

Bell, Duncan. 2014. "What Is Liberalism?" *Political Theory* 42 (6): 1–34. doi: 10.1177/0090591714535103.

Bellah, Robert N. 1957. *Tokugawa Religion*. Glencoe, IL: Free Press.

———. 1967. "Civil Religion in America." *Daedalus* 96 (1): 1–21. http://www.jstor.org/stable/20027022.

Bernstein, Andrew. 2006. *Modern Passings: Death Rites, Politics, and Social Change in Imperial Japan*. Honolulu: University of Hawai'i Press.

———. 2008. "Whose Fuji? Religion, Region, and State in the Fight for a National Symbol." *Monumenta Nipponica* 63 (1): 51–99. doi: 10.1353/mni.0.0001.

Berry, Mary Elizabeth. 1998. "Public Life in Authoritarian Japan." *Daedalus* 127 (3): 133–65. http://www.jstor.org/stable/20027510.

Bisson, T. A. 1944. "The Price of Peace for Japan." *Pacific Affairs* 17 (1): 5–25. http://www.jstor.org/stable/2751993.

Bix, Herbert P. 2000. *Hirohito and the Making of Modern Japan*. New York: HarperCollins.

Blair, Tony. 2014. "Religious Difference, Not Ideology, Will Fuel This Century's Epic Battles." *Guardian*, 25 January 2014. http://www.theguardian.com/commentisfree/2014/jan/25/religious-difference-ideology-conflicts-middle-east-tony-blair.

Blankenship, Anne. 2014. "Religion and the Japanese American Incarceration." *Religion Compass* 8:317–25. doi: 10.1111/rec3.12135.

Borovoy, Amy. 2016. "Robert Bellah's Search for Community and Ethical Modernity in Japan Studies." *Journal of Asian Studies* 75 (2): 467–94. doi:10.1017/S0021911815002107.

Borup, Jørn. 2013. "Aloha Buddha: The Secularization of Ethnic Japanese-American Buddhism." *Journal of Global Buddhism* 14:23–43.

Bradley, Mark. 2016. *The World Reimagined: Americans and Human Rights in the Twentieth Century*. New York: Cambridge University Press.

Breen, John. 2010a. "'Conventional Wisdom' and the Politics of Shintō in Postwar Japan." *Politics and Religion Journal* 4 (1): 68–81.

———. 2010b. *A New History of Shintō*. Chichester; Malden, MA: Wiley-Blackwell.

———. 2010c. "Resurrecting the Sacred Land of Japan: The State of Shintō in the Twenty-First Century." *Japanese Journal of Religious Studies* 37 (2): 295–315. http://nirc.nanzan-u.ac.jp/nfile/3020.

Bromley, David G. 2004. "Perspective: Whither New Religions Studies? Defining and Shaping a New Area of Study." *Nova Religio* 8 (2): 83–97. doi: 10.1525/nr.2004.8.2.83.

Brown, Wendy. 2006. *Regulating Aversion: Tolerance in the Age of Identity and Empire*. Princeton, NJ: Princeton University Press. Kindle edition.

Bunce, William K. 1955. *Religions in Japan: Buddhism, Shintō, Christianity*. Rutland, VT: Charles E. Tuttle Company.

Burnidge, Cara Lea. 2016. *A Peaceful Conquest: Woodrow Wilson, Religion, and the New World Order*. Chicago and London: University of Chicago Press.

Bush, George W. 2001. Speech to Congress on 20 September. http://www.washingtonpost.com/wp-srv/nation/specials/attacked/transcripts/bushaddress_092001.html.

Calhoun, Craig, Mark Juergensmeyer, and Jonathan van Antwerpen. 2011. "Introduction." In *Rethinking Secularism*, edited by Craig Calhoun, Mark Juergensmeyer, and Jonathan van Antwerpen, 3–30. Oxford: Oxford University Press.

Canepari, Zachary, and Andrea Cooper. 2015. "The Family Dog." *New York Times*. 17 June 2015. http://www.nytimes.com/video/technology/100000003746796/the-family-dog.html.

Capra, Frank, dir. 1945. *Know Your Enemy: Japan*. US Office of War Information.

Cavanaugh, William T. 2009. *The Myth of Religious Violence: Secular Ideology and the Roots of Modern Conflict*. Oxford and New York: Oxford University Press.

———. 2014. "Religious Violence as Modern Myth." *Political Theology* 15 (6): 486–502. http://dx.doi.org/10.1179/1462317X14Z.00000000094.

Chamberlain, Basil Hall. 1912. *The Invention of a New Religion*. London: Watts & Co. (published for the Rationalist Press Association, Limited).

Chidester, David. 1988. *Salvation and Suicide: Jim Jones, the Peoples Temple, and Jonestown*. Bloomington: Indiana University Press.

Chikazumi Shin'ichi. 2009. "Kyūdō Kaikan/Kyūdō Gakusha no kiten o tomo ni shita Bukkyō seinentachi." In *Kindaika no naka no dentō shūkyō to seishin undō: Kijunten to shite no Chikazumi Jōkan kenkyū*, edited by Iwata Fumiaki, 5–10. Japan Society for the Promotion of Science Midterm Report of Research Findings (Basic Research [C]) for 2008–9, Research Topic #20520055.

Clark, Scott. 2006. Guide to the William P. Woodard Collection. http://archiveswest.orbiscascade.org/ark:/80444/xv82095.

Claxton, P. P., Frank F. Bunker, W. W. Kemp, Parke R. Kolbe, and George R. Twiss. 1920. "A Survey of Education in Hawaii." *Department of the Interior, Bureau of Education Bulletin* 16. https://files.eric.ed.gov/fulltext/ED543381.pdf.

Cohen, G. Daniel. 2012. "The Holocaust and the 'Human Rights Revolution': A Reassessment." In *The Human Rights Revolution: An International History*, edited by Akira Iriye, Petra Goedde, and William I. Hitchcock, 53–72. Oxford and New York: Oxford University Press.

Collcutt, Martin. (1986) 2014. "Buddhism: The Threat of Eradication." In *Japan in Transition: From Tokugawa to Meiji*, edited by Marius Jansen and Gilbert Rozman, 143–67. Princeton, NJ: Princeton University Press.

Comerford, Milo, and Rachel Bryson. 2017. "Struggle over Scripture." Tony Blair Institute for Global Change. https://institute.global/sites/default/files/inline-files/TBI_Struggle-over-Scripture_o.pdf.

Constitution Investigation Council. 1962a. "The Constitution and Religion [Proceedings of the Constitution Investigation Council Meeting on 9 March 1960]." *Contemporary Religions in Japan* 3 (2): 103–15. http://nirc.nanzan-u.ac.jp/nfile/3303.

———. 1962b. "The Constitution and Religion [Proceedings of the Constitution Investigation Council Meeting on 9 March 1960]." *Contemporary Religions in Japan* 3 (3): 220–33. http://nirc.nanzan-u.ac.jp/nfile/3314.

———. 1963a. "The Constitution and Religion [Proceedings of the Constitution Investigation Council Meeting on 9 March 1960]." *Contemporary Religions in Japan* 3 (4): 314–33. http://nirc.nanzan-u.ac.jp/nfile/3322.

———. 1963b. "The Constitution and Religion [Proceedings of the Constitution Investigation Council Meeting on 9 March 1960]." *Contemporary Religions in Japan* 4 (1): 79–92. http://nirc.nanzan-u.ac.jp/nfile/3066.

Cotter, Christopher R., and David G. Robertson. 2016. *After World Religions: Reconstructing Religious Studies*. London and New York: Routledge.

Covell, Stephen G. 2005. *Japanese Temple Buddhism: Worldliness in a Religion of Renunciation*. Honolulu: University of Hawai'i Press.

Crane, Burton. 1947. "Shintō Spreading throughout Japan." *New York Times*, 5 February.

Curtis, Finbarr. 2016. *The Production of American Religious Freedom*. New York: New York University Press.

Dai Nippon Bukkyōto Dōmei Kai. 1900. *Shūkyō hōan hantai iken*. Publisher unknown.

Dallas Morning News. 2014. "Editorial: Intimidation from Open-Carry Proponents." 22 May. http://www.dallasnews.com/opinion/editorials/20140522-editorial-intimidation-from-open-carry-proponents.ece.

D'Angelo. 2014–15. *Black Messiah*. RCA Records.

Date Kiyonobu. 2015. "Isurāmu wa itsu, ikani shite Furansu no shūkyō ni natta no ka." *Shūkyō kenkyū* 89 (2): 107–32.

Davis, Winston. 1992. *Japanese Religion and Society: Paradigms of Structure and Change*. Albany: State University of New York.

Dawson, Stephen. 2013. "The Religious Resurgence and International Relations Theory." *Religion Compass* 39 (4): 201–22.

Desch, Michael C. 2013. "The Coming Reformation of Religion in International Affairs? The Demise of the Secularization Thesis and the Rise of New Thinking about Religion." In Desch and Philpott 2013.

Desch, Michael C., and Daniel Philpott, eds. 2013. "Religion and International Relations: A Primer for Research." University of Notre Dame, July. http://rmellon.nd.edu/assets/101872/religion_and_international_relations_report.pdf.

Dewan, Shaila, and Richard A. Oppel Jr. 2015. "In Tamir Rice Shooting, Many Errors by Cleveland Police, Then a Fatal One." *New York Times*, 22 January. http://www.nytimes.com/2015/01/23/us/in-tamir-rice-shooting-in-cleveland-many-errors-by-police-then-a-fatal-one.html?_r=0.

Dorman, Benjamin. 2004. "SCAP's Scapegoat? The Authorities, New Religions, and Postwar Taboo." *Japanese Journal of Religious Studies* 31 (1): 105–40. http://nirc.nanzan-u.ac.jp/nfile/2826.

———. 2012a. *Celebrity Gods: New Religions, Media, and Authority in Occupied Japan*. Honolulu: University of Hawai'i Press.

———. 2012b. "Scholarly Reactions to the Aum and Waco Incidents." *Japanese Journal of Religious Studies* 39 (1): 153–77.

Dower, John W. 1986. *War without Mercy: Race and Power in the Pacific War*. New York: Pantheon Books.

———. 1993. *Japan in War and Peace: Selected Essays*. New York: New Press.

———. 1999. *Embracing Defeat: Japan in the Wake of World War II*. New York: W. W. Norton & Co./New Press.

———. 2003. "A Warning from History: Don't Expect Democracy in Iraq." *Boston Review*, February/March 2003. http://bostonreview.net/world/john-w-dower-warning-history.

Dressler, Markus, and Arvind-Pal S. Mandair. 2011. "Introduction: Modernity, Religion-Making, and the Postsecular." In *Secularism and Religion-Making*, edited by Markus

Dressler and Arvind-Pal S. Mandair, 3–36. Oxford and New York: Oxford University Press.

Dudden, Alexis. 2005. *Japan's Colonization of Korea: Discourse and Power*. Honolulu: University of Hawai'i Press.

Dyke, Ken R. [ghostwritten by W. K. Bunce]. (1945) 1966. "Memorandum on State Shintō to the Chief of Staff (3 December 1945)." *Contemporary Religions in Japan* 7 (4): 321–60. http://nirc.nanzan-u.ac.jp/nfile/3176.

Fitzgerald, Timothy. 2000. *The Ideology of Religious Studies*. New York and Oxford: Oxford University Press.

Fujishima Ryō'on [Tangaku]. 1899. *Seikyō shinron*. Kyoto: Kōkyō shoin.

Fujitani, T. 1996. *Splendid Monarchy: Power and Pageantry in Modern Japan*. Berkeley and Los Angeles: University of California Press.

———. 2011. *Race for Empire: Koreans as Japanese and Japanese as Americans during World War II*. Berkeley: University of California Press.

Fukuda Shigeru. 1993. "Kenshō: GHQ no shūkyō seisaku." In *Senryō to Nihon shūkyō*, edited by Ikado Fujio, 521–60. Tokyo: Miraisha, 1993.

Gallagher, Eugene V. 2007. "Compared to What? 'Cults' and 'New Religious Movements.'" *History of Religions* 47 (2–3): 205–20. doi: 10.1086/524210.

Garon, Sheldon. 1986. "State and Religion in Imperial Japan, 1912–1945." *Journal of Japanese Studies* 12:273–302. http://www.jstor.org/stable/132389.

Gluck, Carol. 1985. *Japan's Modern Myths: Ideology in the Late Meiji Period*. Princeton, NJ: Princeton University Press.

Gordon, Sarah Barringer. 2010. *The Spirit of the Law: Religious Voices and the Constitution in Modern America*. Cambridge, MA, and London: Belknap Press of Harvard University Press.

Griffis, William Elliott. 1915. *The Mikado: Institution and Person*. Princeton, NJ: Princeton University Press.

Gulick, Sidney L. 1914. "The American-Japanese Problem." In *Two Addresses by Sidney L. Gulick on A New Immigration Policy and the American-Japanese Problem*. [Federal Council of Churches?] Bulletin no. 10, 18 February.

———. 1918. *American Democracy and Asiatic Citizenship*. New York: Charles Scribner's Sons.

Guthmann, Thierry. 2017. "Nationalist Circles in Japan Today: The Impossibility of Secularization." *Japan Review* 30:207–25. http://publications.nichibun.ac.jp/region/d/NSH/series/jare/2017-07-24/s001/s017/pdf/article.pdf.

Haj, Ahmed, al-. 2013. "Officials: U.S. Drone Strike Kills 13 in Yemen." *Washington Post*, 12 December 2013. https://www.washingtonpost.com/world/officials-us-drone-strike-kills-13-in-yemen/2013/12/12/3b070f0a-6375-11e3-91b3-f2bb96304e34_story.html?tid=a_inl.

Hansen, Olaf. 1963. Foreword to *The New Religions of Japan*, by Harry Thomsen, 9–10. Rutland, VT: Charles E. Tuttle Company.

Hardacre, Helen. 1984. *Lay Buddhism in Contemporary Japan: Reiyūkai Kyōdan*. Princeton, NJ: Princeton University Press.

———. 1989a. "The *Lotus Sutra* in Modern Japan." In *The Lotus Sutra in Japanese Cul-*

ture, edited by George J. Tanabe Jr. and Willa Tanabe, 209–24. Honolulu: University of Hawai'i Press.

———. 1989b. *Shintō and the State, 1868–1988*. Princeton, NJ: Princeton University Press.

———. 2003. "After Aum: Religion and Civil Society in Japan." In *The State of Civil Society in Japan*, edited by Frank J. Schwartz and Susan J. Pharr, 135–53. Cambridge: Cambridge University Press.

———. 2011. "The Formation of Secularity in Japan." Paper presented at "Secularism beyond the West" conference, Oñati, Spain. Digital Access to Scholarship at Harvard, http://nrs.harvard.edu/urn-3:HUL.InstRepos:8843159.

———. 2017. *Shintō: A History*. New York: Oxford University Press.

Haring, Douglas G. 1963. "Daniel Clarence Holtom, 1884–1962." *American Anthropologist* 65 (4): 892–93. http://onlinelibrary.wiley.com/doi/10.1525/aa.1963.65.4.02a00080/pdf.

Hartley, Ryan. 2015. "The Politics of Dancing in Japan." *International Institute of Asian Studies Newsletter* 70 (Spring). http://www.iias.nl/sites/default/files/IIAS_NL70_0405.pdf.

Hastings, Michael. 2012. "The Rise of the Killer Drones: How America Goes to War in Secret." *Rolling Stone*, 16 April 2012. http://www.rollingstone.com/politics/news/the-rise-of-the-killer-drones-how-america-goes-to-war-in-secret-20120416.

Havens, Norman. 2006. "Shintō." In *The Nanzan Guide to Japanese Religions*, edited by Paul L. Swanson and Clark Chilson, 14–37. Honolulu: University of Hawai'i Press.

Hayashi Makoto. 2006. "Religion in the Modern Period." In *The Nanzan Guide to Japanese Religions*, edited by Paul L. Swanson and Clark Chilson, 202–19. Honolulu: University of Hawai'i Press.

———. 2009. "Kindai Bukkyō no jiki kubun." *Kikan Nihon shisō shi* 75:3–13.

Hayashi Makoto and Isomae Jun'ichi, eds. 2008. "Tokushū: Kindai Nihon no shūkyōgaku: Gakuchi o meguru naratorojī." *Kikan Nihon shisōshi* 72.

Hayashi Makoto and Ōtani Eiichi, eds. 2009. "Tokushū: Kindai Bukkyō." *Kikan Nihon shisō shi* 75.

Hayashi Makoto and Yamanaka Hiroshi. 1993. "The Adaption of Max Weber's Theories of Religion in Japan." *Japanese Journal of Religious Studies* 20 (2–3): 207–28. http://nirc.nanzan-u.ac.jp/nfile/2515.

Heisig, James W., and John C. Maraldo, eds. 1994. *Rude Awakenings: Zen, the Kyoto School, and the Question of Nationalism*. Honolulu: University of Hawai'i Press.

Henry, Todd A. 2014. *Assimilating Seoul: Japanese Rule and the Politics of Public Space in Colonial Korea, 1910–1945*. Berkeley, Los Angeles, and London: University of California Press.

Hoffmann, Stefan-Ludwig, ed. 2011a. *Human Rights in the Twentieth Century*. Cambridge: Cambridge University Press.

———. 2011b. "Introduction: Genealogies of Human Rights." In *Human Rights in the Twentieth Century*, edited by Stefan-Ludwig Hoffmann, 1–26. Cambridge: Cambridge University Press.

Hollinger, David. 2017. *Protestants Abroad: How Missionaries Tried to Change the World but Changed America*. Princeton, NJ: Princeton University Press.

Holtom, Daniel Clarence. 1922. *The Political Philosophy of Modern Shintō: A Study of the State Religion of Japan*. Chicago: University of Chicago Libraries.

———. 1927. "The State Cult of Modern Japan." *Journal of Religion* 7 (4): 419–46. http://www.jstor.org/stable/1195452.

———. (1938) 1995. *The National Faith of Japan: A Study in Modern Shintō*. London and New York: Kegan Paul International.

———. 1943. *Modern Japan and Shintō Nationalism: A Study of Present-Day Trends in Japanese Religions*. Chicago: University of Chicago Press.

———. 1945a. "The Japanese Mind." *Republic*, 28 May.

———. 1945b. "Shintō in the Postwar World." *Far Eastern Survey* 14 (3): 29–33. http://www.jstor.org/stable/3022785.

———. 1946. "New Status of Shintō." *Far Eastern Survey* 15 (2): 17–20. http://www.jstor.org/stable/3021509.

Hopgood, Stephen. 2013. *The Endtimes of Human Rights*. Ithaca, NY, and London: Cornell University Press.

Hoshino Seiji. 2009. "Reconfiguring Buddhism as a Religion: Nakanishi Ushirō and His *Shin Bukkyō*." *Japanese Religions* 34 (2): 133–54.

———. 2012. *Kindai Nihon no shūkyō gainen: Shūkyōsha no kotoba to kindai*. Tokyo: Yūshisha.

Howell, David L. 2005. *Geographies of Identity in Nineteenth-Century Japan*. Berkeley and Los Angeles: University of California Press.

Howland, Douglas R. 2002. *Translating the West: Language and Political Reason in Nineteenth-Century Japan*. Honolulu: University of Hawai'i Press.

Hubbard, Jamie, and Paul L. Swanson, eds. 1997. *Pruning the Bodhi Tree: The Storm over Critical Buddhism*. Honolulu: University of Hawai'i Press.

Huber, Toni. 1997. "Green Tibetans: A Brief Social History." In *Tibetan Culture in the* Diaspora, edited by F. J. Korom, 103–19. Vienna: Verlag der Österreichischen Akademie der Wissenschaften.

Hur, Nam-lin. 2007. *Death and Social Order in Tokugawa Japan: Buddhism, Anti-Christianity, and the Danka System*. Cambridge, MA: Harvard University Asia Center.

Hurd, Elizabeth Shakman. 2008. *The Politics of Secularism in International Relations*. Princeton, NJ: Princeton University Press. Kindle edition.

———. 2013. "What's Wrong with Promoting Religious Freedom?" *Foreign Policy*, 12 June. http://mideastafrica.foreignpolicy.com/posts/2013/06/12/whats_wrong_with_promoting_religious_freedom.

———. 2015. *Beyond Religious Freedom: The New Global Politics of Religion*. Princeton, NJ: Princeton University Press.

Hylkema-Vos, Naomi. 1990. "Katō Genchi: A Neglected Pioneer in the Study of Japanese Religion." *Japanese Journal of Religious Studies* 17 (4): 375–95. http://nirc.nanzan-u.ac.jp/nfile/2436.

Ichikawa Hakugen. 1970. *Bukkyōsha no sensō sekinin*. Tokyo: Shunjusha.

Ienaga Saburō. 1965. "Japan's Modernization and Buddhism." *Contemporary Religions in Japan* 6 (1): 1–41. http://nirc.nanzan-u.ac.jp/nfile/3143.

Ikado Fujio, ed. 1993. *Senryō to Nihon shūkyō*. Tokyo: Miraisha.

Ikeda Eishun. 1976. *Meiji no shin Bukkyō undō*. Tokyo: Yoshikawa Kōbunkan.

Imaizumi Yoshiko. 2013. *Sacred Space in the Modern City: The Fractured Pasts of Meiji Shrine*. Leiden: E. J. Brill.

Imamura Yemyō. 1918. *Democracy According to the Buddhist Viewpoint*. Honolulu: Publishing Bureau of the Honolulu Hongwanji. Included in Imamura 1921.

———. 1921. *Beikoku no seishin o ronzu*. Tokyo: Kaneo Bun'endō.

Imhoff, Sarah. 2016. "The Creation Story, or How We Learned to Stop Worrying and Love Schempp." *Journal of the American Academy of Religion* 84 (2): 466–97. doi: 10.1093/jaarel/lfv060.

Inboden, William. 2008. *Religion and American Foreign Policy, 1945–1960: The Soul of Containment*. Cambridge and New York: Cambridge University Press. Kindle edition.

Inoue Egyō. 1972. *Shūkyō hōjin hō no kisoteki kenkyū*. Tokyo: Daiichi Shobō.

Inoue Nobutaka. 1991. "Recent Trends in the Study of Japanese New Religions." In *New Religions*, edited by Inoue Nobutaka and translated by Norman Havens, 4–24. Tokyo: Institute for Japanese Culture and Classics.

———. 1992. *Shinshūkyō no kaidoku*. Tokyo: Chikuma Raiburarii.

———. 2002. "The Formation of Sect Shintō in Modernizing Japan." *Japanese Journal of Religious Studies* 29 (3–4): 407–27. http://nirc.nanzan-u.ac.jp/nfile/2789.

Inoue Nobutaka and Sakamoto Koremaru, eds. 1987. *Nihongata seikyō kankei no tanjō*. Tokyo: Daiichi Shobō.

Inoue Tetsujirō. 1893. *Kyōiku to shūkyō no shōtotsu*. Tokyo: Keigyōsha.

International Human Rights and Conflict Resolution Clinic (Stanford Law School) and Global Justice Clinic (Nyu School of Law). 2012. *Living under Drones: Death, Injury, and Trauma to Civilians from US Drone Practices in Pakistan*.

Iriye, Akira, Petra Goedde, and William I. Hitchcock, eds. 2012. *The Human Rights Revolution: An International History*. Oxford and New York: Oxford University Press.

Ishizu, Teruji. 1965. "In Memoriam of Prof. Hideo Kishimoto." *Numen* 12 (1): 70–73. http://www.jstor.org/stable/3269318.

Isomae Jun'ichi. 2003. *Kindai nihon no shūkyō gensetsu to sono keifu: Shūkyō/kokka/Shintō*. Tokyo: Iwanami Shoten.

———. 2013. "Religion, Secularity, and the Articulation of the 'Indigenous' in Modernizing Japan." In *Kami Ways in Nationalist Territory: Shintō Studies in Prewar Japan and the West*, edited by Bernhard Scheid with Kate Wildman Nakai, 23–49. Vienna: Austrian Academy of Sciences.

———. 2014. *Religious Discourse in Modern Japan: Religion/State/Shintō*. Leiden: E. J. Brill.

Itō Hirobumi. (1889) 1906. *Commentaries on the Constitution of the Empire of Japan*. Tokyo: Igirisu-Hōritsu Gakkō.

Ives, Christopher. 2009. *Imperial-Way Zen: Ichikawa Hakugen's Critique and Lingering Questions for Buddhist Ethics*. Honolulu: University of Hawai'i Press.

Iwata Fumiaki. 2014. *Kindai Bukkyō to seinen: Chikazumi Jōkan to sono jidai*. Tokyo: Iwanami Shoten.

Jackson, Michael. 1979. *Off the Wall*. CBS, Inc.

———. 1982. *Thriller*. CBS, Inc.

Jaffe, Richard. 2001. *Neither Monk nor Layman: Clerical Marriage in Modern Japanese Buddhism*. Princeton, NJ, and Oxford: Princeton University Press.

Jakobsen, Janet, and Ann Pellegrini, eds. 2008. *Secularisms*. Durham, NC: Duke University Press.

Johnson, Sylvester. 2017. "The FBI and the Moorish Science Temple of America, 1926–1960." In *The FBI and Religion: Faith and National Security Before and After 9/11*, edited by Sylvester A. Johnson and Steven Weitzman, 55–66. Oakland: University of California Press.

Johnson, Sylvester, and Steven Weitzman. 2017. "'True Faith and Allegiance'—Religion and the FBI." In *The FBI and Religion: Faith and National Security Before and After 9/11*, edited by Sylvester A. Johnson and Steven Weitzman, 1–16. Oakland: University of California Press.

Josephson, Jason Ānanda. 2006. "Taming Demons: The Anti-Superstition Campaign and the Invention of Religion in Japan (1853–1920)." PhD dissertation, Stanford University.

———. 2012. *The Invention of Religion in Japan*. Chicago and London: University of Chicago Press.

Josephson-Storm, Jason Ānanda. 2017. "The Superstition, Secularism, and Religion Trinary: Or Re-Theorizing Secularism." *Method & Theory in the Study of Religion*, advance article: 10.1163/15700682-12341409.

Juaregui, Andres. 2012. "Soineya, Japanese 'Cuddle Club,' Lets Patrons Sleep with Strangers." *Huffington Post*, 2 October 2012. http://www.huffingtonpost.com/2012/10/02/soineya-japanese-cuddle-club_n_1932314.html.

Katō Genchi. 1926. *A Study of Shintō, the Religion of the Japanese Nation*. Tokyo: Meiji Seitoku Kinen Gakkai.

———. 1935. *What Is Shintō?* Tokyo: Japanese Government Railways Board of Tourist Industry.

Katō Totsudō. 1899. *Bukkyō kokumin zakkyo go no kokore*. Tokyo: Kōmeisha.

Kerry, John. 2015. "Religion and Diplomacy: Toward a Better Understanding of Religion and Global Affairs." *America Magazine*, 14 September 2015. http://americamagazine.org/issue/religion-and-diplomacy.

Ketelaar, James Edward. 1990. *Of Heretics and Martyrs in Meiji Japan: Buddhism and Its Persecution*. Princeton, NJ: Princeton University Press.

King, Christopher S., and Sallie B. King, eds. 1996. *Engaged Buddhism: Buddhist Liberation Movements in Asia*. Albany: State University of New York Press.

Kishimoto Hideo. 1934. "The Task of Buddhism." *Journal of Religion* 14 (1): 77–84. http://www.jstor.org/stable/1196759.

———. 1960a. "From the Editorial Board." *Contemporary Religions in Japan* 1 (1): 3–4. http://nirc.nanzan-u.ac.jp/nfile/3062.

———. 1960b. "The Problem of Religion and Modernization in Japan." *Contemporary Religions in Japan* 1 (3): 1–19. http://nirc.nanzan-u.ac.jp/nfile/3240.

———. 1961. *Shūkyōgaku*. Tokyo: Daimeidō.

———. 1963. "Arashi no naka no Jinja Shintō." In *Sengo shūkyō kaisō roku*, edited by Shinshūren Chōsa Shitsu, 195–281. Tokyo: PL Shuppansha.

Kitagawa, Joseph. 1964. "Kishimoto Hideo, 1903–1964." *History of Religions* 4 (1): 172–73. http://www.jstor.org/stable/1061879.

Kitamura Jōshō, ed. 1899. *Sugamo kangoku kyōkai mondai enzetsu yōryō*. Hyōgo Prefecture: Takahashi Kappansho.

Kitaura Keitarō. 1947. *Zukai kenpō*. Nara: Nara Nichinichi Shinbunsha.

Klautau, Orion. 2008. "Against the Ghosts of Recent Past: Meiji Scholarship and the Discourse on Edo-Period Buddhist Decadence." *Japanese Journal of Religious Studies* 35 (2): 263–303. http://nirc.nanzan-u.ac.jp/nfile/2960.

———, ed. 2014. "The Politics of Buddhist Studies in Early Twentieth-Century Japan." Special issue, *Japanese Religions* 39 (1–2).

Kōno Seizō. 1938. *Waga kokutai to Shintō*. Tokyo: Naikaku Insastu Kyoku.

Krämer, Hans-Martin. 2011. "Beyond the Dark Valley: Reinterpreting Christian Reactions to the 1939 Religious Organizations Law." *Japanese Journal of Religious Studies* 38 (1): 181–211. http://nirc.nanzan-u.ac.jp/nfile/3040.

———. 2015. *Shimaji Mokurai and the Reconception of Religion and Secular in Modern Japan*. Honolulu: University of Hawai'i Press.

———. 2017. "Reconceiving the Secular in Early Meiji Japan: Shimaji Mokurai, Buddhism, Shintō, and the Nation." *Japan Review* 30: 63–77. http://publications.nichibun.ac.jp/region/d/NSH/series/jare/2017-07-24/s001/s007/pdf/article.pdf.

Kruse, Kevin M. 2015. *One Nation under God: How Corporate America Invented Christian America*. New York: Basic Books.

Kuroda Toshio. 1981. "Shintō in the History of Japanese Religion." *Journal of Japanese Studies* 7 (1): 1–22. http://www.jstor.org/stable/132163.

———. 1996. "The World of Spirit Pacification: Issues of State and Religion," translated by Allan Grapard. *Japanese Journal of Religious Studies* 23 (3–4): 321–51. http://nirc.nanzan-u.ac.jp/nfile/2607.

Kushner, Barak. 2006. *The Thought War: Japanese Imperial Propaganda*. Honolulu: University of Hawai'i Press.

Laborde, Cécile. 2014. "Three Approaches to the Study of Religion." *The Immanent Frame*. http://blogs.ssrc.org/tif/2014/02/05/three-approaches-to-the-study-of-religion/.

Lah, Kyung. 2010. "Buddhist Monks Use Hip Hop, Alcohol to Attract Followers." *CNN* 21 January 2010. http://www.cnn.com/2010/WORLD/asiapcf/01/21/japan.hip.monks.buddhism/.

Landman, Isaac. 1919. "The League of Nations and the Jews." *American Hebrew and Jewish Messenger*, 13 June.

Larsson, Ernils. 2017. "Jinja Honchō and the Politics of Constitutional Reform in Japan." *Japan Review* 30: 227–52. http://publications.nichibun.ac.jp/region/d/NSH/series/jare/2017-07-24/s001/s014/pdf/article.pdf.

Lavigne, Avril. 2013. "Hello Kitty." Epic Records. Music video at https://youtu.be/LiaYDPRedWQ.

Lewis, James R. 2004. "Overview." In *The Oxford Handbook of New Religious Movements*, edited by James R. Lewis, 3–15. Oxford: Oxford University Press.

Lindkvist, Linde. 2017. *Religious Freedom and the Universal Declaration of Human Rights*. Cambridge and New York: Cambridge University Press.

Lucas, Philip Charles. 1997. "Introduction, Acknowledgments, and Announcement." *Nova Religio* 1 (1): 6–9.

———. 2008. "A Retrospective: Reflections on the Tenth Anniversary of *Nova Religio*." *Nova Religio* 10 (4): 8–16. doi: 10.1525/nr.2007.10.4.8.

Lum, Kathryn Gin. 2018. "The Historyless Heathen and the Stagnating Pagan: History as Non-Native Category?" *Religion and American Culture: A Journal of Interpretation* 28 (1): 52–91. doi:10.1525/rac.2018.28.1.52.

MacCaughey, Vaughan. 1918. "Americanization and the Schools of Hawaii." *School and Society* 8:24–26.

———. 1919. "Some Outstanding Educational Problems in Hawaii." *School and Society* 9:99–105.

Maekawa Michiko. 2015. *Kindai Nihon no shūkyō ron to kokka: shūkyōgaku no shisō to kokumin kyōiku no kōsaku*. Tokyo: Tōkyō Daigaku Shuppan Kai.

Mahmood, Saba. 2005. *Politics of Piety: The Islamic Revival and the Feminist Subject*. Princeton, NJ: Princeton University Press.

———. 2006. "Secularism, Hermeneutics, and Empire: The Politics of Islamic Reformation." *Public Culture* 18 (2): 323–47. doi: 10.1215/08992363-2006-006.

———. 2010. "Can Secularism Be Other-Wise?" In *Varieties of Secularism in a Secular Age*, edited by Michael Warner, Jonathan VanAntwerpen, and Craig Calhoun, 282–99. Cambridge, MA, and London: Harvard University Press.

———. 2012. "Religious Freedom, the Minority Question, and Geopolitics in the Middle East." *Comparative Studies in Society and History* 54 (2): 418–46. doi: 10.1017/S0010417512000096.

———. 2016. *Religious Difference in a Secular Age: A Minority Report*. Princeton, NJ: Princeton University Press.

Mahmood, Saba, and Peter Danchin 2014a. "Immunity or Regulation? Antinomies of Religious Freedom." In Mahmood and Danchin 2014b, 129–59. doi: 10.1215/00382876-2390455.

———, eds. 2014b. "Politics of Religious Freedom: Contested Genealogies." Special issue, *South Atlantic Quarterly* 113 (1).

———. 2014c. "Politics of Religious Freedom: Contested Genealogies." In Mahmood and Danchin 2014b, 1–8. doi: 10.1215/00382876-2390401.

Markoe, Lauren. 2014. "Wanted: A New Ambassador-at-Large for Religious Freedom." *Religion News Service*, 15 January. http://www.religionnews.com/2014/01/15/wanted-new-ambassador-large-religious-freedom/.

Maruyama Masao. 1969. *Thought and Behavior in Modern Japanese Politics*. Translated by Ivan Morris. London, Oxford, and New York: Oxford University Press.

Masuzawa, Tomoko. 2005. *The Invention of World Religions*. Chicago: University of Chicago Press.

Maxey, Trent. 2014. *"The Greatest Problem": Religion and State Formation in Meiji Japan*. Cambridge, MA: Harvard University Asia Center, 2014.

Mazower, Mark. 2004. "The Strange Triumph of Human Rights, 1933–1950." *Historical Journal* 47 (2): 379–98. doi: 10.1017/ S0018246X04003723.

———. 2011. "The End of Civilization and the Rise of Human Rights: The Mid-Twentieth-

Century Disjuncture." In *Human Rights in the Twentieth Century*, edited by Stefan-Ludwig Hoffmann, 29–44. Cambridge: Cambridge University Press.

Mazzetti, Mark, and Eric Schmitt. 2016. "In the Age of ISIS, Who Is a Terrorist and Who Is Simply Deranged?" *New York Times*, 17 July. http://mobile.nytimes.com/2016/07/18/world/europe/in-the-age-of-isis-whos-a-terrorist-and-whos-simply-deranged.html?smprod=nytcore-iphone&smid=nytcore-iphone-share&referer=https://t.co/sLOo7KyyHK.

McAlister, Melani. 2013. "Engaging Religion at the Department of State." *The Immanent Frame*. http://blogs.ssrc.org/tif/2013/07/30/engaging-religion-at-the-department-of-state/.

McCarthy, Charles J. 1921. "Calls Jap Ascendancy Danger to Hawaii: Ex-Governor Declares That Problems Are Handicapped at Washington." *LAT*, 6 November 1921.

McCurry, Justin. 2016. "G7 in Japan: Concern over World Leaders' Tour of Nationalistic Shrine." *Guardian*, 24 May. https://www.theguardian.com/world/2016/may/25/g7-japan-world-leaders-tour-shrine-cameron-obama-abe.

McCutcheon, Russell. 1997. *Manufacturing Religion: The Discourse on Sui Generis Religion and the Politics of Nostalgia*. Oxford and New York: Oxford University Press.

———. 2001. *Critics Not Caretakers: Redescribing the Public Study of Religion*. Albany: State University of New York Press.

———. 2004. "'Just Follow the Money': The Cold War, the Humanistic Study of Religion, and the Fallacy of Insufficient Cynicism." *Culture and Religion* 5 (1): 41–69. https://doi.org/10.1080/0143830042000200355.

McFarland, H. Neill. 1958. "The Present Status of the Religions of Japan." *Journal of the American Academy of Religion* 26 (3): 222–31. https://doi.org/10.1093/jaarel/XXVI.3.222.

———. 1960a. "The New Religions of Japan [Part I]." *Contemporary Religions in Japan* 1 (2): 35–47. http://nirc.nanzan-u.ac.jp/nfile/3129.

———. 1960b. "The New Religions of Japan [Part II]." *Contemporary Religions in Japan* 1 (3): 30–39. http://nirc.nanzan-u.ac.jp/nfile/3247.

———. 1960c. "The New Religions of Japan [Part III]." *Contemporary Religions in Japan* 1 (4): 57–69. http://nirc.nanzan-u.ac.jp/nfile/3261.

———. 1967. *The Rush Hour of the Gods: A Study of New Religious Movements in Japan*. New York: MacMillan Company.

McGarry, Molly K. 2013. "Crimes of Moral Turpitude: Questions at the Borders of Religion, the Secular, and the U.S. Nation-State." In *Religion, the Secular, and the Politics of Sexual Difference*, edited by Linell E. Cady and Tracy Fessenden, 175–94. New York: Columbia University Press.

McLaughlin, Levi. 2012. "Did Aum Change Everything? What Soka Gakkai Before, During, and After the Aum Shinrikyō Affair Tells Us about the Persistent 'Otherness' of New Religions in Japan." *Japanese Journal of Religious Studies* 39 (1): 51–75. http://nirc.nanzan-u.ac.jp/nfile/4110.

McMahan, David. 2008. *The Making of Buddhist Modernism*. Oxford and New York: Oxford University Press.

McNeill, David. 2013. "Back to the Future." *Asia-Pacific Journal: Japan Focus* 11 (50): 1–8. http://apjjf.org/2013/11/50/David-McNeill/4047/article.html.

Melton, J. Gordon. 2004a. "An Introduction to New Religions." In *Oxford Handbook of New Religious Movements*, edited by James R. Lewis. Oxford: Oxford University Press.

———. 2004b. "Perspective: Toward a Definition of 'New Religion.'" *Nova Religio* 8 (1): 73–87. doi: 10.1525/nr.2004.8.1.73.

Mills, Elliott Evans. 1905. *The Decline and Fall of the British Empire: Appointed for Use in the National Schools of Japan, Tokio, 2005*. Oxford: Alden & Co., Ltd. Bocardo Press.

Minobe Tatsukichi. 1947. *Shin kenpō gairon*. Tokyo: Yūhikaku.

Miyamoto Takashi. 2006. "Kokkateki Shintō to kokumin dōtokuron no kōsaku: Katō Genchi no 'Kokutai Shintō' no imi." In *Kokka Shintō saikō: Saisei itchi kokka no keisei to tenkai*, edited by Sakamoto Koremaru, 317–54. Tokyo: Kōbundō, 2006.

Miyaoka Tsunejirō. 1918. "The Safeguard of Civil Liberty in Japan." *CLJ* 87 (17): 294–302.

Miyoshi Akira. 1967. *Arima Shirōsuke*. Tokyo: Yoshikawa Kōbunkan.

Moore, Ray A. 2011. *Soldier of God: MacArthur's Attempt to Christianize Japan*. Portland, ME: Merwin Asia.

Mori Arinori. 1872. "Religious Freedom in Japan: A Memorial and Draft of Charter." Privately printed.

Moriya Tomoe. 2005. "Social Ethics of 'New Buddhists' at the Turn of the Twentieth Century: A Comparative Study of Suzuki Daisetsu and Inoue Shūten." *Japanese Journal of Religious Studies* 32 (2): 283–304. http://nirc.nanzan-u.ac.jp/nfile/2878.

———. 2008. "Buddhism at the Crossroads of the Pacific: Imamura Yemyō and Buddhist Social Ethics." In *Hawaii at the Crossroads of the U.S. and Japan before the Pacific War*, edited by Jon Thares Davidann, 192–216. Honolulu: University of Hawai'i Press.

Moyn, Samuel. 2010. *The Last Utopia: Human Rights in History*. Cambridge, MA: Harvard University Press.

———. 2014. "From Communist to Muslim: European Human Rights, the Cold War, and Religious Liberty." *South Atlantic Quarterly* 113 (1): 63–86. doi: 10.1215/00382876-2390428.

———. 2015. *Christian Human Rights*. Philadelphia: University of Pennsylvania Press.

Mullins, Mark R. 2010. "How Yasukuni Shrine Survived the Occupation: A Critical Examination of Popular Claims." *Monumenta Nipponica* 65 (1): 89–136. doi: 10.1353/mni.0.0109.

———. 2012a. "The Neo-Nationalist Response to the Aum Crisis: A Return of Civil Religion and Coercion in the Public Sphere?" *Japanese Journal of Religious Studies* 39 (1): 99–125. http://nirc.nanzan-u.ac.jp/nfile/4108.

———. 2012b. "Secularization, Deprivatization, and the Reappearance of Public Religion in Japanese Society." *Journal of Religion in Japan* 1 (1): 61–82. doi: 10.1163/221183412X628442.

Murakami Shigeyoshi. (1968) 1980. *Japanese Religion in the Modern Century*. Translated by H. Byron Earhart. Tokyo: University of Tokyo Press.

———. 1970. *Kokka Shintō*. Tokyo: Iwanami Shinsho.

———. (1982) 2006. *Kokka Shintō to minshū shūkyō*. Tokyo: Yoshikawa Kōbunkan.

Nagaoka Kōtarō. 2010. "Tomeoka Kōsuke no risō teki kyōkōshi zō to sono haikei." *Aoyama Gakuin Daigaku kyōiku gakkai kiyō "kyōiku kenkyū"* 54:37–47.

Nagasawa Hitoshi, ed. 1946. *Shin kenpō tokuhon: Zenjōbun kaisetsu*. Tokyo: Shinkō no Nihonsha.

Nakai, Kate Wildman. 2013. "Coming to Terms with 'Reverence at Shrines': The 1932 Sophia University–Yasukuni Shrine Incident." In *Kami Ways in Nationalist Territory: Shintō Studies in Prewar Japan and the West*, edited by Bernhard Scheid with Kate Wildman Nakai, 109–53. Vienna: Austrian Academy of Sciences.

———. 2017. "Between Secularity, Shrines, and Protestantism: Catholic Higher Education in Prewar Japan." *Japan Review* 30: 97–127. http://publications.nichibun.ac.jp/region/d/NSH/series/jare/2017-07-24/s001/s009/pdf/article.pdf.

Nakamura Masanori. 1992. *The Japanese Monarchy, 1931–1991: Ambassador Joseph Grew and the Making of the "Symbol Emperor System."* Translated by Herbert P. Bix, Jonathan Baker-Bates, and Derek Bowen. Armonk, NY: M. E. Sharpe.

Nakamura Motosuke. 1897. *Naichi zakkyo junbi no shiori*. Nagoya: Nōninsha.

Nakano Tsuyoshi. 1993. "Amerika no tainichi shūkyō seisaku no keisei." In *Senryō to Nihon shūkyō*, edited by Ikado Fujio, 27–72. Tokyo: Miraisha.

———. 2003. *Sengo Nihon no shūkyō to seiji*. Tokyo: Hara Shobō.

New York Times. 1945. "Progress in Japan." 9 October.

———. 1949a. "For Religious Freedom: Group to Protect It in World Is Organized Here." 15 February.

———. 1949b. "The Great Schism." 17 July.

———. 1951. "The Text of Truman's Talk to Pilgrims." 28 September.

Nitta Hitoshi. 1999a. "Kokka Shintō ron no keifu: Jō." *Kōgakkan Ronsō* 32 (1): 1–36.

———. 1999b. "Kokka Shintō ron no keifu: Ge." *Kōgakkan Ronsō* 32 (2): 23–59.

———. 2000. "Shintō as a 'Non-Religion': The Origins and Development of an Idea." In *Shintō in History: Ways of the Kami*, edited by John Breen and Mark Teeuwen, 252–71. Honolulu: University of Hawai'i Press.

Nongbri, Brent. 2013. *Before Religion: A History of a Modern Concept*. New Haven, CT: Yale University Press. Kindle edition.

O'Brien, David M., and Ohkoshi Yasuo. 1996. *To Dream of Dreams: Religious Freedom and Constitutional Politics in Postwar Japan*. Honolulu: University of Hawai'i Press.

Ōhara Yasuo. 1989. "Shintō shirei to sengō no seikyō mondai." In *Kokka to shūkyō no aida: Seikyō bunri no shisō to genjitsu*, edited by Ōhara Yasuo, Momochi Akira, and Sakamoto Koremaru, 9–102. Tokyo: Nihon Kyōbunsha.

Ōhara Yasuo, Momochi Akira, and Sakamoto Koremaru. 1989. *Kokka to shūkyō no aida: Seikyō bunri no shisō to genjitsu*. Tokyo: Nihon Kyōbunsha.

Ōishi Shūten. 1964. "Review: The New Religious Sects of Japan." *Contemporary Religions in Japan* 5 (1): 45–80. http://nirc.nanzan-u.ac.jp/nfile/3099.

Okumura Takie. 1917. *Taiheiyō no rakuen: Paradise of the Pacific*. Tokyo: San'eidō Shoten.

Okuyama Michiaki. 2009. "Kishimoto Hideo no Shōwa nijū nen." *Tōkyō Daigaku shūkyōgaku nenpō* 26:19–34. http://repository.dl.itc.u-tokyo.ac.jp/dspace/bitstream/2261/26755/1/rel02602.pdf.

———. 2011. "'State Shintō' in Recent Japanese Scholarship." *Monumenta Nipponica* 66 (1): 123–45. doi: 10.1353/mni.2011.0019.

Ōmi Toshihiro. 2009. "Chikazumi Jōkan ryaku nenpu." In *Kindaika no naka no dentō shūkyō to seishin undō: Kijunten to shite no Chikazumi Jōkan kenkyū*, edited by Iwata

Fumiaki, 11–12. Japan Society for the Promotion of Science Midterm Report of Research Findings (Basic Research [C]) for 2008–9, Research Topic #20520055.

———. 2012a. “Kindai Shinshū to Kirisutokyō: Chikazumi Jōkan no fukyō senryaku.” In *Kindaika no naka no dentō shūkyō to seishin undō: Kijunten to shite no Chikazumi Jōkan kenkyū*, edited by Iwata Fumiaki, 50–64. Japan Society for the Promotion of Science Report of Research Findings (Basic Research [C]) for 2008–11, Research Topic #20520055.

———. 2012b. “Seinen bunka to shite no Bukkyō nichiyō gakkō.” In *Kindaika no naka no dentō shūkyō to seishin undō: Kijunten to shite no Chikazumi Jōkan kenkyū*, edited by Iwata Fumiaki, 65–79. Japan Society for the Promotion of Science Report of Research Findings (Basic Research [C]) for 2008–11, Research Topic #20520055.

——— [as Ohmi Toshihiro]. 2014. *Kindai Bukkyō no naka no Shinshū: Chikazumi Jōkan to kyūdōsha tachi*. Kyoto: Hōzōkan.

Orbaugh, Sharalyn. 2015. *Propaganda Performed: Kamishibai in Japan's Fifteen Year War*. Leiden: Brill.

Orsi, Robert. 1998. “Snakes Alive: Resituating the Moral in the Study of Religion.” In *In Face of the Facts: Moral Inquiry in American Scholarship*, edited by Richard Wightman Fox and Robert B. Westbrook, 201–26. Cambridge and New York: Cambridge University Press.

Ōsawa Kōji. 2009. “*Seikyō jihō* kaidai.” In *Kindaika no naka no dentō shūkyō to seishin undō: Kijunten to shite no Chikazumi Jōkan kenkyū*, edited by Iwata Fumiaki, 13–21. Japan Society for the Promotion of Science Midterm Report of Research Findings (Basic Research [C]) for 2008–9, Research Topic #20520055.

———. 2013. “Shūkyō dantai hō no seitei to kanryō seido.” *Bukkyō bunka gakkai kiyō* 22:1–18.

Ōtani Eiichi. 2008. “Hansen/han-fashizumu no Bukkyō shakai undō: Seno'o Girō to Shinkō Bukkyō Seinen Dōmei.” In *Kokka to shūkyō: Shūkyō kara miru kingendai Nihon*, vol. 1, edited by Arai Ken and Tanaka Shigeru, 447–81. Kyoto: Hōzōkan.

———. 2009. “Meijiki Nihon no ‘atarashii Bukkyō’ to iu undō.” *Kikan Nihon shisō shi* 75: 14–35.

———. 2012a. *Kindai Bukkyō to iu shiza: Sensō, Ajia, shakai shugi*. Tokyo: Perikansha.

———. 2012b. “Takashima Beihō to Heigo Shuppan.” In *Kindai Nihon ni okeru chishikijin shūkyō undō no gensetsu kūkan: “Shin Bukkyō” no shisōshi/bunkashi teki kenkyū*, edited by Yoshinaga Shin'ichi, 103–26. Japan Society for the Promotion of Science Final Report of Research Findings (Basic Research [B]), 2008–11, Research Topic #20320016.

———. 2014. “The Movement Called ‘New Buddhism’ in Meiji Japan.” In *Modern Buddhism in Japan*, edited by Hayashi Makoto, Ōtani Eiichi, and Paul L. Swanson, 52–84. Nagoya: Nanzan Institute for Religion and Culture.

Owen, Suzanne. 2011. “The World Religions Paradigm: Time for a Change.” *Arts and Humanities in Higher Education* 10 (3): 253–68. doi:10.1177/1474022211408038.

Parrott, Lindsay. 1949. “Japanese Are Returning to Shintō Shrines; Occupation Theory Apparently Incorrect.” *New York Times*, 8 January 1949.

Payne, Richard. 2013. “Foreword.” In Fabio Rambelli, *Zen Anarchism: The Egalitarian Dharma of Uchiyama Gudō*. Honolulu: University of Hawai‘i Press.

Potsdam Declaration. 1945. Issued 26 July. http://www.ndl.go.jp/constitution/e/etc/c06.html.

Preston, Andrews. 2012. *Sword of the Spirit, Shield of the Faith: Religion in American War and Diplomacy*. New York and Toronto: Alfred A. Knopf. Ebook.

Queen, Christopher S., and Sallie B. King, eds. 1996. *Engaged Buddhism: Buddhist Liberation Movements in Asia*. Albany: State University of New York Press.

Rambelli, Fabio. 2013. *Zen Anarchism: The Egalitarian Dharma of Uchiyama Gudō*. Honolulu: University of Hawai'i Press.

Reader, Ian. 2005. "Perspective: Chronologies, Commonalities and Alternative Status in Japanese New Religious Movements; Defining NRMs outside the Western Cul-De-Sac." *Nova Religio* 9 (2): 84–96. doi: 10.1525/nr.2005.9.2.084.

———. 2012. "Globally Aum: The Aum Affair, Counterterrorism, and Religion." *Japanese Journal of Religious Studies* 39 (1): 179–98. http://nirc.nanzan-u.ac.jp/nfile/4117.

Reader, Ian, and George J. Tanabe Jr. 1998. *Practically Religious: Worldly Benefits and the Common Religion of Japan*. Honolulu: University of Hawai'i Press.

Robbins, Thomas. 2000. "'Quo Vadis' the Scientific Study of New Religious Movements." *Journal for the Scientific Study of Religion* 39 (4): 515–23. doi: 10.1111/j.1468-5906.2000.tb00013.x.

———. 2005. "Perspective: New Religions and Alternative Religions." *Nova Religio* 8 (3): 104–11. doi: 10.1525/nr.2005.8.3.104.

Roemer, Michael. 2009. "Religious Affiliation in Contemporary Japan: Untangling the Enigma." *Review of Religious Research* 50 (3): 298–320. http://www.jstor.org/stable/25593743.

Roosevelt, Franklin Delano. 1941. Four Freedoms Speech. http://www.fdrlibrary.marist.edu/_resources/images/sign/fdr_30.pdf.

Rots, Aike. 2017. *Shintō, Nature, and Ideology in Contemporary Japan: Making Sacred Forests*. London and New York: Bloomsbury.

Rots, Aike, and Mark Teeuwen. 2017. "Introduction: Formations of the Secular in Japan." *Japan Review* 30:3–20. http://publications.nichibun.ac.jp/region/d/NSH/series/jare/2017-07-24/s001/s004/pdf/article.pdf.

Sakaino Kōyō. 1910. *Shin Bukkyō jūnen shi*. Tokyo: Shin Bukkyōto Dōshikai Shuppan.

Sakamoto Koremaru. 1994. *Kokka Shintō keisei katei no kenkyū*. Tokyo: Iwanami Shoten.

———. 2000. "The Structure of State Shintō: Its Creation, Development, and Demise." In *Shintō in History: Ways of the Kami*, edited by John Breen and Mark Teeuwen, 272–94. Honolulu: University of Hawai'i Press.

———. 2005. *Kindai no jinja Shintō*. Tokyo: Kōbundō.

———, ed. 2006. *Kokka Shintō saikō: Saisei itchi kokka no keisei to tenkai*. Tokyo: Kōbundō.

Saperstein, David. 2015. Remarks at the Release of the 2014 Report of the US Commission on International Religious Freedom. http://www.humanrights.gov/dyn/2015/10/ambassador-saperstein-at-the-release-of-the-2014-report-on-international-religious-freedom/.

Sawada, Janine Tasca. 2004. *Practical Pursuits: Religion, Politics, and Self-Cultivation in Nineteenth-Century Japan*. Honolulu: University of Hawai'i Press.

Scheid, Bernhard. 2013. "Introduction: Shintō Studies and the Nonreligious-Shrine Doctrine." In *Kami Ways in Nationalist Territory: Shintō Studies in Prewar Japan and the West*, edited by Bernhard Scheid, with Kate Wildman Nakai, 1–22. Vienna: Austrian Academy of Sciences.

Scheid, Bernhard, with Kate Wildman Nakai. 2013. *Kami Ways in Nationalist Territory: Shintō Studies in Prewar Japan and the West*. Vienna: Austrian Academy of Sciences.

Schilbrack, Kevin. 2011. "Religions: Are There Any?" *Journal of the American Academy of Religion* 78 (4): 1112–38. doi:10.1093/jaarel/lfq086.

———. 2013a. "After We Deconstruct 'Religion,' Then What? A Case for Critical Realism." *Method & Theory in the Study of Religion* 25 (1). Brill: 107–12. doi:10.1163/15700682-12341255.

———. 2013b. "What *Isn't* Religion?" *Journal of Religion* 93 (3): 291–318. doi: 10.1086/670276.

Schonthal, Benjamin. 2016. *Buddhism, Politics and the Limits of Law: The Pyrrhic Constitutionalism of Sri Lanka*. New York: Cambridge University Press.

Sehat, David. 2011. *The Myth of American Religious Freedom*. Oxford and New York: Oxford University Press.

Selden, Mark. 2014. "Bombs Bursting in Air: State and Citizen Responses to the U.S. Firebombing and Atomic Bombing of Japan." *Asia-Pacific Journal* 12 (3[4]): 1–10 (my pagination). http://japanfocus.org/-Mark-Selden/4065.

Shah, Timothy Samuel, with Thomas F. Farr, Matthew J. Franck, Gerard V. Bradley, Jennifer S. Bryson, William Inboden, Jennifer Marshall, Margarita Mooney, Joseph Wood, David Novak, Nicholas Wolterstorff, and Abdullah Saeed. 2012. *Religious Freedom: Why Now? Defending an Embattled Human Right*. Witherspoon Institute Task Force on International Religious Freedom. Princeton, NJ: Witherspoon Institute. Kindle edition.

Sharf, Robert H. 1995. "The Zen of Japanese Nationalism." In *Curators of the Buddha: The Study of Buddhism under Colonialism*, edited by Donald Lopez, 107–60. Chicago: University of Chicago Press.

Sherriff, Patrick. 2015. "How To Write about Japan: 10 Infallible Rules." *Medium*, 22 October. https://medium.com/@patricksherriff/how-to-write-about-japan-593c77b85f38#.d3zlwhiw5.

Shields, James Mark. 2011. *Critical Buddhism: Engaging with Modern Japanese Buddhist Thought*. Farnham and Burlington, VT: Ashgate.

———. 2012. "A Blueprint for Buddhist Revolution: The Radical Buddhism of Seno'o Girō (1889–1961) and the Youth League for Revitalizing Buddhism." *Japanese Journal of Religious Studies* 39 (2): 333–51. http://nirc.nanzan-u.ac.jp/nfile/4207.

———. 2017. *Against Harmony: Progressive and Radical Buddhism in Modern Japan*. New York: Oxford University Press.

Shimada, Noriko. 2008. "Social, Cultural, and Spiritual Struggles of the Japanese in Hawaiʻi: The Case of Okumura Takie and Imamura Yemyō and Americanization." In *Hawaii at the Crossroads of the U.S. and Japan before the Pacific War*, edited by Jon Thares Davidann, 146–70. Honolulu: University of Hawaiʻi Press.

Shimazono Susumu. (1992) 2006. *Gendai kyūsai shūkyō ron*. Tokyo: Seikyūsha.

———. 2006. "Teikō no shūkyō/kyōryoku no shūkyō: Senjiki Sōka Kyōiku Gakkai no henyō." In *Nichijō seikatsu no naka no sōryokusen*, edited by Kurasawa Aiko, Sugihara

Tōru, Narita Ryūichi, Tessa Morris-Suzuki, Yui Daizaburō, and Yoshida Yutaka, 239–68. Tokyo: Iwanami Shoten.

———. 2009. "State Shintō in the Lives of the People: The Establishment of Emperor Worship, Modern Nationalism, and Shrine Shintō in Late Meiji." *Japanese Journal of Religious Studies* 36, no. 1: 93–124. http://nirc.nanzan-u.ac.jp/nfile/2981.

———. 2010. *Kokka Shintō to Nihonjin*. Tokyo: Iwanami Shoten.

Shimizu, Naoko. 1998. *Japan, Race and Equality: The Racial Equality Proposal of 1919*. London and New York: Routledge.

Shimoma Kūkyō. (1927) 2002. "Shūkyō hō gaisetsu." In *Shakai seisaku taikei*, vol. 10, edited by Hasegawa Ryōshin, 1–95. Tokyo: Nihon Tosho Sentā.

Shin Nihon Shūkyō Dantai Rengō Kai Research Division, ed. 1965a. "Reminiscences of Religion in Postwar Japan [Part I]." *Contemporary Religions in Japan* 6 (2): 111–203. http://nirc.nanzan-u.ac.jp/nfile/3149.

———. 1965b. "Reminiscences of Religion in Postwar Japan [Part II]." *Contemporary Religions in Japan* 6 (4): 382–403. http://nirc.nanzan-u.ac.jp/nfile/3156.

———. 1966a. "Reminiscences of Religion in Postwar Japan [Part III]." *Contemporary Religions in Japan* 7 (1): 51–80. http://nirc.nanzan-u.ac.jp/nfile/3161.

———. 1966b. "Reminiscences of Religion in Postwar Japan [Part IV]." *Contemporary Religions in Japan* 7 (2): 166–88. http://nirc.nanzan-u.ac.jp/nfile/3167.

———. 1966c. "Reminiscences of Religion in Postwar Japan [Part V]." *Contemporary Religions in Japan* 7 (3): 217–74. http://nirc.nanzan-u.ac.jp/nfile/3171.

Shinshūren Chōsa Shitsu, ed. 1963. *Sengo shūkyō kaisō roku*. Tokyo: PL Shuppansha.

Shweder, Richard A. 2009. "Shouting at the Hebrews: Imperial Liberalism v. Liberal Pluralism and the Practice of Male Circumcision." *Law, Culture, and the Humanities* 5:170–204. doi: 10.1177/1743872109102491.

Silva, Noenoe K. 2004. *Aloha Betrayed: Native Hawaiian Resistance to American Colonialism*. Durham, NC, and London: Duke University Press.

Skya, Walter. 2009. *Japan's Holy War: The Ideology of Radical Shintō Ultranationalism*. Durham, NC, and London: Duke University Press.

Smith, C., B. Vaidyanathan, N. T. Ammerman, J. Casanova, H. Davidson, E. H. Ecklund, J. H. Evans, et al. 2013. "Roundtable on the Sociology of Religion: Twenty-Three Theses on the Status of Religion in American Sociology—a Mellon Working-Group Reflection." *Journal of the American Academy of Religion* 81 (4): 903–38. doi:10.1093/jaarel/lft052.

Smith, Jonathan Z. 1982. *Imagining Religion: From Babylon to Jonestown*. Chicago: University of Chicago Press.

Smith, Steven D. 2014. *The Rise and Decline of American Religious Freedom*. Cambridge, MA: Harvard University Press.

Stark, Rodney, and William Sims Bainbridge. 1979. "Of Churches, Sects, and Cults: Preliminary Concepts for a Theory of Religious Movements." *Journal for the Scientific Study of Religion* 18 (2): 117–31. doi: 10.2307/1385935.

Stone, Jacqueline I. 1990. "A Vast and Grave Task: Interwar Buddhist Studies as an Expression of Japan's Envisioned Global Role." In *Culture and Identity: Japanese Intellectuals during the Interwar Years*, edited by Thomas J. Rimer, 217–33. Princeton, NJ: Princeton University Press.

———. 1994. "Rebuking the Enemies of the *Lotus*: Nichirenist Exclusivism in Historical Perspective." *Japanese Journal of Religious Studies* 21 (2–3): 231–59. http://nirc.nanzan-u.ac.jp/nfile/2544.

———. 1999. "Review Article: Some Reflections on Critical Buddhism." *Japanese Journal of Religious Studies* 26 (1–2): 159–88. http://nirc.nanzan-u.ac.jp/nfile/2673.

———. 2014. "The Atsuhara Affair." *Japanese Journal of Religious Studies* 41 (1): 153–89. http://nirc.nanzan-u.ac.jp/nfile/4334.

Strenski, I. 1993. "Lessons for Religious Studies in Waco?" *Journal of the American Academy of Religion* 61 (3): 567–74.

Su, Anna. 2016. *Exporting Freedom: Religious Liberty and American Power*. Cambridge, MA: Harvard University Press.

Sueki Fumihiko. 2004. *Kindai shisō saikō I: Meiji shisōka ron*. Tokyo: Toransubyū.

Sullivan, Winnifred Fallers. 1994. *Paying the Words Extra: Religious Discourse in the Supreme Court of the United States*. Cambridge, MA: Harvard University Press.

———. 2005. *The Impossibility of Religious Freedom*. Princeton, NJ, and Oxford: Princeton University Press.

———. 2014. "The Impossibility of Religious Freedom." *The Immanent Frame*. http://blogs.ssrc.org/tif/2014/07/08/impossibility-of-religious-freedom/.

Sullivan, Winnifred Fallers, Elizabeth Shakman Hurd, Saba Mahmood, and Peter G. Danchin, eds. 2015. *The Politics of Religious Freedom*. Chicago: University of Chicago Press.

Sullivan, Winnifred Fallers, Robert A. Yelle, and Marco Taussig-Rubbo, eds. 2011. *After Secular Law*. Stanford, CA: Stanford University Press.

Suzuki Daisetsu. 1896. *Shinshūkyōron*. Kyoto: Baiyō Shoin.

Swaine, Jon. 2014. "Ohio Walmart Video Reveals Moments before Police Killed John Crawford." *Guardian*, 25 September 2014. https://www.theguardian.com/world/2014/sep/24/surveillance-video-walmart-shooting-john-crawford-police.

Swanson, Paul L. 2014. "Takagi Kenmyō and Buddhist Socialism: A Meiji Misfit and Martyr." In *Modern Buddhism in Japan*, edited by Hayashi Makoto, Ōtani Eiichi, and Paul L. Swanson, 144–62. Nagoya: Nanzan Institute.

Takagi Kiyoko. 1993. "Kishimoto hakase to senryō jidai no shūkyō seisaku." In *Senryō to Nihon shūkyō*, edited by Ikado Fujio, 423–36. Tokyo: Miraisha, 1993.

Takagi-Kitayama, Mariko. 2008. "In the Strong Wind of the Americanization Movement." In *Hawaii at the Crossroads of the U.S. and Japan before the Pacific War*, edited by Jon Thares Davidann, 217–39. Honolulu: University of Hawai'i Press.

Takahashi Hara. 2008. "Tōkyō Daigaku Shūkyō Gakka no rekishi: Senzen o chūshin ni." *Kikan Nihon shisōshi* 72:153–69.

———. 2012. "Andō Masazumi." In *Kindai Nihon ni okeru chishikijin shūkyō undō no gensetsu kūkan: "Shin Bukkyō" no shisōshi/bunkashi teki kenkyū*, edited by Yoshinaga Shin'ichi. Japan Society for the Promotion of Science Final Report of Research Findings (Basic Research [B]), 2008–11, Research Topic #20320016.

Takashima Beihō. 1946a. "Shin Bukkyō undo no kaikō: Ge." *Daihōrin* (May): 29–33.

———. 1946b. "Shin Bukkyō undo no kaikō: Jō." *Daihōrin* (April): 34–37.

Takayama, K. Peter. 1993. "The Revitalization of Japanese Civil Religion." In *Religion and Society in Contemporary Japan: Selected Readings*, edited by Mark R. Mullins, Shimazono Susumu, and Paul L. Swanson, 105–20. Nagoya: Nanzan Institute for Religion and Culture (published by Asian Humanities Press).

Takeda Dōshō. 1991. "The Fall of Renmonkyō, and Its Place in the History of Meiji-Period Religions." In *New Religions*, edited by Inoue Nobutaka and translated by Norman Havens, 25–57. Tokyo: Institute for Japanese Culture and Classics.

Takemae, Eiji. 2002. *The Allied Occupation of Japan* (formerly titled *Inside GHQ: The Allied Occupation of Japan and its Legacy*). Translated by Robert Ricketts and Sebastian Swann. New York: Continuum.

Takemura Makio. 1993. "Senryō seisaku to Bukkyō dantai." In *Senryō to Nihon shūkyō*, edited by Ikado Fujio, 267–90. Tokyo: Miraisha, 1993.

Takenaka, Akiko. 2015. *Yasukuni Shrine: History, Memory, and Japan's Unending Postwar*. Honolulu: University of Hawai'i Press.

Tan Reigen, ed. 1897. *Bukkyō enzetsu shū: Naichi zakkyo no junbi*. Tokyo: Kōbunsha.

Taylor, Charles. 2007. *A Secular Age*. Cambridge, MA: Belknap Press of Harvard University Press.

Tebbe, Nelson. 2017. *Religious Freedom in an Egalitarian Age*. Cambridge, MA, and London: Harvard University Press.

Teeuwen, Mark. 2002. "From Jindō to Shintō: A Concept Takes Shape." *Japanese Journal of Religious Studies* 29 (3–4): 233–63. http://nirc.nanzan-u.ac.jp/nfile/2782.

Teeuwen, Mark, and John Breen. 2017. *A Social History of the Ise Shrines: Divine Capital*. London: Bloomsbury Academic.

Terasawa Kunihiko. 2012. "Modern Japanese Buddhism in the Context of Interreligious Dialogue, Nationalism, and World War II." PhD dissertation, Temple University.

Thelle, Notto. 1987. *Buddhism and Christianity in Japan: From Conflict to Dialogue, 1854–1899*. Honolulu: University of Hawai'i Press.

Thomas, Jolyon Baraka. 2014a. "The Concept of Religion in Modern Japan: Imposition, Invention, or Innovation?" *Religious Studies in Japan* 2:3–21. http://jpars.org/online/wp-content/uploads/2013/12/RSJ_2014_Thomas.pdf.

———. 2014b. "Free Inquiry and Japanese Buddhist Studies: The Case of Katō Totsudō (1870–1949)." *Japanese Religions* 39 (1–2): 31–51. http://www.japanese-religions.jp/publications/assets/JR39%201&2_Thomas.pdf.

———. 2014c. "Religions Policies during the Allied Occupation of Japan, 1945–1952." *Religion Compass* 8 (9): 275–86. doi: 10.1111/rec3.12117.

———. 2016a. Review of *Religious Discourse in Modern Japan: Religion, State, and Shintō*. *Monumenta Nipponica* 71 (1): 186–91. doi: 10.1353/mni.2016.0019.

———. 2016b. "Varieties of Religious Freedom in Japanese Buddhist Responses to the Yamagata Religions Bill." *Asian Journal of Law and Society* 3 (1): 49–70.

———. 2017. "Big Questions in the Study of Shintō." H-Japan, H-Net Reviews. http://www.h-net.org/reviews/showpdf.php?id=48924.

———. 2018. Review of *Against Harmony: Progressive and Radical Buddhism in Modern Japan*. *Journal of the American Academy of Religion* 86 (2): 568–71. https://doi.org/10.1093/jaarel/lfx075.

Thomas, Marlo, and Friends. 1972. *Free to Be You and Me*. Bell Records.

Thomsen, Harry. 1963. *The New Religions of Japan*. Rutland, VT: Charles E. Tuttle Company.

Tōgō Ryōchō. 1899. *Sugamo kangoku kyōkai mondai enzetu yōryō*. Hyōgō: Takahashi Kappan Sho.

Tony Blair Faith Foundation. n.d. http://www.tonyblairfaithfoundation.org.

Totani, Yuma. 2008. *The Tokyo War Crimes Trial: The Pursuit of Justice in the Wake of World War II*. Cambridge, MA: Harvard University Press.

US Department of State. 2013. "Remarks at the Launch of the Office of Faith-Based Community Initiatives." 7 August. http://www.state.gov/secretary/remarks/2013/08/212781.htm.

US House of Representatives. 1921. *Labor Problems in Hawaii: Hearings before the Committee on Immigration and Naturalization*. House of Representatives, 21–30 June and 7 July. Washington, DC: Government Printing Office.

US War Department, Information and Education Division, dir. 1945. *Our Job in Japan*.

van der Veer, Peter. 2014. *The Modern Spirit of Asia: The Spiritual and the Secular in China and India*. Princeton, NJ: Princeton University Press, 2014. Kindle edition.

Vásquez, Manuel. 2011. *More than Belief: A Materialist Theory of Religion*. Oxford and New York: Oxford University Press.

Victoria, Brian D. 1997. *Zen at War*. New York: Weatherhill.

———. 2014. "Sōka Gakkai Founder Makiguchi Tsunesaburō: A Man of Peace?" *Asia-Pacific Journal: Japan Forum* 12 (37). http://apjjf.org/-Brian-Victoria/4181/article.pdf.

Ward, Ryan. 2009. "*Shinkai kengen* kaidai." In *Kindaika no naka no dentō shūkyō to seishin undō: Kijunten to shite no Chikazumi Jōkan kenkyū*, edited by Iwata Fumiaki, 27–30. Japan Society for the Promotion of Science Midterm Report of Research Findings (Basic Research [C]) for 2008–9, Research Topic #20520055.

Warner, Michael, Jonathan VanAntwerpen, and Craig Calhoun, eds. 2010. *Varieties of Secularism in a Secular Age*. Cambridge, MA: Harvard University Press.

Washington, Garrett. 2013. "Fighting Brick with Brick: Chikazumi Jōkan and Buddhism's Response to Christian Space in Imperial Japan." *Cross-Currents: East Asian History and Culture Review* 6:95–120. http://cross-currents.berkeley.edu/sites/default/files/e-journal/articles/washington_0.pdf.

Wedemeyer, Christian. 2013. *Making Sense of Tantric Buddhism: History, Semiology, and Transgression in the Indian Traditions*. New York: Columbia University Press.

Weiner, Isaac. 2014. *Religion Out Loud: Religious Sound, Public Space, and American Pluralism*. New York and London: New York University Press.

Weingarten, Victor. 1946. *Raising Cane: A Brief History of Labor in Hawai'i*. Honolulu: International Longshoremen's and Warehousemen's Union.

Weitz, Eric D. 2013. "Samuel Moyn and the New History of Human Rights." *European Journal of Political Theory* 12 (1): 84–93. doi: 10.1177/1474885112450999.

Weitzman, Steven. 2017. "Allies against Armageddon? The FBI and the Academic Study of Religion." In *The FBI and Religion: Faith and National Security Before and After 9/11*, edited by Sylvester A. Johnson and Steven Weitzman, 269–90. Oakland: University of California Press.

Wenger, Tisa. 2017. *Religious Freedom: The Contested History of an American Ideal*. Chapel Hill: University of North Carolina Press.

Wessinger, Catherine. 2009. "Deaths in the Fire at the Branch Davidians' Mount Carmel: Who Bears Responsibility?" *Nova Religio: The Journal of Alternative and Emergent Religions* 13 (2): 25–60. doi:10.1525/nr.2009.13.2.25.

Williams, Duncan Ryūken. 2006. "From Pearl Harbor to 9/11: Lessons from the Internment of Japanese American Buddhists." In *A Nation of Religions: The Politics of Pluralism in Multireligious America*, edited by Stephen Prothero, 63–78. Chapel Hill: University of North Carolina Press.

Williams, Duncan Ryūken, and Tomoe Moriya. 2010. "Introduction: Dislocations and Relocations of Issei Buddhists in the Americas." In *Issei Buddhism in the Americas*, edited by Duncan Ryūken Williams and Tomoe Moriya, ix–xxi. Urbana, Chicago, and Springfield: University of Illinois Press.

Woodard, William P. 1972. *The Allied Occupation of Japan 1945–1952 and Japanese Religions*. Leiden: E. J. Brill.

Yamaguchi Teruomi. (1999) 2005. *Meiji kokka to shūkyō*. Tokyo: Tōkyō Daigaku Shuppankai.

Yasumaru Yoshio. 1979. *Kamigami no Meiji ishin: Shinbutsu bunri to haibutsu kishaku*. Tokyo: Iwanami Shinsho.

Yomiuri Shinbunsha. 1946. *Shin kenpō tokuhon*. Tokyo: Yomiuri Shinbunsha.

Yoshinaga Shin'ichi, ed. 2009. "The *New Buddhism* of the Meiji Period: Modernization through Internationalization." Special issue, *Japanese Religions* 34 (2).

———, ed. 2012a. *Kindai Nihon ni okeru chishikijin shūkyō undō no gensetsu kūkan: "Shin Bukkyō" no shisōshi/bunkashi teki kenkyū*. Japan Society for the Promotion of Science Final Report of Research Findings (Basic Research [B]), 2008–11, Research Topic #20320016.

———. 2012b. "*Shin Bukkyō* to wa nani mono ka? 'Jiyū tōkyū' to 'kenzen naru shinkō.'" In *Kindai Nihon ni okeru chishikijin shūkyō undō no gensetsu kūkan: "Shin Bukkyō" no shisōshi/bunkashi teki kenkyū*, edited by Yoshinaga Shin'ichi, 27–43. Japan Society for the Promotion of Science Final Report of Research Findings (Basic Research [B]), 2008–11, Research Topic #20320016.

Zhong, Yijiang. 2014. "Freedom, Religion, and the Making of the Modern State in Japan, 1868–89." *Asian Studies Review* 38 (1): 53–70. doi: 10.1080/10357823.2013.872080.

———. 2016. *The Origins of Modern Shintō in Japan: The Vanquished Gods of Izumo*. London: Bloomsbury Academic.

INDEX

Page numbers in italics refer to figures.